EMILIE BARNES'

15

MINUTE

House and Budget

Manager

EMILIE BARNES'

15

MINUTE

House and Budget

Manager

Two Bestselling Books in One Volume

EMILIE'S CREATIVE HOME ORGANIZER

THE 15 MINUTE MONEY MANAGER

Emilie Barnes
Bob Barnes

Inspirational Press · New York

Contents

Emilie's
CREATIVE HOME ORGANIZER

EMILIE BARNES

This book is dedicated to the many women who have mailed me helpful hints and ideas on organizing a home and solving household problems.

Lovingly,

Emilie Barnes

Introduction

Please come into my home through the pages of this book. I wish you could really visit and share a cup of tea. We could lean back on the sofa cushions, nibble a cookie, and talk.

Talk about what? About home. Not necessarily "house beautiful," but a home filled with the spirit of loveliness—the spirit of warmth and caring. Let's talk about my home, which I love and which I love to share with others. And let's talk about your home—and you.

Your life situation may not be like mine. Maybe you're newly married, just starting out in a tiny apartment with a sprinkling of furniture and a few wedding presents. Maybe you live in a simple tract home with a struggling lawn, a few baby trees, and a houseful of little children. Maybe you're single, in a suburban condo with security patrol and silent neighbors, or maybe you've just moved to a much smaller place after the kids have left home. Maybe your home is just a room in somebody else's house!

Your tastes may not be like mine. You may prefer clean, modern lines to the chintz and china that I love in our country home. Maybe you cannot live without a piano and wall-to-wall bookshelves. You may prefer chunky pottery mugs to the dainty china cups I collect.

But if you're like the women I meet in my seminars and through the mail I receive, you long for a home that is warm and welcoming, comfortable and freeing—a place where you can express the uniqueness of your God-given talents and nurture your relationships with people you love. You are hungry for a home that reflects your personality and renews your soul—and for a life that glows with a spirit for the home.

I believe this spirit for the home is already there in your heart. May this book help it shine forth wherever you live and wherever you go.

Moses prayed, "Let the favor of the Lord our God be upon us; and do confirm for us the work of our hands; yes, confirm the work of our hands." (Psalm 90:17 NASB). *Confirm* means "to give meaning, to make permanent." I trust you will find the ideas in this book significant in lightening the load of your everyday routine, and that God will also help you to see the value and importance of what we sometimes consider boring and meaningless. I know from my own personal experience that these ideas do work.

The contents of this book represent years of experience and will save you many hours in research. As you read, may these ideas give you "hope to cope" with life, and may you become a creative home organizer! And may the hours you save give you more valuable time to spend with our Lord and your family.

Emilie Barnes

Laughter in the Walls

I pass a lot of houses on my way home—
some pretty, some expensive,
some inviting—
but my heart always skips a beat
when I turn down the road
and see my house nestled against the hill.
i guess I'm especially proud
of the house and the way it looks because
I drew the plans myself.
It started out large enough for us—
I even had a study—
two teenaged boys now reside in there.
And it had a guest room—
my girl and nine dolls are permanent guests.
It had a small room Peg
had hoped would be her sewing room—
the two boys swinging on the dutch door
have claimed this room as their own.
So it really doesn't look right now
as if I'm much of an architect.
But it will get larger again—
one by one they will go away to work,
to college, to service,
to their own houses,
and then there will be room—
a guest room, a study,
and sewing room

for just the two of us.
But it won't be empty—
every corner, every room,
every nick in the coffee table
will be crowded with memories.
Memories of picnics, parties, Christmases,
bedside vigils, summers,
fires, winters, going barefoot,
leaving for vacation, cats
conversations, black eyes
graduations, first dates,
ball games, arguments
washing dishes, bicycles
dogs, boat rides
getting home from vacation
meals, rabbits and
a thousand other things
that fill the lives
of those who would raise five.
And Peg and I will sit
quietly by the fire
and listen to the
laughter in the walls.

—Bob Benson

Contents

1

Organization

It only takes
15 minutes a day
and you'll be on
your way to becoming a
creative home organizer.

*B*ut everything should be done in a fitting and orderly way.

—1 Corinthians 14:40 (NASB)

Organization

$\mathcal{B}$eing a homemaker, full-time or part-time, is a gift. Every woman should realize that she has the greatest profession in the whole wide world.

How you organize your home and life will determine how effective and efficient you are in this honorable position.

This chapter contains quick ideas that will keep you from backtracking and wasting valuable time. Try to think of time as money. You either save it or waste it, but time does cost you money.

Recently, I saw a sign which read: "I had my home clean last week; I'm sorry you missed it." Even though most of us would like a clean, orderly home because it brings pleasure and peace of mind, we must remember that most homemakers have never had their home in perfect order.

A modern homemaker needs a lot of courage to face the ordinary daily tasks of managing a home. Let's make homemaking an exciting adventure, rather than drudgery and a thankless job that we are stuck with. Let's all learn to find satisfaction in a job done to the best of our abilities and energies.

Organization begins *now*. Do a little each day and you

will be absolutely amazed at what happens in your home. Remember to be consistent with your routine and organization.

The following ideas will help:

• Your inner drive toward order and clarity is much more powerful than the forces of chaos. Remember, the glass is half full, not half empty.

• It takes 21 consecutive days of doing a new task before it becomes a habit. Don't give up on Day 15.

• Simplify and unclutter your life by saying no to good things and saving your yeses for the best things in life. Live a balanced life. Make time for yourself. Stop go-go-go. Be a person of "being" rather than a person of "doing."

• The specific elements of real order include a home that is easy to move around in, with simple systems of handling paperwork and managing money. We must realize that time is money and is limited.

• Any system of organization must be right for you. There is no best way to be organized. Whatever methods you select must fit your life-style.

• Order and organization is not an end that we kill ourselves to attain. It is a way for us to function effectively.

• In order to have order, you must figure out what your goals and purposes are in life. Why do you do what you do?

• People don't plan to be failures, but they do plan if they are going to be a success.

• I have found that my motto "Do the Worst First" helps me get started. Once the worst is done, everything else is so much easier.

• Use the salami method to reach your goal: If the size of your project overwhelms you, tackle it a piece at a time. You wouldn't eat a salami whole, would you? You'd cut it into slices. Do the same thing with your big projects.

• Share your goals with people who really care about you and want to help you.

- A goal is nothing but a "dream with a deadline."
- Studies show that the success rate for people who write down their goals is about 90 times greater than for those who don't.
- Getting organized is not an end in itself. There is no "right" way to do things—unless it's right for you. It must fit your style, your energy, and your schedule.
- Are you a morning person or a night person? Your efficiency may increase if you arrange your tasks as much as possible around the rhythms of your body. Try scheduling top-priority projects during your peak hours, routine work during your "low" time.
- Provide yourself with a notebook—either looseleaf or spiral-bound, and small enough to carry around with you. This notebook will become your "master list"—a single continuous list that replaces all the small slips of paper you're probably used to. Use the notebook to keep track of all errands, things to do or buy, and general notes to yourself about anything that will require action.
- Keep your list with you at all times. A list is worse than useless if you can't refer to it because you may think that you've disposed of a matter when in fact you haven't.
- Beware of the tail-wagging-the-dog situation where your appointment book, budget and expenditures records, filing system, and master list take more time to maintain than working out the problems they're supposed to solve.
- Keep a second, separate notebook to cope with complex, special situations—for example, enrolling a child in college, moving to a new home, or organizing a big family holiday.
- Don't be in a hurry to throw away notebook pages that have been completed. That stove part you ordered two months ago may be all wrong when it arrives, and you may have to call the same people all over again.
- List on paper ten goals that you wish to attain by the end of the year, and do them.

• Keep a daily "to do" list. Make up a new one each morning and include tasks you specifically hope to accomplish—deadlines and appointments, as well as items from your master list. Give each task a priority number—1, 2, 3. Do all the 1's first.

• Assign jobs and responsibilities within the family. Kids ages two to four can put dirty clothes in the hamper or match socks, ages four to seven can dress themselves and clear the table, while those over eight years of age can put away toys and do many chores reasonably well.

• Set up an area for yourself where you keep all your lists, calendars, menus, etc. This is *your* place to work and make schedules.

• The key is to start now—no matter what! If you have a call to make, start dialing. Have a letter to write? Start typing.

• Buy one small basket or a plastic bin (color code the various members of your family) for each person and hang the baskets near the coat closet. Use them for gloves, mittens, winter hats, scarves, and other small but important items.

• Set up an emergency shelf out of reach of small children. Equip it with flashlights, candles (use votive candles in glass holders for safety), matches, a first-aid kit, and an index card with emergency telephone numbers. Make sure baby-sitters know where the shelf is.

• No one has several free hours to clean out a closet. The key is to use the 15-minute segments you do have to accomplish a small task or make a dent in a larger one. For example, file your nails, make an appointment to see the dentist, or clean just one shelf of that closet. You'll double your efforts if you do small tasks (such as writing a thank-you note) while engaged in some other activity like running a bath or waiting for a casserole to heat. Try talking into a small tape recorder to give yourself reminders while putting on your makeup or taking the bus.

• Make a list of three things you want to do. Next to each item write two reasons why you are not doing it. Change the two negatives into two positives. The ability to turn a negative attitude into a positive one is the key to self-organization.

• An easy way to organize your handbag is to have separate little purses—one for cosmetics, one for food items (like mints, gum, suckers), one for bits of papers and business cards. Another can be for Band-Aids, nail clippers, nail file, nail polish, and pills. You can go on and on. All these little bags go into your purses. Just take out whichever bags you need, and you are ready to go.

• Never have time to read all the magazine articles that you would like? When you receive a magazine, quickly go through it and tear out the articles you find interesting and file them away for later reading.

• Five-minute pickup: Pick up and dust in each room for five minutes. Time yourself with a kitchen timer.

• To organize the various booklets and pamphlets that come with cooking and home-care appliances, punch holes into self-sealing plastic bags so that they will fit into a three-ring notebook. Use one bag for each appliance.

• Select one shelf in the den or playroom for storing borrowed library books. You'll know where they are when it's time to return them.

• Get rid of extra paper. Almost 90 percent of the paper in your home or office is never referred to again. Get rid of as much of it as possible.

• The problem with storage closets and kitchen cabinets is remembering everything that is in them. Taping overall lists inside each of these doors saves the time and trouble of searching for something that may be in the back or at the bottom of the closet—or may not be there at all!

• When you get a new reference book (such as a cookbook or gardening manual), attach a pocket inside the cover to

---

Key Questions When Cleaning a Closet

As you weed out a closet, consider each item individually and ask yourself:

1. *Have I used this item in the past year? If the answer is yes, it's worth keeping another year. If no, discard it.*
2. *Does this have either sentimental or monetary value to me? Yes? Then keep it.*
3. *Might this come in handy someday? If you answer yes but have nothing specific in mind, better put the article into a "throw-away," "give-away," or "put-away" box unless you have ample attic or basement storage space. A yes answer usually means that you're hanging onto clutter.*

---

store clippings, notes, or pictures about that subject.

• To help keep track of gift-giving, use an inexpensive monthly planner (purse- or pocket-size). On each special date, note the name of the person, the occasion, and the gift given. Add sizes, color preferences, and any tips for future giving.

• Have a secret shelf for gifts. When you find something on sale or have time to shop, buy gifts in quantity and wrap and tag them for future giving.

• Many household chores can be done during "in-between times"—in between outings, appointments, or TV programs. Once you realize that it takes only 15 minutes to change the sheets, you can fit this and similar tasks into the available time slots.

Sometimes all it takes to eliminate mess, clutter, and confusion are a few hooks here, a basket or two there, and a bit of reshuffling of items on a shelf.

- Use drawstring pouches made from fabric as containers for baby's blocks, puzzle pieces, and other toys with dozens of parts.
- Use a zippered mesh lingerie bag for storing bath toys. Tie with a string, and hang it over the showerhead so toys can drip dry.
- When moving to a new home, order extra labels of your new address. Enclose one of your personalized labels along with each change of address card you send to your friends. Then they can stick the label right in their address books.
- If you conduct a lot of business by mail (like paying bills, sending for free offers, or ordering merchandise), enter each transaction on a large wall calendar in the kitchen and check it periodically. This is especially helpful to verify a payment that may have gotten lost or if too much time has elapsed since placing an order.
- If you cannot find time to do what you want, here is how to make time:
  1. Delegate some of the household work to other family members.
  2. Eliminate some of the work entirely. (You don't *have* to iron certain items.)
  3. Make sure that all your children contribute to running the household.
  4. Use small amounts of time (five to ten minutes) to your best advantage.
  5. Carefully plan the use of leisure time.
     Concentrate on doing those activities that give you real pleasure.
  6. Leave yourself some open-ended time for a spur-of-the-moment activity. Do not cram your appointment book full.
- Do you seem to have a lot of spare time or have trouble making good use of your spare time? You might consider learning a new skill or cultivating a new friendship. Check

your local newspaper to find some groups you could attend that would interest you, or become a volunteer somewhere.

• Write the names in ink and use a pencil to write phone numbers and addresses in your address book. If someone moves, you can easily make the necessary change without messing up your book.

• To keep track of your credit cards, lay them out and photocopy them. All the info is on one sheet.

• It is not what you get that makes you successful; it is what you are continuing to do with what you've got.

• Remember: Your goal is to get organized so that you can work toward your mission in life.

• I practice a 45/15 rule that really helps me. After every 45-minute work cycle, I take a 15-minute break and do something different—take a short walk, go outside for some fresh air, call someone on the phone, get a drink of water. This rule keeps me renewed and fresh.

It's not what you are that holds you back;
it's what you think you are not.

• I have kept a mini-notebook for several years which I call "The Lord Provides." In it I've listed everything that has been given to us as gifts and from whom. Also listed are things we have found and items donated to us. It's beautiful to see how the Lord leads others to meet our needs and desires.

• Having more than one phone can be a frustration as well as a convenience, so I keep a list of frequently called numbers beside each of the phones. Emergency numbers and those of close relatives are a must if you live alone, even if you normally remember the numbers. In a stressful situation you may forget.

• Color code your files for a real time-saver. The red folders can be for "hot" items, for example. Use bright colors—they are more cheerful.

• I had so much data and information around the house that I became a slave to recording and keeping track of everything. A friend of mine urged me to look into a small home computer. At first I balked, but I am so glad I listened to him. Now that I have one, I can't believe how valuable the computer has become. It's a real time-saver.

• Whenever I receive an invitation, I attach it to my kitchen calendar in the month the event will take place. I also write the event on the calendar on the appropriate day. I keep the invitations clipped to the calendar in one stack in chronological order. After each event has taken place, I remove the invitation. Keeping the invitations handy saves me from searching for the time, the place, and especially the spelling of people's names.

• It's important to look professional and not weighted down when making customer calls. I have one leather briefcase that holds my wallet, makeup, calendar, and other business-related files. If I go to lunch and don't want to take my briefcase, I simply take my wallet and go. No more fumbling with briefcase, purse, keys, etc.

• Once you have organized your space, keep it organized by maintaining the space on a regular basis. I find that maintenance is the most important aspect of organization.

It takes time for change to be assimilated.

• Assign convenient permanent locations for small, "restless" items that would otherwise end up on a tabletop or be mislaid. For example, place a hook near the door for keys that you always take when you go out, a small dish on the bureau top to collect loose change or earrings, a mug on the desk to hold pens and pencils.

• If messy housemates are a problem, toss their out-of-place belongings into a big cardboard box. When asked where you put an item, point to the box.

• Some of the most valued "records" that you have are probably personal letters, photographs, and such mementos as newspaper clippings, diplomas, and graduation programs. Don't feel guilty about saving these, but don't be overly sentimental either. Throw out the scraps that will mean little as time passes.

• To protect valuable mementos and records from fire or flood (and to keep them all in one place, as well) store them in a metal strongbox or small footlocker.

• Make sure that you have copies of all birth, marriage, divorce, and death certificates. These records are filed permanently either in a state vital statistics office or in a city, county, or other local office.

• To get copies of a birth certificate, write to the appropriate office of the capital of the state where the birth took place. The office may be listed in the phone book under "Vital Statistics" or "Health Department."

• When storing keepsakes or clothing, number your boxes 1, 2, 3, and so on. Make out 3" x 5" cards and list on each what you're storing in the numbered boxes. Put your 3"x 5" cards in a file box. When you need to look for an item, simply go to your file box and find the card with the item listed. Check the card number and get the corresponding box. The item is found in minutes!

• Use a kitchen silverware tray to store art supplies, children's crayons, pencils, etc.

• Use colored plastic rings to color code your keys. It makes it much easier to locate them. Store keys in one central location so everyone in the family knows where all of them are.

• You might consider a trade-off system. Whenever you add a new item to the household inventory, discard an old one. This works great for wardrobe items.

• Caution! Do not throw out someone else's things unless they ask you to do so. Suggest and encourage, but don't take

Prime Rules of Organization

1. Use a single notebook for notes and basic written information.
   - Jot down five areas of your life that need straightening out. Concentrate on these areas.
   - Isolate these basic five areas. You must learn to focus on the part and not the whole.

2. Divide up difficult problems into instant tasks.
   - When you see a problem area like a messy refrigerator, don't see the whole mess, but start with one area of the whole. Clean one shelf or drawer at a time.
   - If the whole is too large to do in one day, take two to three days to do the task. You will feel so relieved and proud when you finish.

3. Prioritize your projects.
   - Rank them according to importance. Don't get bogged down in this process. Don't worry about ranking each one exactly.

4. Choose a regular time to organize work.
   - We do much better when we are specific in this area.
   - This regular time will soon become a habit.
   - Block out one longer amount of time or several shorter spans of time.

5. The important element is to start.
   - Even if it's the wrong spot, begin.
   - The most important step is to identify the problem. Then you can analyze the solution, prioritize what needs to be done, and finally get started.
   - Remember, these are firm appointments to be kept.

6. Reward yourself for beginning with:
   - A walk on the beach.
   - A new blouse.
   - A new CD.

over. This applies to your parents, spouse, and any children over four years old.

• Be ruthless with your own possessions. Discard all unused junk. When in doubt, throw it out. It takes up space, and you'll just wind up cleaning it and moving it around.

• When the enthusiasm strikes to clean, start from the outside in. Take care of the clutter scattered around the room before digging into the closet. Starting with the closet first makes a double mess.

• To keep mess to a minimum, before you begin cleaning a closet arrange three boxes nearby to categorize those things that shouldn't go back in. Label them "Give Away," "Put Away," and "Throw Away."

• Work on one small section of a closet at a time. Do not empty an entire cluttered closet at once. The resulting chaos is sure to discourage you or put you off entirely.

• The most basic part of organization is knowing what to throw away. Invite an objective friend over to help make those decisions. Less is better than more. It saves you a lot of cleaning.

People don't plan to be failures,
but they do plan for success.

• Keep items used together near one another (for example, tennis rackets, balls, sneakers, and other tennis equipment). Store these related items at or near the place where you use them.

• Make the time to do what you want and need to make your life what you want it to be.

• Buy a handbag or tote bag large enough to hold a paperback book or magazine (for waiting time) and a small notebook for list-making. Attach your keys to a chain that clips to or loops around the strap. Tuck keys inside. Keep cosmetics in a separate bag that closes to keep makeup from falling out. Wrap a rubber band around pens and pencils. Always put your eyeglasses in the same compartment. Remove notes, crumpled tissues, and deposit slips once a week, maybe while you watch TV. Switch bags only when you dress up.

• Before you buy something, ask yourself, "Where am I going to put it?" and make sure that you have a clearly defined place in mind.

• If the phone encroaches on your efficiency, unplug it or let it ring. Can't bear that? An answering machine or service will take your messages and let you return calls at your convenience.

• Keep a pad and pen next to your bed and in your bathroom to jot down ideas, things to do, and supplies and makeup you need.

• Allow time for making beds and tidying the kitchen before leaving the house in the morning. It makes coming home much more pleasant—and sets an example for others in the household.

• If you can't get all your housework done in a reasonable amount of time, hire someone to help you. You'll be surprised at how much more you can accomplish with someone helping out just three hours every week!

• If you can't afford professional help, be creative. Possible sources of assistance include schoolchildren, college students, and neighbors who might be willing to take over one or two jobs, such as housecleaning, ironing, or grocery shopping—and for considerably less than it costs to hire a professional.

• Don't keep an address book for home use. Instead, buy a small 3" x 5" file box. Use 3" x 5" cards to list names alphabetically and file them in the box. You'll never lose the box or spend money replacing old address books. When someone moves or changes a phone number, just replace the card. Add cards when needed. On the back of the card you can write important information about that person: directions to

Using Bits of Time

Most small chores can be accomplished in bits and pieces of time. For instance, while you're waiting in a doctor's office, you can pay bills; while riding the bus, write out your shopping list. The following lists may give you some ideas of what you can do with small chunks of time.

What you can do in 5 minutes
Make an appointment.
File your nails.
Water houseplants.
Make out a party guest list.
Order tickets for a concert or a ball game.
Sew a button on.

What you can do in 10 minutes
Write a short letter or note.
Pick out a birthday card.
Repot a plant.
Hand-wash some clothes.
Straighten your desktop.
Exercise.

What you can do in 30 minutes
Go through backed-up magazines and newspapers.
Work on a craft project.
Polish silver and brass.
Vacuum three or four rooms.
Weed a flower bed.

home, favorite colors, names of family members, birthdays, favorite foods, etc. This will give you a great source of information about that person.

• Make it a habit to return everything to its proper place and remind others to do so. If you do this daily, it takes less time than waiting until the situation is out of control. An even bigger bonus is that you won't need to spend time looking for out-of-place objects.

• Do small chores as needed so that they occupy little time. For example, laundry left until the weekend can consume the weekend; instead, start a load before breakfast, put it in the dryer after breakfast, and it's done.

• Use labor-saving gadgets or appliances whenever they will really save time. But don't overdo it. Chopping an onion with a knife may take no longer than using a food processor and then having to take the machine apart and wash and dry it.

• Leave some slack in your day for surprises, interruptions, or emergencies. Some activities will take longer than expected, no matter how carefully you plan or allow for delays.

• Think before you act—even before you do routine jobs. The way you perform simple, basic tasks is usually the result of habit, not logic. There may be a better way.

• Why does a half-hour job often take twice as long as you thought it would? Probably because you estimated only the actual working time and didn't take into account the preparation (getting out and putting away tools, for instance).

• Install telephone jacks all around the house or get a cordless phone so that you can talk wherever you are in and around your home.

• Establish a message center in your home. It needn't be elaborate—it can be on the refrigerator or on a bulletin board or a door. Encourage everyone in the household to use the message center to list plans, needs for the next shopping trip, and (especially important) all telephone messages.

• Keep the message center current. Throw away outdated notes. Take care of as many items as you can each day, or enter them in your notebook for action later.

• To save time and frustration, whenever possible use the telephone instead of making a trip. Phone to confirm appointments, to check if a store has the item you want, to learn business hours, and so on.

• Learn how to cut off time-consuming calls without hurting people's feelings. For example, it's quite all right to say, "This is a terrible time for me, may I call you back?" (Of course, do call back later.)

• Sometimes a phone call is more timesaving and effective than a letter. Even a long-distance call may be cheaper, especially when you consider how long it takes to write a letter and how much your time is worth.

• Group your errands so that you can accomplish several in a single trip. Try to find a convenient shopping center that has all or most of the stores, offices, and services that you need.

• Whenever possible, do errands when traffic is light and lines are short—usually between 10 A.M. and 3 P.M. on weekdays, in the evenings, and all day Sunday.

• If you have appointments or errands at several locations, schedule them so that you can go from one to the next with a minimum of wasted time and travel.

• Eliminate additional trips by making back-to-back doctor or dentist appointments for family members (or at least for all the kids).

• Try to get the first appointment of the morning so that you won't be delayed by someone ahead of you and you'll still have most of the day left when you finish.

• Take your weekly "to do" list with you whenever you go on errands. You may be able to fit in something that you scheduled for later in the week.

2

Food
Preparation

Meal planning and
a shopping list
is a must

She gets up before dawn
to prepare breakfast
for her household, and
plans the day's work
for her servant girls.

—Proverbs 31:15 (TLB)

Food
Preparation

One of the secrets of success is to enjoy doing whatever we do—not only for stimulation for ourselves, but also for the satisfaction of giving of ourselves to others in love.

Where can this be done better in the home than in the kitchen, cooking and preparing nutritious meals for our loved ones? Even if we only cook for ourselves, it's important to approach food preparation as a love ministry to ourselves.

Descriptions of food are found throughout the Bible from the Garden of Eden (Genesis 2:16–3:3) to the discussion of the elements of the Lord's Supper (1 Corinthians 11:23-26). Careful dietary laws are presented in Leviticus 11:1-47. Mealtimes were often celebrations, as in Luke 15:22-32.

Women have long been associated with mealtime in a special way. For example the "victorious wife" or "woman of strength" described in Proverbs 31:10-31 is willing to expend great effort to provide physical nurture for her family. There is no more beautiful time to nourish the family and other people than in those regularly appointed gatherings which provide physical sustenance and spiritual nurture.

Brother Lawrence, a member of the humble, barefooted Carmelite monks in the 1600s, expressed the special

31

opportunity for service in the kitchen: "Lord of all pots and pans and things. . .make me a saint by getting meals and washing up the plates!"

Oh, how our family life would change if we could look upon meals and mealtimes as worthy of God's calling! Remember, we were called to serve and not to be served. What a great opportunity to serve members of our family when we prepare food. Truly make mealtimes a celebration. Do it as unto the Lord.

• Turn menu planning into a family project. Ask family members to list their favorite dishes, then compile menus using these recipes. When given a chance to participate, people enjoy their meals more.
• Perk up your dinners by serving your family a new dish each week, if possible. Exchange recipes with your friends and neighbors. Check food sections of magazines and newspapers. Try unfamiliar fruits and vegetables.
• Notice what your family enjoys at restaurants. Consult your cookbooks and try to duplicate the dishes at home.
• To add interest to a soft-textured meal, serve a crunchy vegetable salad or crisp bread.
• Serve something other than rice or potatoes to accompany gravies and sauces. Try barley, bulgur (cracked wheat), or pasta in unusual shapes.
• Check ads for sales. Plan to go to several stores if the savings are worthwhile and you have enough to buy to make the trip worthwhile.
• Build menus around meat and poultry on sale.
• When shopping, don't deviate from your grocery list unless you find unadvertised sales, such as overripe fruit and day-old bakery items.
• Buy herbs and spices in bulk and store them in your own bottles. You'll save as much as 70 percent on their cost.
• For perfectly shaped fried eggs, press a drinking glass into

the center of a slice of bread and cut out a circle. Place the bread flat in a buttered frying pan. Break an egg into the center of the hole.

• If you have overestimated the hotcake or waffle appetite of your family, you needn't discard the leftover batter. Cook it up, but brown very lightly. Freeze with foil between, then pop in the toaster or oven on a morning when you don't have time to cook.

• When cooking vegetables in water, leave them whole; they'll retain more vitamins and minerals. And they're much easier to chop or slice after they're cooked.

• When cooking a hot cereal, use low-fat or skim milk as part or all of the liquid, and you'll greatly improve the nutritional value.

• Raw fruits and vegetables have more useful fiber than those that have been peeled, cooked, pureed, or processed.

• Drink lots of liquids when you eat foods containing fiber, or the fiber may be constipating instead of stimulating to your bowels.

• Generally, coarse fiber is more effective than the same fiber finely ground. Look for the words "whole grain," "whole wheat," or "whole oats" when you buy breads, cereals, and crackers.

• Your body needs only one tablespoon of dietary fat a day, but most people eat far more. Much of it is hidden in meat, cold cuts, pastries, other commercial baked goods, and such prepared foods as potato chips, French-fried potatoes, and frozen dinners.

• To avoid saturated fats (the kind that clog your arteries), buy margarine that lists liquid oil as its first ingredient. The second ingredient should be partially hydrogenated vegetable oil.

• Because they help to reduce the cholesterol levels in your blood, polyunsaturated or monounsaturated oils are the best choice for salads and for cooking. Safflower oil is the most polyunsaturated. Others in descending order are sunflower, soybean, corn, and sesame oil. Olive and peanut oils are monounsaturated.

• Bottled salad dressings may be loaded with saturated oils and preservatives. Make your own by mixing three or four parts polyunsaturated vegetable oil, olive oil, yogurt, or buttermilk with one part vinegar or lemon juice, and seasonings.

• In place of high-fat gravy, serve broth. Instead of butter, season foods with lemon or lime juice, vinegar, spices, or herbs.

---

*Peaceful mealtimes aid both the
digestion and the disposition.*

• To prevent freezer burn, remove as much air as possible before sealing. Never freeze meat in store packaging, since it's neither airtight nor moisture-proof.

• Store food in a single layer to allow proper air circulation and to speed the freezing process. Set the thermostat at 0°F.

• Defrost the freezer when frost buildup reaches a thickness of one-quarter inch.

• Before freezing fresh bagels, cut them in half. When you're ready to use them, they will defrost faster and can even be toasted while they are still frozen.

• Because the yolk of one large egg contains a day's quota of cholesterol, limit yolks to three or four a week, including those in prepared and processed foods (you can only guess how much egg yolk is in such foods).

• Eat as many egg whites as you wish. They're a fine low-calorie source of protein. Omit the yolks of hard-boiled eggs in salads.

• In preparing eggs, give every other yolk to your dog. In other words, make your omelet with two whites and one yolk. Do the same with pancakes or French toast. You

The Family That Dines Together
Has Better Nutrition

Children who eat meals with the family have better nutritional habits, says a registered dietitian for the California Dietetic Association.

"Children learn good eating habits from the examples set by adults. Left to choose their own meals, they are less likely to make nutritionally balanced selections essential for proper growth and health."

And the children agree. According to a recent Gallup survey, children who rate their own nutritional habits the best are those who dine with their families most frequently.

To make family dining workable and enjoyable, the association suggests the following:

- Pick at least one meal of the day when your chances for getting everyone around the table are best. If one meal each day is still too demanding, compromise. Set a goal of eating as a family four or five days a week instead of seven.
- Set a regular mealtime when everyone is at home.
- Make healthy eating fun by serving a variety of foods and trying new preparation methods.
- Involve your children in cooking. They will learn different cooking techniques and how to prepare nutritious meals.

For a free brochure to help you manage your children's food choices, send a self-addressed stamped envelope to Helpful Hints for Healthy Children, 3170 Fourth Avenue, Suite 300, San Diego, CA 92103.

won't notice the difference, but your dog will develop a beautiful, shiny coat.
• Although eggs contain a good deal of iron, this iron is poorly absorbed by the body and may interfere with the absorption of iron from other sources.
• Many of our friends and family members have broken the mealtime salt habit. When I have guests for dinner and set out salt and pepper shakers, I also place a small dish of lemon and lime wedges on the table as a healthy seasoning alternative.
• Don't throw away a soup or stew that has turned out too salty. Instead, add a cut raw potato, and discard the potato slices when they are cooked. The potato will absorb most of the salt.
• How many times have you opened the refrigerator to find a key ingredient for the next meal missing, "stolen" by some greedy snacker? To save the meal, the day, and your nerves, try using red warning dots. Any food you want to save should receive one of these attention-grabbing self-sticking labels before it gets stored in the refrigerator.
• If you take out all ingredients at the beginning of a cooking project and put them away as used, the cleanup is easier and there's no doubt whether or not you have used an ingredient.
• Try placing turkey stuffing in cheesecloth and loosely inserting it into the bird before roasting. It can be removed intact, leaves the bird clean inside, and makes it easier to store leftovers.
• To crisp salad greens, wash and roll them in a terry-cloth towel and refrigerate or place in a lingerie bag and run it through the spin cycle of your washing machine. Don't leave the machine—you might forget that your lettuce is in there. Make sure all the water is out of the lettuce.
• Never store carrots with apples. Apples release a gas that gives carrots a bitter taste.

Tasty Tips to Please Even Picky Eaters

Even the most delicious, nutritious meal won't do any good if your children refuse to eat it. Some youngsters are naturally finicky eaters, according to the American Dietetic Association, which shares these tips to make meals pleasant for everyone:

• *If your child doesn't like one group of foods, try offering a nutritional substitute. For example, if the child won't eat vegetables, try serving fruit instead. Substitute low-fat cheese or yogurt for milk.*

• *To boost the nutritional value of prepared dishes, combine foods in unique ways, like adding nonfat dry milk to cream soups or puddings or mixing grated zucchini and carrots into quick breads, muffins, meat loaf, and lasagna.*

• *Cut foods into interesting shapes. Draw a smiling face on top of a casserole with cheese, vegetables, or fruit strips. Make Mickey or Minnie Mouse pancakes. (The batter needs to be a little thinner for ease in pouring.)*

• *Let children help with food preparation. Helping to prepare food makes eating it a lot more fun. Have a special chef's hat and apron for the cook.*

• *Set a good example by eating well yourself and, whenever possible, eat together as a family.*

• *Preparing foods in a different way can capture kids' interest. Make grilled cheese sandwiches fun. Prepare them in the usual way, but instead of grilling the sandwiches in a skillet, put them in a waffle iron.*

• Slice raw tomatoes vertically so the inner pulp holds its shape for salads.

• To avoid residue when measuring sticky liquids (honey, molasses), rinse the measuring cup in hot water first.

• The easiest way to slice cheesecake is with dental floss. Press a long strand of tautly held unflavored floss through the cake. Pull it out without pulling it up again.

• Favorite recipes that you use often, whether cut from magazines or written on recipe cards, can be taped to the inside of your kitchen cabinet doors. When you're ready to cook, there's no need to rummage through clippings in envelopes or boxes. Just open your cabinet door!

---

*Offer a prayer of thanksgiving together
to bring to your heart gratitude,
peace, and warmth around the table.*

• Our family loves BLT (bacon, lettuce, and tomato) sandwiches. Whenever I fry or microwave bacon, I cook a few extra pieces and put them into a plastic freezer bag and freeze. They are ready for the next BLT sandwich.

• To avoid contamination of food in containers, always use a clean utensil to scoop out mayonnaise, peanut butter, and tomato paste.

• When serving leftover meat or fish, don't just reheat it. Instead, prepare it in a different form. For example, grind it and shape it into patties, dice it for casseroles, or slice it thin and add it to stir-fry dishes or to a white sauce.

• People who regularly substitute caffeine-type beverages, such as coffee, tea, and cola, for milk are not only limiting their intake of calcium, they also may be losing calcium. For example, the caffeine in one cup of coffee can cause six milligrams of calcium loss through the urine beyond the amount the body normally loses.

• For those of you who hate searching through your

cookbook collection for favorite recipes, here's a solution. Stick colorful self-adhesive dots from the dime store next to your favorite recipes on the pages of each cookbook. When you flip through the pages, the dots will catch your eye.

• For those times when you can't cook, prepare a small book entitled "Mom's (or Dad's) Helpful Hints," in which you record your favorite easy-to-prepare recipes. Carefully note each step for every recipe and include some special cooking tips. Your family will really appreciate it.

• Start a "hope chest" recipe card box with all the family favorites for your daughters and sons who enjoy cooking or will soon be living on their own. This truly is a gift filled with love and fond memories.

• Try satisfying your sweet tooth with dessert breads containing relatively little sugar. Add nourishing ingredients such as whole-wheat flour, oatmeal, nuts, raisins, and a fruit or a vegetable such as pumpkin, zucchini, cranberries, or carrots.

• Grease and flour baking pans in one step. Thoroughly mix one-half cup shortening and one-fourth cup all purpose flour or wheat flour; then use a pastry brush to apply the coating to the pans. Store any leftovers in a covered jar at room temperature.

• To take the skin off a whole chicken in a jiffy and make it less fatty, remove the wings and cut the bird down the breastbone. Lay it out flat with the back up and pull off the skin.

• Sautéed diced vegetables make a delicious low-calorie topping for pasta, baked potatoes, or rice.

• Pureed vegetables make excellent low-fat sauces for fish, poultry, or pasta.

• Mix powdered salad dressings into plain yogurt instead of using oil or sour cream. Or add buttermilk, cottage cheese, or tomato juice to the dressings. Use yogurt instead of sour cream for dips.

- Pie lovers can save approximately 150 calories per serving by eating single-crust fruit cobblers instead of two-crust pies.
- Eat slowly. Taste your food. Put down your knife and fork after every two or three bites. Make each meal last 20 or 30 minutes.
- Postpone that second helping for about 20 minutes. You'll realize you don't need it, and you'll feel less hungry, too.
- Have some cooked meat left over, but not enough for an entire meal? Chop it up small, add a small amount of mayonnaise, bell pepper, celery, etc., and you have a great salad spread for sandwiches.
- Don't forget to use your microwave, even when making a conventional recipe. Let it melt butter and chocolate, soften cheese, toast nuts, cook bacon, and thaw frozen vegetables.

Turning off distracting noises creates an
air of calm, which allows conversation
to focus on building relationships,
generating peace, expressing love,
and providing encouragement.

- Make your own cracker crumbs in your blender.
- An easy way to make bread crumbs is to take frozen hamburger buns and scrape the inside of the buns with a dinner fork.
- When you find yourself out of bread crumbs in the middle of a recipe, reach for packaged croutons and the potato masher. It is quick, saves you a trip to the store, and there is no blender to wash.
- You can store homemade bread crumbs in an old salt carton and pour out what you need. Feed them into the carton through a funnel and store in the freezer.
- Make oat flour by whirling oatmeal in a blender. Use for

crumb crust in pies. To make the crust, use one cup oat flour, one-fourth cup butter or margarine, and two teaspoons sugar. Blend together with a fork.

• To get more juice out of a lemon, place it in your microwave oven on "high" for 30 seconds. Squeeze the lemon, and you will get twice as much juice—and the vitamins won't be destroyed.

• Oatmeal made from steel-cut or rolled oats (not the instant variety) leads the pack in food value for hot cereals because oats contain the most protein of any of the commonly eaten grains.

• Prolonged exposure to light produces a greenish tinge on potatoes. To prevent this discoloration, store potatoes properly in a dark, humid, well-ventilated place at a cool 45°F to 50°F. They should keep for weeks.

• To easily remove shish kebab meats and vegetables from the skewers, give the skewers a light coating of salad oil or vegetable cooking spray before you put the meat on them. It also makes for easy cleanup.

• To keep wax paper from curling up or slipping around when rolling a pie crust, wipe the countertop with a damp cloth or sponge before placing the wax paper on it. The moisture will keep the paper flat and prevent it from sliding.

• Since the leavening ability of baking powder diminishes with age, always test the powder. Place one-half teaspoon in one-fourth cup hot water. If the powder is fresh, the water will bubble actively.

• Buy walnuts, almonds, pecans, and other recipe-type nuts after the holidays at sale prices. Shell, then store them in individual plastic bags in the freezer. The nuts won't stick together, so it's easy to remove only what you need for each recipe.

• Get in the habit of serving fruit—preferably fresh fruit— for dessert. A fresh fruit cup can't be beat for appearance and taste. If you must rely on canned or frozen fruit, look

How to Save Money at the Supermarket

1. Shop with a purpose and a list.
   - *Plan your menus for the entire week and organize your shopping list accordingly.*
   - *Arrange your shopping list to correspond to the layout of your regular supermarket.*

2. Control impulse buying.
   - *Don't fall victim to media pressure.*
   - *Stick to your shopping list.*
   - *Don't buy last-minute magazines, candies, and gum at the checkout stand.*

3. Get your shopping done within a half hour.
   - *Don't shop during rush hour.*
   - *Shop during early mornings or late evenings.*

4. Shop alone, if you can.
   - *Children and spouses can cause you to compromise your shopping list.*

5. Never shop when you are hungry.
   - *Hunger will cause you to break the discipline of your shopping list.*

6. Use coupons wisely.
   - *Discipline yourself to use only those coupons that relate to products you regularly use.*
   - *Try to shop where they offer "double coupon" value.*

7. Be a smart shopper.
   - *Become acquainted with the psychology of the market industry.*
   - *Audit your receipt to check for any errors and for coupon credit.*

8. Use unit pricing.
   - *Carry a small calculator with you to figure out unit prices.*
   - *Don't be misled by the size of the packaging.*

9. Avoid foods that are packaged as individual servings.
   - *Individual servings usually increase prices.*

10. When buying meat, consider the amount of lean meat in the cut as well as the price per pound.
    - *Chicken, turkey, and fish are good bargains for the budget buyer.*

11. Buy vegetables and fruits in season.
    - *Canning produce yourself gives you the greatest economy.*

for brands packaged in water instead of sweetened syrup.

• Read food labels for clues on sugar content. If the word *sugar, sucrose, glucose, maltose, dextrose, lactose, fructose,* or *syrup* appears first on the label, then sugar is the ingredient used in greatest quantity in this product.

• Instead of buying cakes, pies, or cookies, make your own and cut the sugar in the recipe by a third or even a half.

• When you are packaging hamburger, take it off the plastic meat tray and flatten the meat out. Then put it in a freezer bag. You can place flat packages of meat side by side in the freezer, which uses less space.

• To cut up canned tomatoes quickly, use kitchen shears and snip the tomatoes right in the can.

• To separate frozen fruits and vegetables easily, put them in a colander and rinse them under hot tap water.

• When cutting grapes for a salad, working in front of a light will make removing seeds a lot easier. The light shining through the grape makes the seeds more visible and quicker to remove.

• When a recipe specifies "dot with butter," it's easier to use a vegetable peeler to shave thin curls from a frozen or very cold stick of butter or margarine.

• Protect your thumb with a rubber fingertip (available in office supply stores) when peeling hot potatoes or other just-cooked vegetables in their skins.

There is no more beautiful time to nourish the family and others than in those regularly appointed gatherings which provide physical sustenance and spiritual nurture.

• To avoid splatters when using your hand-held beater, especially when whipping cream, take a paper plate and punch two holes in the center with a knife. Insert the blade posts through them before connecting to the beater. The plate will cover the bowl while the beater does its work.

• When whipping cream, chill the bowl and beaters so the cream will not sour while being beaten.

• When making soup stock, use a spaghetti cooker, placing pieces of chicken or meat bones in the strainer along with vegetables and seasoning. When the stock has simmered long enough, lift out the strainer along with the vegetables and bones, leaving just the clear stock in the bottom pot.

• Use clean, squeeze-type catsup and mustard containers to decorate cakes. Their narrow spouts are great for writing and drawing with icing.

• The few extra tablespoons of fruit juice left in the bottom of the bottle are a perfect baste for poultry.

• When preparing graham crackers or wafers for a crumb crust, place the crackers in a plastic bag and use the side of your meat tenderizer hammer to pound the crackers into crumbs. All the mess stays confined inside the bag, and you can pour the crumbs into your baking pan.

• When a recipe calls for dry ingredients, cooking oil, and honey or syrup, always measure the dry ingredients first, then the oil followed by the honey. In this way, your measuring cup stays clean for the next ingredient. The dry ingredients won't stick to the cup and, as the honey is measured last, it will flow freely since the cup was first coated with oil.

• To avoid a pot boil-over, apply a thin coat of cooking oil around the top of the inside of your pot.

• A great way to clean fresh mushrooms is to add three to four tablespoons of flour to a medium-size bowl of cold water. Wash the mushrooms in the water. The dirt adheres to the flour particles almost like magic. The mushrooms come out very clean.

• Put a drop of vegetable or salad oil in boiling water before adding macaroni, noodles, or spaghetti. The oil keeps them from sticking together.

• After you open a container of ice cream, cover it with a

plastic freezer bag before you put it back in the freezer. This will help protect against freezer burn and keeps the ice cream fresh much longer.

• Whenever you make a brown-bag lunch, wrap the lettuce for your sandwich in a damp paper towel and pack it in a separate plastic bag. At lunchtime, simply add the lettuce to the sandwich.

• Cooking a lot of tacos? Use your dish drainer. It can hold the shells safely upright while you fill them "production line" fast.

• When placing things in the freezer, be sure to wrap and date them. Place new items in the back of the freezer and move older items to the front.

• An inexpensive way to make breakfast cereal is to buy an inexpensive brand of corn or wheat flakes and a box of raisins. Each time you have a bowl of cereal, add two scoops of raisins. It really lasts a long time and is much cheaper than the cereal that contains raisins.

• To microwave-heat a frozen dinner that comes in a foil tray, pop the frozen food out and place it in a glass pie plate. Invert another glass pie plate over the top and heat (usually five to seven minutes on high will do). Easy, fast, and delicious!

• The cardboard from medium-size pizzas makes great giveaway cake plates. Cover the cardboard with aluminum foil, and your cake, pie, or batch of cookies is ready to travel to a friend or bake sale.

• Store the remainder of a banana (unpeeled) in a tightly closed jar in the refrigerator. Believe it or not, it won't turn dark.

• When you bring home a bag of flour or a box of cake mix that won't be used immediately, slip a bay leaf into the box or bag to keep the bugs out.

• When cooking rice, prepare a large batch and freeze the

How to Use Aluminum Foil Effectively

Try baking apples in cups shaped from aluminum foil and placed in a shallow pan. It's a quick and easy way to serve the apples when you put them on your dessert dishes, and there's no sticky pan to wash.

Make a quick liner for the baking pan: Shape the foil over the outside of the inverted pan and then slip the preformed foil inside.

When you're preparing a meal of assorted leftovers, are you fed up with trying to juggle the pots and pans? Next time, try putting each leftover into a bowl shaped from aluminum foil. Put these bowls in one big pan, add a little water, cover, and steam.

You can keep rolls hot and protect your bread basket from grease stains by placing a piece of aluminum foil under the napkin in the basket.

When you accidentally crack an egg, you can still soft- or hard-cook it. Wrap it in aluminum foil before immersing it in boiling water.

When you have a lot of cookies to bake and are short on oven space and time, try a foil assembly line. Cut aluminum foil to fit your cookie sheets, place the cookie dough on the foil, and slip the foil over your cookie sheets. You can prepare all the cookies ahead of time and just slip the foil sheet liners on as soon as the sheets come out of the oven.

---

leftover rice, two servings to a bag. The next time you want to serve rice, pull the needed number of bags out of the freezer and heat them in a steamer basket over boiling water.

• Keep a large saltshaker full of flour near the stove for times when you need only a spoonful. This saves the time and bother of opening a big canister, and you will never have spills where you don't want them.

• Keep at least one dated, brown-bag lunch in the freezer as a backup. You can save a few valuable minutes in the morning and a couple of dollars in the lunch line.

• When canning jams, use Saran Wrap stretched tightly over the mouth of the jar. Then screw the lid on tightly. No need to use paraffin again. One woman has used this method successfully for over ten years.

Consider your mealtimes a celebration. Enjoy the food, friends, and family. Have fun!

Smart Cooking Tips

• Carefully monitor leftovers. Use them as snacks or for lunch, or freeze them to use another time.

• Try to include "filling" food on your menus for the hearty eaters in your family. Chili, stew, soup, sandwiches, and slow-cooker dishes are good choices.

• Remember that *sometimes* quantity counts more than quality. For instance, you can serve two packages of chicken franks for almost the same price as one package of beef franks. But don't substitute foods your family won't eat.

• Prepare hot cereals for breakfast. They're more economical and filling than cold cereals.

• Plan a "bake day" when everyone can pitch in. Assign kitchen tasks so family members can help prepare inexpensive homemade snacks to freeze or refrigerate.

• Substitute boneless chicken breasts or turkey cutlets in recipes calling for expensive veal cutlets.

• Make your own salad dressing by the bottle and keep it in the refrigerator.

• Save time *and* money with one-dish salad meals. Combine diced leftover meat, fish, or poultry with fresh vegetables.

• Don't waste milk by using it for scrambled eggs or omelets. Milk makes eggs watery because it won't blend

Shaking the Salt Habit

Go easy on such salty foods as potato chips, pretzels, salted nuts, popcorn, snack crackers, commercial frozen dinners, pickled foods, cured meats, canned tuna or crab, sauerkraut, steak sauce, soy sauce, and garlic salt.

Read labels on processed foods; often such foods contain sodium in forms other than table salt. Be aware of these ingredients: sodium nitrate, sodium bicarbonate (baking soda), monosodium glutamate (MSG), sodium benzoate, and sodium phosphate.

with them. Use water, which makes eggs fluffy.
• Create healthful, low-cost meals based on dried beans with leftover meats and fresh vegetables.
• Be innovative with whatever vegetables are in the refrigerator. Try cooking several together.
• Include a relish/pickle platter with a meal, made up from what's on hand.
• Doctor up canned chili by adding canned beans and serving it over a bed of rice. Garnish with shredded cheese, chopped green onions, and sour cream.
• Use grilled cheese sandwiches to extend soup menus.
• Turn a simple pasta side dish into a meal by serving it with a salad.
• Pizza can be made from practically anything on hand. Use cheddar, Swiss, or Monterey Jack cheese to replace the mozzarella. If you don't have cheese, use canned tomatoes, green and red sweet peppers, olives, or onions to create a vegetarian pizza.
• Use mixed grains (rice, wheat, and millet) to make a nutritious side dish. Sauté broken spaghetti with the grain before adding the broth.
• Use dumplings to extend soups and stews.

• For a quick dessert, use canned and frozen fruits for topping ice cream or sherbets.

Ideas for Leftovers

Don't throw out your leftovers. The following ideas can help you recycle scraps of food:
• Spread almost-stale bread with butter or margarine and sprinkle with grated cheese. Toast and top with a poached egg.
• Leftover pound or sponge cake makes a wonderful dessert. Top with custard or fruit sauce, or crumble over ice cream.
• Freeze heavy cream for later use in quiches, tart fillings, cream soups, and sauces. Remember: Once frozen, cream no longer whips.
• Freeze coffee in ice-cube trays. Add the cubes to iced coffee for an extra-strength brew. Or whirl the cubes in the blender with ice cream for a coffee slush. You can also enrich meat gravies with coffee for a robust flavor. Coffee in cake frosting makes for a luscious mocha cream.
• When I have a few crumbs left in a bag of potato chips or box of crackers, I save them. After I lightly coat them with butter and toast them in the oven until brown, they make a tasty topping for casseroles and baked vegetables.
• To help keep a vegetable salad from becoming soggy, place a saucer upside down in the bottom of the bowl before filling it with the ingredients.
• If you make dip that's too runny, add some bread crumbs for extra body and flavor.
• Bring limp celery back to life by immersing in ice-cold water for just a few hours.
• For the two of us I bake six large potatoes. We eat them baked the first night. The second serving is sliced and fried in a bit of butter. The last two potatoes are cubed and served in a cream sauce with some cheese.

What Food Labels Don't Tell You

1. What standardized foods contain.
   - *Over 350 standardized foods require no labeling by the FDA.*
2. How much sugar is in some products.
   - *Due to the nature and variety of sweetness ingredients, which are listed separately, it's hard to know just how much total sugar is contained.*
3. How "natural" a product is.
   - *The term "natural" is very misleading.*
   - *Many of these foods can be highly processed and full of additives.*
4. Specific ingredients that may be harmful.
   - *Coloring and spices don't have to be listed by name.*

- You can make your own condensed milk. To one-half cup of boiling water, add three tablespoons of butter or margarine, one-half cup of sugar, and $1^1/_2$ cups of powdered milk. Beat all together. Makes $1^1/_3$ cups.
- Make homemade TV dinners from leftovers. Label them as follows: "Goulash/Date/Micro: High—one minute/Salad and Bread." By suggesting the cooking time and menu complement, you'll find that leftovers are eaten, meals are rarely skipped, and money is saved.
- To save time in the kitchen, freeze homemade soup in family-size portions in a bowl. When they are frozen, remove the rounds and place them in plastic bags. When it is time to reheat the soup, the frozen rounds fit perfectly into a big soup kettle.
- Quickest-of-all sauces: Deglaze a pan with a bit of wine. Here's how: When you finish browning meat or fish, remove it from the pan. Pour in a little wine while the pan is still hot and scrape up browned bits left in the pan

with a wooden spoon. Reheat the wine for just a minute.
• To make meatballs that are wonderfully moist, put a small ice cube in the center of each ball before browning. Cook as usual.
• To prevent sauces from burning or cooking too fast, place a heat diffuser on the burner. It evens out and reduces the heat.
• Use peanut oil for frying. It can withstand high temperatures without burning and won't alter the taste of the food because it's flavorless.
• Cooking with part butter and part peanut oil will give the flavor of butter with less saturated fat. The oil also helps to keep the butter from smoking.
• Freeze lunch box sandwiches. They can be made up by the week. Put on all ingredients except lettuce. It will save time and effort.

Even when dining alone, mealtime can be a time to rest, to reflect on God's blessings.

• To measure cooking oil more accurately and avoid drowning a salad or stir-fry dish in a sudden deluge, don't remove the seal from a new bottle of oil. Cut a slit in the seal and pour through that—you'll be able to measure even a teaspoonful without a spill.
• Try replacing the oil required in recipes for bran, whole grain, or oatmeal muffins with an equal or slightly larger amount of unsweetened applesauce. You'll have a moist, low-fat variation of these mealtime favorites.
• Don't flour meat when you're browning it for a stew or casserole. You'll end up browning only the flour and the meat won't get the color or flavor of browning. Instead, heat

Perfect Peeling

Four quick and easy ways to peel:

- Onions: *Cut off the bottom, then the top. Cut a slash in the side of the onion and remove the first outer peel, including the skin.*
- Tomatoes: *Turn a fork-held tomato over a gas burner until the skin begins to darken and blister. It will peel right off.*
- Tomatoes: *Place tomatoes in boiling water and remove the pan from the heat. Let it sit for one minute. Remove the tomatoes from the pan, plunge them into cold water, and strip off the skins.*
- Garlic: *With the palm of your hand, crush the entire head of garlic so that the cloves fall apart. Select one clove and place the flat side of a large knife over it; hit the knife gently with your hand. The clove skin will come off immediately. To get the smell of garlic off your hands, rub them in used coffee grounds.*

the pan, add a bit of oil, and sear or brown the meat very quickly.
- Read your recipes carefully before you begin; then gather the ingredients and utensils you will need.
- Be sure to keep a good supply of staple foods for last-minute meals.
- Chill foods quickly by placing them in the freezer for 20 to 30 minutes.
- Don't toss out that last half-inch of French, blue cheese, or Russian salad dressing! Transform it into a new dressing. Just add two teaspoons of vinegar or lemon juice (or one of each, if you prefer). Recap and shake vigorously. Now gradually add one-half cup mayonnaise or sour cream, shaking as you add. You will have a brand-new, tasty dressing!
- Fruits such as melons, cantaloupes, watermelons, and

bananas make delicious frozen pops. Blend the fruit till smooth in a food processor or blender. Place the fruit puree in small containers and freeze till ready to use.

• Keep unpopped popcorn in the freezer to minimize the amount of unpopped kernels when you prepare it.

• Hot peppers, also known as chilies and frequently used in Mexican dishes, contain a colorless substance called capsaicin that can seriously irritate skin and eyes. Wear rubber gloves and avoid touching your face or eyes. Wash the gloves and your hands thoroughly afterward.

• After opening, refrigerate wheat germ, pure maple syrup, vegetable shortening, salad dressing, jams, jellies, and shelled nuts.

• In warm weather (unless your kitchen is air-conditioned) consider storing whole-grain flours, crackers, and breads in the refrigerator or freezer, unless you can use them quickly.

New Food Labels

The new food labels are here and, believe it or not, they are a huge improvement over the old ones.

The Food and Drug Administration's new labeling regulations require that manufacturers indicate in clear and understandable language exactly what you will be eating if you buy their products. A serving size, for example, must reflect what a person would normally eat. And you must be able to tell at a glance whether a food is high in fat, cholesterol, sodium, carbohydrates, and protein. At the bottom, each label must indicate the Daily Value of vitamins A and C, iron, and calcium. A manufacturer has the option of listing other nutrients that are present in significant amounts.

Processed foods must carry the new labels, with a few exceptions: ready-to-eat deli and bakery food that is prepared on-site, plain coffee and tea, some spices, restaurant food, and products made by small manufacturers.

To get the most from the new information, the consumer still has a few responsibilities. The labels are based on consumption of 2000 calories per day with 30 percent of those calories (65 grams) derived from fat. So you will need to know how many calories you take in per day. The 2000 is a bit high for the average woman, but it is lower than the average of 2335 calories for Americans aged 20 to 49. If you eat less than 2000 calories a day, or if you want a lower percentage of fat in your diet, you should adjust the percentages accordingly. Since the labels don't provide fat content as a percentage of calories, you might want to keep your daily fat tally at 50 grams total. The calcium figure may be especially helpful, since it is based on the needs of an adult female.

Here, then, are the basic components of the new labels. For more information, call the FDA, toll-free, at 800-FDA-4010.

3

The
Kitchen

A gathering place
for family, friends,
and guests to meet
and enjoy each
other's presence.

*S*he watches carefully all that goes on through-out her household, and is never lazy.

—Proverbs 31:27 (TLB)

The
Kitchen

$\mathcal{T}$he heart of a good home—the most sweetly rewarding part of a woman's domain and family responsibilities—is the kitchen.

If you don't find your kitchen such an enjoyable place, it can and should be. The secret is in learning to do things the easiest way possible and to have the proper tools. There is a way to make most tasks more pleasant by learning to "top clean."

Get rid of the excess clutter in your kitchen. Not only does this give you more room in which to work, but it also makes for easier cleaning. Clean up as you go—don't wait till the end of the meal. Otherwise, you will get discouraged, and the task will become too much of a burden.

Keep stacks from collecting on the counters and tables. Keep the big items picked up and the cupboards arranged—have a place for everything. If you don't have a place to store something in the kitchen, consider not purchasing it (or get rid of it if you don't use the item regularly).

I find that one or two "kitchen overflow" boxes come in handy. Place items like picnic utensils, Thanksgiving and Christmas pots, plates, and dishes into these boxes and store them in the garage, attic, basement, spare room—even under a bed. This will clear a lot of needed space for new everyday tools. Don't be stuck with doing things the traditional way. Do your chores the easiest and most convenient way for you.

Don't do without those basic tools that make homemaking and cooking easier. Spend a few dollars and buy yourself good knives, can openers, good pots and pans, and a few things which help so much to keep the kitchen a pleasant place to work.

If you find your kitchen drab and boring, spruce it up a little. Fresh paint, a few flowers, a little wallpaper, and a candle do wonders for this area of your home. A small radio sets the tone for what's happening here. Have a favorite FM station that plays soothing music. Many of the local Christian radio stations afford an excellent menu of good, uplifting music. Make the environment look appealing, and you might even get volunteers to help out!

Learn to delegate some jobs to other members of the family. If you are going to have responsible children in your home, you have to give them responsibilities.

Make the kitchen the place to be. Make it fun and enjoyable.

• If your kitchen is too small to accommodate a table and chairs permanently, install a pull-out extension table or work space that slides back into a "drawer." Or, make a flip-up counter and eating area that folds back down when not in use.

• To make the most of available space when storing tapered glassware, position every other glass upside down.

• A wall-hung canvas "apron" with lots of pockets makes a decorative and space-saving holder for all sorts of kitchen gadgets and utensils.

• If you hang your sharp knives inside or on the side of a high cabinet, you'll save drawer space and keep these

Cooking Tricks in the Bag

Zip-top plastic bags are not just for food storage. They also can make other kitchen tasks easier and less messy.

● Marinating meat and poultry: *Put marinade ingredients in a large bag (you may need only half as much as usual). Seal bag, shake to mix ingredients, then add meat, press the air out of the bag, and reseal. Refrigerate, turning the bag occasionally.*

● Making deviled eggs: *Put hard-cooked egg yolks and other ingredients into a zip-top bag, then knead until blended and smooth. Press mixture into one corner of the bag, cut off the tip, then squeeze mixture into egg-white halves.*

● Coloring cookies: *Put plain vanilla or sugar-cookie dough in the bag. Add a few drops of food coloring, press out air, seal and knead until the color is blended. (No dyed hands!)*

● Freezing for fast thawing: *Fill bags with ground meat. Place on countertop and press into a flat layer that fills the bag. Seal, label, and freeze.*

utensils out of the children's reach.

● To economize on drawer space, arrange wooden spoons and other utensils bouquet-style in a handsome pitcher, canister, or wooden bucket near the range or on the counter.

● If you lack drawer space for kitchen linens and towels, store them in attractive baskets on the counter.

● Staple plastic berry baskets to the pantry wall or the inside of a cabinet door to hold small packages of sauce mixes, seasonings, and cold drink mixes.

● If you don't have cabinet space for your pots and pans, put a small wooden ladder—painted to match your kitchen—in a corner and place the pots and pans on the steps.

● Hanging mugs on cup hooks underneath your cabinets saves shelf space.

● To save space in the kitchen, hang pots, pans, and other

items from the ceiling. Use hooks meant for hanging swag lamps and screw them directly into the joists.

• When you are defrosting the refrigerator, put an old bath mat in front of the fridge. It will help catch spills.

• A great way to repair those nicks on your kitchen cabinets is to go over the nicks with a marker that matches the finish of the cabinets. You can polish over them with clear fingernail polish.

• Arrange your kitchen for maximum efficiency. Position often-used utensils in convenient drawers and cupboards. Make your dishes do double duty (for example, use a saucepan as a mixing bowl, then use the same pan for cooking).

• Cut the lid off an egg carton and place the cups in a kitchen drawer. You can then organize your cup hooks, small nails, paper clips, thumbtacks, and other small items— no more junky drawers.

• When you are in need of extra ice cubes for party or summer use, simply fill your egg cartons with water and freeze.

• To find spices quickly, put them on a double-decker lazy Susan. When storing your spices, simply alphabetize them on the racks: the top layer can be A-K, the bottom L-Z. Then when your family members or guests are looking for a specific spice, it will be easy to find.

• A trash can under the kitchen sink takes up some very valuable storage space. Take a large decorative basket, line it with a plastic bag, and leave it in the open. The bag is easy to lift out when full. Train several family members to help take the trash out.

• To cover kitchen cabinet shelves, I apply easy-to-install vinyl floor squares by just peeling off the backing. They are particularly good for lower shelves where pots and pans are usually stored. They cut easily and do not tear or wrinkle.

• Put a decorative hook by the sink. Hang your watch and rings on it while you work.

• Use glass or ceramic pans for baking; you can reduce your oven temperature by 25°F.

---

*A sense of direction, a plan, can make
the difference between responsible family
living and just surviving.*

• If your dishpan leaks, don't throw it away. Use it as an under-the-sink storage bin for waxes, brushes, and soaps. It will slide in and out like a drawer.

• If you keep your brooms, mops, and buckets hanging on hooks inside the broom closet, they won't fall out every time you open the door.

• You can cut counter clutter with stackable plastic canisters or a four-in-one turntable canister.

• Purchase food storage containers that do several jobs. Freezer-to-oven casserole dishes are more useful than freezer containers that store casseroles adequately but can't be used in the oven.

• If your kitchen and dining room area are combined and you dislike looking at the pots and pans while you eat, install a ceiling-hung venetian blind to separate the two areas.

• Place the plastic lids from coffee cans under bottles of cooking oil to keep cabinets clean. When the lids get dirty, just throw them away.

• Mark your bowls and their covers with the same number, using a marking pencil. Then you won't be looking for a matching cover for the bowl when putting away leftovers. All you have to do is match the numbers.

• Use pressure cookers, microwaves, or electric pans when you can. They use less energy than your stove or oven.

• To keep a bowl steady when whipping or mixing ingredients, place it on a wet, folded cloth.

• Keep an aloe plant growing in your kitchen. The gel

Seven Top Tips

Smart eating strategies from the ADA:

1. Calm your cream cravings. *Trick your fat tooth by using plain low-fat yogurt instead of sour cream, whipped cream, or mayonnaise.*

2. Spice up your meals. *Stock up on fat-free seasonings and condiments (spice mixes, fresh herbs, flavored vinegars, salsa, and mustards). Experiment with low-fat ethnic seasoning combinations (garlic, ginger, and soy sauce—Japanese; cumin and cilantro— Mexican; or garlic, basil, and oregano—Italian).*

3. Bake with fruit in, fat out. *Cut up to half the butter, margarine, oil, or sugar from your favorite dessert recipes. For extra moistness in quick breads and muffins, substitute applesauce, pureed prunes, or mashed bananas, ounce-for-ounce, for some of the fat.*

4. Make more of your meat. *A two- to three-ounce portion of chicken, fish, or meat will look like a lot of food if you cut it into chunks or strips and pile it loosely on your plate. Or make dishes combining vegetables with meat, chicken, or fish, like stir-fried chicken or beef and vegetables.*

5. Fill up on fiber. *Eating plenty of fiber-rich breads, cereals, and other whole-grain products leaves you less room for fatty foods. Another bonus: Carbohydrate foods rich in soluble fiber, such as oatmeal, are digested and absorbed more slowly, providing you with a long-lasting supply of energy.*

6. Get the best from bread. *If you can't gauge the portion size of crackers, light bread, bread sticks, cereals, and other bread-group foods, check the calorie information on the package label. One serving from the bread group should have about 80 calories.*

7. Get the nutrients you need. *Don't skimp on the number or size of the servings specified in ADA meal and snack lists—you might miss out on essential vitamins and minerals. You may also become hungry and start to overload on more fattening foods.*

squeezed from a leaf can soothe insect bites, prickly heat, or sunburn.

• Washing your ice cube trays occasionally in hot, soapy water will keep the cubes from sticking.

• A rubber-coated plate rack makes a great cookbook holder.

• Save screw-top glass containers for storing dry goods in the pantry.

• A small glass saltshaker makes an excellent container for lemon juice because you can sprinkle exactly the amount you need without the risk of pouring too much and ruining the flavor of a dish.

• The shaker bottles and containers that some spices come in can be filled with flour for no-mess flouring of cutlets and other foods. If you add seasonings to the flour, you've got an instant seasoned coating mix.

• Recycle those tall, cylindrical potato chip containers for picnic food. They'll hold cutlery, rolled up paper napkins, apples, or the baby's food jars (put folded paper towels between the jars for cushioning).

• Well-scrubbed empty bleach bottles are great household helpers, too. Cut them to shape as flour or sugar scoops or as sun shades for the seedlings in your garden. The bottoms make good stands for indoor plant pots, too.

• Make a knife holder out of your empty thread spools. Insert screws in the spool holes and attach them to a cabinet door. Place the spools in a row, one butted right next to the other. The blades will fit in the gaps between the spools while the handles rest on the spools.

• If you have nowhere to hang a memo board for your notes, paint part of your kitchen door with three coats of blackboard paint.

• A phone center with a writing surface can be installed between two wall studs in your kitchen. Cut the wall between the two studs and build the center to fit the space.

• You can mend a crack in a china cup with milk. Just immerse the cup in a pan of milk, simmer for three-quarters of an hour, and then wash and dry the cup. The protein in the milk is what works the miracle.

• To keep recipes clipped from newspapers and magazines so they will be readily available, fold them into an envelope fastened to the inside cover of your cookbook.

• Even when soap bars wear down, they're still useful. Slit a sponge to make a pocket to hold the slivers. Wet and squeeze the sponge for foamy suds. Or fill a sock with soap slivers and use it the same way.

• Thin, leftover soap bars can be tossed into a blender with water and transformed into creamy, liquid soap. Pour this substance into empty squeeze bottles, and keep one at each sink.

• If you store your dishes in open dish racks instead of in cabinets, position the racks over the sink. That way you can wash the dishes, put them in place, and they'll drip-dry into the sink.

• Napkins, paper towels, or cloth protectors placed between pieces of fine china when stacking will help prevent scratching.

• Mesh bags, wire baskets, and even old nylon stockings make good storage containers for potatoes and onions because they allow the necessary air circulation.

Begin to organize your kitchen
so that you can prepare tasty,
easy, healthful meals.

• To chop parsley successfully in the food processor, make sure the leaves are very dry by first whirling them in a salad spinner or patting them dry with a heavy towel.

• Citrus zest used in a dessert recipe can be chopped in a

food processor with a steel blade if some of the sugar from the recipe is placed in the work bowl with the zest.

• Cook as many foods in the oven at one time as you can to save money on the utility bill.

• Match the size of the pan to the heating element so more heat will get to the pan.

• A rubber jar opener (or rubber gloves) gives you easy access to anything in a tightly closed jar.

• If you keep plastic wrap in your refrigerator, it won't cling to itself when handled.

• If the rubber gloves you're wearing won't come off because you've forgotten to sprinkle powder on your hands, hold your gloved hands under cold tap water. The gloves will slip right off.

• An electric beater won't sound so loud if you put a damp dishcloth under the bowl to muffle the noise.

• To slice soft cheeses (such as Swiss or mozzarella) in the food processor, place the cheeses in the freezer for about 10 to 15 minutes before slicing. The firmness of the cheese will make more even slices with less strain on the machine.

• When grinding hard cheese (such as Parmesan or Romano) in the food processor, be sure the cheese sits at room temperature for several hours before processing. Then cut the cheese into small cubes and—with the machine running—drop them through the feed tube.

• Here's a little trick to prevent tightened caps and lids of containers from getting stuck. Coat the rims of the containers with petroleum jelly before tightening the caps or lids. Works great on latex paint cans, tubes of artist's paint, nail polish bottles, and (especially) glue containers.

• To keep bugs out of your flour canister, put a stick of spearmint gum in the flour and it will be bug-free.

• When postage stamps are stuck together, place them in the freezer. They will usually come apart, and the glue will still be usable.

Fresh Start For Broken Parts

Need a new mixing bowl for your older mixer? Trying to replace a broken carafe for your favorite coffeemaker?

Some folks "retire" older appliances when they can't find replacement parts or accessories. But now there's a hassle-free way to locate those parts and keep that "old friend" on the job—just call Culinary Parts Unlimited.

This California company has genuine replacement parts from Oster, Kitchen Aid, Norelco, Hamilton Beach, Proctor Silex, and many other manufacturers.

If you'd like to order a replacement part for one of your small kitchen appliances, call Culinary Parts Unlimited toll-free at (800) 543-7549 (California residents, phone (800) 722-7239).

- If you have a gas stove, make sure the pilot light is burning efficiently with a blue flame. A yellowish flame needs adjustment.
- Cook with a clock or timer. Don't open the oven door continually to check food.
- After making pies or pastry buns, sprinkle the counter with salt. The counter wipes off easily and the dough does not stick to your dishcloth.
- Keep parsley fresh and crisp. Wash the parsley and put a bunch of sprigs into a jar, stem ends down. Pour in an inch or two of cold water—enough for the stems to stand in without the leaves touching the water. Tighten the lid, set the jar in the refrigerator, and enjoy crisp parsley for up to two weeks.
- To slice flank steak, pork tenderloin, or boneless chicken breast in your food processor, partially freeze the meat before slicing. The meat will cut evenly into thin slices.
- Almost any recipe can be adapted to the food processor.

Carry out all the recipe directions involving dry ingredients first and then just wipe the bowl clean with a paper towel. Process the wet ingredients last.

• Use stewed chicken or turkey (picked off the bones) in casseroles, salads, sandwiches, and creamed dishes.

• To make full use of the catsup in a nearly empty bottle, rinse the bottle out with a little warm water and add the water to baked beans or any dish requiring a tomato base.

• Glue a 12-inch square of cork to the inside of the cabinet door over your kitchen work area. On the cork tack the recipe card you are using and newspaper clippings of recipes you plan to try within a few days. It keeps them at eye level and they stay spatter-free.

• When using your electric can opener, help save your fingers from cuts by placing a refrigerator magnet on top of the can before opening it. This magnet will give you a good grip when you lift off the lid.

• Select cooking pans that are durable and made from a good heat conductor, such as copper, cast aluminum, heavy rolled steel, or cast iron. Specially treated aluminum pots and porcelain-lined cast iron pans won't react to acid or cream foods.

• Top-quality carbon steel or combination carbon and stainless steel knives are essential to good cooking. Knife edges should be sharpened on a steel or ceramic sharpener before each use. Knives should be reground professionally every four to six months.

• When cooking with a wok on an electric stove, position the ring so the narrow opening is on the bottom. This will bring the wok closer to the high heat needed for successful stir-frying.

• The best type of pastry bag is plastic-lined. The canvas makes the bag easy to grip, and the plastic lining makes it easy to clean.

• Keep a small plastic shaker bottle filled with baking soda with your dishwashing supplies. It is handy to take a stain out of a coffee cup or polish chrome-finished small appliances while you wash dishes without getting the soda box soggy with damp hands. Be sure to clearly label the bottle.

• Leftover orange, lemon, or lime rinds are great garbage disposal deodorizers.

• Create extra counter space when cooking for a crowd or baking for a holiday by placing trays or cookie sheets across pulled-out drawers.

• If you put marbles or a jar lid in the bottom of a double boiler, their rattling will alert you if the water boils away.

God delights to turn weakness into strength and to bring order from chaos.

• Add cold water immediately to pans, dishes, and utensils that were exposed to raw eggs, hot milk, cooked cereal, or other sticky starches.

• Leftover linoleum can be cut with scissors into place mats of any size.

• To make a tray of fresh ice cubes quickly, leave three or four cubes in the tray when you refill it. The already-frozen cubes help cool the fresh water and speed the freezing process.

• To prevent ice cube trays from sticking to the freezer shelf, line the shelf with wax paper.

• To be sure that cake tins are completely dry before you store them, place them in a warm oven for a few minutes.

• If one drinking glass is tightly nested inside another, don't try to force them apart. You may crack both. Rather, fill the top glass with cold water and immerse the lower one in hot water. The top glass will contract slightly and the bottom one will expand, so they'll come apart easily.

• Lemons and limes get hard and dry when left at room temperature or loose in the crisper, but if you refrigerate

Smart Food Shopping

To be sure your family gets only fresh, high-quality foods from your local grocery store, consider these smart shopping tips from the University of Wisconsin Extension Service:

• *Always use your senses when shopping (eyes, nose, and fingertips—when appropriate) to determine the freshness of raw meats and produce.*

• *Select sound packages. Avoid items that are in torn, dented, or damaged containers.*

• *Make sure refrigerated and frozen foods are below the cold line in their respective cases.*

• *Visit your store late in the evening occasionally to see if deli personnel have removed fresh prepared food displays so dishes and cases can be cleaned.*

• *Buy cold and frozen foods last, right before you check out.*

• *Put meat, poultry, or fish in plastic bags so they don't drip on your other groceries.*

them in a tightly closed jar, they stay fresh for weeks.

• Add a small amount of lemon juice to your whipping cream and it will whip more quickly.

• You can improvise a sink or tub stopper from the plastic cover of a coffee can. Lay the cover across the drain, and suction will hold it firmly in place.

• Is the key or tab on a can missing or damaged? Just turn the can over and open it with an ordinary can opener.

• You can do more with toothpaste than brush your teeth or remove spots. It also works as an adhesive, perhaps for hanging lightweight pictures and posters on your kitchen walls. When you eventually remove the pictures or posters, just wipe away the toothpaste with a damp cloth. There will be no nail holes to repair.

• The one-dozen-size egg carton fits perfectly in the bottom of a large grocery sack. When tea bags, coffee grounds, and wet items are thrown away, the carton absorbs the liquid and prevents drips from trash bags on your carpet or linoleum.

• If salt pours out of your salt shaker too liberally, plug up some of the holes with clear nail polish.

• Put a few grains of rice in your salt shaker to keep the salt from caking.

• If you put a dab of butter under the spout of a pitcher, the contents won't run down the side after you pour.

• To reduce odors and stains on countertops, coat the surface with vegetable-oil spray before cutting up onions or berries.

• New drinking glasses sometimes crack when you pour hot liquids into them. They won't if you "season" them this way: Put the glasses in a large pot filled with cold water, bring the water slowly to a boil, and then turn off the heat and let the water cool.

• When you buy an electric coffeemaker, look for one with water markings on the inside. They're easier to read than markings on the outside.

• Pot holders protect against cold as well as heat, so wear your kitchen mitts to protect your hands when rearranging frozen foods in the freezer.

• Selling your goodies at a bake sale? They'll move faster if you include the recipe. People like to know the ingredients—and how to duplicate your goodies.

• To keep your SOS pad from rusting, place it in something airtight. Make sure to put the lid on tightly. Place the airtight container in the freezer.

• A nutcracker is a great twist-on bottle-cap opener. It unscrews the caps with ease.

• My mother always took time to make simple things extra special. I have happy memories of asking for an orange and then delighting to see she had cut the skin into a lovely basket shape and filled it with small pieces of the fruit. This made me feel special and loved.

• Never refrigerate those pale, off-season tomatoes. Let them ripen on the kitchen counter or windowsill until ready to eat. Refrigeration kills the taste.

• If you have too much frosting left over after icing a cake, spread the leftovers between two graham crackers and freeze for dessert treats.

• When onions are in season, nice and sweet, buy extra. They will last a month or so. Keep in a dry, cool place.

• For sweet, fresh pineapple, simply prop the pineapple upside down on its head for 24 hours before cutting. This allows the juices and natural sugar to saturate the entire pineapple.

• Rather than making the first day of school a time to dread, I decorate the kitchen with crepe paper, make a special breakfast, and leave new pencils at each child's place setting.

• When preparing fruits and vegetables, lay an old newspaper on your counter to catch the peelings. (But don't lay the peeled vegetables on the newspaper.) When you are finished, just roll up the paper and throw it out, or add the vegetable waste to your compost pile.

• When driving home from the store, strap seat belts that aren't being used around bags containing items that could be spilled or broken.

• You can sharpen garbage disposal blades by running ice cubes through them.

• Because instructions on bottle labels are frequently in tiny, almost unreadable print, it's a good idea to keep a magnifying glass handy.

• For a quick shine between waxings, dust mop with a piece of waxed paper attached to the bottom of your mop. The dirt will also stick to the waxed paper.

• To avoid a smelly garbage disposal, run cold water and the disposal at the same time for a while with each use.

• To speed up a sluggish drain, first run hot tap water down the drain, then pour in three tablespoons of baking soda and one-half cup of distilled white vinegar. Stop up the drain

---

Make the Most of Your Microwave

Even though they're not the best choice for cooking all foods, microwave ovens can be helpful kitchen tools. The National Frozen Food Association shares these microwave strategies:

- *Use the defrost cycle for readying frozen meats for the broiler or oven.*
- *Start with the shortest cooking time given. Add time as necessary to get the food the way you want it.*
- *Arrange foods in a circle to cook evenly. Stir casseroles and vegetables halfway through cooking. Let food stand a few minutes before serving to allow the heat to penetrate evenly.*
- *Most foods should always be covered while microwaving. This helps heat and steam created in the food penetrate all parts for even cooking.*
- *Don't use any metal in the microwave (a fire could start).*

---

and wait 15 minutes. The baking soda and vinegar will foam up, reacting with each other, and will eat away at whatever is slowing the drain. Finally, flush the drain with hot tap water.

- Have fresh lemon juice all year long. Squeeze lemons and freeze juice in ice cube trays. Transfer the frozen cubes into freezer bags. Defrost for fresh lemon juice anytime.
- Never slice your onion to make soup; just peel and put the whole onion in to make a sweeter pot.
- Do not store cookies, cereal, or other "bait" by the stove. Children can get burned climbing on the stove to reach an item overhead.

Smooth communication, effective problem-solving, successful task management, and coordination of life's pursuits relate more to meaningful interpersonal relationships than to juggling and sorting activities.

• If you're using an inexpensive dishwashing detergent but find that it leaves spots on the dishes, simply put a few tablespoons of vinegar in the rinse water.

• At least once a year pull the plug on your refrigerator and give it a thorough cleaning. Rinse with clean water after cleaning with baking soda (one tablespoon baking soda to one quart water). Let it air dry.

• Instead of using the dry cycle on your dishwasher, open the machine and pull out the top shelf just an inch or so to prop the door slightly open. The escaping steam helps to dry the dishes almost as well as the dry cycle. It's much faster, and it saves energy and money.

• Want spotless dishes whenever you use the dishwasher? Then be careful at the supermarket. Shake the box of dishwasher detergent; it should sound loose and powdery. Old, lumpy detergent won't do the job properly.

• Purchase a large, plastic lazy Susan to store cleaning items under the kitchen sink. I also use lazy Susans in the linen closets, sewing room, baby's room, office, and refrigerator. They are also great to use under bathroom sinks for shampoos, hair spray, creams, etc. The same large size lazy Susan can also be used for pots and pans.

• To renew the shine and clean the top of a toaster or toaster oven, simply heat the appliance and wipe it with a damp dishcloth. It will clean and shine fast.

• You never clean the top of the refrigerator because you're only five-foot-two and you can't see the top of the refrigerator? Cover it with a towel. Then when it does occur to you to investigate, just whip off the towel and replace it.

• If wax has built up on the felt pads of your floor polisher, place the pads between several thicknesses of paper toweling and press with a warm iron. The towels will quickly absorb the old wax.

• If the children spill cooked rice on the floor, try to resist the temptation to clean it up immediately. It will be much easier to sweep up when it has dried.

- Hard lime deposits around faucets can be softened for easy removal by covering them with vinegar-soaked paper towels for about an hour before cleaning.
- The fastest and cheapest way to remove stains from non-stick coated cookware is to mix two tablespoons baking soda with one cup water and a half cup liquid bleach. If you boil the solution in the pan for several minutes, the stains will disappear. After washing the pan, wipe the inner surface with cooking oil to reseason it.
- It's usually possible to remove burned-on foods from a pan by coating the burned-on food generously with baking soda that's barely moistened with water. Leave the paste on overnight and then wash the pan as usual.
- Another way of removing burned-on foods from a pan is to fill the pan with water, drop in one or two fabric-softener sheets, and let the water stand for an hour or so. The food crust will lift right off.
- To remove heel marks on your linoleum, wipe the spots with kerosene and turpentine.
- To protect your wok from rust when not in use, coat it lightly with cooking oil before storing it.
- To retard tarnish on polished brass, rub it with a cloth moistened with olive oil. When it eventually tarnishes, clean it by rubbing with a lemon wedge dipped in salt. Rinse with water and dry with a soft cloth.
- To rid a teakettle of lime deposits, fill it with a mix of half water and half vinegar and boil the mixture. Let it stand overnight, and then pour the cooled-off liquid—and the lime—down the drain.
- Keep a jar of hot, soapy water in the sink when you're cooking and slip dirty silverware into it. Rinse quickly, and the utensils will be clean again.
- You can get rid of rust marks in a stainless steel sink by rubbing them with lighter fluid. Afterward, thoroughly

Must-Have Kitchen Equipment

Mortar and pestle. *We use a mortar and pestle for garlic all the time at the restaurant, to make a puree that can go very easily and smoothly into a mayonnaise. Using a mortar and pestle mashes the flavors together, which is very different from chopping.*

Sharp knives. *All work in the kitchen is made easy with some sharp knives. You don't need a whole range, but it's important to use the right knife for the right purpose.*

How many should you have? I think you need a boning knife, a chef's knife—it could be smaller or larger, depending on what you feel comfortable with—and a paring knife or a couple of little paring knives. And, of course, you need a serrated bread knife, which also works for a lot of other things, too.

My knives are stainless steel. I never use knives that react to the ingredients (garlic and shallots, for instance, are especially sensitive to carbon steel).

The fewer knives you have, the more care you can take sharpening and keeping them clean. The best way to sharpen knives is with a sharpening stone.

wash the sink and your hands.

● Banish sink odors by washing the sink with a strong salt solution or with laundry bleach.

● A good way to remove odor from plastic containers without spending a cent is to crumple a piece of newspaper into the container, secure the lid tightly, and leave overnight. The newspaper takes the odor away very effectively.

● Metal-trimmed china should not be soaked for long periods. Soaking will damage the trim.

● Be sure the water is not too hot when you rinse glazed dinnerware. Boiling water will cause the glaze to craze, or develop minute cracks.

- Use a crumpled sheet of newspaper to soak up excess grease from a pan before cleaning the pan in the regular manner.
- Loosen leftover egg and cheese residue on dinnerware by soaking in cool water.
- A soiled white porcelain sink will gleam like new if you line it with paper towels, spray them until soaked with household bleach, and wait an hour before rinsing.
- Scorched pans (other than aluminum) can be cleaned by bringing one teaspoon baking soda and one cup water to a boil in the pan. Allow to cool, then wash. For aluminum pans, substitute vinegar for the baking soda.
- When washing delicate objects such as precious glassware or fragile plates in the sink, guard against breakage by padding the sink bottom with a towel. Wrap another towel, held in place with a rubber band, around the faucet.
- You can remove all traces of fish, onion, or other odors from your hands if you wet them and sprinkle on baking soda. Work the paste over your hands, and then rinse away both soda and odor.
- For stains on acrylic kitchen utensils, wipe at once with a damp cloth. If the stains persist, use an all-purpose cleaner or moistened bicarbonate of soda. Always act as quickly as possible, and never use harsh abrasives.
- Soft cheeses can be cleaned from a grater by rubbing a raw potato over its teeth and openings. (A lemon rind or a toothbrush also do a first-rate cleanup job.)
- One way to clean porcelain surfaces is to rub them with cream of tartar sprinkled on a damp cloth. You can remove rust spots from metal surfaces the same way.
- A paste made of baking soda and water is very effective in removing stubborn soil and stains from plastic and rubber utensils, and it deodorizes them at the same time. Apply the paste with a synthetic scouring pad and watch the stains disappear.

4
Storage

Any closet, cupboard,
or shelf can hold
more and be
more convenient.

*P*lans fail for lack of counsel, but with many advisers they succeed.

—Proverbs 15:22

Storage

What to store and where to store it is high on the family conflict list. Why leave for work with a knot in your stomach when you can stop the morning madness with a few simple storage solutions?

The cry of each person is to have more storage. There are never enough cabinets, cupboards, and shelves.

Men like to store magazines, tools, books, and broken parts that may come in handy for a repair someday. Women want to store unfinished craft projects, old clothing, holiday decorating items, photo albums, etc.

It's bad enough when there are no children, but when the family starts, the need for storage increases. Not only does each child save things, but having children adds a purpose to your saving. You become even more likely to hang on to loose photographs and completely useless items that may turn into valuable antiques during your children's lifetime.

The three major storage concerns are:
- What to store
- Finding room
- Keeping whatever you store safe from dust, dampness, insects, fire, or flooding

Analyze your needs—each storage problem has its own

solution. Things to consider may include:
• Can you rearrange existing space?
• Do you need different sizes of storage boxes? (Read my books, *More Hours in My Day, Survival for Busy Women,* and *The 15-Minute Organizer* for added information in this area—published by Harvest House Publishers.)
• Is there wasted air space?
• Can added shelves, poles, or hooks solve your problem?
• Can wall space below a window be used for low bookcases or a window seat?
• Can space underneath the stairs, in the garage, or in the basement be used more efficiently?
• Can your wardrobe closets be rearranged to give you more space?
• Can pegboards and plastic containers be used in the garage?
• Can most garden tools be stored in a central area by sticking long-handled tools (shovels, brooms, rakes, hoes) upside down in a 55-gallon trash bin?
• Can bicycles be suspended in space by hooks that are affixed to rafters in the garage?

Here are some handy ideas that will help you with your storage problems. Be creative in your solutions to your unique situations. (If all else fails, you can rent a storage shed near your home to store the excess!)
• Stationary shelves are the strongest; however, adjustable shelves are more flexible.
• To store sweaters so they keep wrinkle-free, simply lay the sweater front side down and fold in half so the bottom meets the top, then cross each arm over the width.
• Before putting coats and boots away when winter's over, wax their zippers with a candle. The zippers won't be stuck or hard to pull closed next year.
• If you store clothes and other items in boxes on high

shelves, put a finger hole in the front of the box near the bottom. It's great for sliding the box off the shelf.
• Organize various kinds of plastic bags by wadding and tucking them into cardboard rolls from paper towels. You can label the tube with the kind of bag in each: small, produce, freezer, and so forth.

Give one item away every day.

• Install drawer runners and slide-in drawers under open stairs for linens, clothes, and more.
• A three tier basket, which I recommend for the bath, can also be used at baby's changing table to hold small toys and pacifiers, etc., and in the kitchen to hold small tools.
• If it's deep enough, a landing may hold a wardrobe containing out-of-season clothes or be converted into a mini home-office area.
• Cover apple-type storage boxes with calico fabrics and use for storage in bedrooms and closets.
• Use leftover wallpaper for shelf liners in pantry, cupboards, linen closets, and on kitchen shelves. The paper gives new life to old, drab shelving.
• Used gym lockers can be bought, repainted, then put in a child's room to store bats, helmets, skateboards, and toys.
• Night tables can hold out-of-season clothing or extra linens. Buy a large garbage pail, have a round plywood top made, and cover the plywood with a circular cloth. Order a round glass top to put over the cloth to keep it looking fresh.
• Drawers from a discarded dresser can be used for under-bed storage. Fasten casters to the bottom and the drawer will be easy to roll in and out.
• Stow blankets between the mattress and box spring.
• To organize photos, make subject dividers out of 4" x 6" cards. Organize the photos by subject. For example: Henry,

---

Order, Order Everywhere

Your storage will look and work better for you if you use some common sense:

1. *Things should be where they are most convenient. Store like items together: coffee tools and equipment, gardening supplies, laundry and sewing items, outdoor picnicking supplies, athletic equipment.*
2. *Things you use often should be easy to see. Save your inaccessible places for what you seldom use.*
3. *Things that are needed at the same time should be in the same place (for example, store your stationery items next to your stamps, pens, and stapler).*
4. *Everything should have its own place. Get away from forming stacks and piles. Don't put it down; put it away.*
5. *Label containers. Take away the mystery of having to open everything and look inside.*
6. *Keep items covered (keeps out dust) and in uniform storage boxes. They stack easier and give a sense of order.*

Margaret, vacation, animals, home. Then file in a shoe box.
• Purchase or build a coffee table that's a hinged-top bin or that contains drawers.
• Pegs, hooks, rods, and shallow shelves can be hung on backs of doors. So can fold-away ironing boards.
• Store quilts, blankets, Christmas presents in November, and out-of-season sports equipment in unused suitcases or duffel bags.
• You can buy plans for easy-to-build outside storage buildings or outside tool chests. Build one to keep extra flower pots and barbecue tools out of the way on the patio.
• Always keep items separate from one another: tools separate from extension cords, screws separate from picture

hangers. If everything is in a jumble, you won't want to use it.

• In packing my dishes for moving, I found that paper plates were perfect to sandwich between china plates to cushion them. The smaller ones worked for dessert plates or saucers. With just a little newspaper between the stacks, they were ready to go.

Remember that by using small bits of time faithfully, you can accomplish great things.

• If you find that your wardrobe closet is full and you have nothing to wear, it's time to do a major reconstruction job.

1. Take everything out of the closet. You'll find things you thought you had lost.

2. If time permits, do this project in one session. This is one job that needs continuity. Small work sessions don't work best here.

3. Have a friend help you!

4. If you haven't worn something for at least one season, consider getting rid of it. If you have not worn it for two years, get it out of your closet. (See my "Total Mess to Total Rest" chapter in *More Hours in My Day*. I go into a lot of detail on how to sort your things that will go into three bags: "Give Away," "Throw Away," or "Put Away."

5. Get rid of the garment if it is:
   — Too small, too dated, too faded, torn or not mendable, or if it doesn't match anything or is not "you" anymore.
   — If the garment needs repairs, set it aside to take to the laundry room to stitch.
   — Less is best. It's better to have a few basic clothes that you will wear than a closetful that just takes up space.

6. Hang clothes in categories: pants, shirts, tops, dresses,

jackets, suits, athletic clothes, lingerie, sweaters, accessories.

7. Group items in each category by color.

8. Put shoes on a shoe rack at the bottom of the closet, or build special slots in your newly designed closet.

9. Put your belts, scarves, and other accessories where you can see them.

10. Hang your shirts on individual hangers.

11. Replace your wire hangers with good plastic hangers. (Swivel heads are best—they allow you to put the garment on the hanger any way you wish and still hang the clothing facing the same direction.)

12. If you put a strip of Velcro at the end of the hanger, the grip will keep thin straps from sliding off.

13. Remodel and paint your closet. There are many wardrobe organizers on the market that will give you more space.

14. Put a square mirror tile on the closet ceiling to check the contents of the top shelf without a ladder.

Jesus sent out His disciples and organized them in teams of two and gave them specific directions—See Mark 6:7.

• A new thought for lining drawers and cupboards: Instead of putting the contact paper down on the bare wood, first measure the area to be covered and then cut a piece of cardboard, poster board, or mat board to fit. Cover the board. Slip the covered board into the drawer or onto the shelf. Easy to cover, easy to remove for cleaning, and when or if you move, you can take them with you! Easy to use every scrap of contact paper too—no waste.

• Store out-of-season clothes in large, plastic-lidded trash cans. Not only will your clothes be mothproof, they will stay dry in damp basements.

• To prevent moth damage, be sure to mothproof wools

> ## Tidy Tips
>
> *Try these space-saving ideas:*
>
> - *Replace a single hanging bar with several bars at different heights. Jackets, blouses, trousers, and skirts can be hung in tiers.*
> - *Build high shelves to store items that are used only occasionally or seasonally (such as ice skates), leaving lower shelves and storage areas for more frequently used items.*
> - *Build shelves or cubbyholes to accommodate shoes, sweaters, bulky clothing, and sports equipment.*
> - *Fit children's closets with adjustable rods to "grow" with the child.*
> - *Think creatively. If there isn't enough room for bed linens in a hall or bedroom closet, put them in an empty dining-room sideboard. Or place Christmas items on the top shelf in the pantry.*

and wool blends, especially during summer months. Don't forget your sweaters. Use tissue paper to prevent clothing from coming into contact with moth proofers.

- Add a cabinet under the sink, one that rests on the lid of the toilet tank, and/or a set of those new, tall, ultra-slim bookcases (as little as 12" wide) to hold towels and other items.
- An extra wall-mounted medicine cabinet is an inexpensive and very helpful way to add space.
- Inside the medicine cabinet, glue small magnets to the door to hold nail files and cuticle scissors.
- Hang caddies over the shower head. Over the curtain rod, slip new double hangers—one hook faces the shower wall, the other hook faces out. They can hold both bath sheets and/or robes. Install wall dispensers of shampoo and hair conditioner inside the shower.
- Shoe bags on the back of the bathroom door or three-tier kitchen baskets suspended from the shower rod can hold soaps, disposable razors, shampoo, cotton balls, etc.

Where to Put the Towels

Roll them: *Keep them in a basket or rattan wine rack.*

Rod them: *Increase hanging space by installing a long closet rod the length of the tub wall.*

Rack them: *Use hotel-type racks that stow towels horizontally.*

Hook them: *Install pegs instead of bars (which your family probably never uses anyway) and you'll have room for many extra towels. Put name tags above the pegs to help family and guests know which towel is whose.*

Bar them: *Install a rod behind each bedroom door and have family members hang big towels in their bedrooms to dry. This eliminates clutter, reduces bathroom moisture, and humidifies the bedroom.*

Sack them: *Do away with towels entirely. Give everyone in the family a terry robe which they can hang on a hook in their own room. You won't be washing a lot of bath towels—just the terry robe once a week.*

• Take an under-shelf basket (the kind made of vinyl sprayed on wire) and bend the hooks in the opposite direction so it will hang over the side of the tub. Use it to hold shampoo and tub toys.

• Install a second shower-curtain rod level with the first and over the tub far enough to clear a moving shower curtain. It's great for drip-drying clothes, hanging laundry, or holding the rubber bath mat while it dries.

• The worst thing in the world—okay, one of the worst things—is to find yourself in a bathroom where there's no toilet paper. Keep a roll handy under one of the plastic covers made to fit a tall, square tissue box. Or stow two rolls on their sides in one of the rectangular tissue holders. Or put up a long dowel, meant to hold paper towels, instead of a conventional toilet tissue dowel—it will hold two rolls.

• A favorite trick for making sure you don't run out of paper goods like toilet tissue and paper towels is to buy one roll in a color you don't ordinarily use and put it at the back of the storage cabinet. If that roll shows up in the bathroom or kitchen, you know it's time to stock up!

• My mother-in-law came up with a great idea. She stores things in apple-type boxes, piling them three high. She went to the lumber yard and had a 24-inch-diameter plywood tabletop made, set it on the boxes, and covered everything with an adorable cloth that reaches to the floor. With a lamp on top, she now has end tables with storage!

• Leather handbags store well if stuffed with tissue. Wrap in tissue—never plastic—and place in a storage box or fabric bag. Plastic will dry out leather.

• One of the worst results of a fire is the loss of family photographs. Keep all your film negatives in your bank safe-deposit box. In the unfortunate event of a fire, you can have pictures reprinted and save precious memories.

• Rather than keep bed linen in the bathroom linen closet and lingerie in bureau drawers, reverse it. It is so much easier because linen is then available in the bedroom and lingerie is right at hand to slip into after you shower.

• The small space between the refrigerator and wall may be wide enough to hold a narrow cart on casters.

• Canisters that are square don't waste space.

• Flatware can be hung in slings beneath a cupboard. Stem glassware can be hung upside down so that the bottoms slip into tracks (as in many bars).

• Small cabinets fastened together can make a base for a kitchen table.

• My friend Karen bought a bunch of letters and numbers from old printing presses—they're in antique shops everywhere—and attached them at random to the cupboards. When anyone asks where to find a plate or a soda glass she points them toward cupboard A or cabinet 7.

- Use the entire front of the refrigerator as a message center (with a waterproof marking pen) or use a piece of black contact paper as a blackboard.
- Odd flatware pieces collected at yard sales make interesting drawer and cabinet pulls. Lacquer or polyurethane them so they don't require polishing.
- Stow a folding table pad under the table. Find hooks or angle irons and install them so pads can rest on them.
- Build a narrow ledge all the way around the room and use it to store dishes as they did in old taverns. (A groove in the ledge, or molding around the edge of it, will hold the dishes in place.)
- Cardboard boxes for storage and moving are clumsy to pick up and carry. Take a knife and cut a half circle in each end or side of the box. These openings will serve as handles and the box will be much easier to manage.
- You can build a strip of bookshelves high on the wall, just below the ceiling.
- Slightly below the ceiling of a garage, you can make a loft platform on top of your 2" x 6" framing. Go to the hardware store and purchase sheets of economical 4' x 8' plywood. Use common sense in what you store overhead, and watch the total weight—no accidents, please.
- The doorway to your basement can make a temporary coat closet when you entertain. Install brackets and buy a clothes pole to fit (or buy a chinning bar with brackets). Put the pole up when it's needed and dismantle it when it's not.
- I saved our family photos in a storage box over the years. Then one day I got some albums and put together a "This Is Your Life" album for each of the children from birth to college. I gave the albums to them as Christmas gifts. They absolutely loved them and cherish the albums to this day.
- When mailing cookies, pack in popped popcorn or Styrofoam popcorn to help keep them from crumbling.
- Place a piece of chalk in your jewelry box to prevent costume jewelry from tarnishing.

Shelf Storage

• *When shopping for a wall system, check to see if the shelves are structurally attached to the cabinet, rather than resting on movable pins; the unit will support more weight.*

• *If you own freestanding bookcases and storage units but would prefer a built-in look, you can add decorative moldings at the top and bottom and paint or stain the units to match the walls. Or you can refinish the wall to match the storage units.*

• *Check your local hardware stores to see if they already have a pre-built storage unit (much cheaper than custom-building one).*

• *Even narrow wall space can be used to store compact discs and videocassettes.*

• To keep pots and pans neat, line shelves with plain or light-colored adhesive wallpaper.
   — Determine the best possible position for each pan.
   — Draw an exaggerated outline of the pans on the paper with a black felt-tip pen.
• Many women go into shock when the refrigerator is mentioned.
   — Look at it as just another closet.
   — Fruits and vegetables should be put into plastic containers with lids, in special vegetable bags that breathe, or in refrigerator doors.
   — Cheeses and meats go on the coldest shelf (use all types of see-through containers with tight lids).
   — Remember to rotate the oldest eggs to the front or to the right depending on whether you have a drawer or shelf for eggs.
   — Lazy Susans in the refrigerator are great space-savers. They will hold fat-free sour cream, cottage cheese, jellies, peanut butter, and yogurt.

Cutting Out Clutter

Get rid of clutter to lighten your workload and need for added storage:

• *Designate one area or room where the inevitable clutter can accumulate (a place where puzzles can be left out, where the sewing machine can stay open, where model Lego projects can wait for completion).*

• *Place containers where clutter collects (a large toy box in the playroom, a basket for newspapers and magazines in the living room, a file cabinet for mail that otherwise may collect on the kitchen counter or hall table).*

• *Put up easily accessible hooks and shelves for hats, coats, schoolbooks, and other everyday items that usually end up on the floor or a chair.*

• *Throw bulk junk mail away immediately. (Don't even take the time to open the envelope.)*

• *Sort through your belongings a few times each year and give or pack away anything you haven't used recently.*

• *Place a wastebasket in each room.*

• *Use throw rugs outside each outside door. (They will catch a lot of dirt before it comes into your home.)*

5
Cleaning

No more
sticky streaks

*I*n everything you do,
put God first, and he
will direct you and
crown your efforts
with success.

—Proverbs 3:6 (TLB)

Cleaning

Cleaning house, while necessary, is a very personal issue. Don't worry about other people's standards. Decide what "clean" means to you and keep house accordingly. Above all, use your time effectively. Here's how:

Establish priorities. Identify which tasks absolutely have to be done, which ones should be done, and which ones would be nice to get done. Work on them in that order, and forget about all others.

Set time limits. You can accomplish quite a bit in several 15-minute periods. Keep your cleaning schedule flexible so you can change it if something unexpected comes up. Do what you can *when* you can.

Delegate. Teach your kids how to fold laundry, vacuum, dust, unload the dishwasher, make their beds, and how to prepare their breakfasts, lunches, and snacks. Enlist teens to help with big jobs like washing windows and floors and cleaning cabinets and woodwork.

Finish tasks. Complete one project before you start another.

Reward yourself for a job well done.

Time management is not just keeping busy. It is finding

God's focus for you—choosing a direction and moving ahead to accomplish your goals. Success in this endeavor is one of the most difficult yet helpful skills a woman can develop. Remember: By using small bits of time faithfully, you can accomplish great things.

The Proverbs woman arose early (Proverbs 31:15) to plan for the day's activities, and just as she had "maid-servants," women today have appliances and cars, as well as utility and telephone service. These blessings of God are ready to help and serve women in daily, mundane tasks, giving them a maximum amount of time to serve others and to spend with the Lord.

Often women are overwhelmed by too many things to do because there are many good choices for using our time (Ecclesiastes 3:1-8). Priorities determine what is important to you and how your time is to be apportioned—who and what will take precedence over other parts of life.

One very practical way of accomplishing this awesome goal is to list all the tasks before you, prayerfully consider each one's merit and timeliness, arrange them in order of importance, then proceed as planned (see 1 Corinthians 14:40).

Here are some cleaning tips to get you started:
• To clean windows and mirrors with no streaks, wipe off cleaner with newspaper instead of paper towels.
• Rub floor scratches away with fine steel wool dipped in floor wax.
• For a grass stain, use liquid detergent and sponge the area. If the spot is stubborn, apply rubbing alcohol, rinse, and wash. Use bleach if the fabric allows.
• To clean mini-blinds, remove from the window and put into a bathtub of warm, sudsy water. Slosh them around, rinse, and rehang. To maintain, use a feather duster on your mini-blinds weekly. They should only need major cleaning annually.

• To polish copper, mix vinegar with salt and you will have beautiful, shining copper.

• Waterless cleaners are ideal for cleaning some wood surfaces because they won't cause wood to swell. The cleaners come as a paste that you apply with a sponge or rag, then rub or wipe, using more product as needed until the surface is clean. You can get waterless cleaners in auto supply stores and supermarkets.

• Water rings or hot-dish rings can be removed by making a thick paste of equal portions of salad oil and salt. Rub it on the spot with your fingers and let it absorb for a couple of hours. Then rub it off with a soft cloth.

• Scorch that beautiful linen cloth? Simply rub the scorched area with a raw onion, soak in cold water for a couple of hours, then wash the linen as usual.

• If the odor of cigarettes, cigars, or pipe smoke is in a room, dampen a dish towel with vinegar and wave it around the area. Small bowls of vinegar will keep a room deodorized, and filling ashtrays with fresh cat litter will not only put out cigarettes but will also get rid of smoke odors.

• A piece of clothing that smells smoky can be put in the dryer for five to ten minutes with a couple of fabric softener sheets. The controls should be set to "air only" or "cool."

Homemade Cleaning Formulas

All-purpose cleaner. Pour one-half cup ammonia and one cup baking soda into a clean plastic gallon jug. Add two cups warm water, cover, and shake. Then add 12 more cups of water. Label the jug so everyone knows it's cleaner. Use one-half cup to a bucket of water for large jobs, full strength in a spray bottle for appliances and tile.

All-purpose nonpolluting cleaner. Add two tablespoons baking soda to one quart warm water and you have a wash that will clean plaster, tile, and porcelain. Plain baking soda

Cleaning Tools:
Basic Shopping List

You will definitely need:

Brooms—push broom for outdoors, smaller for indoors
Dustpan
Pails (2)
Mops with replaceable heads (2); buy a spare (you'll
need it every 3-4 months)
Vacuum cleaner
Hand-held vacuum cleaner
Dust wand and polishing cloths
Scrub brush (with 6" handle)
Sponges
Paper towels
Rubber gloves
Spray bottle
Toilet brush (one per bathroom; get one that comes
with its own holder)
Tile brush (to scrub grout in bathroom. More abrasive
than a sponge)
Toothbrush (for scrubbing small areas)
Squeegee (to clean windows or tile walls; the best ones
are brass or stainless and have a 10" to 14" rubber
blade)

You will probably need:
Wax applicator
Floor polisher
Dust mop

will substitute for scouring powder all over the kitchen, on appliances, even in the toilet bowl. Or mix two teaspoons borax and one teaspoon liquid dishwashing soap in one quart water for a cleaning spray.

All-purpose pine cleaner. Mix two quarts of water, one cup of pine oil, and two cups of soap flakes (like Ivory Flakes) in an empty gallon jug. (This is toxic—keep away from kids and cap tightly.) For kitchen floor and ceiling, use full strength. For walls and ceilings in other rooms, use diluted.

Ceramic tile cleaner. Mix one-fourth cup ammonia, one-half cup baking soda, and one gallon warm water.

Chandelier cleaner. Combine two teaspoons rubbing alcohol, one pint warm water, and one tablespoon dishwasher antispot agent (like Jet Dry) in a spray bottle. Make sure the lights are off and the fixture is cool, then drench the chandelier and let it drip dry. Water will sheet off.

Fixture cleaner. Pour eight ounces of ammonia and one quart of denatured alcohol into a spray bottle. Spray and wipe with tissue and use on small kitchen appliances, chrome faucets, and other greasy surfaces.

Furniture polish (lemon-scented). Mix a teaspoon of lemon oil (from craft or herb shop) with a cup of mineral oil. Pour into a clean spray bottle. Before using, shake well. Use a thin coat and buff well, or the oil will collect more dust!

Furniture polish (earth-friendly). Olive oil works well on stained (but not lacquered or painted) wood. Rub in with a clean cloth until there is no stickiness left.

Polishing cloths. Cut soft cotton or terry cloth into 9" squares. Moisten them with water and put them in a large plastic container. Mix ¼ cup water, a cup of mineral oil, and a teaspoon of lemon oil (which you can buy from a craft shop or herb shop). Shake well, and pour over the cloths while the oil and water are in solution. Wipe furniture with the cloth, then buff off excess with a clean cloth. The cloth can be washed and reused.

Wall cleaner. Combine one-half cup borax, two table-spoons soap flakes (like Ivory Flakes), one table-spoon ammonia, one gallon warm water. Store in plastic jug. Use full strength in spray bottle or add two cups to a pail of warm water. Or mix one-half cup ammonia, one-fourth cup white vinegar, and one-fourth cup baking soda for every gallon of water.

• A cover-up apron with two large pockets is great to wear on housecleaning days. I can go from room to room and use one of the pockets for pickups and the other pocket to hold my dust cloth. Just remember to empty the pockets before washing the apron.

Don't put it down; put it away.

• For no more rusty scouring pads (and for a great job for your children), when you get home from the market, hand the kids the box of pads and a pair of scissors. Instruct the kids to cut the pads in half. You usually only use one-half pad per job.

• To remove lipstick, liquid makeup, or mascara from fab-rics, soak in dry-cleaning solution and let dry. Rinse and wash.

• For ballpoint-pen ink stains, put a towel under the stain and blot the spot with rubbing alcohol. Moving the towel to a cleaner section, continue to blot until the spot is removed. Then wash as usual.

• Make double use of your time. Straighten the coat closet while waiting for the car pool. Clean kitchen counters while talking on the telephone.

• For washing windows inside and out, measure two gal-lons of the hottest water your hands can bear into a pail. Add two measuring tablespoons of cooking cornstarch and stir well. This solution can be used until it cools. (This sounds like a lot of water changes, but you can do many windows before cooling occurs.)

• Next time you want to paint something with oil-base paint, choose paint thinner (mineral spirits) instead of turpentine for wiping up smudges and cleaning brushes. Paint thinner costs less, and its smell isn't as heavy as "turp's."

• Use Windex spray to shine scuffed patent-leather shoes. Just take a clean cloth and wipe clean.

• A good way to keep stainless-steel range hoods clean is to pour undiluted liquid dishwashing detergent onto a damp sponge and thoroughly clean the grease off the hood. Rinse with a clean, damp sponge, then dry the hood with a clean, soft cloth. Afterward, go over the surface with a spray protectant usually used to protect vinyl in cars. Every day or so, wipe off the hood with a *dry* cloth. Repeat the application of the protectant every few weeks or as needed.

• Need a great cleaner for those extra-hard-to-clean clothes—ones that are stained with blood, grass, ink, grease, paint, or dirt? Use multipurpose Goop hand cleaner with a toothbrush (you might have to go over the spot more than once). It does clean.

• When using a sink full of hot water to rinse the dishes, add a capful of vinegar to cut any excess grease or soap. This will give your dishes a clean, sparkling look.

• To prevent lime buildup in teakettles, put a marble in the bottom. As it rolls around, it keeps the lime from accumulating.

• To keep your closets smelling fresh and clean, use a box of scented fabric softener sheets.

• Pregnant ladies or elderly people can clean their bathtubs easily by using a mop. It saves on bending.

• Nail-polish remover takes off price tag stickum just great.

Removing Mildew

In a perfect world, it would be easy to grow flowers and hard to grow mildew, but in our world the opposite is true.

Mold grows in damp, uninsulated attics, crawl spaces,

Working With Rubber Gloves

• *If you have trouble pulling off you rubber gloves, put your hands under cold tap water.*
• *If you have long nails, protect the inside tip of each rubber glove finger with a small piece of electrical tape.*
• *If you rip the right glove on every pair, save the one that's left. Use it turned inside out on your left hand.*
• *You can make very strong elastic bands by cutting strips from old rubber gloves.*

---

drain systems, tubs, refrigerator drip pans, humidifiers and air conditioners, duct work (of forced-air heating systems, in particular), and foam rubber furnishings. And if there is any water damage in the house, mold spores are probably present.

While mildew loves dampness, it can also thrive in an airtight and under-ventilated building—particularly when there is a lot of cooking, a lot of toilets, and a lot of people.
• Since mildew is especially common in closets, leave a low-wattage bulb burning and/or buy a desiccant (moisture remover) such as activated charcoal (or a similar product) from your hardware dealer. Some disinfectants also prevent mold.

All of the following mixtures remove mildew but may harm some surfaces or cause colors to bleed, so always test on an inconspicuous surface first.
— Rubbing alcohol: Mix half alcohol and half water.
— Hydrogen peroxide: Use two tablespoons per gallon.
— Tri-sodium phosphate: Use four to six tablespoons per gallon.
— Chlorine bleach: Use one-half to one cup per gallon of water.
• *For mildew stains:* Wash in bleach if the fabric is safe to use

bleach on. Or rub the spot with lemon juice and salt, let it dry in the sun, and then wash as usual. Or scrape off the mildew and sponge the fabric with alcohol and a mild detergent.

More Cleaning Tips

• To clean the inside of your washing machine and remove soap scum, run the machine through a rinse cycle with two cups of vinegar.

• If clothes show rust marks, check the washing machine (or dryer) drum to see if it needs a coat of paint. (Paint store specialists can tell you which type to buy.)

• Ever wonder when to use sudsy ammonia and when to use clear? One manufacturer explains that the sudsy product cuts through tough grease and grime quickly, but may leave streaks on shiny materials. The clear formula is preferable for use on glass, stainless steel, chrome, and other shiny surfaces.

• When the shower mat begins to look grungy, it's time to soak it in a tubful of warm water and distilled white vinegar. Then give the mat a good scrubbing with a stiff-bristle brush, rinsing thoroughly.

• Don't throw out barely-used paper napkins. Retrieve them and keep them with cleaning supplies. They make thrifty and handy paper towel substitutes.

• To prevent soap buildup, cut a sponge to fit the soap dish by the sink. After using the soap, place it on the sponge. This makes for easy cleaning later.

• For those nasty stains in your toilet bowl, use a pumice stone (can be purchased at a beauty supply shop or drugstore). Rub the pumice stone over stains in the toilet bowl and presto. . .the stain comes off. Be sure to clean under the inside rim of the bowl, too.

• To prevent the nozzle on a can of spray paint from becoming clogged, turn the can upside down after each use

and depress the spray head until the air is clear of paint.
● Gum can be removed from fabric, hair, and so forth, by
using lighter fluid on a piece of cotton. Rub gently and it
comes off easily. Don't use around fire or heat.

Your Personal Cleaning List

No matter how casual you are about cleaning, there are
some jobs you have to get to. These are not necessarily the
jobs that make the house look nice but the ones that keep
away the germs and insects and keep the things you own in
reasonably good shape. If you don't clean the air conditioner filter, the thing may get clogged up and break down.
If you never turn a mattress, it may quite literally split down
the middle. On the list of routine jobs on page 103, I've
marked these essential jobs with a star. On a scale of 1 to 10,
they are the 10s.

If you put the spread on the bed in the morning, go off to
work, and then carefully remove and fold it at night, you
probably don't need to clean the spread more than once a
year. But if the kids and the dog are rolling around on it regularly, I'm sure you'll want to clean it more often than that.

In my house, the pictures and photos get dusted and
cleaned about once every two weeks. On the other hand, I
never have the drapes cleaned since I think they will never
look or hang the same again. I just vacuum them periodically to get rid of the dust and when they start looking worn
and dingy, I replace them.

To make you feel better about what you're doing (or not
doing), I would like to remind you that despite the rumors,
nowhere in the Bible does it say "cleanliness is next to
godliness." Being a little deficient in the dusting and wiping
departments may displease your mother, but it won't get
you into trouble in the afterlife.

Cleaning Checklist

Weekly

★ Vacuum high-traffic areas of hard-surface floors and carpets.

★ Dust and polish furniture.
   Empty wastepaper baskets.

★ Change bed linens.

★ Kitchen cleanup (described earlier).

★ Bathroom cleanup (described earlier).
   Living-room cleanup (described earlier).

Every Two Weeks

★ Clean or replace the air conditioner filter (summer only).

Monthly or As Needed

★ Wash bathroom rugs.

★ Clean TV screen, mirrors, pictures.

★ Clean oven.

★ Vacuum all floors.

Every Two or Three Months or As Needed

★ Polish silver.

★ Wipe windowsills.

★ Dust knickknacks.

Semiannually or As Needed

★ Defrost refrigerator/freezer (or when ice is more than one-fourth inch thick).
   Clean lamp shades.
   Wipe out kitchen cabinets.

Cleaning Products: Basic Shopping List

You will definitely need:
- *All-purpose cleaner (such as Top Job, Lestoil, etc.)*
- *Borax*
- *Baking soda*
- *Vinegar*
- *Ammonia*
- *Scouring powder*
- *Liquid abrasive cleaner*
- *Steel wool pads*
- *Medium-rough nylon or fiber scrubbing pad*
- *Light-duty plastic scrubbing pad*
- *Sanitizer (such as Lysol without phenol)*
- *Bleach*
- *Spray furniture polish*
- *Liquid dishwashing detergent*
- *Dry-cleaning solvent stain remover (for carpet)*
- *Solvent- or water-based floor cleaner, plus stripping solution (depending on type of floor you have)*

You will probably need:
- *Automatic dishwasher detergent*
- *Oven cleaner (if oven isn't self-cleaning). Odorless products are weaker but less dangerous. You can also use plain ammonia.*
- *Mineral and lime remover (if you have white scales on tiles, tub, etc.)*
- *Mineral spirits (a solvent; often used in stain removal for waxed wood floors)*
- *Naphtha soap (a petroleum distillate and great degreaser)*
- *Rust remover*
- *Silver polish*
- *Brass and copper cleaner*
- *Foaming bathroom cleaner (such as Dow)—good for a variety of quick cleanups*
- *Wood cleaner (such as Preen), if you have woodwork*
- *Very heavy-duty cleaner (such as TSP or Mex Multi-Purpose Cleaner) for walls, ceilings, brick and concrete*
- *Other items recommended in sections of this book that cover specific cleaning jobs*

Polish furniture.
Dust electrical outlets, pictures and frames, tall things, books, lamps.
Clean windows and screens.
Clean light fixtures.
Wash walls and woodwork.
Wash mattress pad and pillow covers, air pillows.
★   Turn the mattress.
Wash shower curtain.
Clean out floor of closet; organize closet.
Vacuum drapes and upholstery.

Annually or As Needed

★   Shampoo carpets and rugs; turn rugs (for even wear).
Vacuum rug pads.
★   Strip and reseal hard-surface floors.
Wash curtains and blinds.
Clean drapes or toss them into dryer on "air only."
Wash bathroom walls.
Wash bedspreads, blankets, and slipcovers.
Clean out and organize workshop.

More Cleaning Tips

• After becoming extremely frustrated with tub-and-tile spray cleaners, I decided to try an easier way to clean the tile around my tub. I filled my plastic plant watering can with laundry detergent, liquid bleach, and hot water, and "watered" the tile around the tub with it. Almost instantly the tile became bright and shiny—even before I began to scrub!

• An easy way to remove the price tag from vases and dishes is to put two to three drops of cooking oil on the tag

---

Money Saver

One way to save big on cleaning supplies is to buy from a janitorial supply company. You can buy generic cleaning solutions that cost a lot less than supermarket brands. There are also cleaning tools that you'd never see in a supermarket.

If your town doesn't have any such company, a local church, school, or small manufacturer may order from such a place and can piggyback your order with theirs. Or get together a group to buy in bulk.

---

and rub it a bit. It comes right off.
• To keep silverware tarnish-free, put a piece of blackboard chalk in the silverware box.
• In life, you start at the bottom; in cleaning, you start at the top.
• When cleaning the glass doors on your fireplace, use a standard window cleaner on the glass for the easy-to-remove grime. Where the soot is baked on, dip a damp paper towel into the fine wood ash on the floor of the fireplace. When this mixture is rubbed over the burned-on stains—presto! Off they come with no ill effects to the door's transparency.
• For those hard-to-reach places around the bathroom faucet, use a toothbrush. It gives a nice shine, too!
• Those beautiful cut-glass vases, bowls, and glasses will sparkle if you wash them in soapsuds and one tablespoon of bluing.
• To remove water spots from your shower tile and glass doors, use non-steel wool scrubbers. Rub scrubbers on the walls while they are dry and then wipe them down with a damp towel.
• To clean those yucky glass shower doors, take a small pail and add one and a half cups of blue fabric softener. Do not dilute. Using a sponge, go up and down the door, over and

To Make the Air Fragrant

• *Simmer a potful of stick cinnamon, orange peel, and whole cloves, add water as needed—place small bowls of vinegar around the room.*

• *Put your favorite spice blend into a length of panty hose tied at both ends, then place it inside a heating vent.*

• *Add some spices (even kitchen spices that are too tired to use in food) to the vacuum cleaner bag.*

• *Add a couple of tablespoons of potpourri to a can of water and place it (or an adhesive air freshener) inside your heat register to spread moisture as well as scent throughout the house.*

• *My favorite way to make a house smell good is with a trick I call "faking baking." Sprinkle some cinnamon on a pan and warm it on the stove. But you'd better make sure you have some food on hand. This tends to make everyone hungry.*

over. Do not rinse. Let it air-dry, and all the yuck will be gone.

• Put a sachet in the bag of your electric broom so the room will smell fresh and sweet after you sweep it.

• Having tried everything to remove adhesive left by the decals that slip-proof the tub, I found the solution by accident. My drain had backed up, so I poured liquid drain cleaner into the tub. After the solution drained, I began to wipe out the tub and found that the glue came right off.

• Clean the glass globes of your light fixtures in the dishwasher.

• Wash your kitchen floor right before you're ready to go to bed to minimize inconvenience and foot traffic.

• Wear white canvas work gloves sprayed with furniture polish to speed up cleaning. Wash and reuse each week. The children love to do this.

• Clean rooms in a clockwise pattern, starting at the door that leads to the next room you want to clean.

• Don't clean everything every time. Deep-clean one room each week—dust the mini-blinds, pull out furniture, flip cushions, polish furniture. Quick-clean the rest of the rooms.
• Place a nylon stocking over your dust mop. Throw it away after using and you can keep your dust mop clean.

An organized home will give you more time to do other things that are more valuable.

In my book *Things Happen When Women Care*, I gave my readers several charts to help them with their scheduling. So many of my readers have expressed to me how helpful those were to them. See if these charts on page 109-11 will also help you out.

TOTAL MESS TO TOTAL REST CHART
Suggested Areas To Clean

D	= Daily
EOD	= Every Other Day
W	= Weekly
M	= Monthly

Q	= Quarterly
Y	= Yearly
Bi	= Twice a Year

🐾 KITCHEN	Freq.	Est. Time		Freq.	Est. Time
Dishes			Clean cupboard drawers		
Wash dishes			Clean window over sink		
Dry dishes, put away			Wash countertops		
Fill dishwasher			Wash canisters		
Empty dishwasher			Clean knickknacks		
Clean dishwasher			Wash/polish woodwork		
Wash pots/pans			Clean fan		
Scour sinks			Walls/ceiling; Paint/wash		
Polish fixtures			Wash/dry-clean curtains		
Floors			Clean toaster/can opener		
Sweep/damp-mop floor			Clean cutting board		
Wash floor			Empty garbage		
Wax floor			Clean light fixtures		
Strip old wax			Clean telephone		
Shake scatter rugs			Clean ceiling fans		
Vacuum kitchen carpet					
Shampoo kitchen carpet					
Range/Oven					
Scour/replace drip pans			🐾 BATHROOM		
Cover drip pans in foil			Clean tub		
Scour rims			Clean sink		
Clean under drip pans			Clean toilet		
Clean knobs/clock			Clean shower stall		
Clean range hood			Wash shower door/curtain		
Clean oven inside/outside			Wash scatter rugs		
Microwave inside/outside			Wash/dry-clean curtains		
Refrigerator/Freezer			Clean out medicine cabinet		
Defrost freezer			Wash mirror		
Clean inside/outside/top			Wash walls/ceiling (paint)		
Clean drip pan			Clean/polish tile		
Cupboards/Drawers			Clean mini-blinds		
Under sink					
Empty/wash shelves					
Dump anything dead					
Change shelf paper					

TOTAL MESS TO TOTAL REST CHART

	Freq.	Est. Time		Freq.	Est. Time
❦ BATHROOM CONTINUED			Clean mirrors		
Floors			Dust lamp shades		
Wash floor			Move furniture to clean		
Wax floor			Wash walls		
Strip old wax			Paint walls		
Vacuum carpet			Remove cobwebs		
Shampoo carpet			Clean furnace vents		
Cupboards/Drawers			Change furnace filter		
Clean/organize			Change air conditioner filter		
Clean/polish woodwork					
Polish countertops			❦ LAUNDRY		
Clean brushes/combs			Wash/dry		
			Fold/put away		
❦ BEDROOMS ▢ ▢ ▢ ▢ ▢			Mend/iron		
Make bed			Do hand washables		
Turn mattress					
Wash mattress pad/bedding			❦ PET CARE		
Clean under bed			Bathe dog		
Vacuum			Change kitty litter		
Polish furniture			Clean bird/hamster cage		
Dust furniture					
Dust picure frames			❦ MISCELLANEOUS		
Clean closets/drawers			Prepare meals		
Wash window (inside)			Set table		
Wash blinds			Polish shoes		
Clean mirrors			Bake		
			Change sheets		
			Water plants		
❦ LIVING ROOM/FAMILY ROOM			Clean fingerprints from walls		
Vacuum carpet			Clean light switches		
Shampoo Carpet			Dust high places/ledges		
Dust furniture			Clean purse		
Polish furniture			Sort seasonal clothing		
Clean fireplace			Clean out car		
Window (inside)			Wash car		
Dust picture frames			Polish/wash purses		
Wash ornaments					
Wash/dry-clean drapes					

TOTAL MESS TO TOTAL REST CHART

	Freq.	Est. Time		Freq.	Est. Time
❀ OUTDOORS			Read		
Sweep patio			Study		
Sweep porch/walks			Fun shopping		
Mow lawn			Lunch out		
Do gardening			Hobbies/sewing/crafts		
Clean up leaves			❀ EXERCISE		
Do pruning			Jog		
Wash windows (outside)			Walk		
❀ SPECIAL PROJECTS			Tennis		
Plan vacations/birthdays					
Plan Christmas			❀ CLASSES		
Write letters			Bible study		
Sew			Women's ministries		
❀ FAMILY			❀ PERSONAL GROOMING		
Family Counsel			Shower		
Dinner/breakfast out			Shampoo		
Fun activities with children			Makeup (one card)		
Church			Shave legs/underarms		
Children's lessons			Manicure		
Candlelight dinner			Pedicure		
Love basket			Haircut		
			Permanent		
❀ FINANCE					
Balance checkbook			❀ VISITING		
Do bookkeeping/budget			Friends		
			The elderly		
❀ PERSONAL ACTIVITIES			Shut-ins		
Bible reading			Telephoning		
Prayer			❀ ERRANDS		
Doctor			Banking		
Dentist			Dry cleaners		
Church			Return recyclables		
Choir			Post Office		
Sunday School			Grocery shopping		
Meetings			❀ HOME ORGANIZATION		
Youth Group			Menu planning/check freezer		
Bible study			Compile grocery list		

6

The Garage

Don't be a coward.
Get rid of
that clutter.

*W*e can make our plans, but the final outcome is in God's hands.

—Proverbs 16:1 (TLB)

The Garage

"*H*elp! I'm in the garage! Over here. No, silly, not over there—in the middle of the garage, third heap on your left. Come fast! Help! I'm under the newspapers and magazines. Look at all this mess. Can you believe it? We really do need to clean this garage."

What You'll Need

1. Trash bags
2. Jars—mayonnaise, peanut butter, and jelly size
3. Small metal cabinets with plastic drawers—you can purchase these at a hardware store to take the place of jars.
4. Large hooks—the type you hang bicycles on
5. Boxes—cardboard-type used for apples and oranges. Most supermarkets have them (or use *More Hours in My Day* "perfect boxes").
6. Broom and rake hooks—hardware stores will have these, too.
7. One to four plastic trash cans, for uses other than trash.
8. Two to six empty coffee cans.
9. Black marking pen.
10. Three trash bags marked "Put Away," "Throw Away," and "Give Away."

Safety Tips for Your Garage

- *Throw away paint- or oil-stained rags or store in metal containers.*
- *Dispose of combustibles such as newspapers, magazines, boxes, and old furniture.*
- *Install extra lighting in work areas, especially where power tools are used.*
- *Make sure ladders are sturdy and have nonslip treads on rungs.*
- *Check that each electrical fuse is the proper size; never use any substitute for the proper fuse.*
- *Keep flammable and volatile liquids in tightly capped safety cans, far from any heat source. Gas fumes travel. Never store gasoline in the home.*
- *Power tools should have double insulation and/or grounded plugs.*

How to Begin

1. Call a family meeting and set a date. (Example: Saturday, 9 A.M.) Ask the family to help "poor Mom" clean the garage.
2. Make a list of all jobs.
3. Delegate responsibilities to each member of the family. Responsibilities could be written on pieces of paper and put into a basket. Have each family member, friend, neighbor, cat, dog (or whomever you can get to help) draw three jobs from the basket.

An Example

1. Jenny: Sort the nails and screws into different jars or into the metal organizational cabinet with the plastic drawers (that you purchased last week).
2. Brad: Separate hammers, screwdrivers, wrenches, and small tools into piles, then put them into the empty

coffee cans (that you have pre-labeled with the black marking pen).

3. Husband Bob: Sort your possessions—papers, pipes, bolts, etc.—and put them into jars and cardboard boxes. Label with the black marking pen.

4. Craig: Neatly roll up the hoses, extension cords, wires, ropes, and any other roll-up type of materials. Put all gardening tools with long handles (such as rake, shovel, edger, broom, etc.) down into one of the trash cans, or hang these tools on a wall in the garage with the special hooks purchased especially for them.

5. Bradley Joe: Empty the large bag of dried dog food into another of the plastic trash cans with a tight lid. It will keep fresh and prevent little animals such as mice from enjoying the food.

6. Mark (our ten-year-old neighbor boy): Collect all the clean rags, old towels, sheets, etc., and put those into a trash can with a lid or into a cardboard box marked accordingly.

7. Mom: Label the cardboard boxes and arrange them on shelves (hopefully you have some) in the garage according to priority. (For example, you don't need the Christmas ornament boxes on the lower shelf because you will only get them down once a year, so they should be put on a top shelf.)

Suggestions

• Bicycles can be hung on rafters with the large hooks you purchased at the hardware store. Most regular cars will easily drive under them. These are for bicycles not used every day. Maybe Dad or an older son could make a bike rack for the other bikes used most often.

• The partially used bags of cement, fertilizer, and other dry materials can also be stored in the plastic trash cans with lids. This will prevent the materials from getting wet.

• Gardening pots, bricks, flats, etc., can be neatly stored on a shelf in the garage or outside the garage in a convenient spot—or build a few shelves outside just for those things. Winter weather won't hurt them, and you have little need for them during those months, anyway.

• Whenever we have a garage sale we let the children keep whatever money comes from their items (such as outgrown games and toys, ice skates, clothing). This encourages them to clean out and get rid of little-used items. Be careful, however, because children can get overexcited and sell their bed, desk, cat, or even baby brother!

• The Put Away trash bag will have items you'll need to store in cardboard boxes, such as athletic equipment (mitts, baseballs, baseball caps, Frisbees, cleats). Another box will house the ice skates, mittens, snow caps, ski sweaters, thermal underwear, and wool socks. Be sure to throw in a few mothballs and label the boxes as to what's inside.

• Another good way to label the boxes is to mark the items on 3" x 5" white cards and tape or staple the cards on the front of the boxes.

• When storing clothing, you may want to put the clothes in a small trash bag with a few whole cloves, then into the cardboard storage box. This prevents silverfish and other little critters from having a picnic.

• Spray-paint cans and smaller paint cans can be put into a storage box and labeled, too.

• Are you beginning to feel all boxed up? Great! That will free you from the guilt feelings of garage disorganization, and you'll now know where everything is.

• Sweep and hose out any leftovers. Put hamburgers on the barbecue, then kick back and enjoy your family, being thankful that you worked well together!

• Charities such as the Salvation Army, Goodwill, your local church mission project, or many local agencies would be glad to receive your castaways. Look in the yellow pages

Garage Sale Checklist

First, consider asking neighbors and friends if they want to join you. Sales advertised as "several families" or "neighborhood" attract more buyers.

1. Check with your city to learn if there are any garage sale restrictions in your area, and if you need to get a permit.
2. Advertise in local newspapers, noting several of the best or most unusual items for sale in the ad.
3. Separate clothing by size and hang it up for easy pickings.
4. Mark prices on each item so that people don't have to ask. If you know you will have a sale when you are cleaning closets, stick prices on discards immediately so you won't have so many to price the week before the sale.
5. Price items objectively and reasonably. If several families are participating in the sale, use colored stick-on tags with a different color for each family. Then as you sell an item, remove the tag and stick it in a notebook; each family will know exactly how much it has earned.
6. Place large, eye-catching items on the lawn or driveway to attract customers.
7. Have boxes, newspapers, and paper or plastic bags to package sold items.
8. Be ready for the "early birds" who show up an hour or two before the sale to get the best bargains.
9. Keep someone at the money box at all times and arrange the tables so that buyers have to pass the "checkout" as they leave. Of course, never leave the cash unattended.
10. Don't accept personal checks unless you know the buyer. Also, have plenty of change ready at the beginning of the sale. You can keep coins in muffin tins.
11. Since the object of the sale is to get rid of the stuff, be ready to bargain with buyers. You earn no money at all if you give or throw away the items, so why not give discounts?
12. Give leftover items to a charity.

of your phone directory. When you give items away, get a receipt for your tax records.

• For those old antiques that are just gathering dust, call your local dealer to come to your home and offer a purchase price. You may even want to assign them to the dealer for a consignment price. Be sure you are dealing with a reputable dealer. Obtain a receipt.

• Systemize your garage by installing shelves, sturdy hooks and a drawer system. Check around your local area to locate garage cabinets. Go to the added expense to have doors installed (it makes the garage more attractive).

• Have a workbench installed to do your basic repairs. Make sure it is near natural light and/or install a fluorescent fixture over the work area.

• Save floor space in your garage by storing storm windows or screens overhead in a simple storage rack attached to existing ceiling joists.

• To soften the blow in case you accidentally collide with the garage's rear wall when parking, cushion the wall with an old tire hung at bumper height.

• As a last resort, try removing a stain on the garage floor with full-strength laundry bleach.

• If all cleaning attempts fail, you can camouflage garage floor drippings with paint. Apply a black stripe the width of the space between the car's tires. The stripe doubles as a parking guide.

• Maximize garage floor space by painting white lines on the floor to outline parking areas for bicycles, the lawn mower, and other large objects. Then they'll be out of the way when you want to park the car.

• Garage floor oil and grease spots can be cleaned with paint thinner. Apply thinner and cover overnight with cat litter, dry portland cement, or sand; then sweep. Repeat if necessary.

• Some automotive oil spots can be lifted with baking soda

Garage Security

• *If you frost or cover your garage windows, burglars won't be able to tell if your car is gone.*
• *Keep your garage door closed and locked even when your car is not there.*
• *If you are worried about someone entering your home through your attached garage, a C-clamp can provide extra security if the garage door lifts on a track since the door cannot be opened if you tighten the C-clamp on the track next to the roller.*
• *Another way to increase garage security is to install a peep hole in the door separating the house from the garage. If you hear suspicious sounds, you can check without opening the door.*

---

or cornmeal. Sprinkle on and sweep off. Repeat as necessary.
• If you need to maximize garage floor space, try hanging items such as rakes and shovels on the walls.
• To keep the garage floor free from grease and oil spots, place a drip pan under the car. Use a cookie sheet filled with cat litter, and replace the litter when it's saturated. Or cut a piece of corrugated cardboard to fit the cookie sheet and change it as necessary.
• Luminous stripes painted on the rear garage wall can help you center your car when parking.
• A "padded" garage can help you avoid scratching your car when pulling in and out. Attach sections of inner tube to both sides of the entrance way, if that is your problem area, or anywhere else that there's a danger of scratching the car.
• Because a great deal of heat is conducted through large garage doors, a significant amount of heat can escape from a home that has an attached garage but no insulation between the house and the garage. An insulated and weatherstripped garage door can save you money, even if the attached garage is unheated.

• If you don't want to put old curtains or draperies on garage windows, you can buy window-frosting paint or apply frosted adhesive-backed plastic for privacy and security. Hint: To apply plastic, hold a piece of the adhesive-backed plastic up to one of the panes and cut with a razor for a perfect fit. Remove the backing carefully, smoothing out wrinkles. If you get a small bubble, let air out with a tiny pinprick and press down.

• You can't avoid getting rid of things by packing them into cartons and stacking them in the garage. This only postpones the day of reckoning. Your car—not your unused possessions—belong in the garage.

• You clean out your garage in order to:
  — have less housework
  — save time and money
  — avoid being a hoarder
  — get rid of the 80 percent you don't need

7
The Laundry

Don't Throw in the
Towel — There
Is Hope!

She selects wool and flax and works with eager hands. She sets about her work vigorously; her arms are strong for her tasks.

—Proverbs 31:13,17

The Laundry

Doing laundry is less of a chore and can fit into even the busiest schedules when good equipment is close by. The area for the laundry can be anywhere: in the basement, upstairs, in a special room designed for laundry, or in a closet with a stack washer-dryer. All you need is access to electricity, plumbing, drainage, and a vent to the outside of the home for your dryer.

Often this area of homemaking becomes such as awesome task that a lot of stress is created due to our inability to keep up with the volume of clothing. I remember one lady with ten children telling me that one of her loads of laundry had 78 pairs of socks. That's a lot of socks! If we don't have some organization in this area of our home, it will cause us a lot of frustration.

Laundry is one area of our organized home that can be delegated to various members of our family—all the way from the simplest task of sorting to the most difficult task of ironing. Children can be taught the "hows" of good laundering. The least *you* need to know about laundering is:

- What needs special care
- Sorting the wash
- Setting the right controls

- Selecting the right detergent
- Spot and stain removal

These are skills that can be learned and taught. Start early giving these responsibilities to your children. (Yes, dads can help too.)

With the cost of clothing and fabrics these days, we need to know what we can do to keep our clothing fresh and new, especially if we are spending money on fairly expensive clothing.

- White vinegar will remove permanent creases when rehemming pants or skirts. Simply dampen with vinegar and press with a warm iron. Repeat if necessary.
- Use warm water to sprinkle your clothes. It penetrates them better. Allow clothes to absorb the moisture at least three hours before ironing.
- If your steam iron clogs up, fill it with a mixture of one-fourth cup of vinegar and one cup of water and let it stand overnight. Heat the iron the next day. Remove the mixture and rinse with clear water.
- Divide your laundry into three cloth bags. These can be made from fabric or three king-size pillowcases with a draw-string. Bag 1 is white for the soiled white clothes. Bag 2 is dark (brown, navy, black) for the dark soiled clothes (jeans, washcloths, etc.) Bag 3 is multicolored for the mixed-color clothes. Colored plastic trash cans can also be used. Label the cans "colored," "white," and "dark." Show all members of the family how to sort their own dirty clothes by putting them in the proper bags or cans. Each child or bedroom could have its own laundry bag. From there they take the clothes to the central sorting area, then sort their own into the three bags. (Or each day *all* dirty clothing goes to the sorting area.) On wash days (or whenever the bags become full), it's a simple matter of dumping each bag into the machine and swish, swash, the wash is done.

ph!�

Is Your Water Hard?

To determine whether your water is hard (and if so, how hard), consult your local water-supply office. If your water comes from another source, have it tested by a water treatment company. There are several indications that you have hard water:

- Fabrics look dull and gray.
- Fabrics feel stiff instead of soft.
- Soaps and detergents don't lather well.
- A "ring" settles around your bathtub.
- A white residue appears and remains around drains and faucets and on glassware.

Remember, it's not what you *expect* but what you *inspect*. So be sure to teach the method to your children and then inspect from time to time to see if they are doing it properly. Whatever goes *in* the bags inside out will come *out* inside out.

- Each family member can also have his or her own bright-colored bin for clean folded clothes. Christine's is pink, Chad's is blue, Bevan's is white, mom's is red, and dad's is green. Or you can use all white bins (or dishpan-type bins) and color code them with stick-on dots or colored felt markers with each family member's name on them.
- Whoever folds the clothes places each person's items in his or her proper bin. It is then the responsibility of each family member to take his own bin to the drawers and empty the bin. Should the bin not return to the folding area, no clothes will be folded for that person.
- Plan your wash days and start washing early in the day.
- On wash day use cold water, if possible—especially on colored clothes. This will help them to stay bright longer.
- Wash full loads rather than small ones. This saves energy—and your appliances, as well.

- Never leave the washer or dryer running when you aren't home. A machine leak or short circuit can cause damage or, worse yet, start a fire.
- If using a dryer, remove the clothes as soon as it stops, then hang and fold. Clothes will be less wrinkled, and many times you won't have to iron items.
- Forgot to take out the clothes in the dryer? Simply throw in a damp towel or washcloth and turn on the dryer again for five to ten minutes. The dampness from the towel will freshen the load and remove any wrinkles.
- Hang as many clothes as possible on hangers, especially permanent-press garments. This helps cut down on ironing. Put up a few hooks near the laundry area or string an indoor clothesline.
- I recommend using plastic-colored hangers rather than metal ones. They prevent marks and creases on your garments. Using colored hangers can also be a way to color code your family.
- Schedule at least one day a week for ironing, or three 15-minute slots per week.
- To help ironing time go quickly, pray for the person whose clothing you are ironing.
- Label your linen closet shelves so that whoever puts the sheets and towels away will know just the right spot for them. This prevents confusion, keeps your closet looking neat, and saves time in finding king-size or twin-size sheets.
- When your iron sticks, sprinkle a little salt onto a piece of waxed paper and run the hot iron over it. Rough, sticky spots will disappear as if by magic.
- Always wash your throw rugs in cool or lukewarm water. (Hot water will cause the rubber backing to peel.) Let the rug dry on a line instead of in the dryer. You can fluff it up when it is dry in the no-heat cycle of your dryer.
- *Here's a little trick to make ironing easier:* Using pieces of wax candles in an old cotton sock, swipe your iron every so

often while ironing. The wax makes it glide smoothly, and your ironing goes faster.

• Instead of using expensive fabric-softener sheets, pour one-fourth cup *white* vinegar in the last rinse of the washing cycle. This eliminates static cling, helps remove wrinkles, gives clothes a fresh smell by removing soap, and cleans the drains of the washer by removing soap scum and lint.

• *Another way to remove garment wrinkles*: Hang wrinkled garments on the curtain rod in your bathroom and run very hot water from the shower. Close the bathroom door and let the water run for a couple of minutes. The steam will fade the wrinkles from your clothing. Great for those who travel!

We can make our plans, but the final outcome is in God's hands— Proverbs 16:1 (TLB).

• A neat way to use liquid laundry detergents on "ring-around-the-collar" is to pour a small amount of detergent into a cup and use a small paintbrush or toothbrush to apply it to the collar. This eliminates waste and helps you get the detergent where you want it.

• Hang a whisk broom on a hook beneath your ironing board. Use it to remove lint when pressing clothes.

• When your panty hose are new, take them out of the package, wet them thoroughly, put into a plastic bag, and freeze. They will last longer, saving you money. I also have heard that to resist runs, panty hose should be lightly starched.

• Keep the crinkles crisp in seersucker by adding a small amount of starch to the rinse water when laundering. The fabric will look fresher.

• Use small safety pins to keep socks paired during the wash and dry cycles. Weight keeps socks from clinging to other laundry and saves time in matching socks when folding laundry. (Or do as one mom did and purchase only white socks for the children, one size fits all!)

Plan your work, then work your plan.

• Rotate your various items of clothing as much as possible so they can regain their shape. I have a friend who rotates her garments by hanging them after each wearing at the right end of the closet. The next day she picks the skirt or pants that are on the left end of the closet. That way she knows how often they are worn. This works especially well with men's suits.

• Have you ever thought of Scotchguarding your new fabrics? It's very effective and will last until the garment is cleaned or washed (then you must spray it again). You can also use Scotchguard on fabric shoes.

• Mend your garments as soon as they are damaged. Sew on those buttons and repair those rips and loose hems. My Bob has a tendency to tear out the seat of his pants, so I triple-stitch and zigzag the seams when they are new, even before they are worn. That keeps embarrassing moments to a minimum.

• Keep sweaters in a drawer or on a shelf rather than on a hanger (to prevent stretching).

• Skirts and pants are best hung on hangers with clips; or you can use clothespins on wire hangers.

• Even very good jewelry can discolor your clothing, so just dab the backs with clear nail polish. The polish can also be painted on jewelry with rough edges that could pull fibers of fabrics.

• Brush suede shoes with a suede brush that brings up the nap. You can use a nail file to rub off any little spots.

• If your shoes get wet, stuff them with paper towels or newspaper and allow to dry away from direct heat.

• Shoe trees are great to keep the shape in your shoes.

Stop! Don't Put That in Your Dryer

Do not put items in your dryer that are spotted with or have been in contact with paint, machine oil, gasoline, or any flammable fluids or solids. They are fire hazards, and their fumes can ignite. Line-dry instead.

Once all traces of flammables and their fumes are removed, dry as usual.

• When storing leather handbags or shoes, never put them into plastic bags, since this can cause the leather to dry out. Instead, use fabric shoe bags or wrap the shoes in tissue and put them into shoe boxes.

• Always wash knitwear inside out, either by hand or machine, to avoid snags.

• To stop a run in your panty hose, use hair spray or clear nail polish.

• When you wash curtain panels, use a laundry marking pen to mark each drapery as you take it down to indicate which window it belongs on.

• Dampen a washcloth with liquid fabric softener and toss it in the dryer with your clothes. It works well and is much cheaper than commercial softener sheets.

• If your children manage to get holes in their clothes almost as soon as they get them, use fleecy bathrobe velour to patch the clothes. It is inexpensive, 100-percent synthetic, less plushy, and comes in many colors. It wears very well.

• To get stains out of colored polyester clothes, presoak in one-fourth cup automatic dishwashing detergent to one gallon hot water for several hours. Then launder as usual.

• When I want to wash a rug that sheds, I put it in a pillowcase (an old one that I keep just for this purpose) and tie the top well. Then I have no mess in the washer. Just shake out the pillowcase.

• When wringing water out of corduroys, velveteens, or woolens, gently squeeze fabric and lay it on heavy towels, shaping it to the original size of the garment.

• I wash all my panty hose at one time by putting them in a pillowcase, folding the open end over, and fastening it with a safety pin. I put the pillowcase in the washing machine with other delicate items. I then place the pillowcase in the dryer on low heat.

• A great way to freshen and fluff pillows is to throw them into the dryer and run them through without heat (just air) for a few minutes. The tumbling will get rid of the dust and freshen pillows at the same time.

• To dry a bulky sweater faster and more safely, place it between two fluffy bath towels and roll lightly with a rolling pin. Then remove the sweater and put a hand towel inside it before flattening and shaping it to dry. The hand towel absorbs still more moisture.

• When washing panel curtains, wash them in Woolite in cold water and it won't be necessary to press them.

Managing time takes maximum effort and realistic planning. First, you must acknowledge that you have 24 hours a day—the same amount God has given to everyone. You, with God's help, must determine how to use your time.

• I have tried reusing fabric-softener sheets in the dryer but could never remember how many times I had used them. I finally hit on the idea of tearing off a small corner each time I put a sheet in the dryer.

• To make your blankets fluffier, add two cups of white vinegar to a washer tub of rinse water.

• A cloth dipped in two percent peroxide and used as a pressing cloth will remove most scorches.

• Iron dark cottons, rayons, and woolens on the back of the

fabric to avoid shine marks from the iron.

• To remove wrinkles from anything plastic around your household, such as tablecloths, shower curtains, or shelf paper, use your hand-held blow-dryer.

• Fold towels lengthwise, then double. They will be ready to place on racks. If folded widthwise, they will need to be opened and refolded.

• To clean the lint filter out of the washer or dryer, use a hair pick. It works great, especially if the lint is wet.

• Launder your blankets in the summer and store them for winter in clean paper sealed with gummed tape.

• I'm always dropping socks, underwear, and combs between my washer and dryer where I can't reach. I solved my problem by placing a narrow piece of carpet on the floor between the two appliances. When something falls, I pull out the strip and the article comes with it.

• A great "closet organizer" for socks, scarves, mittens, and swimsuits is a cardboard juice carton with dividers. Take off the top lid; cover the box with colored decorative adhesive paper. Place the box on its side on a wardrobe shelf and you have some great cubbyholes for those little items. Also keep a similar box in your laundry room so each rag has its own cubbyhole.

• To freshen laundry, add one-third cup baking soda to the wash or rinse cycle. Clothes will smell sweeter and cleaner.

• In cold weather, wipe your clothesline with a cloth moistened with vinegar to prevent your laundry from sticking to the line. Wax the line once a month to keep black marks off your clothes.

• Wet shoes can dry quickly without increasing the electric bill. Place shoes with inside or top of shoe facing the exhaust side of the refrigerator.

Bleach Basics

For White Fabrics:
Mix one tablespoon chlorine bleach with one quart water; soak for 15 minutes.

For Colored Fabrics, Silk, or Wool:
Mix two tablespoons hydrogen peroxide in one one gallon water; soak 30 minutes.

NOTE: *Always test any method or solution on a hidden part of the fabric first.*

The foremost challenge a woman faces is not to orchestrate her life or to plan her year but to order each day—allowing for sufficient rest, proper nourishment and exercise, and a quiet time spent with the Lord.

• As you sprinkle your clothes for ironing, sort them. Separate those materials needing a high, medium, or low temperature. This will save you from having to root through the basket as you iron.

• When ironing double thicknesses—collars, cuffs, hems, or pockets—iron on the wrong side first and then on the right side for a much smoother finish.

• Ironing boards never seem to have enough padding. When the cover on your ironing board is ready to be thrown out, leave the pad on the board. Just add your new pad and cover over the old.

• When machine washing or drying delicate items, place them in a net bag or a pillowcase (tied closed or pinned with rustproof safety pins).

Bleaching Dos and Don'ts

- Wear rubber gloves when hand washing with bleach.
- Read fabric and bleach labels.
- Test bleach before use:
  - Chlorine bleach—mix one tablespoon bleach with one-fourth cup cold water. Place a drop on a hidden area; leave for one minute. Blot to see if there is any color change.
  - All-fabric oxygen bleach—mix one teaspoon bleach with one cup hot water. Place a drop on a hidden area; leave for ten minutes. Blot to see if there is any color change.
- Thoroughly rinse out bleach.
- Keep bleach away from children.
- Don't let chlorine bleach come in direct contact with fabrics.
- Don't put all-fabric/oxygen bleach directly on wet fabrics without testing for colorfastness first.
- Don't use chlorine bleach if your household water supply has a high iron content. It can draw out the iron and deposit it as spots on clothes.
- Don't use bleach and ammonia in the same wash. The combination can create hazardous fumes.
- Don't use more of either kind of bleach than recommended on the package or bottle label.
- Starches and sizings restore body to fabrics that become limp (such as cotton and linen) when washed or dry-cleaned.
- Starch comes in powder, liquid, and spray forms. Mix the powder and liquid with water. If using the powder, mix to the desired thickness—thin for light starching, thick for heavy. When washing cottons and linens, add it to the final rinse. Spritz spray starches on during ironing.
- Lighter than starch, sizing is applied to some fabrics by manufacturers for protection and body. General wear, moisture, perspiration, and cleaning will break down sizing,

but you can reapply it. Spritz it on before ironing.

• If you just want to starch selected items, remove them from the washer and soak in a basin in a starch solution for the time recommended on the starch package. Squeeze out excess moisture before placing them in the dryer.

• Harden chewing gum stuck to fabric with an ice cube, then gently scrape off as much as possible with a dull knife. Soak in dry-cleaning solvent until remaining gum is loosened and scrape again. Wash in warm suds. Rinse.

• Add detergent or soap as the washer fills, and then add the clothes.

• Wait until the rinse cycle to add fabric softener, bluing, or liquid starch, as needed.

• Don't use fabric softener with other laundry products that contain softeners.

• Distribute clothes evenly, balancing large and small pieces, and make sure that nothing is wrapped around the agitator.

• Wash chocolate/cocoa stains in warm suds with a few drops of ammonia added. Rinse. If stain remains, sponge or soak in dry-cleaning solvent, then use the appropriate bleach. *Wool: Sponge with glycerine. If unavailable, use warm water.

• Butter/margarine stains usually come out with ordinary laundering. If a greasy residue remains after washing, sponge or soak in dry-cleaning solvent, then wash in warm suds. Rinse.

• Harden candle wax stuck to fabric with an ice cube, then gently scrape off as much wax as possible with a dull knife. Sponge the area with dry-cleaning solvent to remove as much as possible. Place the stain between paper towels. Press with warm, dry iron, changing towel as the wax is absorbed. Launder as usual. If stain remains, use the appropriate bleach.

• If you are unable to iron all your damp clothes (and to

prevent mildew), store them in the refrigerator wrapped in a terrycloth towel until you resume.

• Allow the iron to heat long enough to generate steam before you press the steam spray button. Otherwise, there may be drips that can spot the fabric.

• Use a damp, lint-free cloth (such as a handkerchief, diaper, or old cotton sheet) for a pressing cloth.

• You can cut your ironing time if you smooth seams, pockets, and pleats as garments dry on a hanger or line, or immediately after you take them from the dryer.

• Wrap masking tape around your hand three or four times with the sticky side of the tape facing out. Pat or brush the garment with the tape. This is a great, inexpensive lint remover.

• Soak fresh alcoholic beverage stains in cool water, then wash in warm suds. Rinse. For old, brown stains or any remaining stain, soak in an appropriate bleach. *Wool*: Place a towel under the stain. Gently rub with a cloth soaked in carbonated water (like club soda).

• Rub liquid laundry detergent into antiperspirant stains. Wash in warm suds. Rinse.

• When hand washing items other than silk, add a capful of white vinegar to the next to the last rinse. The vinegar removes any soap or detergent residue in the water or on the fabric.

• You don't have to buy expensive "delicate wash" detergents for sweaters and washable silks. Use shampoo.

• Candles make great pin cushions. The waxed pins slip through material more easily.

• Place heavy-duty aluminum foil between your ironing board cover and pad. The foil reflects the heat and makes ironing quicker.

• Refresh your tired-looking silk ties by using a little steam. Hang the tie in a steamy bathroom, or wrap a damp piece of cloth over the sole plate of your iron and pass the steaming iron over the tie.

Stain-Fighter Supplies

Keep the following stain-removal supplies on hand and follow the label instructions:

Acetone: *pure acetone (not nail-polish remover)—available at pharmacies*

Ammonia: *household*

Bleach: *both chlorine and all-fabric/oxygen varieties*

Carbonated Water or club soda

Color Remover: *available where fabric dyes are sold*

Dry-Cleaning Solvent: *available at supermarkets*

Enzyme Detergent

Glycerine: *available at pharmacies*

Hydrogen Peroxide

Oxalic Acid Solution: *or rust remover—available at pharmacies*

Paint Remover

Petroleum Jelly

Prewash Spot Remover

Sodium Thiosulfate or sodium hyposulfite—*available in photography shops*

White Vinegar

• Having a hard time telling everyone's clothing apart? Use an indelible pen or laundry marker to identify each garment with the owner's first initial.

• Sorting linens after washing will be easier if you buy whites, colors, and prints to help you distinguish among twin, regular, and queen sizes.

• When ironing large items, use the wide end of the ironing board. To help keep the item clean, lay a plastic tablecloth on the floor beneath the board.

8
The Automobile

The worst fault of a
motorist is his belief
that he has none.

Be sure you know the condition of your flocks, give careful attention to your herds; for riches do not endure forever, and a crown is not secure for all generations.

—Proverbs 27:23,24

The
Automobile

As in all phases of life, the three most important parts of any project are to PLAN, PLAN, PLAN. Usually things go wrong when we don't spend enough time in our planning phase. Don't be in such a hurry that you forget to plan. Plan to have your car regularly checked by a reliable mechanic and before starting off on that all-important trip. Many times we think of vacations only in the summer months. But depending upon your schedule's flexibility, you might well take your trip any time of the year.

Having your car checked regularly is the best way to prevent major car problems down the road when you are really counting on your car to perform properly. A combination of getting your car in shape and then paying close attention to the warning signals your car gives to you are key in assuring a car's smooth performance and longevity.

Without giving it a second thought, we jump into our car, turn the key in the ignition, and expect our faithful buggy to start up and take us wherever we want to go.

But a car is an expensive piece of machinery and, like our bodies, it needs care to run well. Being stuck with car trouble is no fun and can often be avoided.

You're dressed in your finest Sunday clothes waiting for

the family to join you in the car for church. You jump in your car, turn the key—and the car plays dead. If you've ever had that happen to you, you know the empty feeling you have.

The children arrive on the scene and, of course, ask 100 questions, which makes matters worse. What are you to do? Call a friend? A neighbor? A taxi? Or cancel the church service?

Here is a checklist to help you keep your car in tip-top shape. It's especially important to give your car a checkup before going on a vacation or an extended trip.

Warning!

• Do not remove the radiator cap quickly when the engine is hot, especially if the air conditioner has been used. Turn the cap slowly to let the steam escape. Otherwise you will be severely burned by hot water and steam.

Routine Maintenance Checklist

The following items need to be checked, especially before taking a long trip or vacation. Other than taking a trip, check these things twice a year. (The frequency of checkups depends somewhat on the type of climate you live in.)

If you take your car to a service station, don't assume that they automatically check these items. You'll need to ask for some of these services:
• Engine oil changed and filter replaced
• Air filter cleaned or replaced
• Emission control devices checked
• Headlights and brake lights inspected and adjusted
• Differential fluid level checked and changed (if applicable for your car)
• Transmission fluid level checked
• Wheel bearings inspected and repacked (once a year)
• Brakes inspected (once a year)

- Air-conditioning system checked and serviced once a year
- Cooling system hoses checked and coolant/antifreeze replaced once a year
- Power steering fluid level checked
- Shock absorbers tested
- Battery inspected
- Drive belts checked
- Windshield wipers checked. Even in summer you will need to replace these if needed, in case of summer rainstorms.
- Tire tread depth and inflation pressure checked
- Exhaust system inspected for leaks
- Tune-up. Refer to owner's manual for manufacturer's suggestion for how often a tune-up is needed.

Emergency Organization List

These items should be carried in your car at all times in case of emergency:

- Fire extinguisher
- Jumper cables
- First-aid kit (bee sting kit)
- Towel(s)
- Flashlight with extra batteries
- Ice scraper
- Spare fuses for electrical system
- Can of tire inflater/sealer
- Flares and/or highway triangular warning signs
- Spare drive belts, fan belts, air-conditioner belts, and air-pump belts
- An empty approved gasoline container. *Do not carry extra gasoline in the trunk.*
- Container of water
- Warm blanket
- Metal or wire coat hanger

- Distress flag
- Plastic drop cloth for working under car
- Toolbox with the following: pliers, screwdriver, adjustable wrench, small socket wrenches, hammer, cleanup wipes for hands, clean rag.
- Winter Tools: Chains, small shovel, can of sand, extra blankets or heavy coat for emergencies, heavy boots, and gloves.

It may seem overwhelming at first to furnish your car with these items, but it's well worth it. Being prepared could save a life or get you out of a dangerous or difficult situation. Besides, being ready for emergencies and keeping your car tuned up will relieve another whole area of stress in your life.

When Your Car Won't Start

The American Automobile Association says failure of cars to start was the most common emergency last year.

Two ways a car can fail to start are 1) the starter motor may turn, but the engine refuses to catch, or 2) the starter motor may be sluggish, perhaps not turning at all.

Let's deal with the second case first.

- If you twist the key and you hear only a click, at least you know the ignition switch works. If there was a click and your car has an automatic transmission, move the shift lever into neutral and then back to park and try starting the car again. Sometimes a little switch—that prevents you from starting your car while it's in gear—sticks.

Still no start? See if the headlights light and the horn honks. If they seem weak, the battery is either dead or has a bad connection.

1. Find where the battery is—usually under the hood.
2. Look closely at the two terminals and the ends of the two cables, positive (+) and negative (-), that attach to them.

3. Are they clean and firmly secured?
4. If not, remove the negative (-) cable (it's usually black) *first*, followed by the positive (+) cable (usually red).
5. Scrape them with a knife or screwdriver and firmly reattach them.

If your car still won't start, you can either push-start it (but only if it has a stick shift) or jump-start it using cables attached to another car's battery. To push-start, you'll need:

1. A couple of strong children or neighbors, or
2. An experienced driver who is willing to give you a push from the rear of the car.
3. Get in the car; turn on the ignition.
4. Put your foot on the clutch and put the shift lever in second gear.
5. When the car reaches about 5 mph, let out the clutch and the car should start.

If you are attempting to jump-start your car, be sure to refer to the owner's manual. Great care should be taken when jump-starting your car.

After the car starts, drive to your mechanic's to check out why the battery was low and wouldn't start the engine. You may need a new battery or it may just need to be charged.

The second area to check if your starter turns but the engine won't start, is the fuel or the ignition system. Be sure to check that you have gas in your tank!

If your car has fuel injection, you will probably want to have the car towed to your mechanic, because these are very hard for the average layman to service. But if it has a carbureted engine:

1. Pump the throttle pedal three times and try to start the car.

2. Still no response? Open the hood.
3. If you smell gas, you have flooded the carburetor.
4. Wait a few minutes.
5. Press the gas pedal all the way to the floor. Hold it there—*don't pump!*
6. The engine should sputter a bit and then start up.

Cold and damp weather present special challenges to a slumbering engine. On a cold day if the starter turns and if you have a carbureted engine:

1. Open the hood and find the air cleaner (usually big and round on top of engine, although sometimes rectangular).
2. Take off the wing nut or retaining clips and lift off the cover of the air cleaner.
3. Spray a little ether starter fluid (available at auto parts stores) down the carburetor throat.

Another useful elixir to carry in your truck is WD-40—it absorbs moisture. On a damp day, spray some on the coil, some on the spark-plug wires and on the distributor and some inside the distributor—if you can get the lid off. Then give the starter another turn.

If on a hot day your car refuses to start after it's been running, it may have a "vapor lock." If your car has a mechanical fuel pump (most carbureted engines do), pour cold water on the pump and nearby gas lines, and that should get you on your way.

If you don't have a very difficult problem, you should get to church in time to participate in the services. Try to relax and not get too uptight.

I will turn their mourning into gladness; I will
give them comfort and joy instead of sorrow.
— Jeremiah 31:13b

Save Money When Buying a Car

• *Have a plan and don't weaken.* Determine one or several models of cars you would like to own. Window-shop (don't get sucked in by a good salesman) the new-car lots to get a better idea of what you want.

• *Hunt the classifieds for your ideal car.* Shop the automobile classified section of your newspaper or your local *Auto Trader* magazine.

• *Buy your next car from an individual instead of a dealer.* A private-party seller is usually the most motivated of all sellers. After several days of advertising, phones ringing, and people making ridiculous offers, the seller is happy to talk to a reasonable person. You are in the driver's seat because there are hundreds of cars for sale by individuals, and you are one buyer.

• *Buy the car you want, but only after it is 2 to 2 ½ years old.* In fact, by using this strategy you will not only save money but also get a better car than if you buy new.

When you buy a brand-new car, it depreciates about 20 percent as soon as you drive it off the lot. Yes, for a $15,000 car you automatically lose $3,000. In the first two years your new car will depreciate approximately 40 percent. Let someone else lose this 40 percent, but not you. You also miss all the nonsense charges of extra freight, rustproofing, fabric coating, added warranties, etc.

• *Don't finance your car at the dealership.* We live in a world of convenience, and it is certainly convenient to get everything done at the time of purchase, but when you do you will be paying extra interest for your loan. The dealer is really just a middleman for the finance company. You as a consumer can go directly to your bank or credit union and get a much better deal. Go to your bank or credit union and get pre-approved for a loan before you go out to buy that car.

• *Stay out of the finance office of the dealership.* That's where you weaken, because you have already agreed on a price and the monthly payments, but a sharp manager can add another $25 per month without you getting too excited. "What's $25 a month? I can certainly afford that." A quick calculation is that $25 a month over 60 months is an additional cost to you of $1500 over the life of the loan.

• *Never use a dealer's blue book.* Many buyers get a copy of a blue book and think they have all the information they need to really lock in on a price. Or they ask the salesperson to bring out his copy (which is usually marked up higher than your copy) and you negotiate from that. A better guide is the "National Automobile Dealers Association (NADA) Official Used Car Guide."

• *Use the NADA Official Used Car Guide to determine the value of your car.* You can buy this guide at many bookstores for under $15. It is published in nine geographic regions. Call this number to get a subscription: (800) 544-6232 [(800) 523-3110 in Virginia]. It is most important for you to know exactly what any car you are looking at is actually worth, which is the maximum you will pay for that car. Never buy or sell a car without consulting the NADA Guide, and never pay more than the auction price. The average trade-in is the auction price and represents what a dealer could buy or sell the car for at an auction. With a little practice you will be able to decode this guide book.

• *Use fabric protection on your seat covers yourself and forget the paint sealer.* Fabric coating consists of about $10 worth of Scotchguard, which you could apply yourself. You don't have to pay a dealer several hundred dollars to do the same thing. It will only take you 15 minutes to do the job yourself. Be sure to read the directions on the back of the can.

Your paint will do fine without the paint sealant with just the normal maintenance of washing and waxing your car on a regular basis. If your paint does begin to fade, purchase a can of "fine grit rubbing compound" available at an auto parts store. It will bring back the shine. Remember to read the instructions on the back of the container.

• *Avoid undercoating your car.* You don't need this added expense. The undercarriage of the car is already painted with rustproofing material by the manufacturer.

• *Don't pay inflated delivery and dealer preparation charges.* A dealer can charge whatever he wants for delivery. His sticker price is usually higher than the actual price, since dealers get excellent rates with their railroad and trucking firms. Negotiate this price.

Dealer "setup and preparation charges" should be zero. The only costs are usually a vacuum job and a good washing. You need not pay for these when you purchase a car.

• *Don't fall for low interest rates or rebates.* When manufacturers and dealers have extra inventory, they need to have a way to sell their backlog of cars. One way is to offer you a lower interest rate or a rebate, which is really a "buy-down." Without going into a lengthy explanation of how it works, the bottom line is to negotiate your own deal and do your own financing.

• *Never finance your car for more than 36 months.* Anything over this amount of time means you have a negative balance due on your car (more than it is worth). This means that in two years, if you decide to sell your car, you will find out you owe more than it's worth. The longer the term of your loan, the greater the percentage of each payment that goes to pay interest rather than principal on your loan.

A 36-month loan allows you to pay off your loan faster than your car is depreciating. This way you can sell your car anytime you want to without losing money. You don't owe more than you own.

A Checklist for Your Car Before a Trip

How do you know when your car needs attention? The Car Care Council gives some very practical suggestions.

1. Watch to see if your engine is hard to start, uses too much gas, seems sluggish, smokes, or is excessively noisy.
2. Be sure that your cooling and heating systems are in good condition. Be sure to check your hoses, belts, and antifreeze/coolant.
3. How about those tires of yours? Heavy loads at high speeds are hard on tires. Make sure tires have plenty of tread and are properly inflated.
4. How's your oil? Oil is not only a lubricant, it is also a coolant. Clean, well-filtered oil will help your engine survive the heat as well as the cold.
5. Be sure to check your transmission. Does it slip when you shift gears? Is it noisy? Does it shift erratically? If you are towing a trailer, it is especially vital for your transmission to be in the best working order possible.
6. Be sure that the brakes stop evenly and are not making any strange noises.
7. Watch to see that all lights are working and that they are aimed correctly. Also check turn signals and windshield wiper blades (for smearing or streaking).

After checking these areas of your car, you can feel more assured of a problem-free trip, barring unforseen mechanical failure. If you do find yourself in car trouble in an unknown town and don't know of a good, reputable mechanic, you can look in the yellow pages under "Automotive Repairs" for ASE-certified technicians. These technicians have taken the proper courses to be certified by the National Institute for Automotive Service Excellence. This is an organization that is highly respected in the automotive industry, and is an independent, nonprofit group which gives voluntary certification exams to technicians.

Keep a Regular Maintenance Log

• Place the form on page 153 in a plastic divider in your glove compartment. Use one column each time the car is serviced. Your mechanic or car owner's manual will tell you how often or at how many miles you should service your car.

Travel Smart

Here is a helpful checklist of items to take with you in your car so you'll be prepared and ready to prevent minor roadside difficulties from becoming major ones.

In the glove compartment:
• Maps
• Notepad and pen
• Tire-pressure gauge
• Cleanup wipes
• Sunglasses
• Mirror (best placed above sun visor)
• Extra pair of nylon hosiery for that unexpected run
• Reading material, Bible—you can enjoy prayer and Bible reading during waiting times in the car
• Can opener
• Plastic fork and spoon, for those yummy stops
• Change for phone calls
• Business cards
• Band-Aids
• Matches
• Stationery—again, waiting can be used constructively to catch up on correspondence
• Scissors, nail clippers
• Children's books and/or games

Protect Your Ownership

• Hide a key for the times you lock your keys inside the car. Caution: Don't put it under the hood if you have an inside hood release.
• A good idea to prove ownership of your car is to print your name, address, and phone number on a 3" x 5" file card or use your business card and slide it down your car windowframe on the driver's side. If the car is lost or stolen, it is easier to prove the auto is yours.
• Your rubber car mats can be used to keep windshields from freezing. Put them on the outside of the windows under your wipers to hold them in place, and presto—clean windows and no scraping, either.
• To remove decals and price lists from windows, simply sponge with plenty of white vinegar. Allow vinegar to soak in, and stickers should come off easily.

The time to relax is when you don't have time for it—Sydney J. Harris.

Sell Your Car Yourself

• Use the NADA Guide to determine your car's true value. Determine the average trade-in price, which is the minimum you will take for your car. If your car is exceptionally clean, you can usually sell it for between the trade-in and the retail price.
• Meet with your banker. You will get a lot more telephone calls if you can put in your ad "financing arranged." Meet with your present loan officer on your car and tell him or her of your intent to sell your car. Ask what would be required for someone to take over the loan. You will be told that there would need to be a new application made for the loan, and the prospect would have to have good credit. If the prospect is approved, the bank would be glad to make the new loan.

AUTOMOTIVE INFORMATION AND SERVICING SCHEDULE

Model _____   Make _____   License Number _____

Serial # _____   Insurance Company _____   Telephone # (____) ____

Use one column each time car is serviced	Date Mileage	Date Mileage	Date Mileage	Date Mileage	Date Mileage	Date Mileage
Oil Change						
Lubrication						
Change oil Filter						
Clean Air Filter						
Service Cooling System						
Rotate Tires						
Replace Tires						
Service Brakes						
Plugs, Points Condenser						
Engine Tune-up						
Change Trans. Fluid						
Total Cost	$	$	$	$	$	$

- *Clean your car with a good detailing job.* A $50 investment in a good detailing job is well worth it.
- *Advertise your car.* Run an ad in your local paper. See if there is a special for three or four days. Here are key words which stand out for buyers: low mileage, clean, sharp, like new, must sell, financing available. Include your phone number and when you can be called. Limit the times people can call by saying, "Call 5-7 P.M. weekdays, 10 A.M.-5 P.M. weekends." Put your asking price in the ad. Make your asking price $200 to $400 above the trade-in value in the NADA Guide.
- *Minimize the time people can see your car.* To save yourself a lot of time and hassle, set up one or two specific times for people to see your car. If they call, say, "I'll be home from 5 to 6 P.M. on Saturdays to show the car." This way several people will arrive during a short period of time to give the impression that a lot of people are interested in your car. This also saves a lot of your valuable time.
- *Never give your keys to a potential buyer.* The potential driver should be perfectly free to drive your car, but not alone. If there is a man of the house, he should be the one going with the potential driver. A woman should not go with a stranger.
- *Be excited about your car.* Don't oversell, but be enthusiastic about the car you are selling. Give a reasonable, positive reason for selling it. If the buyer comments negatively about a feature of the car, you might comment, "That's why the price is so reasonable." Be positive.
- *Select a bottom price.* Your ad should indicate a price of $200 to $400 above the rock-bottom price you will take. Once the buyer has negotiated to that price, let him know that you will not sell the car below that price. At that point the buyer will either purchase the car or excuse himself.

- *Have your paperwork ready.* You will need to have all the necessary papers available and ready to give the new buyer, particularly if he or she needs to go to the bank for financing. However, if he doesn't have a bank for a loan, he may need to go with you to your bank to make necessary application for a loan. In some cases a buyer will pay in cash.
- *Accept only cash or a certified check.* Never accept a personal check or a promise. Take the car off the market only when you have a reasonable deposit. If the buyer has only a check, accompany the buyer to his or her bank to cash the check.

If the buyer has financed the purchase of your car, require him to have the necessary insurance, license, and proof of ownership before taking the car. If you have been paid cash on the spot and the necessary transfer papers have been signed (they may be obtained at the bank or the local Department of Motor Vehicles), the buyer may take possession. Remove your license plate before the car leaves your home (unless the plates are to be transferred).

- *Follow your state's transfer regulations.* Contact your state's Department of Motor Vehicles to find out exactly what must be done legally to transfer the car from you to the new owner. Do not let the buyer take the car if your name is still listed as owner; an accident might make you liable for damages. After making a legal transfer, prepare and sign a bill of sale (a stationery store will usually carry these, or you may get them at the DMV). Keep a copy for your records, and the new owner receives a copy.
- *Don't cancel your insurance too fast.* Wait until your loan shows "paid in full" by your lender. Also, be sure to remember to eventually cancel your insurance. If not, you will be paying for services which you aren't using.

Other Automobile Hints

- The noises your car makes are its way of telling you it has a problem. Listen carefully, and you will save time, repair bills, and perhaps even your life. Listen for:

— *A high-pitched tinkling sound when you accelerate.* You could be running your engine on the wrong grade of gas. Check the owner's manual for the recommended grade. If the noise continues, have it checked at a garage.

— *A banging noise in the exhaust system.* That is a backfire and could mean it's time for new spark plugs or that the fuel mixture is too lean.

— *A coughing sound as the engine is turned off.* Your carburetor probably needs adjusting.

— *Squeaking noises from the brakes.* This is often the result of damp weather. If the noise continues or you hear grating and groaning, have all brakes checked.

• When black rubber tape or plastic trim on your car fades or gets white spots, use black shoe polish to freshen the trim. It will look new again.

• As an emergency precaution, apply large strips of flourescent tape diagonally across the inside top of your car trunk. If you need to stop on the highway at night open your trunk, and you have a warning sign.

• When you wash your car, use two large, old bath towels to wipe and dry the windows and car exterior. They get quite dirty, so instead of putting them in the washing machine, put them in a pail of water with detergent. A little up-and-down motion with a drain plunger works like magic. Do the same in the rinse water. (A bucket, plunger, and cold-water detergent should be great for campers to take along, too.)

• When traveling with children, I spread a large sheet over the backseat and floor. When I get gas or come to a rest stop, I just take out the sheet and shake it. That way crumbs, wrappers, and dirt come out of the car. (Remember to pick up the papers and drop them into a trash can.)

• Keep a new, clean chalkboard eraser handy to wipe the

inside windows when moisture collects on them.

• Always keep a few nickels, dimes, and quarters in the glove compartment. It's very handy when you don't have the correct pocket change for the parking meter or the toll roads.

• Most auto accidents occur at speeds less than 40 mph, within 25 miles of home, and on dry roads. The impact of a car accident is over in one-tenth of a second—you have no time to brace yourself, much less to protect your child.

• While traveling, I find it handy to keep a large resealable freezer bag in the car for trash. It keeps the car clean of sticky wrappers and empty containers, and anything left in the containers will not spill during a quick stop.

• I keep a small spray bottle filled with window cleaner and a roll of paper towels in my car. I have found this especially helpful on a long trip when bugs have accumulated on the windshield between stops at service stations.

• Have an extra set of keys. Keep extra house and car keys in your wallet or other accessible place. If you lock yourself out, you'll save time and trouble by using your spare keys.

• Soak tar spots with raw linseed oil. Allow to stand until soft. Then wipe with a soft cloth that has been dampened with the oil.

• Be sure to carry a small dry chemical fire extinguisher in your car. This might save your car from being destroyed by an unexpected fire.

• With three children, car trips used to be an ordeal for my parents. So my dad started presenting each of us with "fun money"—a roll of dimes apiece—when we pulled out of the driveway. For each "How much farther?" or "He's poking me!" or "She's got her leg on my side of the car!" we spoke, Dad would charge a dime. Whatever we had left when we reached our destination was ours to spend. This cut squabbles to a minimum.

• Since I am on emergency call quite often, I can't take the necessary time to pack an overnight tote bag, so I have one packed and in my automobile trunk for those urgent calls. It saves a lot of time.

• Every time I need to get directions, I write them out on a 3"x 5" card. I keep an envelope of these directions in the glove compartment of my car. I also write the return directions on the other side so I don't have to reverse them in my mind on the way back.

I tape a transparent plastic 3"x 5" sleeve to the middle of my steering wheel. When I have to go someplace unfamiliar, I find the right card and slip it in the sleeve. I never have to figure out the directions twice, and with the sleeve, the directions are in sight for quick reference during the trip.

9
Finances

We earn little by little
and we save
little by little.

*Y*ou may say to yourself, "My power and the strength of my hands have produced this wealth for me." But remember the Lord your God, for it is he who gives you the ability to produce wealth.

—Deuteronomy 8:17,18

Finances

_A_re you in debt over your head? Is there too much month left at the end of your paycheck? Do you wonder where all the money went? Are debtors calling and asking when they can expect their money?

For the Christian family, good money management is important because God associates a person's ability to handle spiritual matters with the ability to handle money:

If you have not been trustworthy in handling worldly wealth, who will trust you with true riches?—Luke 16:11

In addition, we are stewards (managers) for God of our lives and possessions, since both belong to Him. It is God who gives us power to obtain money (Deuteronomy 8:18).

Robert J. Hastings wrote, "Money management is basically self-control, for unless one learns to control himself, he is no more likely to control his money than he is to discipline his habits, his time, or his temper. Undisciplined money usually spells undisciplined persons."

We learn self-control in the use of money by obtaining a proper attitude about money. Good money management is

161

not bondage; it is freedom from the "right" to do what we want, giving us instead the *power* to do what we should!

Our goal as Christians should be to obtain financial freedom. This has four characteristics:

1. Our assets exceed our liabilities.
2. We are able to pay our bills as they fall due.
3. We have no unpaid bills. (We are repaying per our agreement.)
4. We are content with where we are.

• Money management is really more about your *attitude toward the use of money* than a systematic plan to which you become a servant.

• A good way to save money is to put aside at the end of each day every bit of change you have in your pockets or in your purse or wallet, including single dollar bills. Faithfully deposit this amount in a bank or a savings association once a week.

• Because you always want your money to be working for you, don't keep more than is necessary in a no-interest checking account, unless maintaining a minimum balance qualifies you for free checking or other benefits.

• Put your money in a bank where interest is compounded semiannually or quarterly rather than yearly. Your money will work harder for you.

• If possible, never withdraw funds from a savings account before the stated interest payment date. If you do withdraw prematurely, you'll lose all the interest due for that particular interest period.

• In case you're hit by unforeseen big expenses (such as unexpected home repairs or a sudden illness in your family), have an emergency fund in your savings account equal to at least two months' income.

• Even after you've paid off a loan, continue paying out the same amount to your own savings account every month.

How to Choose the Right Checkout Line

Successful people play to win. They know the rules, devise plans of attack and follow their plans with discipline, whether it's on the job, in the stock market—or just doing the grocery shopping. To spend less time in the supermarket:

• *Look for the fastest cashier (individual speeds can vary by hundreds of rings per hour).*

• *Look for a line with a bagger. A checker/bagger team will move a line up to 100 percent faster than a checker working alone. When the supermarket uses optical scanning equipment, the bagger increases line speed by more than 100 percent. Note: Two baggers in the same line are barely more helpful than one.*

• *Count the shopping carts in each line. If all else were equal, the line with the fewest carts would be the quickest. But there are other factors to consider. Look for:*

— *Carts that contain many identical items. Two dozen cans of dog food can be checked out faster than a dozen different items. They don't have to be individually scanned or rung into the register.*

— *Carts that contain a lot of items. Because each new customer requires a basic amount of setup time, it's better to stand behind one customer who has 50 items than behind two customers who have 10 items each.*

— *Carts that contain a lot of produce. Each item has to be weighed.*

— *People with bottles to return. This can take a lot of time.*

— *People who look like they're going to cash a check. This, too, can take a lot of time. The most likely check-cashers: women who clutch a purse.*

— *People who have coupons to redeem.*

You are used to making the payment, so you won't miss the amount so much.

• If you find it difficult to save money, force yourself to do so by purchasing United States savings bonds under a payroll savings plan where you're employed, or by means of a bond-a-month plan at your local bank. You can build sizable savings over the years by authorizing small, regular deductions from your paychecks.

• One simple way to keep expenses down is to pay credit card bills before additional service charges become due. You can also make budgeting easier on yourself if you establish when your regular bills come due each month, including credit card accounts, and work out the most convenient order in which to pay them over the course of the month. If you get organized in this way you can avoid service charges wherever possible, and you can avoid being hit with a whole bunch of bills that have to be paid at the same time.

• As a rule of thumb, the maximum amount of credit and installment debt payable monthly should never exceed 25 percent of your monthly gross salary before deductions.

• Banks are now offering customers a wide range of account alternatives, such as super savings and money market accounts and certificates of deposit. Choose the right account to suit your needs by asking yourself: Can I write checks against the account? Are service charges involved? How much interest is earned? Are earnings determined at a fixed rate or does the rate vary? If I withdraw funds, is there a penalty? Is there a minimum deposit? Minimum balance? Can accounts be opened or closed over the phone or by using automatic teller machines?

• Your money earns interest at different rates, depending on the savings account vehicle that you choose. Regular passbook accounts usually earn less interest than certificates of deposit or money market accounts, for example. Certificates of deposit and money market accounts require you to leave the money on deposit for a specified amount of time. Money put into such accounts usually cannot be withdrawn without penalty.

• If you write a lot of checks each month, ordering them directly from a printer rather than purchasing them through the bank will save you money. Your bank may charge you more than $12 for 200 plain checks printed with your name and address. The same number of checks ordered directly from a printer cost just $4.95. Two reliable companies to purchase checks from are "Checks in the Mail" at (800) 733-4443 and "Current, Inc." at (800) 426-0822.

• Sometimes you can find totally free checking if you write very few (typically, six or fewer) checks each month. But that means six checks posted to your account.

• Many people choose to do all their banking with one bank; however, shop around for various services. Banking is very competitive today and you might save some money.

• If your salary is paid or credited by direct deposit, some banks will waive certain fees.

• As an alternative to banks, don't forget your credit union. They usually charge less for most loans.

• If you travel frequently by airplane for business, you're probably already enrolled in a "frequent flier" program. These programs allow you to earn mileage credit toward future flights. Many of the major credit cards will also give you miles on your favorite airline.

• You can send for a list of low-fee, low-rate credit cards by sending $5 to RAM Research, PO Box 1700, Frederick, MD 21702, (301) 695-4660.

• It's smart to obtain maximum lines of credit well in advance of need. If a credit-card grantor opens your account with several hundred dollars' worth of credit, request an increase after six months, even though you may not actually need it. Continue to pump up your credit availability until you achieve the maximum line. That way, it's there when and if you do need it.

• Maintain your credit standing if you're temporarily unable to make a payment on a debt. See your creditor and discuss rearranging the payment schedule with him. Most creditors are understanding about this. They're *not* understanding if you try to avoid them.

• In order to avoid being irritated by a collection notice that you know is due to a creditor's error (a not-uncommon occurrence), pay the item in question if it's less than $25. Immediately forward your statement, with a complete explanation of the error, to the creditor. Your account should reflect a correction within 30 days.

• A good way to keep out of credit binds is to pay off a series of payments completely before committing yourself to a new series of payments for something else.

• Puzzled as to where you stand with your credit accounts? You needn't be. Simply put aside a special place for storing all credit slips. Periodically review the slips to see how much you owe, and determine whether or not you can afford to buy more on credit at that particular time.

• Whatever you do, don't sign a credit contract that contains a "balloon" clause. A balloon clause stipulates a final payment that's much larger than any of the installments that precede it. If you discover such a clause too late, you may lose property after having paid a hefty part of its price, or be forced to refinance at disadvantageous terms.

• Thinking about taking out a second mortgage to finance a vacation, to buy an automobile, or to consolidate bills? Although your home could be used as security for such a loan, it's probably best to take out a personal installment loan instead. Second mortgages should not be used for casual expenditures.

• To conserve money, pay cash for things you'll soon use up, such as food items and cleaning supplies. Use credit only for things you'll continue to use after you've finished paying for them, or for emergencies such as medical bills.

Recognizing Quality in Clothes

    To take advantage of sales, discount designer stores, or consignment shops, look for the details that signal first-class workmanship, label or no label.
- *Stripes and plaids that are carefully matched at the seams.*
- *Finished seam edges on fabrics that fray easily (linen, loose woolens, etc.).*
- *Generous seams of one-half inch or more.*
- *Buttons made of mother-of-pearl, wood, or brass.*
- *Neat, well-spaced buttonholes that fit the buttons tightly.*
- *Felt backing on wool collars to retain the shape.*
- *Ample, even hems.*
- *Straight, even stitching in colors that match the fabric.*
- *Good-quality linings that are not attached all around. (Loose linings wear better.)*

- Offer the best security you can when taking out a loan. When you secure a loan with top-notch collateral, you usually get it at a cheaper rate than on your signature only.
- Always make sure that all collateralized loan balances are less than the collateral's value. For instance, auto loans that entail a lien on the car should be reduced more rapidly than the decline in the car's resale value.

The problem the average housewife faces is that she has too much month left over at the end of the money.

- It pays to use "cents off" coupons when buying food. Little by little, the savings add up over time. Look for such coupons in your daily newspaper as well as in shopper "throwaways" and mailers.

• Save on supermarket costs by preparing shopping lists for a full week of planned menus. Always plan menus so you can make good use of store specials and leftovers.

• You'll come out ahead if you avoid buying nonfood items offered for sale in supermarkets. Shop for such items at discount outlets that specialize in nonfood products, where you'll usually find these products priced lower.

• Trade your extra food discount coupons with neighbors and friends, or form a neighborhood club that meets at intervals to exchange coupons.

• It's convenient to buy sandwich fixings already sliced, but it costs less to buy meats and cheeses in chunks and slice them yourself.

• Take a calculator with you to the store. It makes it much easier to figure out price comparisons and make sure you're getting the best deal.

• If you shop from a grocery list, don't take anyone with you when you shop. The other person will talk you into purchasing impulse items that aren't on your master list.

• Did you know that most supermarkets stock higher-priced items at eye level? The lower-priced items like salt, sugar, and flour are below eye level. Also, beware of foods displayed at the end of aisles, as they may look like they are on sale but many times are not.

• Read labels and check expiration dates. Buy foods that will be usable for the longest time. Check labels for nutritional information.

Many studies show that if you can change a habit or begin a new habit and stick to it for 21 days, you have made a new habit in your life.

• Compare prices of different forms of the same food (frozen, fresh, premixed). You may find one form cheaper than another.

• Pack a sack lunch if you work away from home. You can save a lot of money over a period of several months.

• When marketing, shop quickly with a plan of action and organization (using a marketing list). A study showed that after the first half hour in the market, women will spend at least 75 cents a minute. So get in and get out.

• Shopping by mail can save time, energy, and gasoline, but what happens when something you've ordered for a special occasion arrives too late? Just send it back, unopened, marked "refused." Provided the package is unopened, you will not have to pay the return postage.

• Don't accept a C.O.D. delivery for a neighbor unless you're sure the goods have actually been ordered. If you can't check, or your neighbor has not asked you to accept the package in his or her absence, send the package back.

• When shopping for durable items, save on gasoline and wear and tear on your car by using mail-order catalogs.

• Don't allow yourself to become financially strapped by letting a door-to-door salesperson fast-talk you into signing a sales contract. If you *do* sign, and if the item costs $25 or more, federal law lets you cancel the contract within three business days and receive a full refund within ten days.

• November is a good time to buy men's and women's overcoats at reduced prices. That's when merchants offer bargains to encourage pre-Christmas business.

• When handling rebates, special offers, and mail orders that sometimes never come (and your money is not returned), keep a ledger or file with date and address to whom sent, amount of money sent, and expected date for return of item or rebate (i.e., four to six weeks). Then when it does come, check it off your ledger. Also, note on your canceled check when the company cashed it. If return postage is guaranteed, make sure you get it back from the company on items you send back.

• So that too many family expenditures don't occur

Ways to Reduce Your Energy Bills

• *Reduce overall lighting in nonwork areas by removing one bulb out of three in multiple light fixtures.*
• *Use one large bulb instead of several small ones if bright light is needed.*
• *Install dimmers or hi-lo switches when replacing switches.*
• *If using a three-way lamp, use only the highest setting when reading.*
• *Use white or light-colored lamp shades to get maximum light.*
• *Prevent water from cooling as it travels to your plumbing fixtures by wrapping hot water pipes with insulating material.*
• *Always bring liquids to a boil in a covered pan.*
• *Cook with a timer.*
• *Use pans made of glass or ceramic rather than metal to reduce cooking temperature.*

---

simultaneously, stagger the medical and dental checkups of family members.
• A simple way to budget if there's more than one worker in your household is to use one of your paychecks each month to meet a big expense, such as an installment payment or the rent, and to use all other paychecks to cover the monthly expenses.
• When budgeting, you needn't trace every expenditure down to the last penny. This wastes too much time (and often causes family arguments). Instead, overlook the inevitable small items that you can't seem to track down. Most people have a few dollars' worth of such unaccountable expenses every month. Attempting to pinpoint them entails useless bookkeeping.
• Avoid impulse buying. Watch the ads for off-season sales, which can result in significant savings.

• Go to the country and buy fresh foods in season from the grower. They will taste better and cost less.

• I use my appliances to help beat high heating costs during winter months. After cooking food in the oven, I leave the door open. This puts out quite a bit of heat. I do the same for the clothes dryer. I also open the dishwasher and pull out the racks of steaming hot dishes.

• When you budget, be sure to set both short-range and long-range goals. Goals might include a new car next year, a university education for a child ten years down the road, and retirement for yourself in 25 years. Setting goals gives you the incentive to control your spending.

People are more important than things
(See 2 Corinthians 8:5), and you are wiser to look
for ways to give yourself—that is, your time
and energies—to those you love and even to
those who cross your path than to limit
your investment to money and gifts.

• To prevent the last few postage stamps on a roll from getting stuck together or lost, I place them on envelopes I can use for letter writing or paying bills.

• Check the phone book for small-appliance repair centers. They will sell you replacement parts or fix your broken appliance at a far cheaper cost than that of a new appliance.

• When searching the classified ads for employment or looking for something to purchase, use a colored accent marker to circle the ads you are interested in. This way you will have a quick reference when checking back.

• Make a list of birthdays and anniversaries that require the purchase of greeting cards. Take your list to the card shop and purchase all your greeting cards at one time. Add a few sympathy and get-well cards, too. This saves time and gasoline.

• Does a "50 percent off" sign make your heart beat faster?

Does your credit card burn a hole in your wallet? Think about upcoming birthdays, anniversaries, and other gift-giving occasions. Buy ahead and have the fun of shopping without wasting money.

• Money-wise shoppers take advantage of storewide clearance sales after Christmas, Easter, and July 4th. You'll find bargains galore in linens, clothes, and scores of other items.

• The best time to buy back-to-school clothing for youngsters is at the end of September.

• You can curtail hospital expenses if you try to avoid being admitted on a Friday. Friday admissions result in longer stays than admissions on another day. For the shortest length of stay, try to have yourself (or any family member) admitted on a Tuesday.

• Check the labels on whatever you are buying and make sure that the items don't take special care. Special-care items take up a lot of your time and thus cost you more money.

---

*Say "no" to good things and save
your "yeses" for the best.*

• I receive so many catalogs through the mail that I now shop by phone. It's amazing how much time and money I save. Each catalog seems to specialize in certain styles or fashions.

• Another advantage of shopping by catalog is that each item is described in elaborate detail. You can pick and choose at leisure the product that best suits your needs.

• When you find yourself in the store and in doubt about whether you need a certain item for dinner, go ahead and buy it. It is better to have an extra lemon or box of rice than to have to change the menu or go back to the store again.

• Giving adult and children's clothes to consignment shops is a way to make some small earnings which can be used

---

Where to Buy a Computer

- *Full-service computer dealers.*
  - *— Generally sell at list price, but offer the most assistance in selecting hardware and software.*
  - *— Help customers set up their systems and give the most attention to postsale glitches.*
- *Department stores.*
  - *— Moderate discounts and erratic service.*
- *Discount stores and mail-order houses.*
  - *— Best prices but little or no service or support. (You may not need their support, however, if your system's manufacturer provides a toll-free hotline.)*
- *Buy only from an authorized dealer.*
  - *— That guarantees certain standards of sales and service and ensures future availability of compatible hardware.*

Source: New York Magazine

---

where most needed in your house.

- Save $500 to $1,000 a year by not smoking.
- Save $400 a year by shopping smart. Buy in bulk when items are on sale, not one six-pack at a time at a convenience store.
- Good food often costs less than junk food and saves on medical bills, vitamin pills, and diet pills.
- I get more things done in a day by hiring others to do errands, baby-sitting, secretarial work, housekeeping, bookkeeping, gardening, and anything else I can afford.
- Take a pocket calculator with you when shopping for an expensive item. Ask to be permitted to "work out the numbers" in front of the salesperson who wants to serve you. Then frown thoughtfully while tapping the calculator's keys. This procedure is almost guaranteed to restore an

atmosphere of reasonable give-and-take in a bargaining situation.

• Avoid wasting money on a service contract when you buy an expensive appliance. The contract price will typically be low for the first year when you can reasonably expect that nothing in the appliance is likely to go wrong. However, for each succeeding year, when things are more likely to go wrong, the contract may cost you more than it's worth paying.

• When a repair estimate is more than 15 percent of an appliance's replacement cost, seriously consider buying a new appliance.

• If you really don't need a second car, make do with only one car and rearrange your schedules and appointments accordingly. You'll save a considerable amount of money each year.

• Consider leasing a car rather than buying one. Not only will you tie up less capital, but you won't be burdened by insurance and maintenance costs.

• Having trouble making monthly loan payments? Consider slicing the remaining payments in half by extending them over a longer time period.

• Taking out a loan to finance a vacation? For the sake of personal psychology as well as your budget, make certain you can pay it up within one year. If you can't, you may grudgingly be paying off this year's vacation when next year's vacation time rolls around.

Family must be more important than an occupation since Scripture clearly states that there is no success if the family is lost —see 1 Timothy 3:5; 5:8; Titus 2:4,5.

• It's foolhardy to use emergency funds as collateral for a loan. If you default in payment and the funds are seized, you'll have painted yourself into a corner should any catastrophe occur.

• Keep away from any loan that permits repossession of the property purchased without providing cancellation of the full amount of the indebtedness at the time of repossession.

• The underlying principle in determining priorities is always that spiritual values must overshadow worldly pursuits (see 2 Corinthians 4:18; Matthew 6:33).

• When you purchase furniture, it makes good financial sense to buy the best quality you can afford. Cheap furniture wears out or goes out of style quickly, necessitating the purchase of more cheap furniture. High-quality furniture generally remains in style longer and stays in good condition for many years.

• The best time to buy furniture is in June.

• Cut down on your magazine subscription bills by trading magazines with your neighbors and friends.

Ways To Increase Your Income If You Work for Someone Else

• Increase your skill level, education, or profile in your present job.

• Create a new, better-paying job in your department and fill it.

• Seek promotion to another department.

• Ask for raises as you go the extra mile.

• Change companies for greater opportunities.

• Change to a higher-paying career by getting the necessary skills or education.

Unless you have unlimited resources, you cannot have everything—Ron Blue.

• If you want to save money and time on redecorating

when you're raising kids, use washable wallpapers and semi-gloss paints which are easier to keep clean.

• Small, round end tables with table skirts and overdrapes are much less expensive than antique or even reproduction tables. The fabric will also add color and interest to the room.

• To save money on a dining room table, cover a 48" round commercial conference table with a pretty table skirt. This will seat six comfortably. A rectangular conference table works as well.

• With your doctor's approval, buy generic drugs instead of the brand name variety of your prescription. This can reduce your medical cost by 30 percent. Also, if a drug is needed over a long period of time, buying in quantity can reduce the price even further.

• Before you lock in on a new home mortgage, be sure to consider both a fixed rate mortgage and an adjustable rate mortgage (ARM). The ARM becomes a very good choice if you're planning to be in your new home for less than five years.

• Accelerate the payments on your mortgage and save. Check with your lender to see what is required. A 15-year loan versus a 30-year loan will also save you a considerable amount of interest payment over the life of the loan.

• It makes sense and saves money to refinance a mortgage if the new fixed rate interest is at least two percent lower than your current rate.

• Those who are getting close to retirement might check with their lender about a new mortgage concept called "reverse mortgage." The home serves as collateral for monthly payments that are made to the homeowner, and then the loan is repaid from the estate of the borrower.

• When you pay your child's day-care center, save your receipts. You may be entitled to a federal tax credit of up to 25 percent depending on your income.

10
Time Savings

Managing time takes
maximum effort and
realistic planning.

She is energetic, a hard worker, and watches for bargains. She works far into the night.

—Proverbs 31:17,18 (TLB)

Time Savings

*T*ime management is not just keeping busy but is finding God's focus for you—choosing a direction and moving ahead to accomplish your goals. Success in this endeavor is one of the most difficult yet helpful skills a woman can develop.

Managing time takes maximum effort and realistic planning. First, you must acknowledge that you have time—the same amount God has given to everyone. You, with God's help, must determine how to use your time (Proverbs 3:5, 6). You err in letting others decide your priorities and make your schedule (Romans 12:2). Remember that by using small bits of time faithfully, you can accomplish great things.

The foremost challenge a woman faces is not to orchestrate her life or to plan her year but to order each day, allowing for sufficient rest, proper nourishment and exercise, and a quiet time spent exclusively with the Lord. To focus on what is really important, meaningful time must be assigned for vital relationships, especially with a spouse and children in the home.

To the Hebrews, a day began in the evening—with rest, family fellowship, as well as study and meditation in God's Word. Jesus said, "Seek first His [God's] kingdom and His

Time

Have you wished for wealth while dreaming of a goal
And thought that money was key to the plan?
Well, think again, for in any role
Time—not money—is the true currency of man.

Is it happiness you want, fulfillment of a dream,
Or will only power sate you, who fear to be an also-ran?
Well, reflect again on what success will mean.
It's time—not glory—that's true currency for man.

We are given one day to spend at each morn,
And what we do with this God-given gift
Will determine whether we are reborn
Or just waste away the sands that do sift.

So aim at the real treasure of man.
Think not about money or power or gain.
Rather, use the precious moments you can
And glory in Time, ere it slip by and wane.

—Robert B. Brown

righteousness" (Matthew 6:33 NASB). One way to do that is to devote the evening hours to quiet rest, reflection, and "inner preparing"—in other words, to prepare yourself in the evening for the coming day as well as planning your day's schedule upon rising in the morning.

• If a job is distasteful, such as balancing a checkbook or grocery shopping, see if a friend or relative might be willing to take it on in exchange for a service from you.

• Take advantage of pickup and delivery services offered by neighborhood merchants.

- Hire a teenager (maybe your own child) to run errands for you.
- Exercise while praying or watching TV. Do mending while talking to the children or while helping them with homework. Learn to do more than one thing at a time.
- Plan small projects during waiting periods. Most small chores can be accomplished in bits and pieces of time.
- Consolidate phone calls, bill paying, and correspondence into a single time slot rather than responding to each one separately.
- Use labor-saving devices or appliances as much as possible

Remember that setting goals and planning for
those goals with down-to-earth expectations in
mind is what makes good things happen.
Good things seldom happen by accident.

- Invest in a telephone answering machine (or your local telephone company has an answering service that is comparable in price). It's a great time-saver.
- Break the chronic procrastinator's habit. Whenever you catch yourself thinking, "I can do it later," stop and make a point of doing it now.
- Tell others about your goals so that you'll have extra motivation to accomplish them.
- Make plans that require you to complete your chores by a certain date. This will put you into action.
- Take time out to ask yourself: "Is there an easier way to do this?"
- Don't wait until you have time to finish the entire task. Do as much as you can whenever you can.
- Don't interrupt yourself by starting another task before you've completed the first one.

How to Save Time Each Day

- *Do errands on the way to or from work.*
- *Delegate jobs and responsibilities to other members of your family.*
- *Get up half an hour earlier.*
- *Don't be distracted by the TV. Turn it off.*
- *Cook more than one meal at a time.*
- *Scratch things off your list that aren't a priority.*
- *Learn to say no.*
- *Think about your life in five-year units.*

- Treat yourself to a small reward for each deadline you meet.
- Set your breakfast table the night before. Children love to do this.
- To control the clock better, get up a half hour earlier and decide what you are going to do with the day that is profitable to you and those close to you.
- Don't let work pile up. Decide which projects need to be completed and complete them.
- I've found that if I don't make a decision, I waste time handling problems again and again and again. Save time in the future by making the decision today.
- Since your time is limited, choose to do things that you enjoy or find useful. Don't overload yourself with tasks or responsibilities. Always strive to simplify your life.
- If you are a supervisor or boss, learn to delegate. Moms, as homemakers, don't do anything that someone else in the family can do.
- If you are a traveling salesperson, keep evening meetings to a minimum; however, do take advantage of breakfast and start early in the day.
- Start your meetings on time, even if you have several late

arrivals. Other people appreciate your consideration of their efforts in getting to a meeting on time. Don't reward the late arrivers by delaying the start of the meeting.

• One of the best ways I have found to reduce stress is by saying "No!" It's a hard word to say at times, but so valuable. Try it.

Know that each moment of your life,
once gone, is lost forever.

• A can't-miss reminder system: Staple a note around your purse strap.

• Standardize the way you do chores. Doing them the same way every time makes it easier to streamline them, cutting out even more minutes.

• Pay attention to the time of day when you do your best work. Schedule important activities for that time.

• Don't start with the quick, easy, and enjoyable. Start with what matters.

There's no time like the present.

• Create your own "tickler" file to remind you about upcoming birthdays, anniversaries, and holidays. Buy cards in advance and store them in one of 12 folders labeled by the month of the year. Toward the end of the month, pull the next month's file.

• Don't fill more than 75 percent of your day so you will have time for the unexpected.

• Cut unnecessary long-distance calls by keeping a list of things you want to discuss with the parent/child/friend the next time you telephone. This will also keep you from wasting time trying to remember what you wanted to tell them when you finally do speak.

- Buy a pocket-size electronic data bank to store all business and personal names, addresses, and telephone numbers. Carry it with you.
- Remind yourself with Post-it Notes on your bathroom mirror or on the door you leave by in the mornings—anywhere to get your attention.
- Set the kitchen timer to remind you when to leave for an appointment, do a chore, or make a telephone call.
- Buy a large tote bag to carry your purse, makeup, lunch, important papers, and anything else that needs to go out the door with you each morning.
- Make getting the coffee machine ready for the next morning part of your supper cleanup routine.
- Use a coffeepot with a programmable timer. Fill the pot before you go to bed at night. When you're ready in the morning, your coffee will be ready, too.
- Never spend more than ten seconds looking for your car keys. Keep a spare key in your coin purse for those times when your key ring is missing.
- Always have at least two sets of keys. Pick the best place to put your spares (your wallet, a zippered pocket of your purse, your desk at work, with a neighbor, on a string around your neck or wrist).
- Borrow music tapes or audiotapes of books from the library to listen to during commutes or while fixing dinner, mending, cleaning, or ironing.
- Keep video store membership cards in your car's glove compartment for quick rentals.
- Carry a Swiss Army knife with scissors, tweezers, and nail file in your purse or pocket and handle a million little chores.
- Keep index cards and a pencil handy to keep track of who borrowed which tools.
- Ten minutes a day spent looking for misplaced items adds up to over 60 hours a year. Don't put things down; put them away.
- Never dwell on failures (other than to learn from them). There's nothing you can do about them, so don't waste time

---

Do Things in Small Blocks of Time

What can be done in five minutes:
- *Make an appointment*
- *Make out a party guest list*
- *Fax a note*
- *Write a short letter or note*
- *Water the houseplants*
- *Clean out a drawer*
- *Feather-dust the living room*

What can be done in ten minutes:
- *Pick out a birthday card*
- *Repot a plant*
- *Sort out your desk*
- *Do a short exercise*
- *Call in a catalog order*
- *Reorganize the freezer section of the refrigerator*

What can be done in 30 minutes:
- *Sort today's mail*
- *Skim a report (use a highlighter pen for marking key points)*
- *Skim your stack of magazines that haven't been read*
- *Work on a craft project*
- *Make up a packing list for a future vacation trip*
- *Arrange a school pickup pool, a car pool, or a baby-sitting pool*

---

thinking about them over and over again.

• Save going to the post office by purchasing an inexpensive postal scale and keeping stamps of many denominations on hand.

• Stock up on various types of greeting cards. Keep a supply at home and at the office.

• Fight the urge to call a repairman when electronic equipment or an appliance breaks. Many companies have toll-free numbers and trained representatives to answer questions and guide you through simple repairs over the telephone. Call

the 800 directory [(800) 555-1212] for the phone numbers.
• Have an extra key to your car and house. Place it in a designated area where other members of the family know the location. This will save trips to the locksmith.

*Time—a daily treasure which attracts
many robbers—Ephesians 5:16.*

• The average American spends 27 hours a year at red lights. Listen to an educational cassette tape of a book you've wanted to read.
• Invest in a good cordless phone. It allows you to move around while talking.
• Learn how to program your VCR. Tape your favorite programs so you can watch them when you want to.
• Have a handheld cordless vacuum. Use this for small jobs. It's great for the stairs and the automobile.
• Have direct deposit and automatic teller machines working for you.
• Wash your face and brush your teeth while you're in the shower (men can even shave in the shower, too).
• Buy enough stamps at one time to last a couple of months. (The post office also has provision for mail-order stamps.)

Learn to say no to tasks you do not want to do.

• Film containers make handy holders for spare change. Tuck a few in the car and you'll always have money ready for necessities.
• Greeting cards can make unique postcards. Cut off the picture side and write your message on the back.
• For a change of address, fill out one post office change-of-address card. Then take a package of 4" x 6" blank, unlined

Top Time-Wasters

Trying to do too much at once.
Learn to prioritize your tasks.
Failing to plan.
Successful time managers look at the big picture in order to make a plan and set priorities.
Being unable to say no.
Learning to say no (gently and decently, of course) helps you maintain balance among your personal, family, and work time.
Putting things off.
Don't waste time agonizing over an unpleasant chore—either do it right away, hire it done, or forget it.
Doing everything yourself.
You must learn to delegate certain tasks. You can't do it all.

index cards to the local quick-print shop and have the card duplicated to send to one and all. The cost is worth it in terms of time and energy saved.

• Return only those phone calls in which you are truly interested in what the callers have to offer.

• Fax information on what you want to talk about prior to calling, not after.

Set aside at least an hour of personal time each day to replenish the body and mind.

• Group similar action items (like telephone calls, cooking, planning, letter-writing, research). Schedule blocks of time to get them done.

- Jot down in your notebook ideas that pop into your head. Store them away for a more appropriate time.
- Frequent stores, banks, markets, post office, restaurants during off-hour times.
- Figure out the best way to handle each situation (by phone, by mail, by fax, or in person).
- Promise less; deliver more.
- Eliminate clutter.

I need to be reminded that time is passing;
otherwise I might think that it's always now.

- If at all possible, and if appropriate, return calls and correspondence the same day.
- Remember that you are the master of your life—and your time.
- As much as possible handle every piece of paper only once.
- A trick to conducting short meetings is to have everyone stand.
- Always delay tackling something if you're angry.
- An emergency repair for the missing screw in your glasses is to insert a wooden toothpick through the hinge. Break off both ends of the toothpick, and you are in business for a while.
- If you can't manage your time, you won't be able to manage any other part of your life.
- Time management is self management.
- Our problem isn't time, but how we use it.
- Time management involves habits—breaking bad work habits and developing new ones.
- "Effectiveness" means achieving maximum results with minimum cost (which includes time).
- Focus your efforts on worthwhile, important, strategic matters.
- Without a goal and plans to achieve it, your decisions are

Three Keys to Managing Time

• *Use a single notebook for notes, basic storage of vital information, and calendars.*
- *A basic format of paper size and one filing system will help you keep track of all your basic records and appointments.*
- *You will remember when you write it in your note book.*
• *Divide up a complex problem into manageable segments.*
- *It may involve changing your habits, revising your time schedule, or reorganizing your physical surroundings.*
- *Divide your complex problems on your list into more manageable units.*
• *After identifying a small group of projects, rank them by number according to how aggravating they are.*
- *A problem that creates serious tension is a 1, and one that could wait until next month is a 10.*
- *Before actually tackling the job, set a specific and regular time for organizing work. People are at their best either in the morning, at noon, or in the evening. You decide your best time to solve your problems.*
- *Write your appointments on your calendar.*

left to chance. Who wants to live their life by chance?
• Carry a small tape recorder with you to record a note while driving, waiting for a ride, or sitting in an airline terminal.

Remember, it's not how long you spend on a task, but how effective you are.

• If you're worried about remembering something, wear

your watch on the wrong wrist. You'll be so aware of it, you'll remember why you did it.

• Always buy at least two pairs of socks or gloves. That way if you lose one, you'll still be able to use the one that's left.

• Buy colored plastic key covers so you can identify your keys at a glance.

• Designate a spot in each room (near a door is good) for shoes whenever anybody takes them off. You'll always know where to start looking for them.

• Are you constantly losing or misplacing your reading glasses? Buy two or three pairs and always leave them where you use (or lose) them most—by the TV, on your desk, in the bathroom.

• If your purse seems like a black hole when you're looking for your wallet, buy a bright red wallet or tie a piece of red yarn around it. You'll be able to spot it fast.

• Hang a pair of earrings near the door to grab in case you forget to put a pair on.

• Date numbers as you write them in your phone book to keep it current.

• Group errands together. If you're going to the cleaner's, check your master list to see what else you can do in that part of town.

11

Raising Children

Children need strength
to lean on, a shoulder
to cry on, and an
example to learn from.

Train up a child in the way he should go, and when he is old he will not turn from it.

— Proverbs 22:6

Raising Children

If we are to raise responsible children, we have to give them responsibilities. Too often as parents we try to make life for our children easier than we had it, or we can do the task easier ourselves, or the children complain so much and so loudly that we go ahead and do it ourselves to save the arguments and hassles.

In raising our children we want to focus on raising good, godly individuals who will grow up into fine, responsible adults who know how to solve problems and do not concentrate on finding excuses why they can't do a task.

America needs committed parents who are willing to spend the necessary time to teach the next generation those values and skills which will keep our country great. Yes, it takes more time and effort on your part in training your children, but in the long run the dividends will be tenfold to you and your child.

As a parent we want to be an encourager for our children when they are caught being responsible. For our grandchildren we use a single "Caught Being Good" bear sticker that we give to them when they are caught doing something good (responsible). We are amazed at the smile on their faces and the bright gleam in their eyes when they are given the recognition that they are doing something good and we realize that.

There's no greater calling than to be a responsible mother or father to our children. We desperately need good parents for the children God has given us. Before the foundation of this earth, our children were planned just for us. We must believe and continue as best we know how to raise and prepare our children for God's calling—whatever and wherever that may be.

Jesus spoke so powerfully about little children in Mark 10:14 (NIV), "Let the little children come to me, and do not hinder them, for the kingdom of God belongs to such as these."

God has given us, as parents, these precious children to raise to a full understanding of what Jesus did for us on the cross. May some of these ideas be helpful:

• Try "time-out" by removing your child to a designated chair or area for a brief period (one minute for every year of age is the rule), solely to give a chance for them and you to regroup.
• See that each one of your children are as a delicate, lovely rose, eager to unfold its petals to the sun. Once those petals are torn off by harsh words, criticism, and anger, it's almost impossible to put it all back together again (Ephesians 4:29).
• For safer playing, take children outdoors and talk about playing safe. Define boundaries and show them how far they may go.
• Help your children cope with moving by visiting the new neighborhood, locating schools and involving the whole family in details of the move. Let your children help pack and unpack their belongings.
• Hang a bathroom mirror at child's eye level if you want to start encouraging good hygiene and grooming habits at an early age.

Excuse This House

Some houses try to hide the fact
That children shelter there.
Ours boasts of it quite openly.
The signs are everywhere.

For smears are on the windows,
Little smudges on the doors;
I should apologize I guess
For toys strewn on the floor.

But I sat down with the children
And we played and laughed and read.
And if the doorbell doesn't shine,
Their eyes will shine instead.

For when at times I'm forced to choose
The one job or the other,
I want to be a housewife—
But first I'll be a Mother.

—Author Unknown

• The beach or the mountains aren't the only spots for fun in the sun. Try:
— The local petting zoo
— An amusement park
— A fish pond
— A park with playground equipment (with a special picnic planned and prepared by the kids)
— Ice-skating
— Rent a good classic children's story on video. Have popcorn and drinks.
• Instead of spending hours a year trying to remove felt-tip

marker writing and drawing from walls, spend a couple of minutes putting the markers out of reach of small children. It's also a good idea to restrict potential troublemakers such as crayons, paints, and clay to a specified play area.

• To organize your family's activities and to keep track of everyone's schedule, put up a large poster-sized master calendar that displays a full year. Enter all important family dates (birthdays, anniversaries, holidays) at the beginning of the year. Also enter appointments as they are made for everyone in your family.

Parents need to stay alert to recognize opportunities to teach about God.

• Don't expect a youngster to put in a full day's work. An hour is about all that can reasonably be expected of an 8-year-old. A 14-year-old can probably achieve almost as much as an adult, but this depends on the responsibility level of the teenager.

• Include your youngest child in the housework. It may slow progress, but it's an essential first step in helping that child feel part of the home work force.

• Have your young child dust and sweep along with you at first. The youngster will feel grown up, and you'll get more work done.

• Teach your child step by step how to do a job. Don't assume that the task will be completely learned by watching. Show, teach, and train.

• Once you've given your child certain definite jobs with clear-cut responsibilities, let him work without constant supervision. Check the result when he's finished and compliment him.

• Clearly define the time of day when a child's job is to be completed—either before school, right after school, or by dinner. Don't let tasks hang over into the evening.

• On weekends, make up a list of chores and negotiate assignments over a leisurely breakfast. Break a big job down into steps and be sure the kids' ages and abilities are equal to their assignments.

• Assume that boys and girls will do the housework in equal amounts and without sex designations. Assign their chores accordingly.

• Don't redo a chore that a child has just completed. If you insist that a task be done only your way, then do it and be done with it. Redoing is destructive to a child's ego. Just think back to a time when someone redid something you had just completed!

• Ask your butcher for the end of a roll of butcher paper (or obtain end rolls of newsprint from your local newspaper). Let the children color the paper, paint it, finger paint, or draw on it. Then roll it up again and store it. At Christmas, use this paper for gift-wrapping. The children will be thrilled to see their artwork displayed.

• No matter how well organized I was, my children always seemed to leave for school forgetting something. Plastic dishpans (a different color for each child) were my solution. Into them I put lunch boxes, books, notes to the teacher, homework, and the like. A quick glance tells young students whether or not everything is in the bin.

• Never pay children for doing something for themselves. It actually robs them of self-esteem and is a form of bribery.

• Let your young child play within your sight in the kitchen. Talk, sing, and play together. Have one shelf for the things the child is allowed to use. If you have a small kitchen, keep these toys or pots and pans in a separate box in the garage.

• The more we do for our children, the less they can do for themselves. The dependent child of today is destined to become the dependent parent of tomorrow.

• The happiest, best-adjusted individuals in their present and

---

Making Family Travel Fun

1. Carry a small cooler with snacks and drinks.
2. Make lunch a picnic.
3. Take colored pencils (don't forget a pencil sharpener) instead of crayons. They won't melt.
4. Each child gets a large clipboard and a big pad of drawing paper.
5. Give each child a map so they can follow the route. Use a colored pencil to show how far you have gone.
6. Regularly switch seats.
7. Stop often to stretch, go to the restroom, and get a snack and beverage.
8. Stop driving in the early afternoon so the family can enjoy the swimming pool at the motel.
9. Put a sheet in the backseat over the seat and floor. This will catch all the crumbs and trash. When you come to a stop, take out the sheet and put the debris in a trash can. Your backseat is all clean again. Spread the sheet out again.

---

older lives are those who believe they have a strong measure of control over their lives.

• Save your old magazines. Use the pictures in the magazines to help the children learn to read.

• If you have teenage children who are involved in many different activities, try this: Purchase several duffel bags on sale (three to four dollars). Fill them with the supplies needed for each activity (special shoes, racket and balls, helmets, suntan lotion for the beach). Keep the bags filled and ready to go in the hall closet.

• Assign a designated place where each child can study, and a regular time to do his homework. Make sure there is plenty of light, ventilation, and quietness.

• Divide children's toys into three separate boxes and rotate

the boxes each week to avoid boredom with playthings.
• Let family group pressure maintain standards as much as
possible. When a chore isn't properly done, hold back for a
while and give others a chance to gripe and solve the problem themselves.
• Be sure that you're not imposing too high a standard.
When work is honestly shared, all partners are entitled to a
say in how well it has to be done. If you're the only one who
wants a job done better, reexamine your expectations and
perhaps make some adjustments.
• If your family is uncooperative, consider whether your
standards are too high. If you lower your expectations somewhat, it may be easier to get chores done.
• Try discussing the chores each member of the family likes
least and work around them accordingly. One person may
hate to scrape the dishes but may not mind taking them out
of the dishwasher. Rather than arguing, find something each
person enjoys doing instead.
• Set up a "way station" for the consolidation in one place
of schoolbooks, laundered clothes, toys, mail, and other
odds and ends. Once a day, have your kids pick up their
belongings from the way station and take them to their
rooms. Designate a chair, box, or basket for this purpose and
locate it where they can't ignore it.
• With a two-story house and children, I have found it helpful to have a container at the bottom and top of the stairs. It
saves time by eliminating unnecessary trips.
• Talent Night is a great way for children to show off their
talents—singing, dancing, twirling a baton—for the whole
neighborhood. (Try selling bags of popcorn and soft drinks
for extra pocket money.)
• With a box of giant, colored chalk, children can draw their
own Picasso masterpieces on the sidewalk or driveway.
(They'll wash off with soap and water.)
• Supply your children with squirt guns, a bucket, and a gar-

den hose. Stand back!
- Paint colorful designs on plain T-shirts or sneakers with fabric paint pens or markers.
- Share recorded music. Let each family member pick a piece as dinner music. Talk about what was enjoyable, interesting, or disappointing about the selection.
- Take family walks as opportunities to talk about ideas, observations, and feelings.
- Use dinnertime or another regular time to talk about current events, the day's successes, and/or ideas.

The more responsible a person, the healthier he is. The less responsible, the less healthy.
—*William Glasser*

- According to the most recent studies on drug abuse among teenagers and young adults, there are three cornerstones in the lives of those young individuals who do not use drugs of any kind: religious beliefs, family and extended family relationships, and high self-esteem.
- Tape pictures of socks, T-shirts, and so forth on dresser drawers in your young children's rooms. They then will know where everything goes when putting their clothing away.
- Once a year, I have a baby-sitter swap party. Each attendee must bring the names and telephone numbers of three reliable sitters.
- A tasty variation on the standard peanut butter and jelly sandwich: Make the sandwich as usual, but just before serving, butter the outside of the bread, and brown the sandwich in a hot skillet.
- One most appreciated gift a neighbor gave me after the birth of my first baby was a freshly baked apple pie with a card attached worth eight hours of free baby-sitting. The pie

---

Some Household Jobs a Teenager Can Do

1. Make own bed every day. It may be a little sloppy at first, but it'll improve in the course of time.
2. Put clothes back in the closet or proper dresser drawer.
3. Put toys and games back in the proper areas.
4. Water houseplants.
5. Feed the dog, cat, or goldfish.
6. Set the table.
7. Clear the table, one thing at a time.
8. Empty wastebaskets.
9. Carry out trash cans.
10. Vacuum rugs and floors.
11. Sweep and mop the kitchen floor.
12. Iron own clothes and the family napkins and tablecloths.
13. Polish silver, brass, and copper.
14. Carry in wood for the fireplace.
15. Vacuum the inside of the car.
16. Wash the car.

---

hit the spot, since I was tired of eating all that hospital food, and it was reassuring to know there was someone available close by to baby-sit, if needed.

• Studies of successful young readers show that their parents read to them on a regular basis. Read aloud to each other, or have a special silent reading time when all family members can enjoy their favorite books.

• Encourage everyone to "make up" stories to share based on a picture from a magazine, a fairy tale, a fable, a historical event, or pure imagination.

• Provide your child regular access to a computer.

• Put on family plays. Ham it up in original skits with hand-me-down clothes.

• Here is a little idea for young children at a fast-food store or restaurant: When you buy the tot a soft drink, cut the straw off short so it is easier to hold and drink. There's less chance of a child spilling or dropping the drink, too.

• As a mother and nurse, I know how uneasy and scared children can become over appointments with a doctor. When the need arose for my two-year-old son to be treated at an emergency center, I brought his favorite stuffed monkey along. Since my son was being treated for an eye injury, I had the doctor examine the monkey's eye first, then listen to the monkey's heart. When my son saw the doctor trying to help his monkey, much of his own fear was alleviated.

• When my children were small and I made a pie for dinner, I would use the extra pie dough by forming a ball and rolling it out on a greased cookie sheet. I would sprinkle cinnamon and sugar on it, bake it for ten minutes, then cut it into squares.

• To stimulate my toddler's interest in good dental hygiene, I buy trial-size tubes of toothpaste. These tiny tubes are easy for her small hands to manage, and because they contain her special toothpaste, she enjoys brushing her teeth more.

• Sometimes young children won't take their medicine from droppers or spoons. A useful idea is to take a clean nipple from one of their bottles and measure the medicine into it. The child will suck the medicine very naturally.

• At any age, your children will be influenced far more by what you practice than by what you preach.

• Encourage your children by nine years old to begin saving a portion of their allowance. You can encourage the habit by matching whatever your children put away.

• Look for opportunities to explain how money works. Have them sit down with you when you write checks for your monthly bills, or have them go along when you take out a new loan.

• Help your children broaden their experience and develop good work habits through summer jobs, travel, and part-time after-school work.

• Involve the children when you start planning how the family will pay off college bills.

• Set a time limit on the amount of time (30-60 minutes) per day the children will help around the home. Let the children know in advance there is a light at the end of the tunnel.

• Establish a work-before-play rule at your home. It's easier for children to mop the floor if an afternoon of free time is waiting for them.

It's not what you expect from your child that's important. It's what you inspect.

• Encourage teamwork. It's a lot more fun to work with someone else than by yourself.

• Make work fun. Children love to wear rubber gloves, chef's hats, and aprons, and use feather dusters, spray bottles, sponges, and child-sized mops and brooms.

• Vary your children's chore routines. Variety is the spice of life.

• Encourage children to care for their own belongings. Supply laundry bags, and wall hooks for hats and clothes. Give each child a special place for personal odds and ends.

• From time to time have your children write your shopping list for you.

• Teach your children to write thank-you notes. This is part of teaching good manners.

• Help your children to acquire a pen pal overseas in a country that is of interest to them.

• Use a world map or globe to locate countries that are mentioned in today's TV news reports or today's front-page stories in the newspaper.

• Half eggshells make wonderful plant starters. Fill several eggshells with dirt or planting soil. Put two or three seeds in each. Mark on the outside of the shell what type of seed is in each.

Your Child's Room

Remind your kids that five or ten minutes of effort a day will keep their rooms in pretty good shape. If they save all their straightening up for Saturday, it will take an hour or two and will surely be met with groans and complaints.

Modify children's rooms so that they can help maintain them. Supply child-sized features, such as a low dresser with nonstick drawers and a closet with hangers and hooks at a child's height.

Once you've helped put a child's room together, the room and the objects in it "belong" to the child. If you take over too much responsibility for keeping it neat, the child will feel the room belongs to you and not to her, and she may not take care of it.

A child as young as six can at least "spread up" a bed—it doesn't have to be perfect! Using comforters or quilts on beds will make the job a lot easier.

Ideally, older children's rooms (especially those belonging to adolescents) should be off-limits to any adult interference. Unless the room has reached a level of messiness that threatens to infect the rest of the house, the best policy is hands-off.

• Plan a favorite activity for after homework or instrument practice so the child has something to look forward to.

• Use a timer. Many children tense up during timed tests and may need to practice working under pressure.

• During homework time, parents should be seen and not heard. Helping a child too much undermines confidence in his ability to accomplish something on his own.

• Even a postage-stamp-size garden can produce and provide valuable learning.

• Put family weekend chores in a hat—draw for order of completion. The whole family works at each chore until it is completed.

Questions to Ask When Choosing a
Summer Camp for Your Child

1. Is your child ready for a sleep-away camp?
2. Is the camp accredited?
3. What is the camp's philosophy?
4. Who is directly responsible for your child's supervision while at the camp?
5. Who else can your child go to besides the counselor?
6. How are the counselors screened and trained?
7. How much instruction is provided during each activity period, and how long do activity periods last?
8. Are any trips offered as part of the camp—and what transportation arrangements are made for the trip?
9. How does the camp integrate new campers into the group?
10. What medical facilities are available on-site? Nearby?

• Go to a nursing home and find someone that your family would like to adopt. Make periodic visits to this person, make tray favors for them, write them letters and cards, telephone them. Invite them home for birthdays and holidays if you wish.

• Have a night when all the family gets together to learn a new game. Plan a good dessert.

• Select a time where parents and children can switch roles. Don't try to do this for too long a period of time, though. Take some time afterward to discuss how it felt.

There are no quick fixes in training and guiding children to become responsible; it takes a strong commitment to the task by all concerned and it takes time—Gene Bedley.

Shopping with Kids

• *Establish rules ("Stay close to Mom," "No screaming") before you go. The fewer rules, the easier to enforce.*
• *Eat before you shop. A hungry child is a whiny one.*
• *Limit yourself to one hour per store. (How many stores you can cover depends on your child's age and temperament.)*
• *Ignore pouting, complaining, and crankiness. Do not ignore fighting or infractions of shopping rules.*
• *Enforce rules with a quick verbal scolding in a private place, if possible. If your child has a major tantrum, remove him from the store. When he calms down, go back into the store.*
• *Reward good behavior with verbal praise. Gifts should be the exception, not the rule.*
• *Try to arrange for a pleasant break (ice cream, video games, etc.) in the midst of the outing.*
• *Involve your children. Let them find items, hold things, push carts. Talk about what you are shopping for.*
• *Decide beforehand whether or not your child can pick out a treat. Then stick to your guns. If a child is not going to be allowed to buy something this trip, keep her spirits up by encouraging her to scout for things she might like in the future.*

• I have a great hint for mothers with babies: I know it's hard to pour baby oil. You either get too much, or it spills. I've figured out a convenient way to put on baby oil. Take an empty roll-on bottle (you can get the ball off with a metal nail file), wash it out well, pour the baby oil into the bottle, and replace the ball. The oil will glide on smoothly and won't make a mess.

• Let preschoolers make use of an egg timer to give each of them and their friends a chance to play with a toy. This will add to their fun during playtime. It will also help prevent unnecessary quarreling.

• When sewing buttons on children's clothing, use elastic thread. It makes buttoning much simpler for little fingers.

• Comforters are fast and easy for you and your children to handle while making beds.

• Let your baby hear you pray for him. He will gradually come to know the wonderful Person you are talking to—the One who cares about him.

• A good way to help your older child celebrate the arrival of a new baby is to have the child share the news with his friends. On a paper bag write "It's a boy!" or "It's a girl!" and the name of the new arrival. Inside the bag, place lollipops tied with blue or pink ribbons. The child can take the bag and pass out the candy so everyone can share in the excitement of the new baby.

• Use a pair of adult socks as mittens for infants or small children; they are impossible for children to remove.

• Use children's flat bed sheets of Spiderman, Peanuts, and so forth as party tablecloths. If you desire, spread clear vinyl over them to protect from soiling.

• My son loves to play with his snap-together building set, but come bedtime, he doesn't like picking up the many, many pieces. Solution: We lay out a large sheet for him to play on. When he has to go to sleep, we whisk the floor clear in a jiffy by gathering up the sheet and storing it with all the toy pieces inside till the next time he wants to build something.

• To help children remember the proper way to set the table, tell them that *fork* and *left* both have four letters, while *knife*, *spoon*, and *right* all have five letters.

• Children who grow up in environments full of put-downs, negative nicknames, and criticism often become critical adults. Catch your child doing something good and tell him about it. Be positive and uplifting.

• The most powerful forms of praise are given in private, one-on-one.

• If I pin my children's socks to their outfits, it saves time and eases the frustration of having to dress them in outfits with socks that don't match.

How to Get Along with Your Child

1. "Don't ask me to do something when I'm busy doing something else."
2. "Try to put up with family members' bad moods, because we all have them."
3. "Listen carefully to me."
4. "Listen before you yell."
5. "Give your children some time when they can talk to you without any interruptions."
6. "Plan time with each child alone, once a week."
7. "Even though our problems may seem ridiculous to you at times, don't tell us to forget them. Give us advice."
8. "Lighten up a little."
9. "Trust me with my own money."
10. "Realize that I am my own person. I am not anything like my sister."
11. "Remember, your kids try hard to please you."
12. "Remember to count to 10. . .or 20."
13. "Make sure you tell your kids how much you appreciate having them around."
14. "Admit it when you're wrong."
15. "Be honest with each other."
16. "Show a little happiness."

—Students at Conestoga Valley Junior High

• Instead of a bedtime story, I tell my children the beginning of a dream and suggest they listen with their eyes closed. They are quickly sound asleep and ready to finish the dream.
• To keep several kids' socks straight, assign each child a different color of sock sorters. After washing and drying, distribute socks to the owner of the appropriate color of sorters.
• Put a laundry basket in each child's room. Have each

deliver it full to the laundry room and sort the wash. Children who are tall enough to reach into the bottom of the washer can be taught how to run it.

• I have books from childhood that I cherish deeply. To keep them childproof, I have taken the time to cover each page (and the front and back covers) with clear contact paper. Your child's favorite books can be protected for years to come the same way—a low-cost heirloom.

• When I empty the dishwasher after dinner, I wrap a flatware place setting in a napkin for each family member. This way the children are able to help set the table, and the job gets done faster.

• Have your kids used their crayons to decorate your painted walls? Try baking soda on a damp sponge to remove their murals. With a little elbow grease, your walls will look as good as new.

• When plush toys that aren't machine washable get dirty, spray with dry shampoo, let stand for ten minutes, and brush out with a soft-bristled brush. Refluff the fur with a portable hair dryer set on low.

• When my children get bored (holidays), I send them on a scavenger hunt—either inside the house or out in the yard. My list includes easy- and hard-to-find things (i.e., a small bug or ant, a dead leaf, a red button).

• When my children are riding in the car on a trip, they make up games to amuse themselves. One of their favorites is "I'm looking for. . ." The object can be anything—a red truck, a blue blouse, a pine tree. The first child to see the object picks the next one.

• Decorate your child's room by having him draw pictures of his favorite activities on butcher paper, making a mural, and hang it on the walls around the room.

• A great way to use hand-me-downs is to take the white clothes and dye them pink or blue, depending upon the sex of the new child. If the new child is a girl, you can spruce up

Sorry, No Medal for You, Kid

A teenager came up to me and said, "Gee, Good Adult, why aren't you proud of me? I've never been arrested and I'm a really good kid. It seems that nobody understands me."

You say nobody understands you and then you brag about how you resisted being a bandit, a dropout, and a menace to society. Also, you don't smoke dope or hit your teacher. You work after school and are a joy to your parents.

I do not go around robbing gas stations or shooting people, either. My reward is that I don't get thrown in jail. That is also your reward. You don't punch your teacher and I don't punch my boss. So you get an education and I get to keep my job. You don't hot rod your car and I don't hot rod mine. We both may live longer and that is a pretty nice reward, isn't it?

You work after school. I work after work. We both get money, which is handy when you want to buy something. And don't forget that for many years I have been contributing part of my paycheck to build those schools you brag about not dropping out of.

Your reward for staying in school is an education that will help you get a better job, or maybe be a doctor or a lawyer. Education can help you live a fuller life and be a Good Adult. So stop looking for praise for doing what you are supposed to do. That's what you're here for.

—As printed in Ann Landers' column, January 26, 1990, Press Enterprise, *Riverside, CA*

the old clothes by adding appliques, ribbons, or lace to make them look frillier.

• Keep children busy during dinner preparation with a glob of shaving cream on the counter or high-chair tray. They will love finger playing with it. Since it is soap, they will only taste it once. It is also fun for them to play with in the bathtub. This introduces them to different textures. You can also use toothpaste, whipping cream, or clay.

The only way to predict the future is to create it.
—John Scully

• Here's how to make some inexpensive toy dough for your children to play with:
— Mix together two cups all-purpose flour and one cup salt. Then slowly add two-thirds cup water and some food coloring. Knead until smooth.
• Here's an easy recipe for homemade finger paints:
— Mix one-fourth cup cornstarch with two cups cold water. Bring to a boil.
— Let cool, then pour into paper or plastic cups and add food coloring.
• Many times it is hard to read the ounce measurements on baby bottles, so I paint them with red nail polish.
• Teaching small children to make beds can be easy. Simply use a fitted bottom sheet and a comforter. If the comforter has stripes, it will be easy to throw on the bed and keep the stripes in line with the edge of the bed. A top sheet is not especially necessary with today's beautiful comforters.

12

Good Health

Value your body and
it will give you up to
12 extra years of life.

*H*e himself gives all men
life and breath and
everything else. . . For
in him we live and
move and have our
being.

—Acts 17:25,28

Good
Health

For many of us health has a very narrow definition: foods that we eat. For others the term is much broader than food. It includes such things as exercise, stress management, positive attitude, nutrition, disease prevention, energy level, and more. In the book of Genesis we see a statement that appears after the sixth day of creation: God said, "It was very good." Therefore, we know that in creation God created man and woman to be healthy creatures. Because of the fall of man and our sinful nature, we have taken on habits that have caused us to shorten our lives in both length and quality.

In the last five years the American public is waking up to the fact that America's poor health of its population is costing American taxpayers billions of dollars in extra taxes to underwrite hospital and doctors' care to restore our citizens who have poor health. Not only does good health make sense physically because God created us for that, but it also makes sense economically and gives us a better quality of life.

There are little things that we can do in our own homes that can give each of us a better quality of life. We need to start with ourselves and branch out to our family and future families that our children will have.

Remember, we are not just raising the children of this generation but also children of several future generations. What is taught in our homes can be passed on to the future. In Romans 12:1,2 we read:

> Therefore, I urge you, brothers, in view of God's mercy, to offer your bodies as living sacrifices, holy and pleasing to God—this is your spiritual act of worship. Do not conform any longer to the pattern of this world, but be transformed by the renewing of your mind. Then you will be able to test and approve what God's will is—his good, pleasing and perfect will.

Let's begin today to commit ourselves to a healthier frame of mind so that we can discern what God's will is for our lives.

Live 12 years longer by following these guidelines:

• Eat a healthy breakfast. It's the most important meal in the day. Follow the saying: "Eat breakfast as a king, lunch as a queen, and dinner as a pauper."
• When out in the sun, be sure to apply an adequate amount (at least one ounce) of sunscreen (at least SPF 15, but SPF 30 is preferred). Apply every 60 to 90 minutes while in the sun, after swimming, or after activities that cause perspiration. Get used to wearing a good pair of sunglasses along with a wide-brimmed hat. Taking extra care when you are young will give you beautiful skin as you age.
• Keep a health book for each member of your family (a photo album with self-sticking pages works very well), listing each illness, accident, and doctor's visit, and the date, treatment, medication, and doctor's instructions. Highlight important information, such as allergies to medication and the date of the last tetanus shot. A quick glance at your book

Simple Pleasures

- Feeling the sun on the back of your neck
- Dawn
- The smell of bacon or coffee first thing in the morning
- Singing in church
- Hearing your cat purr
- Finding money in the couch
- Eating bread and tomatoes
- Knowing you did the right thing
- Making a new friend
- Getting into a freshly made bed
- Having all the ingredients on hand when you decide to cook something special
- Getting snapshots back from the processor
- Getting a tax refund
- A great haircut
- Moonlight on the ocean
- Massages, hugs, ladybugs, new shoes, naps, cashmere, making up after a fight
- Knowing you have a full tank of gas
- The smell of fresh-cut grass
- Going home after a bad day
- When the days start to be lighter longer
- Having exact change
- Two scoops
- Having the house all to yourself
- When he does the laundry
- Pink slippers
- Shiny windows and mirrors
- Browsing in bookstores
- Fishing with your dad
- Making someone smile
- Coming home from a vacation
- Watching your kids when they're sleeping
- National public radio
- The sound of rain on the roof, especially when you're under the covers
- Walking on the beach in winter
- Licking the frosting bowl
- Wearing something new
- Being excited about tomorrow

will help you to be well-prepared when you pay a visit to the doctor or emergencies occur.

• Cold beats heat for treating the pain and swelling of minor injuries. For children's cut or bruised lips, keep a frozen fruit treat in the freezer.

• Jot down questions or concerns you want to discuss with your doctor the week before your medical appointment. Write down the answers after the visit.

• Make your appointment for a yearly pelvic exam and mammogram during the week of your birthday so it's easy to remember.

For success in all areas of life, attitude is much more important than aptitude.

• Physicians have found that a positive attitude can result in faster recovery from surgery and burns, more resistance to arthritis and cancer, and improved immune function.

• The best time to exercise for each person depends upon the daily rhythms of his or her body.

— *Morning.* This is the best time for those who have trouble sticking to a fitness regimen. Apparently, excuses accumulate as the day goes by.

— *Midday.* For dieters, vigorous prelunch workouts offer double benefits. Strenuous exercise not only burns calories, it also suppresses appetite.

— *Late Afternoon.* Those looking to reduce stress often prefer end-of-the-day workouts to help them relax.

— *Evening.* Wait at least an hour after dinner to exercise. Also remember that exercise will invigorate you, which could be a problem just before bedtime.

• Don't try to sterilize an open cut or abrasion. Clean a wound with tap water (using a little soap to remove dirt, if necessary). Then apply a loose, dry dressing and leave it

What the Numbers Mean

Blood pressure is measured as two values: systolic over diastolic. Systolic is the highest pressure produced when the heart contracts. Diastolic is the lowest pressure reached when the heart relaxes. A reading of 120/80 used to be considered the most desirable. Recent research suggests even that may be a little high. 110/70 is preferable, but the lower generally the better—there's less work for the heart with every beat.

If high pressure is found during an annual checkup, it should be checked frequently. Blood pressure also varies minute to minute. The best readings are when you are calm and at rest. Here are some important numbers to remember the next time your blood pressure is tested:

- A diastolic of 90-104 means mild hypertension; 105-114 means: moderate hypertension; over 115 means severe hypertension
- A diastolic below 90 but systolic of 140-159 means border-line systolic hypertension; over 160 means elevated systolic hypertension.

alone. (See a doctor if it is an animal bite wound or if you can't clean out the dirt.)

• If after 40 years old you decide to get back in shape, there are several guidelines that will be helpful for your consideration:
— Get your doctor's okay.
— Go slowly.
— Aim for just 30 minutes of sustained activity, three times a week.
— Weeks 1–3: Walk for 15 minutes each time you walk.
— Week 4: Walk for 20 minutes each time you walk.
— Week 5: Walk for 25 minutes each time you walk.
— Week 6: Walk for 30 minutes each time you walk.
• You can boost your energy level by eating the right food

Debugging Techniques

Techniques for removing insects from your skin vary depending on the insect. To remove a tick, grab hold of the pest close to the skin with a pair of tweezers; pull slowly so the head doesn't get left under the surface. To remove a bee stinger, don't use tweezers—they'll only squeeze more venom into your wound. Instead, take a table knife or another object with a straight edge, press it lightly on the skin, and scrape over the stinger in the direction opposite that in which it entered. Then wash the wound with soap and water.

---

at the right times. This can give you the stamina to make it to the end of the day.

— The best thing you can do is to go no more than five hours without food.
— Eating small meals throughout the day provides the body with a steady flow of fuel. Eating more often will cause you not to reach for bad choices of food, plus it can lower your cholesterol levels. (See the informtion in my new book *The 15 Minute Meal Planner* (published by Harvest House Publishers), and in my accompanying six cookbooks.
— These meals aren't the major productions we normally think of as meals. The key is to plan when, what, and how much to eat.
— Plan ahead. Keep fresh fruits and cut-up veggies in the home or office, plus low-fat crackers and low-sodium pretzels. Stock up on nutritious non-perishables like crackers, instant soups, cereal (nonsugared), and canned tuna.
— Be sure you eat plenty of protein. This helps block the buildup that we get from carbohydrate foods.

Hugs

It's wondrous what a hug can do,
A hug can cheer you when you're blue.
A hug can say, "I love you so,"
or, "Gee! I hate to see you go."

A hug is, "Welcome back again!"
and, "Great to see you!" or
"Where've you been?"
A hug can soothe a small child's pain
And bring a rainbow after rain.

The hug! There's just no doubt about it,
We scarcely could survive without it.
A hug delights and warms and charms,
It must be why God gave us arms.

Hugs are great for fathers and mothers,
Sweet for sister, swell for brothers,
and chances are some favorite aunts
love them more than potted plants.

Kittens crave them. Puppies love them.
Heads of state are not above them.
A hug can break the language barrier,
And make the dullest day seem merrier.

No need to fret about the store of 'em.
The more you give, the more there
are of 'em.
So stretch those arms without delay
and give someone a hug today

—Author Unknown

How to Protect Yourself from Insect Bites

1. *Avoid wearing bright clothes, jewelry, and scented toiletries which attract bees and other insects.*
2. *Wear covered shoes rather than going barefooted or wearing sandals.*
3. *Don't walk around outside with food or drinks. This will attract a hoard of pests.*
4. *If someone gets stung, watch out for a sudden rash, hives or swelling, throat tightness, or labored breathing. Be ready for immediate emergency treatment if any of these occur.*
5. *Tuck your pant legs inside your boots or socks, and check your clothes and body when you get inside.*
6. *Wash insect bites immediately with soap and plenty of water.*
7. *Go to a doctor immediately if you have been bitten by a large animal. He can examine to see if you need antibiotics, tetanus or rabies shots, or stitches. You would rather be safe than sorry.*

Serotonin is a brain chemical that causes drowsiness. Good high-protein choices include turkey breast, tuna, tofu, beans, nonfat or low-fat yogurt or milk, egg whites, and nuts (in moderation due to their high fat content).

— Stay hydrated. Drink at least eight to ten 12-ounce glasses of liquids each day. Water is best, but you can substitute juices, soft drinks (decaffeinated), and sport drinks. Read labels to keep track of sugar and calories.
— Use caffeine moderately. Drink no more than one mug of caffeinated coffee per day. Any more than that can lead to shakiness, upset stomach, dehydration, sleeplessness, and impaired nutrient absorption.
— Avoid large, high-fat meals. Fat takes longer to digest

and delays the absorption of protein. A large, high-fat meal will make you tired and listless about an hour after eating.

• In Sunday school and church I've sung the song "Count Your Blessings, Name Them One By One," yet not always realizing how good this process is for our mental health. Asking yourself these questions and answering them honestly is a good way to check how well you know yourself:

— Is anyone a little happier because you came along today?

— Did you leave someone with any concrete evidence of your kindness, any sign of your love?

— Have you learned something new about life, living, or love?

— Have you gone through the day without worrying over what you don't have and celebrating the things you do have?

— Did you help someone feel joy today?

— Did you try to think of someone in a more positive light?

— Did you make someone smile or laugh today?

— Have you forgiven others for being less than perfect?

— Have you attempted to mend a torn relationship?

• Don't shortchange your sleep. Fatigue can lead to overeating.

• People who skip meals have higher body fat levels.

• When tempted by a high-fat treat, take a bite. If it doesn't rate a 10, it isn't worth it.

He makes grass grow for the cattle, and plants for man to cultivate—bringing forth food from the earth: wine that gladdens the heart of man, oil to make the face shine, and bread that sustains his heart— Psalm 104:14,15 (TLB).

How to Have a Good Night's Sleep

1. Don't go to bed too hungry or too full. Limit yourself to a small snack before bedtime, if you must.

2. Limit drinking all liquids a few hours before bedtime. That way you will reduce the chance of having to wake up to go to the bathroom and then fight going back to sleep.

3. Avoid alcohol. It disturbs sleep quality.

4. Cut back on caffeine. It's a powerful stimulant.

5. Stop smoking. Nicotine is an even stronger stimulant than caffeine.

6. Get up at the same time every morning. Regularity helps keep your biological clock in sync.

7. Exercise every day. Get a minimum of 30 minutes of strenuous exercise a day.

8. Set aside time to unwind. Read, listen to good music, exercise, or just wind down before you go to bed.

9. Make your bedroom more inviting for sleep. Reserve your bedroom for sleeping and intimacy—don't turn it into an office or TV room.

10. Invest in a good mattress and pillows. The added cost will be one of your best lifetime investments.

11. Resist the urge to nap. For most people napping makes it harder to sleep at night.

12. Buy a pill box marked with days of the week so you can check at a glance whether you took your medicine.

- At parties, survey the buffet and decide on two or three items, maximum. Don't eat while talking—it's all too easy to down a lot of food without realizing it.
- The healthiest foods are usually on the outside aisles at the supermarket. That's where you'll find fresh and frozen produce, breads, and low-fat dairy products.
- Select single-serving sizes of snacks and desserts to help prevent yourself from eating too-large portions.
- Turn the kitchen into an out-of-bounds area after dinner.
- Invest in new cookbooks that emphasize good, healthy eating. (Try Sue Gregg's and my set of cookbooks that emphasize the latest in nutritional information. See page 376 for ordering information.)
- Bake, steam, or broil rather than fry; use broth to sauté or stir-fry.
- Try oils with strong flavors. Just a teaspoon of sesame oil in a stir-fry or a dash of extra-virgin olive oil in pasta is enough to pep up the taste.
- Chew gum while you cook to discourage unconscious nibbling.
- Every month try at least one new grain or grain-based product.
- Always remove the skin from poultry—you'll automatically reduce calories by about 25 percent.
- Put your salad dressing in a small spray bottle and mist your salads. You'll get the taste without a lot of the calories. Also, have your dressing served on the side, then dip your fork into the dressing first, gather some salad on the fork, put it in your mouth, and chew. This will really cut down on the amount of dressing you eat.
- Substitute club soda for your daily regular soda, and shed up to one pound per month.
- Beat tension eating with this stress-buster: Clench your fists and inhale deeply through your nostrils. Hold for a count of three, then slowly release your breath as you open your fists.

The Most Clever Thief in the World

I invited her into our home for special occasions. We'd become good friends, I thought. And then I began to look forward to our meeting at the end of each day. After a while, we became so friendly I had to see her every evening.

People began to think of us as a couple. Even the police knew our names. Our identities were too closely linked, I thought, so I began to see her on the sly.

At first, she stole small change from my pocket. I wasn't concerned. Before long, she crept into my billfold. I wasn't happy about that, but I enjoyed her company too much to complain.

Friends said I was seeing too much of her and that she had made changes in me they didn't like. I resented their interference and said so. They dropped me.

My wife and children complained about the time I took from them to spend with her. I said, "If you insist that I make a choice, I will choose her." And I did. She began to demand so much of my money that I could no longer afford new clothes. I heard people at work whisper about my shabby appearance. They blamed her. I was annoyed and distanced myself from my colleagues.

She started to visit me at the office. My boss became upset. He said my friend was interfering with my work. After several warnings, I lost my job. We had some heavy arguments after that. I told her to stay away for a while, so I could think. She said, "So long, buddy. You'll come back to me before long." She knew me better than I knew myself. Within three days, I was seeing her again.

Our affair became more intense than ever. We spent every day and night together. I lost my wife, my family, and my job. The next thing to go was my health.

When I became so sick I couldn't eat or sleep, I realized she had taken everything in my life that had meaning. Although I was not religious, I decided to turn to God. He wrapped His loving arms around me and gave me strength I cannot describe to this day. He made me feel whole. My sense of self-worth and sanity began to return. I knew I would never again let my friend back into my life.

Today, although I still bear the scars of that hideous friendship with alcohol, I am on my way back. With God at my side, I know I will make it. My old friend will always be around the corner, waiting for me to weaken and stumble and come back to her, but I am determined to keep her out of my life forever. I have found a magnificent replacement.

—Author Unknown

• Try strength training. The more muscle you build up, the higher your metabolic rate.

• Get active. March in place while you're on the phone, always take the stairs, and walk if you don't have to drive.

• Make an appointment on your calendar to walk three times a week for at least 30 minutes. Be sure to keep your appointment.

• For optimal health, use the general rule of "30 plus 40 plus 50." That is, a minimum of 30 grams of fiber and no more than 40 grams of fat and 50 grams of protein daily.

• Restrict your salt intake.

• Fill up with fiber. Fiber-rich plant foods are filling and high in nutrients, yet low in calories.

• Identify stress-triggering situations and avoid them in the future.

• Allow yourself the luxury of doing nothing. Take vacations and an occasional long lunch hour when you can.

• If possible, stay indoors with air-conditioning during pollution alerts.

• Add houseplants to your home. Studies suggest that they may remove carbon monoxide, benzene, and other indoor contaminants.

• Listen to your body. When it tells you that you're exhausted, don't schedule new activities. Take time to rest.

• Soak in a bubble bath or read a good book.

• Try very hard not to bring home your work. Leave it behind. It will be there tomorrow.

When you are tired, you are attacked by ideas you thought you had conquered long ago.

• For some strange reason, human beings tolerate stress and pressure much more easily if at least one person knows they are enduring it.

• To lift a heavy object from the floor, bend at the knees,

228   Emilie Barnes

grasp the load close to your body, then push straight up with your legs.

• Don't sleep on your stomach because that position forces the back's natural "S" curve into an arch for hours. If you sleep on your back, a pillow under the knees will preserve your spinal curve. Curling up on your side in a fetal position takes pressure off your back.

13
Sewing and Crafts

Look at your home
as an extension of
your personality and
the warmth
of your being.

*S*he sews for the poor,
and generously gives to
the needy.

— Proverbs 31:19,20 (TLB)

Sewing and Crafts

 Today's creative woman finds her closets, drawers, and bedrooms filled with the clutter of craft items, patterns, fabrics, straw flowers, glue guns, and fiberfill. It would be wonderful to have a room devoted exclusively to sewing and crafts. However, most of us must make do with a corner of the bedroom, living room, or even the garage. How can we organize all of this mess and retrieve any item quickly when needed? It's really very simple. Here are some tools and ideas to help you. You will need:

- Several "perfect boxes" for storage. Or if you prefer, use plastic bins, laundry baskets, plastic stacking trays, or wooden boxes.
- Several small jars (baby-food style)
- 3" x 5" cards
- Pen
- Shoe boxes

If you've read the "Total Mess to Total Rest" chapter in my *Survival for Busy Women* book, you'll recognize some of the process. You can add boxes of craft and sewing items to your storage, listing them by number on 3" x 5" cards in the "Storage" section of your card file. This is a simple and fast way of retrieving items quickly.

Let's take your patterns. They can be organized and stored according to size and types (play clothes, dressy outfits, costumes, sport clothing, blouses, pants, etc.). Many fabric stores carry cardboard boxes made specifically for storing patterns, and their cost is low.

The process is the same for fabrics. Put them in piles according to color: prints, solids, stripes, etc. Then place each pile in a separate cardboard "perfect box," number the box, and fill out a corresponding 3" x 5" card. Your cards might look something like this:

Box 1   Calico fabrics
          Reds and pinks
Box 2   Solid fabrics
          Blues, browns, blacks
Box 3   Stripes, polka dots
Box 4   Remnants and scraps, a yard or less

Repeat the process with arts-and-crafts items. Now for some more ideas for organizing all those buttons, pins, hooks, snaps:

• Organize buttons on safety pins, pipe cleaners, or twist ties. Or stick loose buttons and snaps on strips of transparent tape.

• Store bias tape, piping, and hem tape in a shoebox. Don't forget to clearly label the box.

• Store hooks and eyes, snaps, and buttons in baby-food jars. They will look so organized when lined on a shelf, or even when stored in shoe boxes (appropriately labeled, of course).

• If you don't have a bobbin box, string bobbins on pipe cleaners or keep them in a plastic ice cube tray or egg carton. This is also a great way to store safety pins, buttons, and other miscellaneous small items.

• To organize spools of thread, group them according to color and lay them on their sides in a drawer or in shoebox tops. Stack the box tops so that the most frequently used colors are on top.

• Discarded shoeboxes are great for storing sewing supplies and smaller arts and crafts items. Be sure you label the boxes so you know their contents.

• Fabric fill or stuffing and quilting materials can be stored in cardboard "perfect boxes" using the numbering system. So can straw and silk flowers and other such items.

• For craft projects, a hot glue gun is terrific. Be sure to unplug it when not in use and store it out of the reach of children. Let it cool before placing it in its storage area.

• Clamp pattern pieces together with a clothespin until you finish the project and return them to the envelope.

• Baskets are a fun way to store arts and crafts materials. You might consider putting several craft items in a basket and giving it as a Christmas gift to a friend.

• Another gift idea is to spray glue on a "perfect box" and cover it with a patchwork of fabric pieces. It looks country and creative. In fact, you might even do it for yourself! It would be a good way to quickly see what fabrics you've stored in the box.

Learn to say no to requests and jobs that do not fit into your priorities and goals.

• An old bath towel folded and stitched to form a small "pillowcase" makes a perfect cover for a hot water bottle.

• Use Velcro instead of buttons to attach overall straps to overall bibs.

• When in a hurry to hem pants, simply use masking tape for a quick, temporary job.

• It's easy to thread a needle if you spray your fingertips with hair spray and then stiffen the tip of the thread by rolling it back and forth in your fingers.

• Attach your tape measure to the sewing table so that you won't have to rummage through all your equipment to find it.

Buttoned Up

One way to avoid having to sew on buttons entirely is to make sure they don't fall off. Put a dab of Superglue in the middle of the button, over the thread, before you ever wear the garment. That should keep most buttons from ever falling off.

Use elastic thread on a waistband button. If you grow a little, the waistband stretches, too. This is helpful for children's buttons, too. Fishing line (or dental floss) makes really strong thread for sewing buttons on jeans.

• Keep a small magnet in your sewing basket. When needles and pins drop on the carpet while you're sewing, retrieve them quickly with the magnet.

• To help you thread needles, keep a magnifying glass in your sewing basket.

• You can rejuvenate a blunted machine needle, at least temporarily, by rubbing it at an angle across the fine side of an emery board.

• Try making this hang-up sewing center: Insert wood screws or nails across and down a breadboard with a handle, then hang all your spools of thread on it. If you want to hang scissors and other sewing utensils, add a row of cup hooks along the bottom.

• If you have needlework patterns that become frayed because they are loose, try inserting them in 8" x 10" plastic refill pages for photo albums. You can read through the plastic, and the pattern won't tatter and tear.

• I keep an old jar in the wastebasket by my sewing machine. The lid has a small hole and a slot in it. When I have a dull needle or break a needle, I put it in this jar. I also put old razor blades in this jar. When full, I dump the jar in the trash and eliminate possible injuries.

• Cut out several dresses or items at one time and stack them by your sewing machine, then you can sew them when you have little bits and pieces of extra time.

• Sew on shank buttons and metal overall buttons with dental floss to keep them from being torn off.

• Used fabric-softener sheets make wonderfully strong interfacing in cuffs, pockets, and flaps.

• You can use a glue stick instead of pins and/or basting when making lapped seams. Apply the glue to the underside of the overlapping section. Press in place, allow to dry a minute or two, and topstitch.

What lies behind us, and what lies before us are tiny matters, compared to what lies within us.
—Ralph Waldo Emerson

• You don't have time to sew? Maybe you won't have to. Check in your notions department for no-sew hemming tapes, fusible powder that melts into the fabric when you iron, and ready-cut iron-on patches.

• Always remove good-quality buttons before you discard a garment.

• If a pulled-off button leaves a tear in the fabric, reinforce the area by stitching a little patch on the underside before resewing the button.

• If your iron doesn't have button grooves, you can protect buttons by covering them one at a time with the bowl of a spoon as you iron around them.

• Sharpen scissors by cutting through fine sandpaper a few times.

• Time-saver for the seamstress: Make a short apron with pockets to hold pins, scissors, thread, and so forth. Then sew a measuring tape upside down across the bottom inseam. Everything you need is within arm's reach when sitting at your machine, or ironing and measuring hems.

• A bar of soap makes an ideal place to stick needles and pins. It lubricates them so they will go through stiff fabrics with ease.

• If you want a matching quilt or bedspread and curtains, purchase sheets that match the quilt and make into valance and curtains. Pillow slips can be doubled to make tiebacks.

• Having trouble removing a button? Slide a comb under it, then slice through the lifted thread with a razor blade.

• It's easier to repair seams on lingerie fabrics or nylon if you slide a sheet of paper under the seam. Stitch through both the fabric and the paper, and then carefully rip away the paper.

• Thread looks darker on the spool than it will on fabric. Choose a thread a shade darker than the material you'll be using it on.

• After ripping out a seam, pick up all the loose threads with a pencil eraser.

• Save handwork by using iron-on bonding material for hems in lightweight fabrics.

• As your child grows, make notes on favorite patterns about larger and longer waists and arms.

• When knitwear snags, pull the snag through to the wrong side of the garment using a fine crochet hook. Smooth the pulled threads as much as possible in the direction of the snag. If the pulled thread is long enough, tie it in a small knot. If the snag has caused a hole in the fabric, darn the hole.

• For extra-strong stitching when sewing on buttons, double the thread before threading the needle. You'll have four strands of thread for each stitch.

• To keep a four-hole button in place longer, sew through only two holes at a time. If one set of threads breaks loose, the other will hold the button securely.

• Sew an extra button or two to a piece of fabric from a

garment and store it in your button box for easy finding at replacement time.

• An easy way to hem a dress is to have a sink plunger handy to use when marking a skirt for hemming. Mark the handle at the desired length, then move the plunger around the hem. It stands by itself, leaving your hands free to mark or pin.

• After oiling your sewing machine, stitch through a blotter several times to prevent surplus oil from damaging your fabrics.

• Before sewing a zipper, shrink it: Set the zipper in very hot water for a couple of minutes, then let it dry. Repeat the whole process once more before sewing in the zipper.

• When threading a needle, tie a knot in the end of the thread as you begin to pull it off the spool. This helps to keep the thread from tangling. Cut the thread from the spool at an angle. It is much easier to slip through the eye of the needle.

• When counting rows in knitting or crocheting, tie a piece of different-colored yarn every tenth row. This will help you count easily, and the yarn can be pulled out easily.

• A fork makes a great tracing wheel for marking out darts on a pattern with dressmaker's carbon.

• Clear nail polish applied to the underside of the line where you have to cut open a machine-made buttonhole will prevent odd threads from unraveling and will keep the buttonhole firm.

• When buying yarn, check the label on each ball or skein to be sure it's all from the same dye lot; otherwise you could end up with yarn of slightly different shades. Keep a note of the dye lot in case you run short unexpectedly.

• There's an easy test that will tell you whether an unlabeled skein of yarn is wool or synthetic. Put a small piece of the yarn in a large ashtray, and set a match to it. It the yarn burns to ashes, it's wool. Synthetics will harden into a dark lump when burned.

• You can recycle still-usable yarn from knitted items you no longer wear. After unraveling the yarn, wind it loosely around a cake rack, dip the rack into water, and then let the whole thing dry out. All the kinks will be "ironed out" of the yarn, and you can then rewind it.

• Try unraveling an edge of the fabric you're about to mend to get some thread that's a perfect match.

• If you can't find a tracing wheel to transfer a pattern, check the kitchen drawers—a pizza cutter or a pastry wheel may do the job.

• Create your own pattern. Take apart a favorite worn-out garment with the seam ripper and press each piece out carefully.

• On generously cut garments, you may be able to position a dart or seam to "seam out" the problem.

• Try tie-dyeing T-shirts that are badly stained.

• Here's a quick way to mend a garment when appearance is not important. Put a piece of paper under the hole, then darn back and forth with an appropriate stitch on the sewing machine. When you wash the garment the paper will was away.

• To make a handy pin cushion, glue a small sponge to the corner of your sewing machine.

• File your clothes patterns by storing them upright in a shoe box.

• If the foot control of your portable sewing machine creeps on the floor when you sew, glue a piece of foam rubber to the bottom surface and the foot control will stay in place.

• To make a straight cut for a buttonhole on heavy fabric, lay buttonhole section over a bar of soap and cut with a razor blade.

• You can reuse an old zipper by spraying it heavily with spray starch. It will sew in like new.

• To make your patterns last longer, spray a new pattern with fabric protectant. The pattern will last longer, rip less easily, and resist wrinkles.

Sewing Kit for Non-sewers

1 spool white thread
1 spool black thread
1 spool "invisible" thread (matches any color)
1 packet of all-purpose needles, self-threading (or include a threader)
4-hole white shirt buttons (usually come four to a card)
1 iron-on patch kit, lightweight (for sheets)
1 iron-on patch kit, heavier weight (cotton knits, jeans)
1 package Velcro strips, white
1 package Velcro strips, black
small pair of scissors

• If you're sewing a woman's blouse, sweater, or dress that will button down the front, make the buttonholes horizontal instead of vertical. The buttons will always stay firmly shut.

• In order to sew for yourself, you must know your body measurements accurately. Ask a friend to help you, and take measurements over your usual undergarments (not over dresses, blouses, or slacks) using a nonstretch tape measure.

• When you embark on a large-scale dressmaking project, fill a number of bobbins before you start. Then you won't find that just when you've gotten into the swing of it you have to stop to rewind the bobbin (which means you might as well go make a cup of coffee and check the mail, too, and you may not get back to your dressmaking at all that day).

• Give a second chance to a dress. Cut it along the waistline, turning it into a skirt. Add zipper, belt, buttons, or lace to give it a new look.

• Sew a sweater inside a coat as an extra liner.

• To keep metallic yarns from unraveling, dip the ends in clear fingernail polish.

To Keep Thread from Tangling as You Sew

When you're using black or white thread, thread the needle, cut the thread, then tie the knot at the cut. For colored thread, cut the appropriate length from the spool, thread the cut-off end through the needle and tie the knot in the other end. (In the manufacture of all threads, black and white cord is twisted one way while colored is twisted another. I can almost guarantee you will be the only person who knows this in almost every crowd.)

• Attach a paper clip to the page of your knitting book, and move the clip up or down the page to keep your place when following detailed instructions.

• When teaching a beginner how to knit, use a red needle to mark the purl row and a white needle for the plain row.

• When making clothing, dampen a toothbrush and rub across seams that keep opening before they are pressed.

• Don't throw away those old curtain valances. Just cut the valance in half and sew the two pieces together to form the tiers of an apron. For a tie, slip ribbon through the valance casing. It's such a cute idea you may want to buy new valances (on sale, of course) and make these aprons as gifts.

• Spray knees, cuffs, and collars of small children's garments with fabric protectant. Spills and such will bead up, and dirt can be wiped off with a damp cloth.

• Before pressing, sew as many seams and darts as possible at one time. You'll minimize the number of trips to the ironing board and find the project going much faster than if you stitched and pressed each seam individually.

• Plastic egg cartons make convenient storage containers for spools of thread.

• Store tiny buttons in empty pill bottles.

• Sew plastic by placing a sheet of newspaper beneath it so it does not stick to the sewing machine.

• Protect your fingers against needle cuts by coating your fingertips with a few layers of clear nail polish.

• Sequins and tiny beads are often used together to decorate sweaters and other garments. If you get them mixed up, here's a trick for separating them: Drop both sequins and beads into a colander over a bowl; the beads will fall through and the sequins won't.

• When sewing an emblem on a uniform, first position and hold it in place with several dabs of white glue. After the glue sets, stitch the emblem by hand or machine. The glue will wash out with the first laundering.

• You can make your own hem gauge from any lightweight cardboard such as a postcard or index card. Notch the card at the depth required and pin up the hem.

• Clip-type clothespins can be more convenient than pins for holding a hem in place while you sew it.

• Shortening the stitch length when stitching around collar curves reinforces the seam and makes the curves smoother. On collar corners, shorten the stitch length and sew one or more diagonal stitches to reinforce the corners and make room for the seam allowances when the collar is turned.

• When making an elastic waistband, fasten the ends of the elastic with a safety pin for the first few wearings and washings to make sure that the fit of the waistband is comfortable. Elastic sometimes shrinks or relaxes after the first washings. When you are confident that the fit is right, remove the safety pin, stitch the ends of the elastic, and neaten the waistband.

• When making a tablecloth to be used on an outdoor table, put a triangular pocket across each corner. If the wind is blowing when you use the tablecloth, drop a rock in each corner pocket.

• Original eyeglass cases can be made out of purchased pot

holders. Just fold in half and sew one short side and the long side.

• When a design calls for gathering the fabric, test-gather a scrap of your fabric to see if you're getting the desired look. If the gathering is too tight, use a longer stitch.

• When sewing cuffs, you'll have more room for seam allowance when they're turned inside the cuff if you take one or more diagonal stitches across the points of square corners. The heavier the fabric the longer the diagonal needs to be.

• Sheets make great wash-and-wear tablecloths and napkins. One king-size sheet makes one large cloth and 12 napkins or two smaller cloths and six napkins each. A twin sheet will fit most dining room tables perfectly without cutting or hemming. One yard of fabric will make six napkins when cut into 15-inch squares.

• You can make a facing lie flat by stitching it to the seam allowance (not the fabric that will show) just inside the seam. Or simply tack it at the seams. If you tack it all around the edge, the stitching will show on the right side of the fabric.

• To prevent heavy materials from dragging on the floor while you're sewing, support them on an ironing board placed next to the sewing machine table.

• A clean cardboard milk carton with the top cut off (gallon size) makes a great storage file for dress patterns.

• Change a used full-length slip into a half-slip by cutting off the bodice and inserting a narrow elastic band at the waist.

• If you're given a slip that's way too long, turn it into a camisole and half-slip: Cut a little below the waist, then hem the top part, and elasticize the waist of the skirt.

• If hand-sewing strains your back, put a sofa cushion on your lap. You won't have to bend over as far to work on the material.

• For quick and easy access when sewing, hang your scissors from your neck with a loop of fabric, ribbon, or yarn.

• To give new life to an old cloth tape measure, place it between two sheets of wax paper, cover with a paper towel, and press with a hot iron.
• When stitching plastic fabric, rub talcum powder on the needle to avoid sticking.
• To keep a spool of thread neat, tape the thread end down or place a rubber band around the spool.
• A thimble saves wear and tear on your finger when you're stitching heavy, stiff, or multilayered fabrics. Choose one that fits snugly over your middle finger.
• If your thimble's too loose, insert thin strips of adhesive tape on the inside until it fits snugly.
• If wearing a thimble bothers you, protect your fingertip with an adhesive bandage instead.
• If the pull tab on a zipper comes off, replace it with a small paper clip. Wind thread or fine yarn around the clip in a color to match the garment fabric.
• For a temporary repair to a hem that comes unsewn, hold the broken section in place with transparent tape.
• When sewing snaps in place, stitch in the top half and rub a little chalk over its tip. Press it against the other side of the garment to mark the exact spot where you should sew in the bottom half of the fastener.
• If very small snaps slip out of your fingers, tape them in place on the fabric and sew through the tape. Lift off the tape when you're done.
• Before you hem a skirt, a dress, or pants, let the garment hang for a day on a hanger. The fabric will settle, and you'll get a more accurate hem. This is especially important for fabrics with a lot of "give" like knits. If they're not pre-hung, you may find that parts of the hemline drop after a few wearings.
• Always wash all fabric before cutting to allow for shrinkage and for bleeding of colors. Use the same water temperature and drying method you will use for the finished garment.

• Now that you're all organized, you don't have to spend half your time finding supplies and setting up. You can devote your energies to what you do best—creating!

14

Plants and the Garden

One is nearer
God's heart
in a garden.

Then God said, "Let the land produce vegetation: seed-bearing plants and trees on the land that bear fruit with seed in it, according to their various kinds." And it was so.

—Genesis 1:11

Plants and the Garden

$\mathscr{I}$n Genesis 2:8 we read, "Now the LORD God had planted a garden in the east, in Eden; and there he put the man he had formed." We started out in the garden. Maybe that's why green, growing things do so much for us.

The spirit of plants and the garden is the spirit of aliveness, growth, rebirth. Working with plants and soil is a therapeutic experience to our stressed-out lives.

You don't have to have acres of land or an emerald thumb to make the spirit of plants part of your life. Your garden can flourish in whatever space and time you have to give it.

In our first apartment, Bob and I barely had room for ourselves, and no space whatsoever for a garden plot. But I was able to unleash the spirit of the garden even in that tiny place by setting out some small geranium pots in a kitchen window that received early-morning sun. Before long, blooms had brightened our little home. Soon after that, I added pots of herbs on that kitchen shelf. Bob was amazed that I could season our meals with a pinch or two of herbs from my window garden.

That was just the start of our apartment garden. When I went to the market, I would occasionally pick up a potted plant in a gallon container. Those little "instant gardens"

247

Top Garden Catalogs

Send for these catalogs for the best in mail-order plants and flowers.

- Armstrong Nurseries, Box 614, Stevensville, MI 49127. Colorado blue spruce, pines, wonderful new hybrid peaches. Free.
- Breck's, Peoria, IL 61632. Dutch tulips, crocus, etc. Free.
- Brittingham Plant Farms, Box 2538, Salisbury, MD 21801. Twenty-seven varieties of strawberries. Free.
- W. Atlee Burpee Co., 2103 Burpee Building, Warminster, PA 19874. Many varieties of vegetables and flowers. Free.
- Henry Field's Seed and Nursery, 1008 Oak St., Shenandoah, IA 51602. A hundred pages of fruits and vegetables. Free.
- Gurney's Seed Co., 1304 Buffalo Rd., Rochester, NY 14264. Bicolor corn, Cucumbers, melons, and flowers. Free.
- Inter-State Nurseries, 113 E St., Hamburg, IA 51640. All varieties of gladiolas. Free.
- Jackson and Perkins Co., Medford, OR 97501. Bulbs, trees, wide variety of gladiolas. Free.
- J.W. Jung Seed Co., Randolf, WI 53956. Trees, flowers, vegetables. Free.
- Kelly Bros., 281 Maple St., Dansville, NY 14437. Fruit trees, fruit plants, etc. Free.
- Liberty Seed Co., Box 806-A, New Philadelphia, OH 44664. All kinds of garden seeds. Small charge.
- Earl May Seed Co., Shenandoah, IA 51603. Tomatoes, midget vegetables. Free.
- J.E. Miller Nurseries, 510 West Lake Rd., Canandaigua, NY 14424. Fruit trees, vines, berries. Free.
- Musser, Box 53N-A, Indiana, PA 15701. Fine-quality tree seedlings. Free.
- Olds Seed Co., Box 7790, Madison, WI 53707. Flowers from A to Z. Free.
- George W. Park Seed Co., 410 Cokesbury Rd., Greenwood, SC 29647. Complete garden supplies. Free.

- *Rex Bulb Farms, Box 774-E, Port Townsend, WA 98369. Lillies, etc. Small charge.*
- *Spring Hill Nurseries, 110 West Elm St., Tipp City, OH 45371. Widest variety of fruits, vegetables, and plants. Small charge.*
- *Stokes' Seed Catalog, 1733 Stokes Building, Buffalo, NY 14240. Everything. Free.*
- *Van Bourgondien and Sons, Route 109, Babylon, NY 11702. Finest domestic and imported bulbs and plants. Free.*
- *Vermont Bean Seed Co., Garden Lane, Bomoseen, VT 05732. All kinds of vegetables. Free.*
- *Wayside Gardens, 422 Garden Lane, Hodges, SC 29695. Over 1000 varieties of garden plants. Small charge.*
- *White Flower Farm, Litchfield, CT 06759-0050. Everything for the garden. Small charge.*

would travel around the apartment, ending up at the middle of the breakfast table while we ate, on the bathroom vanity while I took a bubble bath, or on the nightstand while we flipped through magazines and dreamed of the beautiful landscaped grounds we would love to have someday.

Today, Bob and I have plenty of room for that magazine garden we wanted 39 years ago. Our home has even been on garden tours in our city. We love to hear people respond, "How beautiful it is!" "How can you ever leave it to travel?" "What a relaxing retreat center!" and especially, "I would love to live here!"

We also hear, "Why go to all the trouble to keep it up?"

For me, the answer to that question goes back to those early years, when God was preparing my heart to appreciate His beauty through our garden. At that point I just knew I wanted a flower in a vase by my bed or in the center of our dining room table. Over the years, Bob used that simple desire to get me out in the garden.

For Bob, who comes from a three-generation farm family, the spirit of the garden goes back even further. Bob truly has a green thumb. It seems that everything he plants grows. He is the one primarily responsible for helping the spirit of the garden flourish so beautifully around our home.

But Bob and I both love being involved with growing things. Even the hard work—weeding, checking for insects, watering—feels purposeful and worthwhile. And then what joy to see a blanket of green outside our door or the bright splashes of color on our patio! What a thrill to pick that first plum, orange, avocado, bean, ear of corn, zinnia, marigold, or squash in our spring and summer garden! We are so much richer because of our love for plants, flowers, and trees and our involvement in their growth.

Flowers . . . have a mysterious and subtle influence upon the feelings, not unlike some strains of music.
—Henry Ward Beecher

• Discourage grass from growing between bricks in a wall or on the patio by sprinkling salt in the crevices.
• Gardens need an inch of water a week. But how do you know how long to water for that amount? Put a can, a pot or a glass under your sprinkler and see how long it takes for the container to collect an inch of water.
• For a no-drip way to water hanging plants, place a few ice cubes on top of the soil (this is okay for all plants except a tropical or tender-leaf variety, like African violets or orchids).
• Protect flowers and vegetables from slugs, snails, cutworms, and grubs by scattering lettuce leaves or citrus rinds around them. The pests will attach themselves to the food, which you remove daily and replace.
• Grass trimmed to two inches high takes less maintenance in the summer than grass mowed to one and a half inches.
• Set baby melons and cantaloupes on top of tin cans in

Flowers That Are Good to Eat

Many common flowers also make gourmet dishes. Here are some suggestions:
- *Calendula (pot marigold): Add minced petals to rice, omelets, chicken soup, clam chowder, or stew.*
- *Nasturtium: Serve leaves like watercress on sandwiches, or stuff flowers with basil- and tarragon-seasoned rice, then simmer in chicken stock and sherry.*
- *Squash blossom: Pick blossoms as they are opening, dip in a flour-and-egg mixture seasoned with salt, pepper, and tarragon, then deep-fry until golden brown.*
- *Chamomile: Dry the flowers on a screen in a dark place to make tea.*
- *Borage: Toss with salad for a cucumber-like taste, or use fresh for tea.*

---

your garden. They'll ripen faster and sweeter.
- Melted snow contains minerals that makes it good for watering your plants.
- Transform an old barbecue grill into a conversation piece by painting it, filling it with soil, and planting flowers or vines in it.
- Vase life for cut flowers is extended by filling the vase with warm water.
- If the seeds you are planting should be set in rows, you can use a broom handle to form the trenches. Press the broom handle into the dirt—about one-quarter inch deep—with your foot. You'll have a perfect row at the right depth.
- Ferns love a tea party. Dump your leftover tea into your fern pots. A used tea bag planted in their soil will also reap beautiful, healthy ferns.
- The simplest way to enjoy the gardening spirit is to make liberal use of houseplants.
- Plants not only please the eye and soothe the spirit, but

Ten Foolproof Houseplants

These hardy species will survive almost anywhere and are a good choice for timid beginners without a lot of sunny windows.

- *Aspidistra (cast-iron plant). This Victorian favorite, known as the "spittoon plant," survived the implied indignity in many a tavern.*
- *Rubber plant. Likes a dim, cool interior (like a hallway). If given sun, it grows like crazy.*
- *Century (Kentia) palm. A long-lived, slow-growing plant that needs uniform moisture. Give it an occasional shower.*
- *Philodendrons. They like medium to low light and even moisture, but will tolerate dryness and poor light.*
- *Dumb cane. Tolerates a dry interior and low light, but responds to better conditions. Don't let your pet chew the foliage or the animal's tongue will swell.*
- *Bromeliads. Exotic and slow-growing, they like frequent misting, but are practically immune to neglect and will flower even in subdued light.*
- *Corn plant (dracaena). Good for hot, dry apartments.*
- *Snake plant. Will survive almost anything.*
- *Spider plant. A tough, low-light plant that makes a great trailer and endures neglect.*
- *Nephthytis. Will flourish in poor light and survive the forgetful waterer.*

they also clean the air of impurities.

- Pots of sweet basil around the patio, swimming pool, or doorway repel flies.
- If roses arrive looking slightly wilted, recut the stems and lay the whole flowers under barely warm water in a sink for an hour or two.
- To make roses last twice as long, fill their vase with one part Sprite soft drink to one part water.

• Place daffodils in a separate vase of water for half a day before combining them in a bouquet with other flowers. They excrete a sap that clogs the stems of other flowers.

• If you have hard water with high mineral content, you can increase the vase life of flowers by switching to distilled or purified water. Do not use softened water, since it contains salts.

• A great investment in your home is to plant a tree. If you don't have a yard, donate a tree to a church, a school, or a city park.

• In a kitchen, where so many hours are spent, one spray of fragrant lilac blossom in a child's battered mug can brighten the day.

• Try using plants as architectural helps—a group of tall plants to divide a room, for instance, or a combination of potted and hanging plants to partially screen a window.

What was Paradise? But a Garden.
—William Lawson

• Repot only when needed. Spring is the best time because it favors new growth.

• To repot a large tree, I placed it in a pail until I prepared the pot. I found it so easy to move the plant about in this pail with a handle that I left the tree in there. I put a few small holes in the bottom for drainage and placed it on a plastic plant tray to catch any water that might drain through.

• Before using an old pot to replant in, clean it thoroughly with hot water with a squirt or two of regular dishwashing detergent. Then let the pot soak for several hours in a solution of one part chlorine bleach to eight parts water. Rinse well and dry, then reuse. This will help to prevent the spread of plant disease.

• Sometimes, people who don't have a green thumb find it

Spring Soil Preparations

When spring arrives, begin to get soil ready for planting. These ideas will help:

1. *With a pitchfork or spade, dig down at least eight inches into the soil, lifting and turning it.*
2. *Remove any debris such as stones and twigs. Besides bringing new soil to the surface, a deep spading buries weeds where they'll decompose, provides air for the soil, and loosens soil for better drainage.*
3. *Check for moisture. Make a ball of freshly dug soil in your fist. It should crumble in your hand. If it sticks together, it's too soon to work the soil.*
4. *Spread two to four inches of organic matter (such as peat moss, leaf mold, compost, or decomposed manure) over the soil and blend in thoroughly.*
5. *Rake the soil to break up soil clumps so that plants will have a smooth bed for their roots.*
6. *Select an all-purpose fertilizer such as 5-10-5 and work into the upper three to five inches of soil. Add two to three pounds per 100 square feet.*

easier to maintain big plants than small ones because they don't need as frequent watering and repotting.

• Give newly potted plants a little less light for the first few days.

• Before you leave for a trip, you can water your indoor plants well, cover the entire pot with a plastic bag, tucking it around the bottom of the pot. The plant should stay moist for at least a week. Very delicate plants might need TLC from a friend or neighbor.

• To make an indoor plant display, cover the floor with a heavy-duty plastic bag to protect it from water or soil stains. Then cover the plastic with ceramic tiles and set your potted plants on the tiles.

• Did you ever grow a sweet-potato garden as a child? Get a

quart-sized jar and a sweet potato, and try it again. (All you have to do is stick the potato in water and wait.) Better yet, share the fun of growing a potato with your favorite child.

Plant a rose bush every year and you
will not have lived in vain.
—*Henry Bowen*

• Four tablespoons of dishwashing liquid in one gallon of water will get rid of red spider mites on your plants. Spray the plant weekly until there are no signs of the mites. I also had mold in the soil of some of my plants. I used a solution of one tablespoon of vinegar in two quarts of water, and watered weekly with the solution until all the mold was gone.

• I'm not one who has great luck with indoor plants, but I have a little hint that helped mine grow. Rather than throw the water out every time I boil eggs, I let it cool down and water my plants with it. It is packed with growth-stimulating minerals.

• A solution of one part lemon-lime soft drink (not diet types) and two parts water provides proper acidity, a bactericide to reduce cloudiness of water, and sugar to "feed" flower buds so they open completely and gives extended life to cut flowers.

• On the kitchen window, a row of herb plants that you can grow from seed or buy in three-inch pots will not only be decorative, but will add distinctive flavor to gourmet dishes.

• On the sun porch, fill an attractive wheeled cart with blooming fibrous begonias.

• Brighten the dining room with an indoor window box of impatiens.

• Plant onions next to beets and carrots to keep bugs away.

• If you plant basil near your tomatoes, worms and flies will be repelled.

Make Your Own Planter Mix

You can make a potting soil that is suitable for most houseplants by mixing together four cups of black soil or potting soil; four cups of leaf mold, peat moss, or spaghnum moss; four cups of coarse sand; two to four cups of activated charcoal; and one tablespoon of steamed bone meal. This mix should be "cooked" in the oven at 200°F for 30 minutes before use. (It will smell awful, but your plants will love it.)

• Going on vacation? Simply put all your houseplants in the bathtub with a few inches of water. They will drink the water as needed.

• Before you water your houseplant, poke three or four holes in the soil with the handle of a wooden spoon. This allows the water to soak the soil thoroughly.

• Pick flowers in early morning before they are stressed by heat. Strip off foliage that will be below the waterline. Fill a broad bowl with water, and use sharp shears to cut about an inch off the bottom of each flower stem. While holding the stem under water, transfer the flower immediately to a vase filled with warm water or preservative solution.

• Schedule your plant feedings (indoors and out) the first of every month. You'll never forget to do it, and your plants will reward you with renewed vigor and beauty.

• Use yellow paint to mark about 12 inches at the end of the hose. Then you can always find the end when the hose is tangled up.

• Herbs can grow in the ground, in hanging baskets, in window boxes, in pots—even in a terrarium made from an old fish tank, large jar, or bowl. Keep close to the kitchen. You will use them more often.

• To avoid bruising tomato plant stems when staking, fasten them to stakes with strips of panty hose.

• Be kind to your knees when working in the garden. Use plastic meat trays as knee pads.

• Because grapes don't continue to ripen after they've been picked, leave them on the vine until the first light frost.

• Are you on a seed catalog list? Send for every catalog you read about. It's an easy way to learn the names of flowers and a great opportunity to see them in color. And browsing through the bright catalogs can color a dreary winter day with hopeful brightness.

• If time or space prohibit a full garden, plant tomatoes and strawberries in a barrel or other large container. You'll be surprised at the yield from just a few plants.

• Order ladybugs from a gardening catalog or nursery and let children help release them around the garden or yard. Ladybugs are God's way of keeping harmful bugs under control—and kids love to help them "fly away home."

• For those plants that like an acidic soil, sprinkle your left-over coffee grounds around the plants.

• For the organic grower, soapsuds can be used as an insecticide. Spray generously.

• Eggshells crushed and spread around your plants will encourage growth. Eggshells are great for getting rid of snails and slugs. Make sure the shells are broken before scattering around the plants.

• To control the weeds and grass that grow between your walkways and cement walled areas, simply pour boiling water containing two to four tablespoons of salt over them.

• I love to garden and have a large vegetable patch. There's always the problem of birds pecking and ruining the vegetables. I found a way to stop them. I take empty soda cans (the type that open by pulling a ring), and I take the tops off with a can opener. I put a string through the holes in the tops and tie the tops to wooden stakes placed crisscross around the garden. When the tops move slightly, they

> *When . . . I go into my garden before anyone is awake, I go for the time being into perfect happiness. . . The fair face of every flower salutes me with a silent joy that fills me with infinite content.*
> —Celia Thaxter

shimmer and shine and it frightens the birds. The tops don't get rusty, so you can use them year after year.

There is only one perfect strawberry in existence and that is the strawberry of memory.
—Stafford Whiteaker

• Pour small seeds into an old spice shaker, put the lid on, and sprinkle over each garden row to evenly spread the small seeds. Cover seeds lightly with soil, water according to package directions, and wait for results.

• Newly planted trees and shrubs need watering every five to seven days. Apply a thorough soaking so that enough moisture gets to the roots and helps them become well established.

• Mulch the soil surface to cut down on weed growth, maintain surface moisture, prevent evaporation of water, and regulate soil temperatures so that you get better root growth.

• On a gardening calendar, note what was planted when; when the plants sprouted; and when they were watered, fertilized, and harvested. Then you can plan the next year by seeing what grew, produced well, and in how much time.

• Take a kitchen timer outdoors with you so that you won't get so absorbed with gardening that you're late for other activities.

• Water bushy plants with a bulb-type meat baster. It allows you to reach through leaves to deliver moisture to the soil, where you want it. This is easier and neater than using watering cans.

• When raking leaves on a windy day, dampen the leaves slightly with a fine spray from the garden hose. They will not blow all over the yard, will be easier to put into a trash bag or container, and more leaves can be stuffed into the bag.

• A rubber garbage-can cover will hold small plants, gardening tools, and other necessities so that you can carry them around the garden and avoid back-and-forth trips.

• When planting seedlings in egg-carton cups or recycled plastic trays, place an eggshell half in the bottom before adding soil; then, it's easy to lift the whole seedling at planting time.

• Paint handles of your rake, shovel, and other garden tools with a bright color of paint so you can see them at a glance if they are left somewhere in the yard. Also, if you lend the tools to anyone, they'll be easily identified as yours.

• Cold winds will increase your heating bills. Shield the windy side of your home with a staggered double row of evergreen trees.

• If you're a bargain hunter, bare-root trees and shrubs may be for you. They are about half the price of balled and burlapped specimens.

• After we water our houseplants, the saucers become full and sometimes overflow onto the floor. We solved this problem by using a turkey baster. As the water drains through, we draw up the excess into the baster and transfer it to another plant. This prevents a mess and protects the finish on the floor beneath the plants.

• Ferns are a bit sensitive to chlorine in tap water, so let the water sit overnight before watering. This allows the chlorine to evaporate. Ferns also like to be misted.

• For beautiful azaleas, simply add two tablespoons of vinegar to a quart of water and use occasionally around your plants. They love acidic soil.

Plastic Mulch

You can keep soil temperatures and moisture constant by mulching plants with black plastic—plants are inserted in holes made in plastic sheeting or plastic sheeting is used to cover soil around them. Or use organic mulch to reduce soil temperature and moisture fluctuations. (In some areas, heavy rainfall can cause rot when plastic mulch is used. Check with your local nurseryman first before using. Make sure your soil has good drainage.)

• Dust plant leaves with a feather duster (or better yet, with your hair blower set on the cool temperature). This method is also good for silk flowers and plant arrangements.

• Cracked walnut shells, marbles, stones, or fruit pits can be used to provide drainage at the bottom of a houseplant pot.

• Misting plants in the evening prompts health, decreases bugs, and is a chore kids love.

• When cultivating the soil in your garden, remember that good soil is slightly lumpy. If you work it until it's too fine, it will pack hard when it rains or blow away in a strong wind.

• If children or pets keep knocking your plants over, try double-potting. Put the plant and its original pot inside another, larger pot with rocks or gravel between the two. This will add both size and weight and should stabilize the plant.

• Cats are territorial animals, so don't position a plant in the cat's favorite place in the sun. Also, if your dog likes to people-watch through the window, leave that spot free.

• Plant a garlic clove beside a houseplant to keep all types of pests away.

• Start a compost pile in fall with dried leaves from the yard. Keep vegetable and fruit peelings, eggshells, tea and coffee grounds, etc. in a plastic bag and empty them onto the pile when the bag is full. Add all valuable organic matter to your garden soil. Kick more leaves over the scraps.

• In order not to dislodge newly planted seeds, place the containers in a shallow dish of water so that moisture can be absorbed from underneath.

• If you're not sure whether a houseplant needs watering or not, poke your index finger an inch into the topsoil. If the soil there is moist, don't water. If it's dry, do.

• Water bulb houseplants from the bottom. Fill a pie pan with water and let the plants sit in it for a while.

• Use a mister to water delicate seedlings.

• Cool the water in which you've cooked spaghetti or potatoes and use it to water your plants. The starch is good for them.

• Water from an aquarium is perfect for fertilizing houseplants, as is water in which fish has been frozen.

• You can "water" a terrarium simply by patting the inside of the glass with a wet paper towel.

• During cold-weather months, a room filled with houseplants will benefit from the moisture provided by a portable vaporizer.

• Tin tops from cans can be used to provide drainage in plant pots. Bend them slightly so that they cover the hole with the concave side down, leaving plenty of room for excess water to drain out.

• Here's a novel but effective way to grow parsley indoors: Slice sponges in half and sprinkle them with parsley seeds. Arrange the sponges on dishes in a sunny location, keep them moist, and watch your parsley grow.

• To speed up seed germination, place seed trays on top of your refrigerator, where the 72°F to 75°F heat emitted will promote steady growth.

• Plants which lower pollution levels in your home are the Chinese evergreen (which looks somewhat like a philodendron), the peace lily, and plants of the peperomia family. However, these don't do quite as good a job of air cleaning as the spider plant.

• Treat an ailing houseplant by dribbling a tablespoon of castor oil on the soil in the pot; then water thoroughly.

• A plant will live longer if you don't let it go to seed. Cut blossoms off when they begin to fade.

• If you think that worms in the soil of your potted plants may be eating away at the roots, place a slice of raw potato on the surface soil in each pot. The worms will crawl out to get at the potatoes, and you can capture and destroy them.

• If you have the space, you can grow vegetables indoors in artificial light. Lettuce does especially well when grown under fluorescent plant lights. Plant your lettuce garden in the basement, the attic, or anywhere the temperature stays between 65°F and 70°F during the day and drops about ten degrees at night.

• Do something special for your plants. Feed them dried blood (high in potassium), ground-up eggshells (which contain calcium and some nitrogen), or a diced banana skin (high in potassium). Work these substances into the soil.

• It's hard work rotating a big, heavy planter so that the plant gets sun all around, but you can simplify the task by sitting the pot on a lazy Susan.

• Old sponges cut into squares are great for covering drainage holes in flowerpots.

• Use a knitting needle to test whether or not your houseplant needs water. If the needle inserted into the soil comes out dry, water the plant.

• To make your own potting soil for plants with very fine roots, decrease the black soil and sand to three cups each, and increase the peat or sphagnum moss to six cups.

• To make your own potting soil for cacti, decrease the black soil and leaf mold or moss to two cups each, and increase the sand to six cups.

Method for Vacation Watering Your Plants

• *Place a couple of bath towels in the bottom of the bathtub. Place the plant pots and one large or several small buckets of water on the towels. Be sure the water buckets sit higher than the plant pots.*
• *Snip cotton string lengths to reach from the inside bottom of the water bucket to the top of the plant pot soil. Gently push one string end into the soil to hold it in place and put the other end at the bottom of the water bucket. Fill the buckets with water. That's all there is to it.*

• You can unwittingly bring bugs into a house by taking houseplants outside for extra sun and then returning them to their places indoors. If you take plants outdoors, keep them isolated from other houseplants for three or four weeks after you bring them back into the house. If you detect bugs on the plants, wipe the stems and leaves with a mild soap-and-water solution.

• If you pinch new shoots at the growing points, you'll encourage branching, which produces more growth for flowering.

• If you suspect that one of your houseplants has a pest problem, attach a pest strip, then cover the plant for a few days with a plastic bag. By the time you remove the bag, the plant should have perked up.

• If you have plants that need to be brought in and potted for the winter, line the pots with plastic. Leave some excess plastic over the edge of the pot, and punch a couple of holes in the bottom for drainage. In spring, when it's time for transplanting, lift the soil and the plant out of the pot by the plastic.

• All plants need adequate light if they are to grow properly. Here's a way to test how much light your plants will get in a given location: Place a sheet of paper where you want to put a plant, and hold your hand a foot above the paper. If your hand casts a sharp, well-defined shadow, you have bright light. If the shadow is fuzzy but recognizable, you have filtered light. If all you get is a blur on the paper, your light condition is shady and you will have to choose your plants carefully or consider supplementing the available light.

• Use pieces of Styrofoam for a lightweight drainage layer in the bottom of a hanging planter.

• Slip shower caps over the bottoms of hanging planters to catch the overflow when watering. The caps can be removed after an hour or so.

15

Beauty

A godly woman
will be honored
for eternity.

*C*harm is deceptive, and beauty is fleeting; but a woman who fears the LORD is to be praised.

—Proverbs 31:30

Beauty

$\mathcal{T}$he old adage "You only get one time to make a first impression" is certainly true. We live in a time in history that stresses personal grooming. As Christians we need to keep moderation in mind and not be out of balance, but we must also be aware that we often conduct ourselves based on how we feel about our personal grooming. As I go shopping, I realize as I look at people that it takes so little to be above average. God wants us to be groomed properly as we go out into the secular world to be ambassadors for Him. Because how we look can affect our personal witness of who we are, I trust that some of these ideas will be helpful for your improved grooming.

Go outside, whatever the weather. Bundle up if it's cold. Take an umbrella for rain, or put on shorts for a sunny summer day. Look around you and take specific notice of five things of beauty created by God for you to enjoy. You may see mist over a pond, red tomatoes on a green vine, sparkles of white snow in the sun, your child's face. Whatever. Just take the time to notice. Beauty is there. Let it refresh and restore you.

Good Sunscreen Sense

"People often compromise the SPF (sun protection factor) in the sunscreen product they use by not applying enough to the skin," says the Skin Cancer Foundation. For example, a too-thin layer of SPF 15 ends up offering protection that is closer to that of SPF 8. An adult of average size should apply about one ounce of sunscreen to all exposed areas of the body; smaller adults or children require proportionately less.

Other Reminders from the Skin Cancer Foundation

• Sunscreen should be reapplied every 60 to 90 minutes while in the sun, after swimming, or after activities that cause perspiration. Reapplication is only a replacement. It does not double the SPF level, nor does it allow you additional time and exposure to the sun's rays.
• Skin damage occurs before sunburn appears, so don't use "redness" as a signal to apply sunscreen.
• Sun exposure is cumulative, therefore small spurts of "incidental" exposure adds up to a lot of skin damage over time. Catching "rays" does not just occur at the pool or beach. It happens during any outdoor activity—even mowing the lawn, walking, or jogging. Use sunscreen daily.
• Most sunscreens have a shelf life of at least two years. An opened bottle will become less effective over time. A change in consistency or odor is a signal to discard the product and buy a new supply.
• It's okay to take advantage of those end-of-summer sales. An unopened bottle will keep its potency over the winter.

Some Simple Pleasures to Enhance Your Beauty

• Watch the sun set over a nearby lake or ocean.
• Teach a child to ride a bike, sew, make chocolate cookies.
• Spend an afternoon in a hammock, sipping lemonade between catnaps.

• Frame baby pictures of all your loved ones and display on a table.

• Toast marshmallows.

• Make a list of all the things you're good at and post inside the medicine chest so you'll see it every morning.

• Do a few hours of volunteer work.

• Call the most harassed mother you know and offer to look after her child (or children, if you can handle it) for two hours.

• Paint tin watering cans and pick flowers to display.

Help me, Lord, to see Your beauty all around me. May my gratitude spill over from a cup full of thanks to You.

• Dark colors are slenderizing. Black, rich brown, and midnight blue all minimize heavier parts of the body. So someone who wants to draw attention away from heavy thighs should wear dark skirts or slacks. Bright colors and patterns draw the eye and should be worn on slimmer parts of the body. For the most slimming look, use monochrome dressing—all one color, or tone-on-tone.

• We all know that the sun's rays are most harmful when the sun is nearly or directly overhead. Here's a tip from the National Cancer Institute to alert you to the danger time: Cover up whenever your shadow is shorter than you are. That way, you'll avoid the sun's most burning rays.

• Hats and ultraviolet light protection: Berets, tams, and other brimless hats offer little protection from the sun. Even baseball caps shield only down to the nose. Hats with brims three to five inches wide that circle the head are better. Most fatal skin cancers originate on the ears, forehead, nose, neck, and other areas of the head.

Shampooing Your Hair

• Lather hair twice only if very oily or very dirty. Otherwise you'll strip your hair of natural oils.

• Don't be surprised if your favorite shampoo seems to leave your hair less bouncy after months of satisfactory performance. No one is exactly sure why but "shampoo fatigue" may be due to a buildup of proteins or other conditioning ingredients. Many people switch brands, only to perceive a drop in performance with the new shampoo within several months. At that point try switching back to the old one.

• When you need a dry shampoo, try bran, dry oatmeal, baby powder, or cornstarch. Use a large-holed shaker or an empty baby powder container to apply. Wash through hair with your fingers and brush out thoroughly.

Conditioning Your Hair

• If you have an oily scalp, but dry or damaged hair, condition hair before you shampoo. Wet your hair, towel it dry, and then apply conditioner, starting an inch from your scalp. Work conditioner through your hair, wait five minutes, and rinse. Then shampoo as usual.

• To revitalize and give luster to all types of hair: Beat three eggs; add two tablespoons olive or safflower oil and one teaspoon vinegar. Apply mixture to hair and cover with plastic cap. Wait half an hour and then shampoo well.

• Here's a hair conditioner that is bound to draw raves! Combine three-fourths cup olive oil, one-half cup honey, and the juice of one lemon and set aside. Rinse hair with water and towel dry. Work in a small amount of conditioner (store leftovers in the refrigerator), comb to distribute evenly, and cover with a plastic cap for 30 minutes. Shampoo and rinse thoroughly.

• When swimming daily in chlorinated or salt water,

alternate hair care, using shampoo one day and conditioner the next.

• Check your portable hair dryer for lint and hair buildup on the air inlet screen. This buildup will cause the motor to get too hot and burn up. Make sure the hair dryer is unplugged.

The most essential element in
any home is God.

• To dry your fingernail polish, spray your nails with Pam (no-stick cooking spray).

Staying Toasty in Bed

Metabolism drops while we sleep; body temperature follows. Cold sleepers have unpleasant dreams and restless nights.

• Sleep on flannel sheets. The brushing process creates insulating air cells, making flannel warmer than regular cotton.

• For cold toes, tuck an old-fashioned rubber hot-water bag (about $4 at discount drugstores) into the bottom of the bed.

• Use an electric blanket with dual controls if you are cold while he's hot. Newer models have reduced electromagnetic field (EMF) emissions. Look for blankets without little bumps, which were the older blanket's safety switches to protect against overheating. Set the blanket on "low" a half hour before going to bed.

• Don't sleep under more than three layers. A third blanket adds virtually no insulation because it squeezes out the air layers. A down or fiberfill comforter over a wool blanket and flannel sheets is another good combination.

• Snuggle up! Humans and animals generate lots of heat. Sleeping with pets on cold winter nights has been a European tradition for centuries.

• While you are supervising a child's evening bath, give

Makeup Dos and Don'ts for
Contact Lens Wearers

- *Put your lenses in before applying eye makeup and take them out before removing makeup.*
- *Use a cotton swab dipped in soap and water to remove eye makeup. Avoid makeup removers; they may leave a residue that can end up on your contact lenses when you put them back in.*
- *Don't use waterproof mascaras, which require removers. Try a brand that does not contain fibers and comes off easily.*
- *Don't put liner inside the lid. It could stain the lens.*

---

yourself a facial, pluck your eyebrows, or do your pre-bed beauty routine.

- A good way to clean out the fragrance when you change perfume in your atomizer is to wash the atomizer well with soap and hot water, fill the bottle with rubbing alcohol, and leave it open overnight.
- If you're tired of spending money on powder puffs, you can make your own. First buy your favorite powder, then get a container. Fill the container with cotton balls. Pour some powder in and shake. Now, whenever you need to powder, just grab a cotton ball.

Cleansing Your Skin

- *To cleanse your face thoroughly, try the following method:* Fill a clean sink with warm water, dip facial soap into the water and rub the bar over your face. Dip the soap back into the water and make a lather in your hands. Massage this lather over your face. Rinse 15 to 20 times with the soapy water. Finish off with several cold-water rinses. Blot your face dry with a towel.
- Excessive stinging or drying are signs that your toner,

astringent, or after-shave lotion is too strong. Change brands or add one teaspoon of mineral water to each ounce of the product.
• *Hot weather tip:* Refrigerate your facial toner, freshener, or astringent for a cool skin treat.
• *Three simple steps for a facial at home:*
  — Wash your face as usual but don't follow with toner or moisturizer.
  — Boil some water and pour it into a large mixing bowl. Create a steam "tent" by draping a large bath towel over your head and the bowl, keeping your face about six inches from the hot water. Steam face five to eight minutes. Steaming softens skin and opens pores.
  — Deep clean your face with a grainy cleanser. You can use a commercial scrub or make one by mixing one teaspoon each of oatmeal, honey, cornmeal, and plain yogurt. Gently massage over face and neck. Rinse thoroughly with warm water and pat dry.
• After having a good cry, my eyes are swollen. I soak cotton balls in cool skim milk, then place them on my closed eyes for five to ten minutes.
• It is always better to arrive for any function looking our best. A first step in good communication is a good appearance. It is a way to make a favorable first impression on people who are important to us until we can project our inner selves through conversation.

Bathing

• In winter, your bath or shower water should be tepid, not hot, since hot water inflames the skin and increases moisture loss afterward. Apply a moisturizing lotion right after bathing while your skin is still damp.
• A simple but effective way to relieve dry skin and winter itch is to completely dissolve one cup of salt in a tub of water and bathe as usual. (For a more luxurious bath, try sea

salt.) Bathing in salt often works better than using expensive bath oils, but if you really want to use oil, a plain mineral oil will generally fulfill your needs.

Moisturizing Your Skin

• Always apply a moisturizer right after cleansing to prevent the surface moisture from evaporating. Moisturizers should last about ten hours. If your face feels tight before that time, freshen it with a toner and reapply your moisturizer. You may need a richer moisturizer.

• Don't forget to moisturize your throat area. If this area is especially dry, heat peanut oil until warm and massage upward into your skin.

• To avoid that cracked, flaky look on your elbows, make it a habit to pay special attention to them at the same time you lubricate the rest of your body.

• If you have begun to get lines around your eyes and want to make them less obvious, rub eye cream between your fingertips to warm it before patting it around the eye area. This makes it easier for the skin to absorb the cream. Do not pull or stretch the skin around the eyes.

• I have oily skin on my nose, chin, and forehead and dry skin everywhere else. To take care of my skin I:
  — Wash with a mild foaming gel to cleanse without overdrying.
  — Sweep some alcohol-free toner over my face with a cotton ball to remove any lingering oil and dirt.
  — Dab oil-free moisturizer on dry areas.

• Once a perfume or cologne is opened, its "life clock" starts ticking. You can prolong the strength of any fragrance by following this advice: Refrigerate a fragrance or keep it cool. Coolness slows the aging process. Purchase two small bottles rather than one large bottle to get greater strength and longevity. Make certain the fragrance has a tight cap. When transferring a fragrance from its original container to a collector's bottle, be sure to cleanse the new bottle first with alcohol.

Devote the evening hours to quiet rest,
reflection, and an inner preparing
for the coming day.

• When my feet are tired, I place them in a basin of warm water with two tablespoons of baking soda or Epsom salts and let them soak for 20 minutes.

• *A great mask for oily skin:* Make a paste of one unbeaten egg white, a half cup of pure lemon juice, and a half cup of oatmeal. Apply to face and let dry completely. Rinse well with warm water.

• To help me relax during my last few months of pregnancy, I made this all-natural recipe for my bathwater: Add two tablespoons of lavender flowers, three tablespoons of bay leaves, four tablespoons of oatmeal, and four tablespoons of bran to a pot of water. Simmer for one hour. Strain and add to bathwater.

• Incorrect shaving of legs can cause rashes and irritations. The right way to shave is to moisten legs with warm water, apply shave cream, and wait three minutes to allow hair to become soft and pliant. Using a fresh, sharp blade, shave in the direction of hair growth for sleek, bump-free skin.

Makeup Foundation

• If you never seem to buy the right shade of foundation, try applying it just under the jawline rather than on the wrist. It should be just slightly lighter than your skin tone.

• To transform a heavy, oil-based foundation into one that glides on more smoothly, add a bit of moisturizer or salt-free mineral water to the foundation. Use your palm or a small dish—not the makeup container—to do the mixing.

Blushers and Powders

• For those "gray" days, mix a drop of liquid blusher with your foundation. Spread this instant glow all over your skin.

• When you're feeling tired and dragged out, use blusher very lightly around the entire outer contour of your face, from the hairline to the chin, blending with a cosmetic sponge.

• Under fluorescent lights, which destroy the rosy tones in the skin and give a yellowish look, apply your blusher a little darker and use a little deeper colored lipstick.

• Store loose powder in an old salt or pepper shaker so that you can shake it into your palm. Then dip a makeup brush or puff into the powder and dust it on.

• Keep all cosmetics you use every morning in one place (on a shelf, in a clear Lucite organizer, or in a plastic zippered bag) so you don't have to think about what to reach for. Keep duplicates in your purse or at work. Don't waste time fishing for them when you are rushing to get ready.

• Put on makeup and eat breakfast before you blow-dry your hair. Your hair will dry faster, stay healthier.

Eye Makeup

• Eye makeup is perishable. Bacteria from your eyes can be introduced to the product. Wash applicators frequently or use cotton swabs. Also, label shadows, pencils, and mascaras with their purchase dates. Replace your shadows and pencils every six months, your mascara every three months.

• If you use liquid eyeliner, try dotting it on along the lash line. It will look less harsh than a solid line.

• To get the sharpest point on your eyebrow, eyeliner, and lip pencils, put them in the freezer for an hour before sharpening.

• Tame unruly eyebrows with a little bit of styling gel or mousse applied with an eyebrow brush.

Dream a dream today. Think of all the
wonderful possibilities that can happen to
you, then go for it.

Remove Makeup

• Never go to sleep without removing every trace of your makeup—except on your wedding night! Habitually sleeping with a layer of dirt, debris, and dead skin cells stuck to your face will leave your complexion looking muddy and dull.
• When you're removing mascara, if it seems to get all over your face, wrap a tissue around your index finger and hold it just under the lower lashes. Remove eye makeup as usual with the other hand.
• Use lemon juice as an astringent, unless you have very dry skin. Lemon juice has a drying effect. It also will whiten the skin. You can mix it with glycerin to make it less sharp.

Removing Hair

• Waxing—you can do this yourself, but many women prefer to have a beauty salon specialist do this for them. Check with your local beauty salon for recommendations.
• Depilatories—this removes hair below the skin's surface and keeps legs smooth longer than shaving does.
• Shaving—there are several good plastic razors that are designed just for women.
• Warm water dries out skin more than cool does. Take short showers instead of long, hot baths (unless you just want to treat yourself to the luxury of a bath). Pat your skin dry—don't rub. Then follow with a moisturizer with sunscreen.

Stretching Your Shower

Wake up muscles with these six stretches to be done while in the shower.
- Neck Stretch. *Drop head forward and hold. Press right ear to right shoulder and hold. Alternate to left side.*
- Shoulder rolls. *Slowly roll shoulders forward, making big circles, then backward, to stretch shoulders, back, chest.*
- Upper Arm. *Bend elbow and raise toward ceiling; push gently on elbow with opposite hand to stretch triceps (at back of upper arm) and deltoids (upper shoulders).*
- Chest. *Clasp hands behind back and lift arms until you feel the stretch.*
- Shoulders. *To stretch upper back, hug yourself, reaching hands toward opposite shoulder blade.*
- Lower Back. *Pull in stomach, bend at waist, knees bent slightly, back straight; hold.*

Lip Care

- Your lipstick will stay on much longer if you use the following method. Layer on in this order: face powder, lipstick, powder, lipstick. Wipe off excess powder with a damp washcloth or a tissue.
- Prepare your lips for color with a lip conditioner or foundation. Lipstick, like makeup, wears better with moisturizer underneath.
- Outline lips with a lip pencil to prevent the color from bleeding.
- For perfect lips, outline the lips with a lip brush and fill in with lipstick. Dust with translucent powder and apply a second coat of the same color lipstick.
- Get the most out of your lipsticks. Try gloss to brighten matte shades, gold over brown tones, or a lighter color on the upper lip.

Five Exercise Tips

• *Any activity is better than nothing. If you aren't into "exercise," at least be more active by walking, working in the garden, parking the car farther away, and/or taking the stairs instead of the elevator.*

• *If you are a "weekend warrior," be sure to refuel your muscles on Saturday night with extra carbohydrates (juices, fruits, pasta, potatoes, breads, frozen yogurt) so that they will have the energy needed for you to enjoy exercise on Sunday. Also be sure to drink plenty of nonalcoholic fluids to replace sweat losses.*

• *If the summer heat gets you down, exercise in the morning or evening, but not in the middle of the day. Try swimming or water aerobics*

• *Drink extra fluids. Drinking enough fluids can be essential to a successful and safe workout. You can tell if you are drinking enough if you void significant amounts of clear-colored urine. Dark urine is concentrated with metabolic wastes, a sign of dehydration.*

• *Choose the right time of day to exercise. Particularly for the allergy sufferer, time of day is an important factor for an outdoor summer workout. Try limiting your workouts to early morning and early evening hours when pollen counts are lowest, and when temperatures tend to be a little cooler.*

---

*We all need periods of reappraisal and renewal,
to take stock and take heart.*

More Beauty Tips

• We would be better off if we engaged in positive solitude—
time alone that is used thoughtfully to benefit mind and soul.

— Solitude provides the opportunity to identify your
most cherished goals and develop ways of achieving
them.
— Regular time alone contributes to a sense of inner
peace and makes you feel more in control of your life.
— We begin to develop a personal philosophy or life
plan.
— Tools that can help in your exploration of who you
are: Read your Bible daily, have daily prayer, start
using a journal to log your thoughts, exercise, listen
to good music, read a good book, turn off the TV.

• Make activity dates for yourself, pencil them into your calendar, and make sure you keep them.

• Using a curling iron is the most efficient way to put
bounce and curl in your hair. To prevent a burnt finger,
wear a glove on your left hand.

• If your hair doesn't hold a set well, curl it with a curling
iron but pin each curl to the head as you remove the iron.
Spray lightly with hair spray, unpin and brush.

• Setting lotions with alcohol listed on the label before
water will be more drying but hold longer.

• With long hair, apply a setting lotion to the roots only.
Too much lotion weighs hair down.

• Use some setting lotion in hair when it's oily and there's no time to wash it. It will make hair look less limp.

• Always try on foundation before buying it. The color in the bottle may look different on your skin. Smooth it onto your jawline in natural light. If there is a noticeable line, choose a different shade.

• Never apply foundation to your neck. You'll only end up with "ring-around-the-collar."

• Use these exercises to relieve eyestrain:
  — Blink and yawn three times.
  — Every hour, look up from your work and focus on an object 20 feet away.
  — Rub your hands together briskly, then cup your palms and place them gently over your eyes for 30 seconds.

• If your eyebrows are naturally sparse or overplucked, use an eyebrow pencil one shade lighter than your brow color.
  — To make your brows appear thicker, use hair spray or mousse on an eyebrow brush and brush the brows straight up.
  — Tweeze under the brow line only and alternate plucking hairs from one brow to the other to ensure a better balance.
  — Always apply an astringent when you are through tweezing.
  — To groom eyebrows, use an old, thoroughly cleaned mascara brush. Brush the brows up, then sideways.

• Stash emery boards and covered elastic bands in the kitchen, in the car, and at work.

• Spend this Saturday doing something you really want to do. I don't mean next month. This Saturday. Enjoy being alive and being able to do something special. You deserve it. There will never be another you. This Saturday will be well spent. Why not spend at least one day a week on you!

• Take time out to ride your bike, build sand castles, fly a kite, smell a rose, walk in the woods, or go barefoot in the sand.

• Find a low-maintenance hairdo.
• Cornstarch is a super soothing dusting powder. To get more mileage from your store-bought dusting powder, just mix half and half.
• When giving yourself a home permanent, protect your tender skin from chemical burn by applying a light film of petroleum jelly to the skin along your hairline and on the top and back of each ear.
• To take a stuck lid off your fingernail polish jar, place in microwave for five to ten seconds. The top will come off easily.

Makeup Dos and Don'ts

• Buy small quantities of makeup and fragrance.
• Don't buy a package that has been opened or appears tampered with.
• Wash your hands and face before applying makeup.
• Don't apply makeup to sunburned or windburned skin, or to skin that has broken out in a rash.
• Don't borrow makeup or share yours with friends.
• Don't moisten makeup with saliva.
• Don't rim your eyes by applying liner inside the lash line.
• Don't overdo mascara. The excess can flake off and irritate your eyes.
• Close your makeup containers securely after each use.
• Don't keep your makeup in sunlight, near hot radiators or air conditioners, or in unventilated bathrooms.
• Don't use a product if it looks dried out, has changed color, or has a disagreeable odor.
• Don't mix leftover products.
• Don't try several new products at the same time. Test them individually so that if you have a reaction, such as redness, itchiness, or swelling, you'll know which product to suspect.
• *Hair blower techniques:* Concentrated blasts on a single section of hair do not do the job. This technique overheats

the hair. You should move the current of air all over your hair, holding the dryer about six inches away from the hair. Combing and drying against the natural growth direction of the hair keeps it from clinging to your head and gives a fuller look.

Nail Pointers

• File nails in one direction, from the side toward the center, working on the undersides of the nails. This helps keep nails from splitting.
• Buff nails before polishing them. It gives a smooth base to work on and makes the nails healthier and stronger.
• Use two thin coats of polish rather than one heavy coat. The polish will wear better, last longer, and be less susceptible to chipping.
• Using basecoat under polish reduces nail discoloration. By itself, it protects nails from the elements and from dishwashing detergent.
• To give nails a longer, more streamlined look, leave a bit of each side of each nail free from polish.
• When polish gets ragged and there's no time for a complete redo, add a darker color and finish off with a topcoat.
• For double strength, apply nail hardener in two directions: side to side, let dry, then up and down. The nylon fibers form a lattice "mesh" that makes a tougher bond.
• Nail stains? Insert your fingertips in half a lemon and "swish" around. This whitens under and around the nails and cleans the cuticles.
• Break in a new emery board by running the coarser side over another emery board. The new emery will be less rough on your nails.
• For ragged cuticles and hangnails, wear protective gloves when washing dishes and keep cuticles well-lubricated by

applying hand cream several times a day. Push cuticles back regularly with an orangewood stick. Also try this once-a-week cuticle "bath": Warm a little olive or almond oil and soak your nails for 15 minutes; the cuticles are instantly softened.

16
Moving

But I'm just
settling in
to this place . . .

They prepared to go up and build the house of the LORD in Jerusalem. All their neighbors assisted them with articles of silver and gold, with goods and livestock and with valuable gifts, in addition to all the freewill offerings.

—Ezra 1:5,6

Moving

One of the most painful statements that can come out of a husband's mouth is, "Honey, I've gotten a promotion and a raise, but we have to relocate!" Oh no, not again! flashes in your mind. You know what that's like, because you've done it several times in the past.

Our moves today are stressful at best and traumatic at worst, whether they be across town or across the continent. With a few helpful ideas, we can certainly reduce the normal stress of relocating.

When Considering a Move

Reasons to stay. . .
- The crime rate in your community is not as bad as in others.
- You enjoy the climate where you presently live.
- You enjoy the friends and neighbors you have now.
- The cost of living is affordable where you are.
- You like your current doctor and hospital.
- The children and grandchildren can visit you.
- A trip now and then will satisfy any need to see new places.

Reasons to go. . .
• Taxes and prices are lower in another place that attracts you.
• Your doctor recommends a different climate.
• You fear that your neighborhood is deteriorating.
• You want to move closer to your children.
• You'd like a new life-style and new friends.
• You want to be closer to modern health facilities.
• Another area has more chances for part-time work in your field.

• When moving valuables, consider carriers other than household movers. Special handling is important for irreplaceable and fragile objects and for jewelry, collections, and currency. Options: air freight, UPS, armored service, registered U.S. mail, move everything yourself.
• When leaving your previous home, empty the children's rooms last, and restructure their rooms first when you've arrived at your new home. This helps them adjust psychologically.
• Type your new address and phone number in columns with two-inch margins and fold on lines above and below each address segment so that you and the children can tear off new-address segments for friends. Then, at the new location, make stationery, envelopes, and stamps available for children to write to their friends. Allow one five-minute long-distance call per month per child (depending on your finances). Each child keeps track of the date and length of call on a calendar placed near the phone and pays for the call with allowance money when the phone bill arrives. Long-distance calls will be kept to the minimum and children will be encouraged to write letters to their friends instead. They will also be encouraged to develop a rewarding lifelong habit of writing.

Safe Trailer Towing Tips

Just like driving a car, towing a trailer is safe as long as the equipment is properly used and maintained. To make your towing adventure as safe as possible, please keep in mind the following:

- Don't overload. Never exceed the rating of the lowest-rated component in your towing system. Your system is only as strong as its weakest part.
- Load the trailer heavier in front. Improper loading can result in trailer instability and sway. Place heavy items on the floor in front of the axle. Then balance the load from side to side, and secure it to prevent shifting. Consult trailer manufacturer recommendations for exact tongue weight.
- Never allow passengers in a trailer being towed.
- Connect safety chains every time you tow. Cross the chains under the trailer tongue and attach to the hitch or the frame of your tow vehicle. Allow just enough slack for turning. Don't let chains drag on the road. Make sure connections are secured.
- Check for proper tire inflation on tow vehicle and trailer before towing. Rear tires of the tow vehicle should be at their maximum rated pressure (usually 32 psi).
- Connect trailer lights, turn signals, and breakaway switch connections every time you tow.
- Check hitch ball, coupler safety chains, retaining pins and clips, and all other connections every time you tow. Re-check at fuel and rest stops.
- Allow extra time for passing, stopping, and changing lanes. The additional trailer weight affects acceleration and braking.
- Drive over bumps and rough roads at slower, steady speeds to prevent damage to your tow vehicle, hitch, or trailer.
- Pull over and make a thorough inspection of your towing system if at any point you suspect damage may have occurred. Correct problems before resuming travel.
- Follow the towing recommendations of the trailer manufacturer.

Packing Your Belongings

• If you're packing yourself, do it a little at a time. Start weeks ahead. Several big cartons are easier to move than many small ones, but (depending on how quickly you'll be unpacking) for certain rooms—like kitchen and bath—you may want smaller cartons, each containing items you may want immediate access to.

• Save space by not packing the unbreakable contents of tightly loaded drawers. Simply tape the drawers in place with strips of wide masking tape. To minimize tape marks, remove the tape as soon as the furniture arrives at your new home.

• Plates are less likely to break if they are packed standing on edge. To minimize breakage of glass items, place the heavier ones on the bottom and the more delicate ones on top. Excelsior or pieces of crumpled newspaper make good packing material. If you have several days to pack before moving, dampen the excelsior so it will shape itself to the china and glassware.

• Get rugs and slipcovers cleaned before you move. They'll come back wrapped and ready to go.

• Small linens such as towels, washcloths, and pillowcases can also serve as packing material for dishes and glassware—and they don't waste space.

• If you pack books so their spines are alternated, they will take up less space. (It may be cheaper to ship books via the United States mail, since the post office offers an inexpensive, fourth-class book rate).

• Number each box for your own inventory list. Have someone in the family check each item as it is loaded onto the truck and again when it is unloaded.

• Make one box for the bedroom (with bed linens, favorite stuffed toys), one for the bathroom (soap and toilet paper, along with medicine cabinet items), one for the kitchen (including detergent for that load you may want to do right away, paper plates, coffeepot), and one with tools. Boxes from the liquor store with dividers are ideal for this purpose since you can pack kitchen tools, workshop tools, and medicine cabinet items in separate compartments where everything is within easy reach. You can use the divider boxes as temporary storage units for days, if necessary.

• Bring a supply of light bulbs.

• Don't bother to pack your hanging clothes. Just put a twist tie around hangers of like items and slip a garbage bag over the top. You can just carry them inside and hang them right in the closet.

• If you're removing shelves, photos, etc., from a wall, use duct or masking tape to tape all the screws (and small bits of hardware) to the item to which they belong.

• Finally, if you move often, it helps to have certain things always in the same place. For example, bills are always put in a particular secretary, the drawer next to the silverware drawer is always the junk drawer, etc.

• As you tape up each packed box, place a piece of kite string underneath the tape, leaving about an inch sticking out. When it's time to unpack, just pull on the string, which will slit right through the tape.

• Take Avery or Dennison colored dots and color code the rooms to your new home:

    Kitchen—green
    Living room—blue
    Master bedroom—red
    Garage—orange

Stick the proper colored dot on the box you are packing. As you get to your new home, you can stick corresponding colored paper in the various areas of the home. The mover doesn't have to keep asking, "Where does this box go?" It saves a lot of time in giving directions.

Moving-Day Countdown

Two to Four Weeks Ahead

☐ *Visit your neighborhood moving company and reserve a moving van.*

☐ *Reserve a utility dolly, piano dolly, furniture pads.*

☐ *Purchase packing supplies.*

☐ *Sell or donate unwanted items. Try a garage sale.*

☐ *Send change-of-address cards to magazines, charge accounts, friends, and relatives. The cards are free at the post office.*

☐ *Collect medical and dental records, eye prescriptions, and pet records.*

☐ *Get copies of school records.*

☐ *Settle all local tax bills.*

☐ *Make arrangements for shipment of pets.*

☐ *Start packing boxes as soon as possible.*

One to Two Weeks Ahead

☐ *Have clothing dry-cleaned. Check on items in repair shops.*

☐ *Close and transfer bank accounts and safe-deposit boxes.*

☐ *Notify utilities and telephone companies at both old and new addresses. Set a date for disconnection and hookup.*

☐ *Return borrowed items and pick up things you have lent.*

Planning a Move

• When notifying people about your move, be sure to include utilities, post office, Social Security, publications to which you subscribe, doctors, insurance companies, and the phone company. If you also go through your address book, you'll be less likely to overlook someone who will want to know you're moving.

• To save time and eliminate confusion when the movers arrive, draw a floor plan of your new home ahead of time.

Two to Seven Days Ahead

☐ *Discard all flammable items such as paint and gasoline.*
☐ *Inspect and service your car.*
☐ *Line up a baby-sitter for moving day.*
☐ *Finish packing. Leave out items for moving day.*
☐ *Buy travelers checks.*
☐ *Empty and defrost refrigerator and freezer.*

One Day Ahead

☐ *Clean range.*
☐ *Pick up moving van in the afternoon to get a head start on loading the following morning if you are moving yourself.*
☐ *Pick up ice and beverages for moving day.*

Moving Day

☐ *Leave young children with a baby-sitter. The older children can help you load up.*
☐ *Turn off water and lights. Lock windows and doors.*
☐ *Be sure to pick up the children from the babysitter before you leave town.*

Sketch in and number your furnishings the way you want them arranged. Tag furniture pieces to correspond to the floor plan so the movers know where to put each piece.

• Moving will go more smoothly if you make a master checklist of everything that must be done in connection with the move. So that you don't fall behind, schedule a deadline for each task.

• For insurance purposes, take photographs of all your possessions and keep them in a metal box or in a safe-deposit box. Then, if any are lost, stolen, or destroyed, you will have proof of having had them.

• Another method of taking inventory is to have someone videotape you while you walk through your house describing and pricing (as best you can) your belongings.

• Under Interstate Commerce Commission (ICC) regulations, all moving companies are required to assume some liability for the value of your goods. Generally, this liability amounts to $1.25 per pound (multiplied by the weight of your shipment). If you want more comprehensive coverage, you have to pay for it. Be sure you understand what extra insurance covers and what deductibles you may face. We had a nicked table and a broken-leg chair, but although we had bought additional insurance, it didn't compensate us for those particular damages.

— For further information and a copy of the ICC regulations on moving, you should contact the Office of Compliance and Consumer Assistance of the ICC. The address is: Room 4133, Interstate Commerce Commission Bldg., 12th St. and Constitution Ave., NW, Washington, DC 20423, (202) 927-5520.

• Since rates are based primarily on weight and distance, now's the time to get rid of big or heavy furniture of dubious value. Do you really want to move that soiled couch from Seattle to Jacksonville? Old furniture looks particularly dirty in a new home, and replacing it may be almost as cheap as moving it.

• Check if your homeowner's property insurance covers items while they are being moved. It probably does not, so take the mover's coverage. The best value is probably the coverage that pays the cost of replacing a damaged or lost item after a one-time deductible of at least $250.

• When contracting with a moving company find out if charges are different for weekday and weekend moves. Ask if they charge overtime rates, and at what hour overtime begins. It may be better to schedule two days to move instead of one with overtime.

• Instead of putting all of your nuts and bolts in one basket, box, or jar when furniture is disassembled, gather all screws, bolts, and brackets for a piece of furniture in a sturdy envelope or bag and tape it securely to the underside of that particular bookcase, desk, etc. Or securely tape the hardware to the underside of furniture with duct tape so that it's ready when you reassemble the furniture at your destination.

Preparing for the Move

• Fill out one post office change of address card, then bring a package of 4" x 6" blank unlined index cards or postcards to the local quick copy shop and have them make duplicates. The small charge is made up for by savings in time and energy. Don't forget to send one to all the magazines to which you have subscriptions and to let your insurance companies know about your move.

• Contact the phone company in the city to which you are moving to get a phone book. Then you can call utility and cable companies to find out what information and fees are necessary to get hooked up in your new location and to set the wheels rolling for faster service. You can look up service people to install appliances and find the name of the local newspaper. Ordering a subscription to the Sunday paper lets you get acquainted with stores, politics, and other facts before you get to the new city. You can check out the chain department stores and know which credit cards will be useful and which to cancel.

— Take your old phone book with you when you move, just in case you leave a few loose ends to tie up. And you'll have your neighbors' street address numbers, too, when you want to send them a Christmas card!

— And if you can get in touch with the new school, see if you can make arrangements for a pen pal for your children in their new community.

• Make a list of items in your refrigerator a few weeks before you leave and use that as a master list for restocking

---

Household Check-Off List

There are so many things to remember before moving time, and it seems like some of them are always forgotten until it's too late. Here's a list to help you remember these necessary details at the right time.

Transfer

- *School records*
- *Automobile and driver's licenses*
- *Bank and savings and loan records*
- *Doctor and dentist records*
- *Eyeglass prescriptions*
- *Pet immunization records*
- *Legal records*
- *Church and fraternal organization records*

Services to Be Discontinued

- *Telephone company (deposit refund?)*
- *Electric power company (refund?)*
- *Water department (refund?)*
- *Gas company (refund?)*
- *Layaway purchases*
- *Home fuel oil company (measure remaining oil)*
- *Milkman*
- *Newspapers*
- *Laundry and dry-cleaning service*
- *Cable TV*
- *Pest control*
- *Water softener company*
- *Garbage collection*
- *Diaper service*

---

in your new home. Put the master grocery list, a list of emergency phone numbers, and any other special lists on a clipboard that's hard to lose.

• *One odd piece of information:* It's illegal for professional movers to transport plants without an inspection sticker

---

Change-of-Address Cards to Send
- *Local post office branch*
- *Magazines*
- *Friends and relatives*
- *Insurance companies*
- *Creditors (charge accounts or credit cards)*
- *Lawyer*

Don't move what you won't need. *Get rid of excess items by running an ad in the local papers or hold a neighborhood garage sale. Consider Goodwill and the Salvation Army.*

Expenses may be tax deductible. *When you donate goods to these charities, ask for signed receipts. You can deduct the new value from your taxes!*

---

from the Department of Agriculture. Call your county agricultural extension agent beforehand and arrange for an inspection a day before you move.

• Don't have the water and lights turned off until the day after you've moved. At the same time, make sure to notify new utility companies to turn water and lights on in your new home.

• If you have assembled any arrangement of photos or pictures on the walls that you're especially fond of, photograph it so you won't have to go through the bother of working it out all over again.

• Allow at least two weeks to pack so you don't have to rush at the last minute. Stress increases your chances of making serious mistakes.

• Write to the Chamber of Commerce to find out about special events and happenings. Some chambers of commerce offer newcomer welcome packets or visitor information packets that are useful to "permanent visitors," too.

• If a family move is coming up, hold a good-bye party and let your children invite all their special friends. Exchange small remembrance gifts and addresses and telephone numbers to assure your children that they will not be completely cut off from old friends.

Moving In

• If you have access to the new home a day or so before the van arrives, you could set off a bug bomb or spray. (Even if you don't see bugs, there probably are some.) This way, you won't worry about the family, your pets, foods, or furnishings during the spraying.

• If you're going to arrive before the movers, consider bringing a book, radio, or portable television with you.

• If you drive to your new location and arrive late, spend the first night at a motel rather than trying to settle in when everyone's tired. Everything will be much more fun in the morning.

• Take a survival package along with the family so you can camp in your new home until the moving van arrives. Include instant coffee, cups, spoons, soap and towels, a can and bottle opener, some light bulbs, a flashlight, toilet paper, cleansing powder, and a first-aid kit. Also be sure that daily medications travel with you, not with the movers.

• Protect carpets from dirt with plastic drop cloths which you can save for later use in the garden or for painting. Protect varnished or new flooring from scratches with old flannel-backed plastic tablecloths, bedspreads, and rugs. *Caution:* Be sure that the floor protection is nonskid.

17

Our
Wardrobe

It requires training
through life-style
and faithful
instruction as we:
. . . sit at home
. . . walk along the road
. . . lie down
. . .get up

*N*o one claimed that any of his possessions was his own, but they shared everything they had.

—Acts 4:32.

Our
Wardrobe

$\mathcal{I}$s your closet a disaster that gives you the feeling of stress and confusion? Take heart. Here's a sensible, easy way to clean it out and put every inch of space to good use. Let's get into our closet and get organized. Let's weed out some of those things we don't need and get our closets in order.

A well-put-together closet makes you more organized and your life just a little bit easier.

Taking Inventory

Now let's start taking inventory. (You can use the Wardrobe Inventory sheet printed on page 321.) As you begin to take your inventory, you'll quickly begin to see what you have and need. For example, you may have way too many pairs of navy-blue pants. You only need one pair of good navy-blue pants and maybe a couple pairs of nice jeans. You can begin to see where you've made your mistakes as you take your wardrobe inventory, and you'll be able to start correcting those mistakes.

Getting Started

How do we get started? We get three trash bags and label

them "Put Away," "Give Away," and "Throw Away." As we walk into each closet, we take everything out. (See the "Total Mess to Total Rest" chapter in my books *More Hours in My Day* and *Survival for Busy Women*.)

As you pull those things out of your closet, keep in mind that if you haven't worn it for the past year it goes in one of those three bags. Either you're going to put it away somewhere else, or you're going to give it away to somebody else, or you're going to throw it away. If you haven't worn it for two or three years, you'll definitely have to give it away or throw it away.

Step 1: Sort clothes into three piles. Hold each item up and ask yourself three questions. Be honest. 1. "Do I love it and wear it?" 2. "Do I feel good in it?" You seldom wear clothes you don't feel good in. You hang on to them because they remind you of the past or because you *may* wear them in the future. Everyone does this. 3. "Am I willing to recycle this?" These are clothes you never wear.

Step 2: Remove the recycle pile. 1. Take the clothes to a used-clothing store and earn some extra money. 2. Give the clothes to a charity, thrift store, Salvation Army, etc. (getting a receipt will give you a tax deduction). 3. Give the clothes to friends or needy families.

Step 3: Create an ambivalence center. Put the clothes you can't decide about out of the way in storage boxes in an attic, basement, garage, or storage closet. You may decide later to recycle these clothes after all, but for now it may be too emotional a decision.

Step 4: You have now only the "I love to wear" pile to deal with. But why put your clothes back in the same old closet? It may be part of the reason your wardrobe seems to get so disorganized. Let's think about this.

The average closet consists of one long pole beneath one long shelf. The old-fashioned single-pole system wastes usable space. Far more efficient is a system with at least three

WARDROBE
Inventory

BLOUSES	PANTS	SKIRTS

JACKETS	SWEATERS	DRESSES

GOWNS	LINGERIE	SHOES

JEWELRY	NEVER WORN	THINGS I NEED

poles and several shelves. By placing poles at different heights, you increase the number of items you can hang in a given area. In a his-and-her closet, this technique can quadruple space. By discarding the one pole, you free space for more shelves. Use these shelves for foldable clothes (enough shelves can eliminate your need for a dresser). By keeping shoes off the floor, you'll eliminate jumbled, dusty shoes. Hats and purses go on shelves to make your closet workable and pleasant (see pages 305 and 306 for suggested diagrams).

You may want to add a light if there is none. If you have the option, avoid sliding doors. It's best to be able to see all your clothes at once. The floor may need a new look. Try inexpensive self-stick vinyl tiles or carpet remnants. Pretty up your closet with wallpaper, wallpaper borders, paint, posters, or eyelet lace glued on the edge of your shelves. Your new closet will save you both time and money. You'll know exactly where to find things and, better yet, where to put them back. It will be easier to mix and match outfits when you know what you have and can see everything clearly. You'll be able to expand your wardrobe using what you already own. Now you will enjoy your organized closet.

One of the reasons most closets are a mess is because people forget about closet organizers. Buy them in notions departments, hardware or dime stores, or use your imagination. These ideas will get you started:

— Mug racks. Good for jewelry, scarves, small purses. Hang vertically or horizontally on closet wall or door.
— Shoebags. Not just for shoes! Use for storing scarves, gloves, stockings. . .anything.
— Hanging baskets. A decorative way to store socks and small, light items.

Storing Extra Clothes

Be sure to number your storage boxes. If you're using file

Hats

Her Tops

His shirts

Their long
Clothes

Her skirts,
pants

His Pants

shoe shelf

shoe shelf

Fighting Mildew

To prevent mildew from forming on stored clothes:
- *Don't put garments away if they're still damp; let them air-dry or iron them at the highest temperature safe for the fabric.*
- *Avoid storing clothes in plastic bags or boxes, which can trap moisture.*
- *Ventilate storage areas when the weather is dry and cool.*
- *Pack storage areas loosely so that air can circulate around clothes.*
- *Don't use starch or fabric finish on items to be stored.*
- *When storing clothes, use a chemical desiccant such as silica gel or calcium chloride, but don't let it touch garments.*
- *Place paradichlorobenzene mothballs or crystals inside closets and drawers. They prevent mildew and absorb moisture.*

cards, number each card to correspond with the number of the box holding your extra clothing. Then list on the card what you have in the box.
- Get boxes with lids and number each box.
- Assign each box a 3" x 5" card with a corresponding number. For example:

Box 1:   Jenny's summer shorts, T-shirts, skirts, sandals
Box 2:   Costume clothing: 1950s outfit, black-and-white saddle shoes, purple angora sweater with holes, high school cheerleader's outfit
Box 3:   Ski clothes, socks, underwear, sweaters, pants
Box 4:   Scarves, belts, jewelry, honeymoon peignoir, etc

Use Your Wardrobe Inventory Sheet

a. Return items to your closet and list them on your

Wardrobe Inventory sheet.
b. Suggested order for your clothes:
   1) Extra hangers
   2) Blouses
   3) Pants
   4) Skirts
   5) Blazers and jackets
   6) Sweaters (these can also be folded and
      put on a shelf or in a drawer)
   7) Dresses
   8) Gowns
c. For each item, put all similar colors together
   (example: light to dark).
d. Coats and heavy jackets can be kept in a hall closet
   or in an extra wardrobe closet.
e. Shoes:
   1. Shoe racks—floor type or hanging
   2. Covered shoe boxes can be put on shelf or
      neatly stacked on the floor.
f. Handbags:
   1. Smaller ones in clear plastic boxes
   2. Larger ones on a shelf above the wardrobe
   3. A hanging plastic shoe bag is also great for your
      handbags. It can be purchased in the notions
      section at any department store.
g. Belts and ties:
   1. Belt rack applied to wall with screws
   2. Hooks are great and easy to use.

The Basics

I don't have time to shop very often, so I need to take
especially good care of my clothing so it will look new and
fresh for several years. Here are some fun ideas and tips to
do just that:
• First of all, I start with three basic items in a solid color:

1. A blazer or jacket
2. A skirt
3. Pants
• To these three basics I then add blouses in prints or solid colors that will coordinate. Next I add a few sweaters and several accessories such as scarves, ribbon ties, boots, jewelry, and perhaps a silk flower. Finally I purchase two pairs of shoes, one for casual wear and one pair for dress (the church type).
• If you do a great deal of traveling, take these six to nine items and a few accessories (plus one all-weather coat) and coordinate them into approximately 12 to 16 outfits that will last 7 to 14 days.
• Pale neutral colors travel the best to the most places. Include off-white, pale gray, beige, caramel, and tan in your wardrobe. They're nondescript colors. Add variety with texture or bright accessories.

Everything in Its Place

• Hang your clothes up as you put them back into your closet. Each piece should have a definite place. For example, all the extra hangers can go at the left end of your closet. Then arrange all your blouses according to color, then your pants, then your skirts, etc. If you have a jacket that matches your pants, separate them (hang the jacket with the jackets and the pants with the pants). This way you can mix or match your clothes and not always wear the same jacket and pants together.
• Your shoes can go on shoe racks. Some neat different kinds of shoe racks are now available, or you can cover shoeboxes with wallpaper or Christmas paper. (Your children can help you do this.)
• Your smaller handbags can go in clear plastic boxes. The larger ones can go up on the shelf above your wardrobe. A hanging plastic shoe bag is great because you can also put

your purses and scarves in it. Belts and ties should go on hooks. Ribbons can be hung on these hooks, too. Or you can just hammer a big nail into the wall. You'd be surprised at how many belts you can get on a nail!

Give Away

• Be sure you give away whatever you're not using. Many people today have limited finances and can't afford some things. If you have clothes that you aren't wearing, give them to someone who will be able to use them. They'll be grateful to you, and you'll feel good about your giving.
• Clothing can be given to friends or family.
• Clothing can also be given to thrift shops, Goodwill-type stores, rummage sales, churches, or missionaries.
• You may want to have a garage sale with friends or a clothes sale.

Throw Away

• Put these items in a trash bag with a twistie on it and set out with the garbage. Use black bags so other members of your family can't see in and try to reclaim items for more clutter to the home.

Wisdom enables one to be thrifty without being stingy, and generous without being wasteful.

Other Wardrobe Hints

• Indisputably, cedar smells better than mothballs. What is debatable is the common notion that the aromatic wood protects clothing stored in cedar-lined closets and chests from snack-hungry moths. The secret to protecting belongings from moth damage is to have the clothes thoroughly cleaned before putting them away for the season in an air-tight unit. Cleaning before storage will destroy any eggs or larvae that could otherwise develop and damage clothing. To restore the fresh scent of cedar, buff the wood lightly with fine sandpaper.

• When I find a photo or illustration of a new use for an old scarf, I cut the picture out and tape it on my closet door. That way I don't forget updated styles.

• Slenderizing fabrics are those that are medium in weight and texture. Patterns on fabrics should be medium in size or in proportion to your height.

• Women with shorter haircuts need softer lines, softer colors, or ruffles rather than man-tailored looks. Use pastels to your best advantage.

• If dark tones makes you feel drab, but you wear them frequently to look slim, wear another flattering color close to your face (a brightly colored blouse under a dark jacket or sweater, or a pretty scarf at the neck can really make a difference).

• *For women who carry a briefcase:* Get a small handbag that fits inside. Don't let too many bags or oversized bags overpower you.

• If you have little occasion to wear a "good" dress or formal outfit, keep the color discreet. Distinctive colors and bold prints are a bit too memorable. A simple outfit or dress lends itself to more creative accessorizing.

• If you have a hard time remembering your family clothing sizes when you go shopping, record them in your organizer notebook. You can also include any fabric swatches from articles you want to coordinate.

• When you shop for clothing, wear the following: garments that are easy to remove; the same type of shoes and undergarments you intend to wear with your new item; a minimum of makeup and jewelry.

• To find the best values, do your shopping at a variety of

How to Get the Best Buys

- Shop early in the day, before crowds have had a chance to pick through the merchandise.

- Make friends with a salesperson who will give you inside information on new shipments, special merchandise, and clearance sales.

- To get the best selection, find out when a shipment is due. Give the store a few hours to get the clothes unpacked and on the racks.

- Some stores are constantly receiving new merchandise, so check back every week or so.

- To make room for new arrivals, many stores "age" merchandise with weekly markdowns of up to 30 percent. Look for tags with multiple reductions for the best buys.

- Check out special clearance racks, where prices may be slashed up to 90 percent. In May you will find big end-of-season clearances on spring merchandise; in August, you will find great summer markdowns.

- To get advance notice, add your name to the store's mailing list and check newspaper ads.

- Compare prices among off-price stores. One may have better buys on swim wear, another on suits or dresses.

- Check for quality fabrics and durable construction, especially for work and school clothes. Crush fabrics and and pull at seams to see how the clothes hold up.

- Irregulars and seconds are not always clearly marked. Check carefully for ripped seams, snags and pulls, broken zippers, missing buttons. A decent discount may make up for certain minor repairs you can do yourself.

places: factory outlets, department stores, thrift shops, mail-order houses, and garage sales.

• If you think a pair of shoes are ruined, check with your shoe repairman before you get rid of them. Repairmen can often work magic. Our dog chewed on Bob's $125 leather shoes. Our shoe repairman made them look like new for under ten dollars.

• Before wearing new leather boots, it is advisable to apply two coats of clear paste wax to protect the leather.

• An easy way to store off-season clothes is to use your empty luggage. Just add a bar of soap so the clothes won't have a musty smell. Store your luggage in a dry area.

• Don't shop when you are depressed. You may buy something thinking the purchase will pep you up. But you may be sorry later for the choice you made.

• Keep your weekend clothes separate.

• Save store receipts, especially if you pay cash. This will save time later should you need to return an item. I tape my new shoe receipts on the inside lid of my shoe boxes.

• Items marked "irregular" may not be perfect in size or color but are free of substantial damage. However, those marked "seconds" or "thirds" often have serious flaws.

• When shopping for clothes, keep in mind that some synthetic fibers, such as those used in sportswear, are as cool as natural fibers.

She selects wool and flax and works with eager hands—Proverbs 31:13 (NIV).

• You can machine wash down-filled vests and jackets using a mild detergent and a gentle setting.

• To prevent dampness in a closet, fill a coffee can with charcoal briquettes. Punch holes in the cover and place the container on the floor. For larger closets, use two or three one-pound coffee cans.

• When you remove your dress, turn it inside out and hang it carefully over a chair or at the end of your bed. This helps rid it of perspiration and body odors.

• Keep good panty hose rolled and in the original envelope, or in a sandwich-size plastic bag. Ones with runs (to be worn under pants), fold double lengthwise and knot in the middle. Sure saves time when you're in a hurry to dress.

• To stop static cling, simply run a wire coat hanger between your slip and dress. This draws out the cling.

• To remove spots from suede, use an art gum eraser.

• After wearing leather shoes, let them air out overnight before placing them in a shoe box and storing on the shelf. To maximize the use of your shoes, you need to rotate two or three pairs.

• To remove lint from clothing, use a damp sponge or a clothes brush.

• Some garments should be folded and stored flat rather than hung up. Generally, the looser, softer, or finer the fabric, the more likely it will benefit from flat storage.

• To keep closets smelling fresh, try the following: Clean clothes before putting them away. Leave the door slightly ajar to allow air to circulate. Put a box of baking soda in the closet to absorb odors. Add a sweet-smelling sachet in the closet.

• To reduce dampness in closets, wrap 12 pieces of chalk together and hang them up.

• To prevent a garment made of very thin fabric from creasing, stuff it loosely with tissue paper before folding it for storage.

• If your slacks are damp from the rain, hang them up by the cuffs or lower hem.

• To protect garments from snags and possible acid damage from wood, line your dresser drawers with quilted fabric or good-quality shelf paper that is ungummed. (Gummed paper attracts insects and is hard to remove.)

• As a safety precaution, make sure that closets can be opened from the inside.

• Consider professional cold storage if you have any of the following: furs or fur-trimmed clothes; a climate that is very hot or humid; inadequate storage space; chronic problems with carpet beetles, silverfish, moths, or mildew.

• Don't dry-clean one piece of an outfit and wash the other, or clean one piece and not the other. The colors may lose their match.

• Use hair clips to keep pleats in skirts. The pleats hold beautifully when the garments are packed in bags for travel.

• Roll the family's T-shirts, socks, shorts, and panties, and put into their drawers. Family members can easily see what they need and find the right color in just one glance.

• At today's cost, it's well worth it to take care of your shoes, using professional products often to protect them.

• Consider using a coin-operated dry-cleaning machine if clothes are sturdy, not heavily soiled, and require little pressing. This is an economical way to ready clothes for long-term storage.

• Dry-clean a garment as soon as possible after it becomes stained. The longer a stain remains, the more difficult it is to remove. If you can, identify the source of the stain to the dry cleaner. It will help him select the best cleaning method.

• When you bring clothing home from the dry cleaner, remove the plastic bag so that the fabric can breathe. If you have small children, tie the bag in several places before throwing it away to prevent accidental suffocation.

• Don't buy shoes strictly by size. Walk around in them for several minutes before making a final decision. Shoe sizes can vary, depending on the style and manufacturer, and your feet can swell up to a half size larger if you've been walking a lot.

• Resist the temptation to wear your new shoes until you have polished them first with a stain-repellent product or plain shoe polish to protect them. (These products tend to darken leather shoe color.)

• Don't slip and slide in your new shoes. Before wearing them, sandpaper the soles or rub them across a rough sidewalk.

• Make your own boot trees. Tie two or three paper towel cylinders together, or use large soda bottles or even rolled-up newspaper.

• Shoes a bit tight? To temporarily solve the problem, saturate a cotton ball with rubbing alcohol and rub it inside the shoes at the tight spot. Then put your shoes on and walk around for a while.

• A more permanent way to solve the problem of tight shoes is to rub alcohol on their insides and put them on shoe stretchers (shoe trees will do in a pinch) for at least two days.

• Shoelaces constantly coming undone? Dampen them before you tie them.

• Typewriter correction fluid makes a great cover-up for scuff marks on white shoes; try a bit of India ink on black shoes.

• Remove light scuff marks with an art gum eraser.

• To remove salt stains from shoes and winter boots, wipe them with a solution of one cup water and one tablespoon vinegar.

• To cover ugly scuff marks, use a matching color in acrylic paint, indelible felt marker, or crayon.

• Spray a fabric protector or starch over new canvas shoes to keep them looking clean.

• Help your canvas tennis shoes keep their shape and wear longer. After washing and drying, stuff them with paper towels, cover with liquid starch, and let dry.

• Clean cloth sneakers quickly with spray-on carpet cleaner. Scrub with a toothbrush, let dry, then brush with a dry brush.

• To steam-clean suede shoes, hold them over a pan of boiling water. Once the steam raises the nap, stroke the suede with a soft brush in one direction only. Allow shoes to dry before wearing them.

• Recycle your old flannel shirts and nightgowns, socks, or

What to Dry-Clean

In general, dry-clean an item if it is:
- *Labeled "dry-clean only."*
- *Soiled with difficult or large stains.*
- *Tailored (for example, a lined jacket or beaded evening gown).*
- *Constructed with two or more fabrics.*
- *Made of sheer or delicate fabrics or trim.*
- *Composed of fabrics with crimped or bouclé yarns.*
- *Unlabeled, but seems to contain wool.*

---

terrycloth towels into first-rate shoe buffers.

• For a speedy clean and shine on patent leather, rub a minute amount of petroleum jelly over your shoes. Then buff them. Or use a spray-on glass cleaner.

• To remove tar and grease stains from white shoes, try a little nail polish remover.

• If shoe polish has hardened, soften it by heating the metal container in a bowl of hot water.

• For a quick shine, rub a dab of hand cream over your shoes and then buff them.

• Avoid messy shoe-polish stains when cleaning sandals; slip the hand holding the sandal into a small plastic bag.

• Give your wooden shoe heels a high shine with an application of lemon oil or furniture wax.

• To maintain the shape of your leather bags, stuff them with tissue or plastic bags. Then, to keep them from sticking together when you store them, place each in a flannel bag or pillowcase.

• Learn to recognize brand names so you will know what kind of quality you're getting. Also note labels that consistently have the look and fit that is best for your figure.

• If you can't find the right size, check the racks with

clothes two sizes larger and smaller than the one you're looking for. Shoppers often stick clothes back in the wrong place.

• Don't buy something just because it's a bargain. Make sure you need it and be certain it looks good on you. A $20 dress may sound like a good deal, but if you don't love it, you probably won't wear it and you'll wind up wasting your money. If you realize you've made a mistake, take it back.

• If you're looking for something specific, a department store is your best bet. You never know what off-price stores will have in stock at any given time.

• Decide what departments you want to cover and go through all the racks before you start trying clothes on.

• If you're shopping with your husband, he can start trying on clothes while you finish looking through the racks closest to the men's dressing room. You save time and stay close enough to help make a decision on style or fit.

• *A surefire way to match something you already own:* Take a clipping from an inside seam. Then when faced with five blouses in five shades of blue, you can make a critical choice and avoid a return trip.

• Examine collars and cuffs for stains. Lipstick and other makeup can be removed, but heavy soil and pen marks mean you should probably pass. Look for fading or discoloration around the shoulders—a definite no-no.

• Minor alterations are definitely worth the time and expense. With what you've saved, you can afford to have them done and still come out ahead. Consider moving the buttons, taking in a waist or back seam, or raising a hem to get a custom-tailored fit.

• When you're looking for simple pullover sweaters, don't ignore discount men's clothing stores. The prices are often lower than for women's clothing and the quality is just as high.

• Sometimes you won't notice a flaw until you try a

garment on again at home. Always keep the register receipt so you will be able to return the garment.

• Always check the care labels. If they say "dry-clean only," you can end up spending more than you saved. Kids' clothes should always be wash and wear.

18
Safety

The low-down
on safety!

So do not fear, for I am with you; do not be dismayed, for I am your God. I will strengthen you and help you; I will uphold you with my righteous right hand.

—Isaiah 41:10

Safety

*I*t was early December and we were decorating our mantel for Christmas. We had just placed our handsome wooden goose, which weighs about 25 pounds, on our sturdy wood mantel. Who would have expected he could jump off and land on my right foot! The goose was repaired in a few minutes. We put a bow around his neck and placed him back in his spot. My foot? Well, it took a little longer to fix—six weeks in a cast and six months before it was fully healed.

The moral of the story: Don't tangle with a wooden goose! Even when we take precautions, accidents can happen. The National Safety Council estimates there is a home accident every seven seconds. Many of them can be avoided.

A house is made of walls and beams;
a home is built with love and dreams.

Kitchen

• Keep knives in knife holders on a wall or in a high drawer.

323

• Place knives with their points down in the dishwasher.
• Never leave a cord plugged into a socket when the other end is exposed. That's an open invitation for a baby to place the cord in his mouth.
• When cooking on a stove top, keep handles facing the back of the stove. Children can easily dump boiling water or hot food on themselves by pulling an exposed handle or swinging a toy overhead. (Incidentally, the best way I've found to treat minor burns is to run cold water over them. Blisters don't usually appear.)
• Always wrap broken glass in paper or place it in an old paper sack before throwing it in the trash. This is also a good rule for razor blades and the lids from metal cans. It protects a child who might inadvertently drop a toy in the trash and try to retrieve it—or the explorer who can't just dump the trash but has to check out every item in the process.
• When cleaning broken glass in the sink or off the floor, dampen a paper towel and it will wipe up all those little pieces of glass. It protects the hands, too.
• Teach children to pour hot water slowly, aiming the stream away from themselves. Be sure to check the lid of a teapot or kettle to make sure it fits tightly and won't fall into the cup and splash boiling water.
• Any poisonous or extremely hazardous products should be kept in a locked cabinet or on a very high shelf.
• Don't store products in unlabeled jars or cans. It's too easy to forget what's inside.
• Never touch an electric appliance or plug with wet hands. Warn your children of this hazard.
• Burn yourself? Apply raw egg white to the burn—this gives quick relief and helps the healing process.
• All medicines in your home are potential poisons and should be kept away from children.
• Keep a coffee can full of baking soda near your stove in case of a grease fire.

Kitchen Fire Procedures

Copy these cautions and put them where you can find them in a hurry.

No Water on an Electrical Fire

Water may spread flames or cause shock. Use a fire extinguisher.

No Water, Flour, or Cornstarch on a Grease Fire.

Use a fire extinguisher, or toss on baking soda or salt. (The baking soda releases carbon dioxide. Salt smothers the fire.)

If the Steak's on Fire

Turn off the flame, pull out the tray, and throw a damp cloth on the meat. If you don't tell the family, you may be able to get away with serving the steak as usual.

Fire in a Pot

Put a lid, another pot, or even a plate on top. That smothers it.

Fire in a Wastebasket

Water is okay to use. The fire is probably from a match.

If the fire is escalating, call the fire department.

• Dispose of smoking materials carefully (not in wastebaskets), and keep large, safe ashtrays wherever people smoke.
• Don't cook over an open flame wearing long sleeves or a flowing nightgown or robe.
• Fill self-sealing plastic bags with water and stick them in the freezer as quick ice packs for aches or bruises. Before applying, pop them in a hand puppet washcloth or wrap in a towel.
• For injured lips and tongues, try sucking on Popsicles! They not only taste good, but also reduce swelling and soothe pain.

• Keep a plastic container filled with basic first-aid supplies like cotton balls, adhesive tape, bandages, sharp scissors, sterile gauze, antiseptic, and tweezers. Keep this handy to take outside or on a picnic.

• Use only dry pot holders. A damp pot holder transmits heat. Also, avoid using dish towels. They're not thick enough to protect you.

• Keep electrical cords and appliances away from the sink and stove.

• If you smell gas, open the doors and windows. Go to a neighbor's house and call the gas company or fire department immediately.

Bathroom

• *Never, absolutely never leave children unattended in the bathtub—not even for a moment.* A lifeguard needs to be on duty at all times. There are too many hazards the youngster faces. If the doorbell or phone rings, take the child with you—or don't answer it.

• Check water temperature before putting children in the tub or shower. It might have started out warm but gotten hotter by someone inadvertently brushing the knob.

• Never allow children to fiddle with the faucets. Scalds happen very quickly.

• Rubber mats can become slippery and are not always skidproof. Once a week turn your mat over and clean it with cleanser, scrubbing off the film. Rinse well.

• Never add hot water to the bathtub with baby in it. Make sure the hot water faucet is turned off tightly. Wrap a washcloth around the faucet for safety when a baby or young child is in the tub.

• Teach every family member that the shower valve is always turned *off* when finished. Otherwise a bather or person cleaning the bathtub risks getting scalding water on the head (not to mention the possibility of Mom ruining her hairdo).

Water Safety

- Swim only in areas supervised by a lifeguard. Unsupervised, unfamiliar areas are likely to be dangerous.
- Wait 20 minutes between eating a normal amount of food and swimming. Remember, the bigger the meal, the longer you should wait. Eating a light snack prior to swimming is safe.
- Never drink alcohol before swimming or engaging in any water sports.
- Dive only in designated areas, never into shallow or unknown waters.
- At the ocean, be cautious of step-offs (holes in the sand that create a sudden drop from shallow to deep water).
- If you have a home pool, be sure to keep doors locked so children can't get near the pool area.
- Make sure that there is adequate supervision before a child is allowed in the swimming area.
- All swimmers must obey the basic rules of the pool—no running, no diving, no shoving, no pushing, no pulling people under the water, etc.
- Send your children to swimming lessons as early as you can.

• When small children are running around the house, keep bathroom doors closed at all times. A latch placed above the knob will eliminate a major source of accidents.

• Be careful of bathroom doors that lock from the inside. Be sure you have an emergency key and know where to find it should Junior lock himself in.

• Door gates are also a good way to close off a bathroom, as well as other rooms and stairs. These gates can be purchased at most stores that have baby departments. Often you can find them at garage sales or through the classified ad section of your newspaper.

• Install plastic cabinet door, cabinet drawer, and toilet seat stops in the bath areas. They can be picked up at most hardware stores and are very simple to install.

• Don't call medicine "candy." Your youngster might like it so much he will take it on his own when you aren't looking. This can result in severe illness or even death.

• Keep a round rubber gripper (designed to open jars) close at hand to use when grabbing the rod to pull yourself out of the bathtub. It keeps your hands from slipping, possibly preventing an accident.

• Childproof the slippery edge of the bathtub by placing a bathmat with suction cups over the side.

• If you must have a lock on the bathroom door, install a doorknob with an outside lock release. This will prevent children from getting locked inside accidentally.

• Prevent bathroom falls by laying scatter rugs with nonskid backing.

• Grab bars in the bathtub or shower and next to the toilet are a help for all and a must for the elderly.

• Avoid using electric appliances, such as space heaters, radios, and hair dryers near water.

• All bathroom outlets should be equipped with GFIs (ground fault interrupters).

Bedroom

• Keep bulb wattage to that recommended on the lamp light fixtures. If not known, limit to 60 watts.

• Keep electric blankets smooth and flat. Don't tuck them in under the mattress. Don't place them on baby or anyone who can't tell you that the blanket is too hot.

• Have the lamp and phone accessible from your bed.

• Make sure all the paint in your house is lead-free.

• Keep windows and screens locked or install window guards if you have young children.

• Place a "child alert" decal on your children's windows

for the fire department.
• Put side rails on small children's beds to keep the children from falling out.

Living Room

• Make sure your extension cords aren't overloaded.
• Install cover plates on all outlets and switches. Call an electrician if any outlet or plate is warm to the touch.
• Shield the fireplace with a screen or heat-tempered glass doors. Keep the area clear of newspapers. Keep the chimney clean, and check it often with a flashlight for cracks.
• Leave airspace around the TV and stereo to prevent overheating.
• Keep fire, police, and poison control phone numbers near the phone.
• Don't run electrical cords under rugs or furniture or in traffic areas. Replace frayed, cracked, or pinched cords.
• Tack down carpets; back rugs with a slip-resistant coating or pads. Use nonslip polish on waxed floors.

Hallways, Stairs, and Landings

• Make sure you have good lighting with three-way switches installed.
• Have a smoke detector on each floor, and one near the bedrooms.
• Keep these areas clear of clutter and of furniture with sharp or protruding parts.
• Treads should have nonskid surfaces. For visibility, use two-inch white tape on the edges.
• Place gates at the top and bottom of your stairways when youngsters are small.

Garage and/or Basement

• Throw away paint- or oil-stained rags, or store them in

Toddler-Proof Your Holiday Home

Many favorite Christmas decorations are too fragile, poisonous, or simply dangerous to have around young children. However, you can still give your home a festive look safely.
* *Keep as many decorations as possible out of your children's reach and establish firm limits about what they can and cannot touch.*
* *Place toxic holiday plants, such as mistletoe and holly, safely out of reach.*
* *Instead of using angel hair, tinsel, and glitter, which can be dangerous, try fabric, paper, and wooden decorations. Don't forget edibles such as popcorn strands and candy canes.*
* *Suspend your glass ornaments from the ceiling above the tree with fishing line.*
* *Move a breakable crèche scene to the mantel, and on the hearth place a straw basket filled with safe-to-handle pinecones and wooden apples.*
* *Buy a small "children's tree" and trim with chains and ornaments they make themselves. Letting them rearrange their tree now and then might discourage them from fooling around with the family tree.*

metal containers. Don't leave old cleaning rags stacked in a pile. This creates an ideal situation to start a fire.
* Make sure ladders are sturdy and have nonslip treads on the rungs.
* Check to make sure that each fuse is the proper size. Never use any substitute for the proper fuse.
* Power tools should have double insulation on grounded plugs. Lock away these tools when not in use.
* Have a general all-purpose fire extinguisher handy.

Safety from the Storm

• Alert your local police department if you discover downed power lines. Set up barricades to keep others away from the area until help arrives.

• Grounding rods (at least two for a small house) should be placed at opposite corners of the house.

• Keep an eye on large trees—even healthy ones—that could damage your house if felled in a storm. Cut them back, if necessary.

• When a major storm is imminent, close shutters, board windows, or tape the inside of larger panes with an "X" along the full length of their diagonals. Even a light material like masking tape may give the glass the extra margin of strength it needs to resist cracking. Exception: When a tornado threatens, leave windows slightly ajar.

• If you live in a storm-prone area, nail down roof shingles or use adequate adhesive to keep them from blowing off in a violent wind. For roofs with shingles that are not the seal-down type, apply a little dab of roofing cement under each tab.

• In your storm shelter, store a lantern, pick, shovel, crowbar, hammer, screwdriver, and pliers. If the exit became blocked, you might have to dig your way out. Store canned food and bottled water, too.

• The basement is not a good shelter during a tornado because it's too close to gas pipes, sewer pipes, drains, and cesspools. A better shelter would be underground, far from the house (in case the roof falls), and away from the gas and sewer system.

• In a hurricane, don't go out unless you have to. However, if flooding threatens, seek high ground and follow the instructions of civil defense personnel.

The best survivor is a prepared survivor.

Basics to Do During an Earthquake

• Stay *calm*.
• *Inside:* Stand in a doorway, or crouch under a desk or table away from windows or glass dividers.
• *Outside:* Stand away from buildings, trees, and telephone and electric lines.
• *On the road:* Drive away from underpasses and overpasses; stop in a safe area and stay in your vehicle.

Basics to Do After an Earthquake

• Check for injuries—provide first aid.
• Check for safety—check for gas, water, and sewage breaks; check for downed electric lines and short circuits; turn off appropriate utilities; check for building damage and potential safety problems during aftershocks, such as cracks around the chimney and foundation.
• Clean up dangerous spills.
• Wear shoes.

Basic Survival Items to Keep on Hand

• Portable radio with extra batteries.
• Flashlight with extra batteries.
• First-aid kit, including specified medicines needed for members of your household.
• First-aid book.
• Fire extinguisher.
• Adjustable wrench for turning off gas and water valves.
• Smoke detectors properly installed.
• Portable fire escape ladder for homes and apartments with multiple floors.
• Bottled water sufficient for the number of members in your household for a week.
• Canned and dried foods sufficient for a week for each member of your household. *Note:* Both water and food

---

Calling for Help

Post these numbers near your telephone:

- *Emergency medical service (in many communities it's not 911)*
- *Fire and police departments*
- *Ambulance and nearest hospital; physician and pharmacist*
- *Poison control center (usually administered by your local health department)*
- *Gas, electric, and water companies (customer service and 24-hour service numbers)*
- *Dependable neighbors*

---

should be rotated into normal meals of your household to maintain freshness. Canned goods have a normal shelf life of one year for maximum freshness.

- Nonelectrical can opener.
- Portable stove (such as butane or charcoal). *Note:* Use of such stoves should not take place until it is determined that there is no gas leak in the area. Charcoal should be burned only out-of-doors. Use of charcoal indoors will lead to carbon monoxide poisoning.
- Several dozen candles. The same caution should be taken as in the above note on portable stoves.
- Matches.
- Telephone numbers of police, fire, and doctor.

Basics You Need to Know

1. How to turn off the gas, water, and electricity.
2. Basic first aid.
3. Plan for reuniting your family.

As with any emergency program that you have for your family, you must review it every three months to make sure the members of your family know what to do in case of an earthquake. The plan for evacuating the home and the plan for reuniting the family if various members of the family are away from home should be walked through so the instructions are thoroughly understood by all members of the family.

Miscellaneous

• Post emergency phone numbers in plain view by the phone for you and baby-sitters.
• Take a first-aid class, including CPR (cardiopulmonary resuscitation), from your local Red Cross.
• Give children swimming lessons at the earliest possible age. Many YMCAs and YWCAs offer great programs for children. If lessons aren't available, work with your children on holding their breath and blowing bubbles under water. It's fun and it will help them become comfortable in water.
• Buy or make up a first-aid kit, if you don't already have one. Store this out of children's reach.
• Never spray liquid insecticides near electrical outlets or exposed connections. Short circuits may result.
• Be sure everybody can reach and operate latches, locks, doors, and chains. Tell your children that they can break a window in case of fire. Instruct them to remove large fragments of glass and cover the sill with a blanket. Draw a floor plan of your home. Include windows and outside features like trees. Mark primary and secondary exits from each room. Designate a meeting place outside of your house where the family will congregate. Mark it on the map. Cover the plan with every family member and walk through the various escape routes from each room. Make sure children understand that they can't hide from a fire but can escape it by following an exit route. Conduct fire drills every six months. With each drill, vary the location of the imaginary fire and instruct family members to alter their escape routes accordingly.

Storm Warnings

If you are in the path of an oncoming major storm:
* *Bring indoors or secure lawn furniture, garbage cans, tools, and other objects that might be blown or washed away.*
* *Clean sinks and bathtubs and fill them with water as a reserve in case you lose your water supply.*
* *Make sure your car is filled with gas and stock the trunk with water, blankets, a first-aid kit, and nonperishable food.*
* *Board up windows with plywood or heavy cardboard or latch shutters over them securely. Keep flashlights and radios on hand; be sure their batteries are fresh.*

* Remember, never squirt lighter fluid into hot barbecue coals, as the flame could be drawn up the stream, causing the fluid to explode.
* For kids who can't read yet but have been taught how to use the telephone, here's a method for easily determining whom to call in case of emergency. Put a poster board on the wall near the phone and use symbols or pictures for the people or places to be called. Then draw a line in a bold color leading to the phone number. For example, for the fire department, use a picture of firemen, for Dad's work number, use a picture of him, and so on.
* If someone is caught on a high-voltage electric wire, throw the main switch or break the contact with a dry piece of wood (such as a wooden broom handle). In no way touch the victim until he is freed from the current.
* When giving a child a pill, raise his head. If he is lying flat on his back when he takes the medicine, it may go down his windpipe instead of into his stomach.
* To prevent your baby from sliding around the seat of a wooden highchair, cut a textured plastic car floor mat to fit the seat. It wipes clean easily and your baby stays securely in place.

Pool Safety

If you have a swimming pool, check local ordinances for proper safety regulations.
- *Enclose the pool with a fence at least five feet high.*
- *Install gates that latch automatically.*
- *Install alarms on the gate or turn on pool alarms (which are activated when anyone falls in the water), when you are indoors or away.*
- *Keep the water level at least three inches from the top so a child can grasp the side and get air.*
- *Cover the pool during the off-season but remove the cover completely when the pool is in use.*
- *Take a course in CPR and water safety at your local YMCA or chapter of the American Red Cross.*
- *Keep electrical appliances and glass away from the pool area.*
- *Store pool chemicals in a locked cabinet.*

- Two tennis wristbands worn like knee pads keep your toddler's knees scrape-free.
- Use laundry baskets as toy boxes. They are durable, economical, and don't have lids that might fall down on little hands or heads.
- Before throwing away an empty product can or unused product, check the label on the container. If it has "caution," "warning," or "poison" on it, follow carefully the directions for the proper disposal of the container.
- Unlike standard playground equipment, which has welded chain links, most retail swing sets have open links. As a result, hair can become tangled or fingers can get cut if a child tries to grasp the chain when falling. To remedy this problem, slip each chain through a three- to four-foot length of hose before hanging the swings.
- A metallic stove or counter mat fastened to the wall

makes a safe bulletin board for young children. Pictures can be hung with magnetic note holders (commonly used on refrigerators) instead of potentially harmful thumbtacks or pushpins. The mat also provides a terrific spot to practice spelling with colorful magnetic letters of the alphabet.

• As a safety precaution before leaving the home on vacation, unplug all electrical appliances except for those lights connected to automatic timers.

• A spare tire in the trunk of your car can be used as a life preserver in an emergency.

I asked God for strength that I might achieve, but I was made weak that I might learn humbly to obey. I asked for health that I might do greater things; I was given infirmity that I might do better things. I asked for riches that I might be happy; I was given poverty that I might be wise. I asked for power that I might have the praise of men, but I was given weakness that I might feel a need of God. I asked for all things that I might enjoy life. I was given life that I might enjoy all things. I got nothing I asked for, but everything I had hoped for. Almost despite myself, my unspoken prayers were answered, and I am among all people truly blessed.

—Author Unknown

The 15 Minute

▲ ▲ ▲

MONEY MANAGER

EMILIE & BOB BARNES

We dedicate this book to all the people who have influenced us to be good stewards of all that God has given us—health, intelligence, talents, marriage, relationships, and money.

Contents

The Road to
Financial Freedom

Emilie and I were both raised in families which gave us the opportunity to work and earn money at very early ages. We learned how to be frugal with our money, how to postpone gratification, how to live within our means, and how to save for the future.

We truly appreciate the opportunity to pass on to you all that we have learned regarding the awesome subject of money. We pray that this book will have lifestyle-changing impact on you. We hope you will be inspired to learn and adopt some of these basic financial principles.

New knowledge will be effective only if you put it into action. Read this book with a highlighter pen in hand so you can mark the areas that speak to you. Don't hesitate to underline or write notes in the margin.

Make a pledge to yourself that each day you will put at least one new idea into practice.

We recognize that we are all very busy people who have difficulty finding time to read or learn new ideas. If that's you and your family, we have written this book just for you!

This 15-minute approach has short, concise chapters for reading while waiting in line, waiting for an appointment, or sitting in bed at night. After reading this book once, you will want to use it as a reference book. Put it on a shelf where it will be handy to consult again and again as you work on the family finances.

Are you in debt over your head? Is there too much month left at the end of your paycheck? Do you wonder where all your money went? Are debtors calling and asking when they can expect their money?

For the Christian family, good money management is important because God associates a person's ability to handle spiritual matters with the ability to handle money:

If you are untrustworthy about worldly wealth, who will trust you with the true riches of heaven? (Luke 16: 11 TLB).

In addition, we are stewards (managers) for God of our lives and possessions, since both belong to Him. It is God who gives us power to obtain money (Deuteronomy 8:18).

Robert J. Hastings wrote, "Money management is basically self-control, for unless one learns to control himself, he is no more likely to control his money than he is to discipline his habits, his time or his temper. Undisciplined money usually spells undisciplined persons."

We learn self-control in the use of money by obtaining a proper attitude about money. Good money management is not bondage; it is freedom from the "right" to do what we want, giving us instead the *power* to do what we should!

Our goal as Christians should be to obtain financial freedom. This has four characteristics:

▲ Our assets exceed our liabilities.
▲ We are able to pay our bills as they fall due.
▲ We have no unpaid bills. (We are repaying per our agreement.)
▲ We are content with where we are.

This book will show you how to make these four elements a reality in your life. But first, there is something you must understand: *Contentment* is absolutely crucial for the other three elements to function properly. Throughout Scripture we are told to be content (1 Timothy 6:8; Hebrews 13:5; Philippians 4:12,13).

We have a saying around the Barnes household: "If we aren't content with what we have, we will never be content with what we want."

Money management is really more about your *attitude toward the use of money* than a systematic plan to which you become a servant. The first half of the book gives a basis for looking at money properly, and the second half offers insight into how to specifically manage your money.

May this book help you on your road toward financial freedom!

PART ONE

A Plan for Your Life

▲ ▲ ▲

Schedule a Plan, Plan a Schedule

$\mathcal{A}$s Emilie and I travel all over the United States and Canada, we find that a majority of individuals, couples, and families have never taken the time to develop a written statement of purpose for their lives.

If you don't know what your purpose, goals, values, and priorities are in life, you will never be able to manage your time, life, self, home, job, or money. You must schedule a plan and plan a schedule.

Charles J. Givens states, "The difference between those who accomplish their dreams and those who only dream of accomplishing them is planning and control."[1]

Many of us don't want to take the time or effort to develop sound strategies to be successful in life. There are those who want to be controlled by life rather than controlling life. These people will usually end up angry, cynical, frustrated, and disappointed with the hand that life has dealt them. On the other hand, people who seem to control life end up satisfied, joyful, and successful. They have a gleam to their radiances.

The second group of people develop a strategic plan to control their lives (with one large segment on knowing how

353

to manage their money). A reporter once asked Helen Keller, "What would be worse than being born blind?" Miss Keller responded, "To be born with eyes, but not to have a vision."

In our Working Woman's Seminar, we give a very simple definition of success: "A Progressive Realization of Worthwhile Goals." In managing money we could paraphrase it into: "A Progressive Realization of Your Financial Objectives on a Timely and Preplanned Basis."[2]

I have a hunch that the two words "progressive realization" already concern you. We have all been conformed by our culture to believe that results must be fast or else we lose patience, become restless, and want to make things happen by our own efforts. However, this concept means a slow realization of financial objectives. Be *patient*—a hard word for Americans to understand, especially young Americans. The products of the '60s, '70s, and '80s have been led to believe "I must have it *now*—no waiting allowed." The recession of the early '90s, however, is showing some return to valuing the "progressive realization" principle of life.

Paul, the writer of Romans, shares with us a basic principle for us to consider:

Do not be conformed to this world, but be transformed by the renewing of your mind, that you may prove what the will of God is, that which is good and acceptable and perfect (Romans 12:2).

As Christians we are at war between "conformed" and "transformed." Everywhere we turn we are pressed into being conformed to the world's mindset. Without a plan for our new lives that is the way we will go. Humans seem to take the road of least resistance. In Proverbs 29:18 we read, "Where there is no vision the people are unrestrained, but happy is he who keeps the law."

This book is meant to challenge you to live a life transformed to godly principles so that you may prove what the will of God is regarding money matters, and what is good, acceptable, and perfect in Scripture.

The next few chapters will develop the four basic components of your plan to create the spirit of "Progressive Realization of Worthwhile Goals":

▲ Developing a purpose or mission for your life.
▲ Developing goals for this purpose or mission.
▲ Planning your goals to accomplish your purpose or mission.
▲ Scheduling these goals to accomplish your purpose or mission.
▲ Developing projects to meet your purpose or mission.

Your *purpose* or mission in life lets you state why you do what you do; your *goals* are simple statements that can be measured to help you reach your dreams with a deadline; your *planning* lets you identify a "to-do list" in implementing these goals and dreams; *scheduling* helps you put some time limits on the accomplishments—one year, three years, five years; *projects* help you visualize what projects can let you develop a master plan to accomplish your purpose or mission in life.

Let's begin by stating a purpose or mission in life.

Why You Do What You Do

No one can serve two masters. Either he will hate the one and love the other, or he will be devoted to the one and despise the other. You cannot serve both God and Money.

—Matthew 6:24 NIV

*M*y father always used to tell me, "It's not how much money you make that counts; it's what you do with what you make." Dad realized that there had to be a method and a plan in managing money. It is much easier to accumulate wealth by wisely using money you save than by going out and earning more money.

I have a very good friend who often uses the familiar saying "Compound interest is the eighth wonder of the world." He and I both have learned over the years the value of "progressive realization." In order to benefit from compounded interest you must have a plan and you must be patient. (In a later chapter we will talk more about this eighth wonder.)

In determining "Why you do what you do," you must have a basic understanding of three basic principles of life:

356

▲ You must have a sense of mastery.
▲ You must have a sense of a calling.
▲ You must be willing to live life on the transformed plane rather than the conformed plane.

A Sense of Mastery

When we have insight into God's overall purpose for His children in this world, we have a sense of direction. In Proverbs we see that God is in control and that He truly has a master plan for our lives:

The plans of the heart belong to man, but the answer of the tongue is from the Lord (Proverbs 16:1).

The mind of man plans his way, but the Lord directs his steps (Proverbs 16:9).

Sometimes in life we take much of the credit for our success when in reality it all belongs to God. He is the Alpha and the Omega, the beginning and the end.

When we begin to realize where everything comes from, and that it is all God's and that He merely loans it to us for a short time, then we can begin to realize a humbling sense of who we are in this thing called life.

A Sense of Calling

In the big picture we must realize that we are called according to God's purpose for our lives: "We know that God causes all things to work together for good to those who love God, to those who are *called* according to His purpose" (Romans 8:28); "[He] called us with a holy *calling*, not according to our works, but according to His own purpose" (2 Timothy 1:9). A sense of calling allows us to see the big picture of God's work in our lives and helps us find meaning in our lives. Understanding our calling and purpose in life has everything to do with our identity. I hear many people today say something like "I'm going to take off six months from my job, my husband, my children, etc. to find out who I am."

When a person makes this kind of comment I realize that he or she doesn't understand that we each have a unique calling from God. By delving into the Bible we soon begin to realize that all of us have been called to serve God according to His purpose rather than ours.

One of the end results of sitting down and writing your mission or purpose in life is that you are confronted with the basic question "Why do I do what I do?" When you are able to answer this question in somewhat clear terms, then you are ready to develop strategy for your life. *This question must be answered first.*

Are you driven by expectations from outside over which you have no control, or are you inner-controlled, choosing to be what you are? When you take control of your life rather than letting life's events control you, you will see a new meaning to your life. Each day will be a new day; you will rise out of bed and vault into a new day. You will excitedly anticipate newness in your life. The Lord says, "God sees not as man sees, for man looks at the outward appearance, but the Lord looks at the heart" (1 Samuel 16:7).

The Transformed Plan Versus the Conformed Plan

In the previous chapter we discussed this concept briefly, but we must come to grips with this contrast, because we will continually be spending wasted energy, money, and time on this wrestling match until we come to grips with this struggle.

As a young man I wanted to be able to straddle the fence and serve both masters, but as I have gotten older (and hopefully more mature and wiser) I see more clearly the giant fight for our mind. We must continually struggle for a transformed mind, or else we will fall back into a state of complacency and be conformed to the world's way of thinking. Our daily choice must be: "Whatever is true, whatever is honorable, whatever is right, whatever is pure, whatever is lovely, whatever is of good repute, if there is any excellence, and if anything worthy of praise, let your mind dwell on these things" (Philippians 4:8).

Another Barnes Motto is: **Who you will be in the next five years depends on three things:**

▲ The books you read
▲ The people you meet
▲ The choices you make

Choose today to live a transformed life!

Developing a Purpose in Life

As we look at our "triangle of success" we notice that the foundation and basic building block is the writing out of our basic purpose for life. You might think of this as being your mission in life. The first step is to create a statement which lets you begin realizing why you do what you do. From this statement you will add the other components which lead to successful financial living.

The biggest reason we don't realize what we want out of life is that we think in the negative. We see what we lack:

▲ Money
▲ Education
▲ Looks

▲ Ability
▲ Encouragement from family and friends
▲ Background

Another Barnes Motto is: **It's not what you are that holds you back, it's what you think you are not.**

The truth is that none of the above six negatives is necessary to possess in order to gain success in life. In reading biographies of past and present successful people we see that many of them started with very little. *It's what you do with what you have that counts.*

In working through this statement you need to think of your values and beliefs. If your statement isn't consistent with these two aspects of what you want out of life, you will continually have conflict in stating what you want out of life.

Values are not facts but simply choices, initially made for us by our parents and our childhood environment. As we grow and mature, our values should tend to become our own choices. The ability to choose our own values is the freedom to choose the direction for our lives.

When you act in accordance with your values you experience emotional balance, a sense of security and pleasure. When your actions are out of alignment with your values, you experience fear, guilt, frustration, and emotional imbalance. Fortunately, you can get rid of those unwanted negative feelings. You can either:

1. Change your actions to align with your values, or
2. Change your values to align with your actions.

Of course, you cannot do either until you identify what your values are.

Values are programs in the mind and can be changed only with constant prodding, attention and affirmation. In other words, to change what you value, even if change is in your best interest, you must reprogram what is in your mind. It is easier, though not usually as rewarding, to change your actions—to get rid of the conflicts and live your life in accordance with what you already value most.

Surprisingly, there are a total of only about 25 major values in life, and these values in different combinations result in the differences in people's actions. The differences in the wants, desires and objectives people set for themselves are the direct result of different values.

By identifying and prioritizing your current values, you will be able to:

▲ Set your goals to enable you to spend more of your life and money doing and experiencing those things that are most important to you.
▲ Eliminate values conflict by making certain no two values are pulling you in opposite directions.

▲ Create an environment of mutual support in your personal relationships by realizing that two people do not need the same values to create a successful relationship, but they must be able to support each other's values emotionally and financially.

▲ Determine how important wealth building is to the success of your total financial plan.

As you can see, values must be identified before goals are set or it becomes all too easy to establish one or more goals that are in conflict with your values. Reaching a goal should create a sense of accomplishment, self-confidence, excitement and a desire to celebrate, but if that goal is in conflict with an important value, there will instead be a feeling of empty achievement, frustration and sometimes even anger.[1]

Emilie and I have chosen a verse of Scripture stating our purpose in life: "Seek first His kingdom and His righteousness, and all these things shall be added to you" (Matthew 6:33). All of our life decisions are tested by this verse of Scripture. Will a particular decision pass this litmus test? If it doesn't, we don't do it.

Our theologian forefathers expressed the chief end of man this way: "The chief end of man is to glorify God and to enjoy Him forever." This too would make a great statement of purpose.

Henrietta Mears once stated, "There is no magic in small plans. When I consider my ministry, I think of the world. Anything less than that would not be worthy of Christ nor His will for my life."

Bill Bright, founder and President of Campus Crusade for Christ, selected in the early part of 1950 his verse to define his purpose for life. It is known as the Great Commission:

> *Go therefore and make disciples of all the nations, baptizing them in the name of the Father and the Son and the Holy Spirit, teaching them to observe all that I commanded you; and lo, I am with you always, even to the end of the age (Matthew 28:19,20).*

Over the past 40 years, Campus Crusade has been led by the statement of this purpose in life. Those who know Bill Bright and Campus Crusade's ministry can testify of their adherence to this statement.

You may want to write out what you want to accomplish in life as a statement that will be your guiding force for establishing goals for your plan.

Remember that a statement is general in nature and is not meant to be stated in strictly measurable terms.

The Barnes' Purpose of Life is stated as: *"Seek first His Kingdom and His righteousness, and all these things shall be added to you."*

In the space provided below, write out your statement of purpose.

My purpose of life is:_____

_____

_____

Hang on to this statement, because everything else we do in this section will be based upon this statement.

You may change your statement of purpose at any time. It is not set in concrete, but is merely a base for all the other decisions in planning for a meaningful life.

Goals: A Dream with a Deadline

What you commit yourself to become determines what you are.

—Tony Campolo

Goals prod us into action. They are a means to an end. A well-stated goal has three qualities:

▲ It states *quantity* (be specific).
▲ It gives a *deadline* (starting and completion dates).
▲ It is *written out* (though not in concrete).

"I want to lose 15 pounds by July 1." That is very brief but it meets the two basic criteria of a goal. Goals are measurable, whereas purposes aren't that specific. I like to tell those who attend our seminars that goals are dreams with a deadline.

These stated goals are specific objectives on which you have decided to invest your time, money, and energy. A goal can be accomplished very quickly or it may take a lifetime. Only state those goals which are in keeping with your value system and which help you meet your stated purpose of life.

Each year between Christmas and the first part of January we take a vacation trip to some place where we can kick back, relax, recreate, and plan for the new year. We each spend the first couple of days writing out two or three goals under the following topics:

▲ **Spiritual goals** Activities to strengthen your spiritual life together

▲ **Physical goals** Things you want to do physically

▲ **Family goals** Activities you want to do to bring closer relationships

▲ **Financial goals** What you want to do with your finances

▲ **Professional goals** Courses to be taken, seminars to attend, books to read

▲ **Mental goals** Projects for the brain

▲ **Social goals** Activities to do which would include your friends, old and new

▲ **Community support goals** Involvements to support the community.

GOALS
(A Dream with a Deadline)

PURPOSE
(Mission in Life)

Schedule a Plan, Plan a Schedule

Emilie does her set of goals and I do mine. On the third or fourth day we come together and discuss each of our goals for the new year. After some time discussing together, we write out the "Barnes Goals" for the new year.

Be committed. Your level of commitment to any goal determines how you will handle interferences along the way. Remember that these goals aren't set in concrete; they can be changed or altered.

Don't just think or dream about your various goals. Put them in writing on paper or enter them into your computer. Somehow the physical activity of writing them out gives greater credibility to their value. Make lists similar to the ones shown in this chapter, but don't just write them and file them away. Keep them where you can refer to them from time to time. Emilie and I keep them in the front of our Bibles, and we review them at least once a quarter. Sometimes we change an entry, and sometimes we confirm that we are on target and move on.

Emilie's book *Survival for Busy Women* provides two charts which are used to track personal goals.[1] One chart is designed for the person who has never kept goals before. It is bite-sized, with no more than three months of goals at a time. Don't overwhelm yourself with too much to do. If you do, you will become discouraged and give up.

Remember that it takes 21 days to create a new habit.

The other chart is more sophisticated and has several new components added. There is room to state what you need to consider for each goal. You may have a wonderful goal stated, but you must take time to consider other people, costs, added education, time away from home, etc. There is also space to rank the goal by priority.

Not all goals are possible for today. Some are "A" priority (which is urgent—top of the list); some are "B" priority (which I call my "maybe items"); some are "C" priority (which I classify as no time, money, or energy given to this today). My B and C items can become A's, but not for now.

Another necessary section for your goal list is space to jot down your steps to completing this specific goal. Think through the various steps necessary, and then jot these down in this area. You also have a space to date the beginning and another space to jot the completion.

Writing Your Financial Goals

E ach of us has similar financial goals, but varying somewhat based upon our personal value system. These goals would include:

1. Income goals—the increases in yearly income we want to achieve.
2. Career goals—the type of work we want to do, the company positions we want to attain, or the business we want to create.
3. Acquisition goals—the things we want to buy and own.
4. Travel goals—the places nationally and internationally we want to visit and experience.
5. Accomplishment goals—the things we want to do and become.
6. Educational goals—the knowledge we want to acquire for personal, financial, and career advancement.
7. Recreational vehicle goals—the "fun" things we want to own for recreation and sports.
8. Investment goals—the income-producing, tax-reducing, or net-worth-increasing investments we want to own.

Income Goals

In order to accomplish these financial goals we have to take a serious look at our income goals. And we need to be realistic in this area. Many couples get into real trouble by being too optimistic when deciding if their present income is going to let them establish attainable goals for their immediate future. If you are single, either male or female, you have little chance of increasing your income substantially unless you get a sizable raise, inherit money, or marry.

When Emilie and I were first married, she worked in a bank for the first three years. It would have been very easy to increase our standard of living with the extra money, but we didn't. We tucked most of it away into a savings account for a down payment on that first home.

Over the last few years about 4 to 5 percent of yearly income has been used to keep up with inflation. If your income doesn't grow by at least this amount you are losing ground to inflation.

A basic question is, "Will your current rate of increase allow you to finance your dreams?" That depends upon two things: 1) the amount of time it will take you to double your income after inflation is factored in, and 2) how much of a hurry you are in to reach your dreams. (Remember, success is a progressive realization of worthwhile goals.)

Ways to Increase Your Income If You Work for Someone Else[1]

▲ Increase your skill level, education, or profile in your present job.

▲ Create a new, better-paying job in your department and fill it.

▲ Seek promotion to another department.

▲ Ask for raises as you go the extra mile.

▲ Change companies for greater opportunities.
▲ Change to a higher-paying career by getting the necessary skills or education.

Ways to Increase Your Income If You Work for Yourself

▲ Increase sales through hiring more salespeople or spending a greater portion of your time selling.
▲ Create a better advertising and marketing campaign.
▲ Cut your expenses in every area without sacrificing net profit.
▲ Expand your line of products or services.

Career Goals

Here are guidelines that will help you determine the directions in which you would like to take your career.

1. Do you want to change careers?   Yes ____ No ____
   To what kind of work?

   1. _____   3. _____

   2. _____   4. _____

2. Do you want your own business?   Yes ____ No ____
   In what kind of work?

   1. _____   3. _____

   2. _____   4. _____

3. Advances you want to make in your present career:

	Position	Annual Salary
Current	_____	$_____
1 year	_____	$_____
5 years	_____	$_____

Acquisition Goals

Make a list of all the things you would like to own, how much they cost, and the date by which you hope to acquire them. Include automobiles, stereos, jewelry, furs, furniture, clothes, etc. Some items will come from your "dreams list."

	Item	Cost (Approx.)	Target Date (Mo./Yr.)
1.	_____	_____	_____
2.	_____	_____	_____
3.	_____	_____	_____
4.	_____	_____	_____
5.	_____	_____	_____
6.	_____	_____	_____
7.	_____	_____	_____
8.	_____	_____	_____
9.	_____	_____	_____
10.	_____	_____	_____

Travel Goals

Make a list of the top ten places which you would like to visit in the United States and abroad. Your list can include the names of countries, states, cities, monuments, or other attractions.

	Destination	Target Date (Mo./Yr.)
1.	_____	_____
2.	_____	_____
3.	_____	_____

4. _____   _____
5. _____   _____
6. _____   _____
7. _____   _____
8. _____   _____
9. _____   _____
10. _____   _____

Accomplishment Goals

Make a list of all the things you want to do and become. Include positions you would like to hold in clubs, groups, your church, and your community. Include sports in which you would like to get involved or to excel, as well as social activities or organizations you want to join. Also, list the awards you want to win or other forms of recognition you want to achieve.

Sport, Activity, or Organization	What You Want to Accomplish	Target Date (Mo./Yr.)
1. _____	_____	_____
2. _____	_____	_____
3. _____	_____	_____
4. _____	_____	_____
5. _____	_____	_____

Educational Goals

Make a list of the courses or programs you would like to take and the estimated cost of each. Examples: Speed-reading courses, night-school course, courses to complete your degree, real estate investing programs.

Program	Approximate Starting Date	Approximate Cost
1. _____	_____	$ _____
2. _____	_____	$ _____
3. _____	_____	$ _____
4. _____	_____	$ _____
5. _____	_____	$ _____

Recreational Vehicle Goals

Make a list of the recreational vehicles you would like to own, when you want to acquire them, and the cost of each.

	Type	Acquire	Cost
1. Sports car	_____	_____	_____
2. Motorcycle	_____	_____	_____
3. Bicycle	_____	_____	_____
4. Snowmobile	_____	_____	_____
5. Sailboat	_____	_____	_____
6. Jet Ski/ wet bike	_____	_____	_____
7. Fishing boat	_____	_____	_____
8. Hobie Cat	_____	_____	_____
9. Sailboard	_____	_____	_____
10. Houseboat	_____	_____	_____
11. Yacht	_____	_____	_____

12. Airplane   _____ _____ _____
13. Hang glider   _____ _____ _____
14. Motor home   _____ _____ _____
15. Camper   _____ _____ _____

Investment Goals

There is only one reason to invest: to accumulate money to buy yourself something in the future that you can't afford now. For some people this means financially safe and secure retirement years. Other people have goals that won't wait until retirement, and investing means eventually having the money to make the down payment on a beautiful home or expensive automobile, or having a cushion to quit a job and start a business. Investment accounts, retirement accounts, and investment in your home and other real estate are all means you can use to achieve your investment goals. Your goals list will help you determine how important your investment plan will become to your future.

Make an Investment Goals Chart similar to the one below to identify where you are now and where you want to be the next year, five years from now, and at age 65. This chart will also help you measure your progress.

INVESTMENT GOALS CHART

	This Year	Next Year	5 Years	Age 65
Cash in bank	$_____	$_____	$_____	$_____
Investment accounts	$_____	$_____	$_____	$_____
Retirement accounts	$_____	$_____	$_____	$_____
Your home	$_____	$_____	$_____	$_____

Real estate investments	$_____	$_____	$_____	$_____
Other investments	$_____	$_____	$_____	$_____
TOTAL	$_____	$_____	$_____	$_____

Here are some suggestions that will help you fill in your Investment Goals Chart:

Cash in bank. Include for this year all money in bank-type savings and checking accounts, money market accounts, or any other cash. Set your goals for the future on the level of available cash that will give you a sense of security.

Investment accounts. Include all stocks, bonds, CD's, government securities, and mutual fund shares you now own, plus what you want to have invested in the future.

Retirement accounts. Enter the amount of money currently in all your retirement accounts. Your retirement accounts will cover the cost of your lifestyle after you are no longer producing income from your job or career. By the time you retire, the amount in your retirement plan should be eight times the annual income you want to have during your retirement years. Although other investments may also produce income during your retirement years, here you will list only the amounts you have and want to have in your retirement accounts, including your IRA, SEP, Keogh, 401(k), 403(b), annuities, federal retirement plan, state retirement plan, and union retirement plan.

Your home. Show the current amount of unmortgaged equity you have in your home—what your home is worth minus what you owe. For future years, estimate what you think your home should be worth. If your goal is to buy a more expensive home, adjust your estimated home equity accordingly. If you own or plan to own a second home, show those figures also.

Real estate investments. Show the equity you have in rental real estate or land and the equity you would like to have in the future.

Other assets. Include the value of such noninvestment assets as automobiles, jewelry, furniture, etc.

I can't overemphasize the importance of putting all your financial goals in writing. Focusing on your goals inevitably means that you will think about how to achieve them. Putting them in writing motivates you to take the necessary actions.

Making Your "To Do" List

Which one of you, when he wants to build a tower, does not first sit down and calculate the cost, to see if he has enough to complete it? Otherwise, when he has laid a foundation, and is not able to finish, all who observe it begin to ridicule him, saying, "This man began to build and was not able to finish."

—Luke 14:28-30

Planning is crucial if we are going to realize our purpose in life. Christ pointed out to His disciples the high cost of commitment to His calling, and we are likewise to realize that planning makes similar demands of our lives.

I am continually told by the women who come to our seminars that their husbands aren't interested in this whole process of planning for the future. Men must wake up and get serious with life.

Procrastination

Many people are paralyzed because of their inability to make a decision and get their gearshift into drive. One of the ways we are ineffective in our lives is by the evil time-waster called *procrastination*.

In adults, procrastination generally signals some kind of internal conflict. After we have made the decision to do something, a part of us still holds us back. Why do we hold back?

▲ We feel overwhelmed.
▲ We overestimate the amount of time needed.
▲ We would rather be doing something else.
▲ We think that if we wait long enough, the task will go away.
▲ We fear failure.
▲ We fear success.
▲ We enjoy the last-minute adrenaline rush.

Ways to Stop Procrastinating

▲ Make yourself a "to do" list. Use the last five to seven minutes of each day to jot down several activities that need to be done tomorrow.

▲ Keep a log of how long various projects take (usually shorter than you thought).

▲ Work with the time available to you, breaking the task into small bites. Call these "instant tasks." You get a lot of satisfaction in completing these small tasks. See Emilie's book *The 15-Minute Organizer* for more ideas on this concept.

▲ Make time by saying no to lesser projects and blocks of time.

▲ Set small deadlines for these small tasks.

▲ Do things as they come to you.

▲ Ask yourself, "Is there a simpler way?"

▲ Eliminate distractions.

▲ Make it easy to work by grouping like things together. Make them handy.

▲ Reward yourself for getting started.

▲ Tell someone else what your deadline is.

▲ Expect problems; things don't always go as expected.

▲ Learn to delegate.

▲ Start today; don't wait for tomorrow!

Scheduling Goals for Peak Performance

There is an appointed time for everything, and there is a time for every event under heaven.
—Ecclesiastes 3:1

*I*f we have a proper overview of life, we realize that there is an appointed time for every event of our lives. Truly there is a God who masterminds all of life's events, there is a calling which we all have, and there is a world of contrast living (conforming versus transforming).

As I look back over life, I realize that there are definite seasons of life. What you do at 50 isn't available to you at 30, and what was available at 30 isn't available to you at 50. The mystery that amazes me is that God's timing is always perfect; there are no flaws or mistakes.

Since people tend to be "now"-oriented, the general public has a very difficult time waiting on the Lord.

When our children were very young, our family attended a summer camp at Forest Home Christian Conference Center in Southern California. One of the speakers addressed the idea that we needed to plan and think what we wanted our children to be as teenagers. At that time Jenny was about seven and Brad was about five years old, and I thought, *No problem, I won't have to think about that for several years.* Wrong! He said, "Start scheduling now." I said, "But Jenny won't be a teenager for another six years!" "Schedule now for the future, it will soon be here," he said.

Many couples say, "I don't know what we are going to do next week, let alone three to five years from now."

I'm so glad that Emilie and I made a commitment during that week to schedule for the future. Once we started thinking several years ahead of time we could think of projects to get us successfully to that point in time.

When we sold our manufacturing company several years ago, I sold my stock and cashed in my profit-sharing funds and was left with no retirement plans for the future. One of my financial goals that year was to set up an Individual Retirement Account (IRA) and a self-directed profit-sharing account (Keogh) to help with Social Security funds for our retirement.

That goal made me future-oriented; I had to get beyond the present and think several years into the future. It takes proper scheduling to be on target for the retirement season of your life. You need to schedule:

▲ Where you will be in five years
▲ Your children's education
▲ The status of your marriage
▲ Your career level
▲ Where you will live
▲ Your retirement
▲ Your children's future mates and their weddings

For about 25 years Emilie and I had been praying for our children's future mates. We knew they were born and living and being raised somewhere. We prayed for God's protection, and for their moral and character development as youngsters. *We* wanted them to be godly and possess a teachable spirit. Do you know what? That's exactly what God gave us in Craig Merrihew for our daughter and Maria McCallum for our son.

The most marvelous scheduling was God's creating me in time. He planned me from the very beginning. The writer of Psalms says, "I am fearfully and wonderfully made" (see Psalm 139:13,14).

There are many financial goals that need to be scheduled *now.* Don't wait until the day actually comes, for then it will be too late to control the situation. Instead, the situation will control *you,* and you will not be the winner.

So activate now! What needs to be scheduled right now? Write it down or it will float away.

1. *Schedule an appointment with my attorney for a will.*

2. *Open an IRA at my bank.*

3. _____

4. _____

5. _____

6. _____

7. _____

Our goals can be designed to be scheduled in three categories: short-term goals, mid-term goals, and long-term goals. Anything less than a month is considered short-term; two months to two years would be mid-term goals; two to five years would be long-term goals.

Lifetime Goals	short-term goals	mid-term goals	long-term goals	Lifetime Goals

Notice that at the front of the diagram is Lifetime Goals and at the tail of the diagram is Lifetime Goals. They are at the beginning of the process as well as the end of the process. As we decided to plan for our children to be free, strong, and committed young people living out their own unique gifts, we had to schedule projects that were short-term (daily) as well as long-term. If not, it would never happen later.

Many authorities on this subject believe that you need to visualize a goal already fulfilled and to store that picture in your mind as one of the most successful ways to reach a goal.

The Wright brothers had a dream to become the first men to fly. Everyone thought they were crazy, but on December 17, 1903, they achieved their personal dream goal.

Write down several goals that would be under each category.

Short-term goals (less than one month)
A. To open a money market savings account by the end of the month.
B.
C.
D.
E.

Mid-term goals (two months to two years)
A. Register for an accounting class by December 15.
B.
C.
D.
E.

Long-term goals (two to five years)
A. Purchase a retirement home within 36 months.
B.
C.
D.
E.

Projects Designed for Success

The greatest thing in the world is not so much where we start as in what direction we're moving.
—Oliver Wendell Holmes

I hope the last few chapters have captured your vision for planning, not only for your life in general but also for the various aspects which make up your life. The rest of this book will deal specifically with projects you can do to increase your financial independence.

Projects are activities which assist us to reach our purpose in life. They will be different for each of us. The project is what puts our focused energy into action. The following listing will give you an idea how it may work.

Area: *Financial*

Goal: *To be able to build our dream home and to finance our three-week vacation*

Ten-Year Goal Activities

1. To move into our 2500-square-foot, three-bedroom home on one acre of land with a mortgage of $90,000 and with no more than a $1200 monthly payment.
2. To enjoy a three-week vacation with the family with no more than $500 being financed for this trip.

Five-Year Goal Activities

1. To purchase our one-acre parcel and begin a five-year payment plan.
2. To plan a two-week vacation in the mountains. Emphasis on the finance and budget for this vacation.

Three-Year Goal Activities

1. To research and investigate the various aspects in purchasing, financing, and designing our new home.
2. To plan a one-week vacation trip to the beach; emphasis on hope to finance the trip.

One-Year Goal Activities

1. To meet with the bank to determine a savings plan that will let us meet our financial goal of building our own home and taking a three-week vacation.
2. To begin a savings plan to meet the two ten-year goals.

Today's Goal Activities

1. To make an appointment to meet with the loan officer of our main branch bank.
2. To visit the main library and talk to the librarian about her recommendation of the two best architect magazines for our style of living.
3. To sit down and talk with the children about how they can help with this plan.
4. To purchase a qualified camping/vacation magazine that describes various planning aspects for successful vacations.
5. To go to the Automobile Club to acquire various maps showing details for our minivacations.

If we are to live life on purpose, our composite of lifetime goals helps us determine what we do today. This way we control life and don't let it control us.

Another Barnes Motto is: **"Successful people do what unsuccessful people aren't willing to do."**

It takes choices for us to live this way. It isn't easy, but the difference is certainly worth the effort. Each day when I wake up I have to choose to make meaningful decisions today. Each of us has 24 hours or 1440 minutes or 86,400 seconds in each day. Those who get the most out of life are those who make wise decisions based upon what life means to them. Live life with a purpose!

People don't plan to fail, but they do plan to succeed. Success doesn't come by luck or accident; it comes because individuals schedule a plan and also plan a schedule.

When it comes to money matters, you must have a plan or you won't be able to make good daily decisions. Today's decisions must be based on your future orientation. No plans for the future muddy the water in deciding what to do today.

Putting Family Life Goals in Writing

I can do all things through Him who strengthens me.

—Philippians 4:13

*T*hroughout the first seven chapters I have referred to writing down the Barnes Life Goals each year. Emilie does hers, I do mine, and then we compile a joint list for each calendar year. It is not overly sophisticated, but it works for us. You may want to design your own form. The important thing is to get started.

THE FAMILY LIFE GOALS

Theme Verse: "_____
_____"

My purpose or mission in life is: _____

1. **Spiritual Goal**   a. <u>To read the book of John</u> _____
                           b. _____

When?

    a. <u>By May 1</u>_____

    b. _____

2. Physical goal   a. <u>To weigh pounds</u>_____

    b. _____

When?

    a. <u>By July I</u>_____

    b. _____

3. Family goal   a. _____

    b. _____

When?

    a. _____

    b. _____

4. Financial goal   a. _____

    b. _____

When?

    a. _____

    b. _____

5. Professional goal   a. _____

    b. _____

When?

    a. _____

    b. _____

6. Mental goal   a. _____

    b. _____

When?

a. _____

b. _____

7. Social goal   a. _____

b. _____

When?

a. _____

b. _____

8. Community   a. _____

   support goal   b. _____

When?

a. _____

b. _____

The most important foundation of this form is stating your purpose or mission in life. From this statement comes the value for all other planning. Make sure your goals are consistent with your statement. If not, drop the goal or change your statement. Statement and goals must be consistent with each other.

PART TWO

The
Right Priorities

▲ ▲ ▲

Four Cornerstones for Money Management

You may say to yourself, "My power and the strength of my hands have produced this wealth for me." But remember the Lord your God, for it is he who gives you the ability to produce wealth.
—Deuteronomy 8:17,18 NIV

A very good friend of ours, Jim De Lorenzo, is a brick-layer par excellence. All of the most discriminating home-owners in Riverside smile with pride when Jim can do their masonry work. He is so good that recently the California Brick Association selected him the outstanding builder for using brick as a building material. Jim has done brickwork for us in each of our homes over the last 20 years. He is the best in his profession.

The first thing he does when he gets on the job is to get out his transit and shoot the grade to make sure he knows where the cornerstone is going to be. From there every-thing will be built from the central calculation. All heights of retaining walls will come from there.

Several years ago we had a new garage built, and the contractor did the same measuring and calculating to determine the four cornerstones and to make sure they are level.

That's the way it is with finances: There are four basic principles that are cornerstones. In order to have a good sense and proper attitude toward money, these principles must be your basic reference for all your money decisions.

Cornerstone 1: Recognize that God Owns Everything

He owns our home, our car, our marriage, our children, our job, our business, and our talents. We may possess them, but we don't own them. Possession is not ownership.

▲ The earth is the Lord's and all it contains, the world, and those who dwell in it (Psalm 24: 1).
▲ Every beast of the forest is Mine, the cattle on a thousand hills. I know every bird of the mountains, and everything that moves in the field is Mine (Psalm 50:10,11).
▲ "The silver is Mine and the gold is Mine," declares the Lord of hosts (Haggai 2:8).

Everything belongs to God. You are merely a steward of His property. God holds you personally responsible to faithfully manage for Him whatever money or possessions He allows you to have.

Often we are tempted to grasp our possessions selfishly, as if they actually belonged to us and not to God. I'll never forget the beautiful blue 1972 Mercedes Benz I cherished for about ten years. I waxed it often to keep it shining brightly, kept it in the garage when I wasn't driving it, and dusted it every day.

Once when Emilie and I were away for a few days, our son Brad and a few buddies came home from college to go skiing. Brad saw my Mercedes in the garage and decided to take it to the mountains to impress his friends and any young ladies they might meet. He strapped the ski rack to the roof, loaded the skis and poles onto the rack, and headed for the slopes.

All went well until they started home. The ski rack vibrated loose and slid off, leaving a dent and a large scratch on the roof of my Mercedes. When I returned home, Brad broke the news. When I saw the damaged car I was angry at Brad for taking my car without asking, and devastated that he had allowed my prized car to be damaged. But it took me only a moment to regain my composure. God was using the incident to test my perspective on my car. "Well, God, Your car has a scratch and a dent," I said. I drove God's Mercedes for another year-and-a-half with the scratched and dented roof. Each time I looked at the damage it reminded me who really owned the car.

As caretakers of God's money and property we must obediently grow and nurture the spiritual fruit of self-control. (See Galatians 5:22,23.)

Take a few minutes and jot down your possessions that God owns.

1. _____   4. _____

2. _____   5. _____

3. _____   6. _____

If you have never given them to God before, you might want to do that now. Turn everything over to him.

Cornerstone 2: The Goal of Financial Responsibility Is Financial Freedom

In order to be financially free you must meet these qualifications:

▲ Your income exceeds your expenses.
▲ You are able to pay your debts as they fall due.
▲ You have no unpaid bills.
▲ Above all, you are content at your present income level.

We mentioned this Barnes Motto earlier: "*If you are not satisfied with what you have, you will never be satisfied with what you want.*"
List three things you intend to do to become more financially free.

1. _____

2. _____

3. _____

Cornerstone 3: Establish a Spiritual Purpose for Your Life

If your spiritual purpose is to serve God (Matthew 6:33), all of your resources become ministering currency toward that end. An example would be Patrick Morley in his book *The Man in the Mirror.* He shares a situation out of his own family's experience:

> Several years ago we began to earn more money than needed live in the manner to which we were accustomed. We live in a neighborhood where our children are happy, secure, and settled. My wife likes the convenient location and the neighbors. One of my daughter's very best friends lives two doors down. No dogs bark in the middle of the night, and no expressway drowns out the conversation when we cook out in the backyard.
> Since we were making enough money to live in a bigger, more expensive house, I began to make plans to

move. That's what people do when they can afford to, isn't it? We can generally slot people's income level by the house they live in, because most people keep trading up to the most expensive one their income will allow. People with a $25,000 income live in homes which $25,000 of income can afford; people with a $50,000 income live in homes which $50,000 of income can afford; people with a $150,000 income live in homes which $150,000 of income can afford.

Yet we loved our neighborhood. And we know that people and relationships were more important than possessions. But the social pressure to buy the bigger house preoccupied my mind. The image of having money, and making sure everyone else knows it, pulls like a tug-of-war against the Christian life view.

One day I noticed I was the only family member pressing for the move. That got me thinking. Finally I yielded my ambition to move to the bigger house and allowed God to work. We decided to redecorate instead.

Over the years we began to give shape and form to the belief that God wanted us to put a cap on our standard of living. And however He blessed us over and above that standard of living, He wanted us to help fulfill His purposes.

This decision evolved. We didn't actually sit down and write it out on a piece of paper. Rather, over time, by our lifestyles and actions, we inbred it into values. Then one day we said it out loud, and that settled the issue.

So now we live a predetermined standard of living. And everything God entrusts to us above what we need to live and save for retirement, we give to His work. I would have guessed that living in a bigger house would have made me feel more significant. Yet the sense of usefulness and the impact that we are having leaves us with a deep confidence that we are truly significant, not for our own self-gratification, but in a way that will last forever.[1]

The more money we give to God's work the more our hearts will be fixed on Him. The opposite is also true: Don't give money to God's work, and your heart will not be fixed on Him.

Write down at least one area of your life where you could change priorities and direct the monies to God's work.

1. _____

_____

Cornerstone 4: Give Money to the Lord on a Regular Basis

Once I heard a comic on TV say, "I've been rich and I've been poor, and I like being rich better." For the Christian, the only reason to be rich is to have resources to carry on God's program. Does God need our wealth? No. Can God's purposes be carried out without our money? Yes! God doesn't need our possessions, but we do need to give.

God doesn't care how much we give as deeply as He cares *why* we give. When we lovingly and obediently fulfill our role as givers—no matter what the amount—God will use what we give to minister to others and we will receive a blessing in return.

The Scriptures clearly show us many directions for our giving:

▲ To God through our tithes, gifts, and offerings (Proverbs 3:9,10; 1 Corinthians 16:2)
▲ To the poor (Proverbs 19:17)

▲ To other believers in need (Romans 12:13; Galatians 6:9,10)
▲ To those who minister to us (Galatians 6:6, 1 Timothy 5:17,18)
▲ To widows (1 Timothy 5:3-16)
▲ To family members (1 Timothy 5:8)

On the subject of giving to God, we have already determined that everything we have is His anyway. The question of how much we should actually give back to God in tithes, gifts, and offerings is debatable among Christians. Some insist on a literal tithe (10 percent) and others claim that grace allows each individual to give as he chooses. Without entering the debate, my point is simply that Christians are clearly instructed to return to the Owner of everything a portion of what He has given to us. I will use 10 percent to represent Christian giving, whether offered as a tithe or a freewill gift.

Second Corinthians 9:6-15 contains three excellent principles on the topic of giving. Read the passage for yourself and note the following principles:

Principle 1: We reap what we sow. If we sow sparingly we will reap sparingly. Plants cannot grow if no seeds have been planted. Cups cannot overflow unless water is continually poured into them. If you want an abundance, you must give an abundance. If you give little, you will reap little.

Principle 2: We are to be cheerful givers. We are not to give because we feel pressured to give, but freely and joyfully as in all other areas of ministry. We have attended a couple of churches which have helped worshipers grasp this truth. In the Mariner's Church in Newport Beach, California, no offering plates are passed. The church leaders believe that if God is working in your life, you will make the effort to place your gift in the mail slot in the wall. Another church we attended called the offering box in the foyer the "blessing box." Leaders in this church taught the principles of giving, then trusted parishioners to respond to God's Word instead of an offering plate. And whenever a special financial need arose, the elders brought it to the congregation and the need was met.

Principle 3: We will be blessed because of our obedience. The world will know we are obedient to God by our faithfulness in giving.

You may ask, "How can I give before I receive? Don't I need to have something before I can give it?" That may be the way we think, but that's not the way God thinks. Luke 6:38 states, "Give, and it will be given to you" (NIV). Only after we give are we ready to receive what God has for us.

Many people ask the question, "What is the right way to give money to the Lord?" I was raised with the concept of the 10 percent tithe, and that has been our guideline for returning a portion of our monies to God's work, both in the local church and to parachurch organizations. This money needs to be set aside as it is earned and then given in a systematic way each Sunday. (Even when away from the church on a Sunday we need to continue to give on a regular basis.)

There are many Christian businessmen and women who give tithes of their companies' earnings to Christian organizations. We have a builder in our city who builds a new church each year as his way of returning profits back to the Lord.

These monies are to be used in the work of the local church, but God may direct you to help other worthwhile groups that aren't church-affiliated.

In general your giving should be done in private to guard against you becoming proud or trying to control an agenda on where it should go. Remember, we are giving to God and not to man, and so we should not look for a blessing from specific churches or people to whom we give.

In order to be effective with your money, so that at the end of the month you don't ask the famous question "Where did all my money go?" you need to:

▲ Recognize that God owns everything
▲ Strive for financial freedom
▲ Establish a spiritual purpose for your life
▲ Give to the Lord's work regularly

Four Little-Known Secrets for Developing Financial Strength

A faithful man will abound with blessings.
—Proverbs 28:20

*W*hat a mystery money is! Many people spend their whole life working for it, and some even die for it, but many aren't happy with it when they get it. Money is like a gun: In the right hands it can be a tool for justice, but in the hands of a criminal it can become a weapon of evil.

Money is simply a commodity for exchange. It enables us to provide an end to a means—the purchase of something.

There are four ways in which we can get money:

▲ We can work for it.
▲ We can loan it to someone else and earn interest on it.
▲ We can subcontract it out to someone else and earn a profit from their labor.

▲ We can invest it (risk it) in order to speculate that we may earn a profit.

There are many experts in the field of Christian money management, most of whom give different formulas and principles on how to use God's resources of money. We have adopted four basic guidelines or secrets to assist us in handling money and developing a sound money-managing strategy.

Secret 1: Earn Little by Little

The writer of Proverbs understood this concept very well, for he wrote, "Wealth obtained by fraud dwindles, but the one who gathers by labor increases it" (Proverbs 13:11). (The NIV reads, "He who gathers money little by little makes it grow.") That's the basic concept behind accumulation of excess money beyond the monthly expenses. In the first section of this book we talked about **Progressive realization of worthwhile goals.** The Lord rewards those who are patient and content with their lives. It is amazing how the consistent plodder advances in life. The prize doesn't always go to the swift. Develop a life of being satisfied with a little at a time.

Secret 2: Save Little by Little

As a young boy delivering early morning papers and only making about $35 per month, I can remember learning this basic principle of saving some money each month. Over the years I can't remember a month when I haven't saved something. In America we are a spending country, but we must turn to becoming a saving country if we are to survive financially. One of the greatest services you can give your children is to teach them how to save on a regular basis. It teaches them to be future-oriented, and they also learn to postpone gratification.

In our country, saving for retirement seems to be on everyone's mind. Even young couples think about this great benchmark in life. We need to start early in life to save for that event.

Patrick Morley has a good chart in his book dealing with "The Nest Egg Principle."

> You can pick the annual retirement income you want. That's right. Pick any income level you want, and then follow this simple plan: Each year of your forty-year career save 10 percent of your desired annual retirement income, put it into a qualified retirement plan, and you can extend your targeted income in perpetuity.
>
> How does that work? Here's an example:

▲ Desired annual income at retirement	$40,000
▲ Amount to save each year	$4,000
▲ Required average annual earnings rate	6.2%
▲ Number of years	40

> Here are the results at retirement, rounded to the nearest thousand dollars:

▲ The nest egg (capital accumulated)	$651,000
▲ Yield required to produce desired income	6.2%
▲ Annual retirement income	$40,000

(Note: Tax and inflation consequences are not considered. Money saved can be sheltered through proper tax planning, and retirement income can be protected through lower tax rates and tax-exempt income instruments, e.g., municipal bonds.)

If you have a late start you can catch up by saving more, earning a higher interest rate, or some of each. Here are the required interest rates you would have to earn for shorter periods of time to produce the same income:

	30 years	20 years	10 years
Yield needed	8.3%	12.8%	27.0%
Capital accumulated	$479,000	$316,000	$147,000[1]

Any desired income level can be extended by saving ten percent of that amount for forty years at 6.2 percent.

Here are several ways to achieve this goal:

▲ Open an IRA account with your bank or any reputable investment broker.
▲ Contribute to your retirement plan at work.
▲ Invest in a reputable no-load mutual fund.
▲ Invest in companies which permit you to reinvest with the dividends that are earned.
▲ Don't take out interest and dividends earned; reinvest again.
▲ Invest in annuities that are tax-deferred until they come due. Then reinvest.
▲ Purchase rental income on a regular basis.
▲ Interview and select a good investment counselor who will assist you in these areas if you are a beginner.

This principle of saving little by little helps develop good Christian character qualities of diligence, industry, prudence, and patience.

A small amount set aside regularly grows faster (even at modest compound interest rates) than the average person realizes. If you set aside $1000 at the beginning of each year, in 20 years it will have grown substantially.

$1000 Per Year Compounded

Rate of Interest	10 years	15 years	20 years
6%	13,972	24,673	38,993
7%	14,784	26,888	43,865
8%	15,645	29,324	49,423

Secret 3: Share Your Blessings

If we live within the basic principles which we have discussed, we will be able to share with others a part of what God has so richly given us. We can:

▲ Give to our local church.
▲ Give to other parachurch organizations (Wycliffe Translators, Billy Graham Association, Campus Crusade for Christ, etc.).
▲ Give to local community needs (Red Cross, American Cancer Association, March of Dimes, etc.).
▲ Give to individuals we meet who have needs.
▲ Give to specific interests when needs arrive (summer camp, choir tour, new piano for church, new songbooks, a short-term missionary tour, etc.).

Secret 4: Stay Out of Debt

Our advertising industry, along with manufacturers of products, have conditioned us to buy, buy, buy. We are consumers, and the economic policy which stimulates this mindset is *consumerism*. Romans 12:2 comes to mind again, because we truly are in a war of either conforming to the world system or being transformed by the renewing of our minds.

The way most of us can get there "bigger than life" is to charge it on our credit cards. Since our culture says, "The man who dies with the most toys wins," we have to discipline ourselves not to go into more debt than we can afford with our present income.

In Secret 2 we talked about saving. Debt is the very opposite of that: in life we either earn interest or pay interest. In debt we have to pay back even when we can't afford to do so. Then the collection fees become an even greater burden to us.

The wisdom of Proverbs speaks specifically about this Secret:

▲ Better is he who is lightly esteemed and has a servant than he who honors himself and lacks bread (Proverbs 12:9).
▲ There is one who pretends to be rich, but has nothing; another pretends to be poor, but has great wealth (Proverbs 13:7).

Credit cards are the "genie in the glass bottle" which lets us enter into the world of make-believe. They let us buy products we can't afford. I'm not saying that everything should be paid by cash, but I'm warning that improper use of debt will prevent us from managing our money properly. We will not be financially free as long as the monster of debt controls our lives.

The remedy for overuse of credit cards:

▲ Use your credit card to your advantage, and not to that of the lender.
▲ Pay off the balance at the end of each statement.
▲ If you're behind at the moment, stop using your card at once.
▲ On large items wait 24 hours before purchasing.

▲ Never purchase a large item on the same day that you have an impulse to do so.

▲ Use only one credit card for all expenses. Stay within your credit line. Use this card for emergencies, for car rentals, when traveling to minimize the risks of carrying cash, and as proof of purchase records, expense accounts, IRS receipt of purchase, etc.

▲ Place your credit card in your safety deposit box. It takes away the impulse to use it irresponsibly.

▲ Freeze your credit card in a container in your freezer. You can't purchase until the ice thaws.

▲ Cut up your cards if you can't manage them.

Give these four secrets a try:

▲ Earn little by little.
▲ Save little by little.
▲ Share your blessings with others.
▲ Stay out of debt.

Good
Money Management
Is Imperative

*F*or the Christian family, good money management is imperative for at least three reasons.

First, God associates our ability to handle money with our spirituality. In Luke 16:11 Jesus stated, "If you have not been trustworthy in handling worldly wealth, who will trust you with true riches?" (NIV). If we want to grow in spiritual responsibility and blessing, we must prove our faithfulness in the area of financial responsibility. God is not going to trust us spiritually if we have been irresponsible with our money.

Second, financial responsibility is important because we are only caretakers of what really belongs to God. Psalm 24:1 declares, "The earth is the Lord's, and all it contains." You may possess many things—home, car, furniture, boat, money—but you don't own anything. Even your ability to earn money comes from God (see Deuteronomy 8:17,18). Everything belongs to Him; you are merely a steward of His property. God holds you personally responsible to

411

faithfully manage for Him whatever money or possessions He allows you to have.

Often we are tempted to grasp our possessions selfishly as if they belonged to us and not to God.

As caretakers of God's money and property we must obediently grow and nurture the spiritual fruit of self-control (see Galatians 5:22,23). Every couple we have counseled over the years regarding money problems had at least one member who lacked self-control. Money problems were just one of many undisciplined areas in their lives, including maintenance of the home, yard, automobile, spiritual life, personal hygiene, children, and on and on. These couples exemplify the "easy come, easy go" generation. They are irresponsible with their money and possessions and consequently always have problems in these areas. God wants to give to us abundantly, but He also wants us to exercise self-control over the management of what He gives.

Third, financial responsibility is necessary to help us avoid a number of major money mistakes. Most couples fall into one or more of the following traps because they have not appropriated biblically based principles for the use of their money and possessions.

1. Getting into debt beyond our means to repay. We live in the now generation, and we don't like to save for something when we can buy it right now on credit. But easily available credit can become a problem when we have no predetermined limits and guidelines for spending. I am not saying that we should never go into debt, but rather that undisciplined credit spending is a big mistake (see Romans 13:8).

2. Living a money-centered life. It is easy in our culture to get caught up in the pursuit of wealth and material possessions. But Scriptures like Matthew 6:19-24 and 1 Timothy 6:6-10 warn us that *God* is to be our focus, not money. Without careful, prayerful money management we can be overly influenced by our money-centered society.

3. Trying to get rich quick. Once a reputable Christian man in our church urged me to buy some stock at $26 per share, promising me it could be sold at $40 per share within a month. I eagerly invested a large sum of money, only to lose it all when the "surefire" company went bankrupt. My overeagerness to make a financial killing cost us dearly. Proper money management will help you keep tantalizing schemes like these in perspective (see Proverbs 28:22).

4. Withholding benevolence. According to Proverbs 11:24,25, if we give generously to God and others, we will receive everything we need. But we often turn that principle around by grabbing and holding onto everything we need and want, and giving only from the leftovers— if there are any. For the Christian, being a grabber instead of a giver is not only unscriptural, but it is financially unprofitable.

5. Using people. When money becomes a high priority in our lives, our relationships often suffer. We use people as steppingstones to promotions or personal gain, or we see people as our customers instead of those we are to love, honor, and care for. We are in trouble when we scramble the saying "Love people and use things" to read "Use people and love things."

6. Misplacing priorities. When we overemphasize money in our lives, we try to beat God's system and do things our own way. The order of the big three priorities in life—God, family, and work—often gets wrongly aligned to read—

Work, family, God
or
Work, God, family
or
Family, work, God
or
Family, God, work

or
God, work, family
until we finally get it right:
God, family, work.

At one point in my working experience I had to ask myself this very basic question: How much of my soul am I going to sell to my boss? Until I answered "no more," I was never satisfied because I was letting other people establish my priorities. When I took control of my life, I established the order of the big three in my life. Only when it was God first, family second, and work third was I really content in my job.

Principles for Financial Responsibility

$\mathcal{F}$inancial responsibility for Christian families can be categorized into three distinct actions: giving, receiving, and spending. When we discover God's principles for these three areas, and implement His principles with practical strategies, our needs will be met and our families blessed. Let's look closely at each area.[1]

Giving

In Chapter 9 we provided a basic overview of Christian giving. You might want to reread this chapter to refresh your mind. Just remember that everything is from God and that we are to have thankful hearts. We give back to God what He has so freely given to us.

It is amazing that we must learn to give before we receive. In the world system it is just the opposite: Receive first, then you may give.

Receiving

As giving Christians, we receive from several sources:

▲ From others giving to us (1 Corinthians 9: 11)
▲ From diligent work (Genesis 3:19; 1 Thessalonians 4:11,12; 2 Thessalonians 3:10-13)
▲ From creative endeavors (Proverbs 31:13,24)
▲ From answers to prayer (Philippians 4:6; James 4:2)

Emilie and I know a couple in Newport Beach who once suffered serious financial problems because the husband was having difficulty finding a job. About ten couples from their church banded together to cover their house payments, food, insurance premiums, car expenses, and household needs while the man was out of work. The couple had always been faithful givers; this was their opportunity to receive. Like them, you may be surprised at times to see how God provides for your needs through the giving of others.

A primary way we receive is in return for our own hard work. With all the government programs for the needy today, sometimes we are tempted to look for a handout instead of a job. But Paul clearly confronted that attitude when he wrote, "He who does not work shall not eat" (2 Thessalonians 3:10 TLB). Your diligence as a worker is an avenue by which God will bless you and meet your needs.

Like the Proverbs 31 woman, couples may sometimes receive supplementary income from their creative endeavors, such as sewing, ironing, typing, woodworking, painting, or baking. Others may have the resources to open a business in their home, such as selling and distributing cosmetics, cleaning supplies, kitchenware, or nutrition items. Maybe you also have a God-given talent that you can use for extra income.

James wrote, "The reason you don't have what you want is that you don't ask God for it" (James 4:2 TLB). Since God owns everything we need, He is the ultimate source of everything we receive. We must ask Him to supply our needs, whether a certain salary, a refrigerator, or a larger home. As we present our needs to Him, He may supply them through the giving of others, a temporary job or over-time, or a completely unknown source. But we must pray to Him and expect from Him because He is our source.

In Mark 10:29,30 Jesus teaches that if we leave houses, farms, and relatives for his sake, we will receive a hundred times as much as we give up. We have proved that this prin-ciple works. We have homes in Newport Beach, Laguna Beach, Santa Barbara and Lake Arrowhead, and vacation homes in Scottsdale, Arizona; Chicago; and Stockbridge, Massachusetts. We have boats at the ocean and private jet planes. These assets didn't cost us one dime. They are at our disposal because they belong to Christian friends who give to us freely because somehow we have touched their lives along the way.

Spending

On the topic of spending, we first need to talk about *spendable income.* When you receive your paycheck, there is a very important number on it called gross income, the amount of money you earned before deductions. In order to figure your spendable income you need to deduct two standard expenses from your gross income.

First, you must deduct your giving to God—10 percent, for example. During a session at one of our seminars a man asked if giving should be figured on the gross or the net. A pastor in the group retorted, "Do you want to get blessed on the gross or the net?" Good point. If you are giving a percentage of your true earnings, you must figure your giv-ing on gross income. When you consider your giving a standard expense which is taken off the top of your earn-ings, you will be more faithful than if you consider it an op-tion.

Second, you must deduct local, state, and federal income taxes, approximately 15 to 35 percent, including Social Security. (Other deductions from gross income, such as medical, dental, or life insurance premiums, credit union payments, payroll savings, retirement contributions, annuities, etc. are figured elsewhere in your spending.) These two deductions equal approximately 25 to 45 percent, and the 75 to 55 percent which remains we call *spendable income.* Your spendable income is the amount you have the most control over.

Some Christian financial advisers suggest that spendable income be allocated according to the 10-70-20 plan. According to this plan, 10 percent of your spendable income should be reserved for savings and investments, including any deductions from your paycheck for these purposes.

General living expenses should be confined to 70 percent of your spendable income. This category includes all of the following:

Housing. Housing consists of all expenses necessary to operate the home, including mortgage/rent, property taxes, insurance, maintenance, and utilities. When budgeting utilities, be sure to average your payments over a 12-month period.

Food. Include all groceries, paper goods, and nonfood products normally purchased at a grocery store. Include items like bread and milk which are often purchased in between regular shopping trips. Do not include lunches or dinners at restaurants, which is another category. If you do not know your actual food expenses, keep a detailed spending record for 30 to 45 days.

Transportation. In this category include car payments, auto insurance, gas and oil, licenses, maintenance, etc. Another transportation expense is for depreciation, setting aside money to repair and/or replace your automobile. The minimum amount set aside should be enough to keep the car in decent repair, and then to replace it every four or five years. If replacement funds are not available in the budget, the minimum amount set aside should cover maintenance costs.

Annual or semiannual auto insurance premiums should be set aside monthly to avoid the crisis of a neglected expense. If you ride a bus or train to work, fares should be budgeted in this category.

Insurance. Include health, life, and disability not categorized under housing or transportation. Also include amounts deducted from your paycheck for these items.

Entertainment and recreation. Include vacations, camping trips, dining out, club dues, sporting equipment, hobby expenses, and athletic events. Don't forget Little League and booster club expenses, etc. The only effective method to budget for entertainment and recreation is to decide on a reasonable amount for your family and stay within it.

Clothing. Determine your monthly budget in this area by dividing a year's worth of expenditures by 12. The minimum amount should be $10 per family member per month.

Medical. Include insurance deductibles, doctor bills, eyeglasses, prescriptions, over-the-counter medicines, orthodontia, etc.

Miscellaneous. This category is a general catchall for items like childcare expenses for working mothers, private education costs, allowances, laundry expenses, gifts, etc.

The final 20 percent of your spendable income should be earmarked for payment of debts (loans, notes, credit cards, etc.) and emergencies. Sometimes called a buffer or margin, this amount consists of any money left over after expenses. Most couples with financial difficulty will not have any money in this account. Those who include a margin account in their budgets find it to be a helpful fund for special projects, offerings, gifts, additional savings, or future education expenses.

For every $1000 earned per month, your 10-70=20 figures would look like this:

Total income	$1000
Less giving (10%)	100
Less taxes (15-35%)	280
Total spendable income	$620
10% savings and investments	62
70% living expenses	434
20% debts or buffer	124

May each of us, with God's help, be good stewards of all His riches. May God say to us as He did to the servant, "Well done, good and faithful slave; you were faithful with a few things, I will put you in charge of many things; enter into the joy of your master" (Matthew 25:21).

Monthly Income and Expense Worksheets

INCOME

Gross income (monthly)

Salary	_____
Interest	_____
Dividends	_____
Notes	_____
Rents	_____
Other	_____

TOTAL GROSS INCOME   _____

Standard Expenses

Giving to God (10%)	_____
Income taxes (15-35%)	_____

TOTAL STANDARD EXPENSES   _____

Spendable Income

(Gross income less standard expenses) _____

_____

EXPENSES

Savings and Investments (10%)

Savings _____

Investments _____

TOTAL SAVINGS
& INVESTMENTS _____

Living Expenses (70%)

Housing _____

    Mortgage/rent _____

    Insurance _____

    Property taxes _____

    Electricity _____

    Gas _____

    Water _____

    Sanitation _____

    Telephone _____

    Maintenance _____

    Other _____

    TOTAL HOUSING _____

Food _____

Transportation   _____

    Payments   _____

    Gas/oil   _____

    Insurance   _____

    Licenses   _____

    Taxes   _____

    Maintenance   _____

    Other   _____

    TOTAL TRANSPORTATION   _____

Insurance

    Life   _____

    Medical   _____

    Other   _____

    TOTAL INSURANCE   _____

Entertainment and recreation

    Eating out   _____

    Amusements   _____

    Babysitters   _____

    Vacation   _____

    TOTAL ENTERTAINMENT
    & RECREATION   _____

Clothing   _____

Medical

    Doctors   _____

    Dentists   _____

Prescriptions _____

Other _____

TOTAL MEDICAL _____

Miscellaneous

Toiletries/cosmetics _____

Beauty/hair care _____

Laundry/cleaning _____

Allowances/lunches _____

Subscriptions _____

Gifts (incl. Christmas) _____

Sanitation _____

Telephone _____

Maintenance _____

Other _____

TOTAL
MISCELLANEOUS _____

Total Living Expenses _____

Debts and Emergencies (20%)

Credit card payment _____

_____

_____

_____

Loan and note payments _____

Emergencies _____

Other _____

TOTAL DEBTS AND
EMERGENCIES   _____

INCOME VERSUS EXPENSES

Total Spendable Income   _____

Total Expenses (10-70-20)   _____

Monthly Bottom Line
(income less expenses)   _____

If income exceeds expenses, where will you direct your surplus income?

1. _____

2. _____

3. _____

If expenses exceed income, where will you increase income?

1. _____

2. _____

3. _____

If expenses exceed income, where will you cut expenses?

1. _____

2. _____

3. _____

PART THREE

Organized for Action

▲▲▲

Create a System for Records

Money is nothing more than a resource, and money management is nothing more than a tool to use that resource.

—Ron Blue

You can have the most elaborate set of goals and a very defined set of Christian principles regarding money, but if you don't properly store your records, you will be ineffective in your overall money management program.

In the last six years we have been audited by the IRS three times. If we did not have a good record-keeping system it would have cost us a lot of time, stress, and money. (The stress is sometimes more of a factor than the other two aspects.)

The IRS auditor was very impressed with our system because with every schedule she wanted answers to, we were able to furnish the records and data to back up our figures. After a short period of time she commented favorably on our record system and the audit was completed much sooner than she anticipated. In one of the audits we had to make a minor adjustment, but on the other two audits we had no adjustments. Without the proper system I would have had major adjustments, plus it would have cost us added money for having our CPA present at $60 an hour.

By creating a simple records system you can organize your important papers in a few hours and then spend a minimum amount of time and effort staying on top of the system.

In several of her previous books Emilie talks about different aspects of record-keeping. This section will be geared to the financial aspects of your record-keeping.

You might be the kind of person who shoots from the hip and has a "sorta system." However, this system is like having no system at all. There are various reasons to have a good record system:

▲ You have total control of your financial life.
▲ You enjoy a savings in time, stress, and money.
▲ You have records to check your progress toward your financial goals.
▲ You can support your insurance claims when losses occur.
▲ You can prove payment when a vendor states he never received payment.
▲ You can support a claim if a lawsuit ever occurs.
▲ You can support your IRS and other legal claims.
▲ You have service warranties and proof of payment for previous services performed.
▲ You have easy access to documents for credit, loan, or refinancing applications.

A good system is fairly simple and doesn't take as much time to establish and maintain as most people think. What peace of mind to know where to find a particular piece of information! With the advent of millions of home personal computers, much of the paper figures can be translated to your own database. However, there are also times when you personally have to produce the original documents.

Creating a Workspace

Find some place in your home or office which you can call your own. You need either a temporary or a permanent workspace—a desk or tabletop and some form of filing cabinet. It need not be fancy or elaborate. (See Emilie's books *More Hours in My Day* or *Survival for Busy Women* to get added information on this aspect of record-keeping.)

In creating your system you will need to:

▲ Purchase an inexpensive printing calculator.

▲ Purchase at least a two-drawer file cabinet if you don't already have one.

▲ Use the top drawer to store your *transitory files*. That would include this year's receipts, bills, statements, personal papers, contracts, and agreements which are still in force.

▲ Use the bottom drawer to store your *permanent files* for previous years' papers, completed contracts, old tax returns and records, etc. You will refer to your history file only occasionally, but when you need past records, you will want them quickly. (See the end of this chapter to see how we store past IRS records.)

▲ Purchase at least 50 letter-size Manila file folders.

Deciding how long to retain transitory records can be difficult because often you don't know how long you'll need them. As a rule of thumb we suggest that you keep all employee records until you leave the job. Other transitory records you want to keep for three to five years include receipts for any major purchases you have made (jewelry, autos, art, stock certificates), plus all tax returns and all receipts for health insurance policies, credit union membership, and company stock ownership plans. Canceled checks not relating directly to specifics like home improvements should be kept for a minimum of three years in case of a tax audit. However, I usually keep these five to six years just to make sure I'm not throwing away any records I might need on a tax audit.

Your tax return, wage statements, and other papers supporting your income and deductions should be kept at least three years (that's the IRS statute of limitations for examining your return). I retain our records six years because the IRS has the right to audit within six years if they believe you omitted an item accounting for more than 25 percent of your reported income, or indefinitely if they believe you committed fraud.

Storing IRS Files

If you are familiar with Emilie's "Total Mess to Total Rest" program, you are aware of her "perfect boxes" and her numbering system of these boxes. We reserve the 15 block of numbers to store all our records pertaining to April 15. We mark them 15, 15A, 15B, 15C, 15D, 15E, etc. In box 15 we store all our past IRS and California state tax forms, and these are filed by year: 1989, 1990, 1991, 1992, etc. The other boxes we use to store various years' documents along with all the backup receipts for that year. For example, the boxes would be marked:

▲ 15A
▲ 15B
▲ 15C
▲ 15D

On a separate 3x5 card we write:

▲ 15A—1989 tax returns
▲ 15B—1990 tax returns

▲ 15C—1991 tax returns
▲ 15D—1992 tax returns

We use one card for each box. I store these 3x5 cards in an appropriate-size 3x5 file box. When I need to look through a certain year's records, I go to my file box in the 15 series and find the year. Suppose it is 1990 returns. I see that it is stored in box 15B. I go to box 15B, flip the lid up, and find all the information I need.

If I have more material than fits in one box, I reserve two or three boxes for the same year and my card would read:

▲ 15A, 15B—1990 tax returns

Every year I review my boxes that house the records that are over six years old. I consolidate my reporting forms to box 15 along with any backup data on home purchases, stock purchases, etc. that have continued tax implications. The other receipts I toss, and I can use the empty box for this year's records.

Suggested Categories for Your System

$\mathcal{H}$ ere is a suggested checklist to begin your filing system. Check those file names you can use. Add to this list any other files you will need. The name of the file folder is shown first. The items that go in the file are shown second.

____ **Asset management account**—monthly statements, prospectuses

____ **Bank account**—monthly statements, correspondence

____ **Children's file**—school papers, birthday and Christmas cards, drawings, awards, diplomas, certificates

____ **Clubs**—health club, country club, business club

____ **Credit bureau report**

____ **Credit card bills/receipts** (one file for each)—monthly statement and phone numbers
Enter names of each credit card you have:

_____   _____

_____   _____

_____   _____

____ **Doctor and hospital bills**—family doctor, address, phone number, medical records, doctor and hospital bills

____ **Education**—night school, correspondence school, work-related courses

____ **Employment records**—employment contract, employee handbook, employee benefits information, retirement plan information

____ **Financial blueprints**—your goals list created in Chapter 8

____ **Guarantees, warranties, instructions**—instructions and guarantees for carpets, tires, stereo equipment, appliances, etc.

____ **Home**—purchase contract, mortgage papers, home improvement receipts, leases and rental agreements, payment book, canceled checks

____ **Home improvements**—records and receipts of any home improvements

____ **Important papers**—birth certificates, marriage license number, passports, diplomas

____ **Insurance, auto**—automobile insurance policy, traffic infractions and accidents, automobile title, driver's license number, license plate information

____ **Insurance, health**—health insurance policy

____ **Insurance, homeowner's**—homeowner's or tenant's insurance policy, umbrella liability policy, personal property inventory list

____ **Insurance, life**—life insurance policies, correspondence with company, insurance quotes

____ **Investments, annuities**

____ **Investments, IRA accounts, Keogh accounts**

____ **Investments, miscellaneous** tax-sheltered annuities, savings accounts, loans to others, IOU's

___ **Investments, mutual funds**—monthly statements, correspondence

___ **Investments, real estate**

___ **Investments, stock and bond certificates**

___ **Personal**—cards, letters, pictures, etc.

___ **Receipts**—miscellaneous

___ **Resume**

___ **Retirement plan**—papers relating to your employment or small-business retirement plan

___ **Taxes, federal and state**—tax-deductible receipts, tax returns and files for last three to seven years (see Chapter 14)

___ **Telephone**—telephone bills and correspondence

___ **Utilities**—electric, gas, water, sewer bills

___ **Will**—copy

The time required to set up and maintain these files is not great, and it will be a great investment of your energy.

Setting Up a Desk and Work Area

A wise man thinks ahead; a fool doesn't, and even brags about it.

—Proverbs 13:16 TLB

$\mathcal{A}$s I began to get my home in order and to eliminate all the clutter I soon realized that I didn't have an area to handle all the mail and literature that came into our home. We have had several mottos to help us focus on our home organization.

One was, **"Don't put it down, put it away."** Much of our clutter was little piles of materials that needed to be put away but we just temporarily put it down until we could put it where it belonged. At the end of the day we had piles sitting all around the home. Now we take it back to where we found it. It's amazing how the piles have disappeared!

Another motto was, **"Don't pile it, file it!"** Somewhere in the corner of the home we had piles of literature that were in no organized order. In our new program we have taken Manila folders and given them one-word headings such as **Insurance, Car, Home, Foods, Patio, Children,**

Utilities, Taxes. Now we file, not pile, our papers. (See suggested headings in Chapter 15.)

During all this change in our home we still had no central desk or work area. Yet we realized we needed one in order to function properly with maximum efficiency.

Efficient paper-handling requires a good physical setting with a practical location furnished with a comfortable working surface and a good inventory of supplies. Ideally, this office will become a permanent fixture where the business life of your home is done. It should have all necessary supplies and files and should be located where other household operations do not interfere. However, if your desk/work area can't be this ideal, don't let this fact stop you from getting started. Your desk might have to be portable, but that's okay—just get started.

Since a desk or work area is so basic to a well-functioning lifestyle, we will give you some practical steps in setting up this area in your home.

Choosing the Location

The selection of your office area depends on how long you spend in your office daily. If you have a business out of your home you need to use different criteria in selecting that special site from the person who needs a place to open mail, answer mail, pay bills, and file papers. Regardless of what your precise need is, you want to choose a location that agrees with your spirit. If after a short while you find you aren't using your new space, but find yourself working in the room with the big window, you might have initially selected the wrong location, one that doesn't fully meet your needs. However, it is not always practical to work in the ideal location, often there needs to be a compromise. In order to choose the proper setting, ask yourself these questions:

▲ Do I need to be in a place where it's quiet, or is it better for me to be near people?

▲ Do big windows distract me or do I like being near windows?

▲ Do I prefer a sunny room or a shaded one?

▲ Do I prefer to work in the morning or in the afternoon?

These last two questions are related because different rooms receive varying amounts of light at different times of the day.

The answers to these questions help narrow your alternatives. Walk around your home to see which areas meet your answers to the four questions. After selecting at least two locations, you might ask yourself another set of questions:

▲ Are there enough electrical outlets and telephone jacks?

▲ Is there enough space for a desk?

▲ Is this location out of the way of other household functions? If not, can they be shifted so they won't interfere with my office hours?

▲ Is the area structurally sound?

Add the answers to these questions to your previously selected alternative and narrow your possibilities down to a final selection. Do you feel good about this selection? Live with it a few days before making a final selection. Walk to and through it several times to see that it feels good. Sit down in the area and read a magazine or book. If it still feels good, then you will probably like your choice.

Don't begin tearing out walls, adding electrical outlets, moving phone jacks, or building bookcases until you're sure you've found the right location.

Selecting Desk, Equipment, and Supplies

After you have selected the location for your office, you need to sketch the floor plan and show the room dimensions. You will use this information when you want to make or select furniture for your new work area.

The Desk

Actually, all you really need is a writing surface of some type. In some cases a portable piece of plywood is all you have or need. Look around, because you may already have around your home a suitable desk or table which would fit into the dimensions of the work area.

If you find a table, it should be sturdy, high enough to write comfortably, and large enough to hold various implements on its surface.

If you can't find a desk or table in your home, buy a desk. It is an investment you won't regret. Check your local classified ads to find a good bargain. One good source is the yellow pages of your phone book under "Office Furniture—Used." You need not pay full price. Many times these stores will deliver to your home free or with a minimum charge.

You should have no trouble finding a desk which has the practical characteristics of office models but is still attractive in your home. Here are a few specifications to keep in mind.

1. **Writing surface.** Your desk should be sturdy and comfortable to use, with a surface that doesn't wobble.

2. **Place for supplies.** Have at least one large drawer in which paper and envelopes can be kept in folders. If you find a desk with large drawers on each side, so much the better. There needs to be a shallow drawer with compartments for paper clips, rubber bands, and other supplies. At

your local stationery store you can purchase small trays with dividers that can store these small items.

3. Files and records. A home office seldom has need for more than one file drawer, or sometimes two. If your desk has at least one drawer big enough to contain letter-size file folders (legal size accommodation is preferable), all your files will probably be comfortably accommodated. If you can't purchase a file cabinet at this time, go back and read "Total Mess to Total Rest" in Emilie's *More Hours in My Day* or *Survival for Busy Women,* where she talks about the **Perfect Box.** These make excellent file boxes until you are able to purchase a file cabinet. Watch your newspaper for stationery "sale" offerings.

4. Typing platform. If you have a typewriter or a personal computer and plan to use it in your work area, try to get a desk with a built-in platform for these to rest on. If you have enough room in your office you might want to designate a separate area in your office for these two functions.

If you don't have enough space for a regular stationery desk in your home, look into portable storage to house your stationery and supplies. Go again to your local office supply store and have them recommend products that will service this need. You will still need a file cabinet or its short-term substitute (the Perfect Box) and a sturdy swivel chair just for the office area. (The swivel chair permits you to turn from one position to another without getting up.)

Other Storage Ideas

▲ Wall organizers are helpful for pads, pens, calendars, and other supplies.

▲ Paper, pencils, and miscellaneous supplies can be kept in stackable plastic or vinyl storage cubes kept under the desk.

▲ Use an extra bookcase shelf for portable typewriter, basket of supplies, or some files.

▲ Decorative objects (such as a ceramic mug) look attractive holding pencils and pens.

▲ Use stackable plastic bins that can be added on to for your expanded needs. Use the small style for stationery and papers, and a larger size (a vegetable bin) for magazines and newspapers.

Supplies

For your shopping convenience I have given you a checklist of supplies that you will need to stock your office. Again, try to purchase these items on sale or at an office supply discount store. Watch your local paper for these sales, or look under "Office Supplies" in the yellow pages. Many times bulk buying is the way you will get your best prices.

____ Address book or Rolodex. I personally like both; the address book I take with me when traveling or on business, and the Rolodex I keep permanently located on my desk. The Rolodex has room for adding other information you might want to use when addressing that particular person or business.

____ Appointment calendar. Ideally the calendar should be small enough to carry around with your notebook, as well as to use at your desk. If you search around, you can find a combination notebook and calendar that isn't too bulky to carry around in your briefcase or purse. The date squares should be large enough to list appointments comfortably. In our "Working Woman's Seminars" we offer an excellent organizer called "Harper House/Day Runner." This product does an excellent job in meeting this need.

____ Bulletin board. This is a good place to collect notes and reminders to yourself. Attach notes with pushpins.

____ Business cards. A must time-saver.

_____ Carbon paper. Make a carbon copy of every business letter you write. Your office supply store can help you with this selection. Every year new formats come on the market.

_____ Computer, desktop. You will need to shop around for this tool if you are inclined to incorporate this in your money management system.

_____ Desk lamp. A three-way bulb will give you a choice of light levels.

_____ Dictionary and/or electronic speller.

_____ File folders. I use colored "third-cut" folders in which the tabs are staggered so they don't block each other from view. The colors give a more attractive appearance to your file drawer.

_____ Letter opener.

_____ Marking pens. I keep on hand a few marking pens in different colors. (I do a lot of color-coding on my calendar.) I also use the "yellow hi-lite" when I want some information to pop out at me for rereading.

_____ Paper clips. Regular and large.

_____ Postcards. These save money on your mailing.

_____ Pencil sharpener. If you use a lot of pencils, I recommend a desktop electric model.

_____ Pencils and pens.

_____ Postage scale. A small inexpensive type.

_____ Rubber bands. Mixed sizes.

_____ Rubber stamp and ink pad. There are all kinds of rubber stamps you can use in your office. These are much cheaper than printed stationery or labels. If you use a certain one over and over, you might consider having a self-inking stamp made for you (a great time-saver).

_____ Ruler.

_____ Scissors.

_____ Scratch paper. Use lined pads for this purpose. 3-M "Post-It-Notes" are also great for this.

_____ Scotch tape and dispenser.

_____ Stamps. In addition to regular stamps, keep appropriate postage on hand for additional weight and special handling.

_____ Stapler, staples, staple remover. If you do a lot of stapling you might consider an electric model (saves time and the palm of your hand).

_____ Stationery and envelopes. Usually the 8½ x 11 plain white paper (with matching business-size envelopes) is all you will need. If you use a printed letterhead stationery you will need to get some plain white or matching colored second sheets. I find that 9x6 and 9x12 Manila envelopes are good for mailing bulk documents, books, or magazines. Sometimes a #6 Jiffy padded envelope can be used to ship items that need some protection from rough handling in transit.

_____ Telephone. An extension right at your desk is great. I use my cordless telephone for this purpose and it works just fine.

_____ Typewriter.

_____ Typewriter correction fluid or paper.

_____ Wastebasket.

You now have an office space that lets you function to your maximum ability. This addition to your lifestyle will make you more efficient in other areas of your life, and it will give you a special feeling of accomplishment.

Me? Balance a Checkbook?

$\mathcal{T}$he one dreaded chore that we all have to face is balancing a checkbook. Unless God has gifted you with special strengths, you find that this monthly exercise is not a great deal of fun. Yet I find this to be one of the important exercises in money management. In our home, Emilie takes care of all the banking for our family expenses and I manage all the finances relating to More Hours in My Day. She balances her checkbook and I balance the business checking account and books.

An absolute rule in our home is to reconcile the bank statements within 48 hours of receiving them. Keeping these up-to-date is very, very important!

There are several ways to maintain a proper record of the checks. They are:

▲ Store them in the Manila file folder labeled "Bank Account."

▲ Store them in a separate check file box intended just for canceled checks.

▲ File checks in order by check number, along with deposit slips, deposit receipts, and your check register.

▲ Don't leave canceled checks and statements lying loose in a drawer.
▲ Don't assume that your statement is accurate just because it is mechanically done. Errors can be made.

Reconcile each monthly statement by using the form found on the back of your statement. If the check is for an item that is tax deductible at the end of the year, I make a copy of this check and file it in my "Taxes" Manila folder. If you don't have access to a copy machine, you can put a red "T" in the upper-right-hand corner of the check for ease in documenting at tax time. At tax time I have quick access to a copy of these and can make quick calculations for our federal and state tax returns. I also photocopy all checks which I need for future verification of major purchases, stock purchases, and contract agreements. I staple this copy to the original document.

The steps in reconciling your bank statements are:

1. Be certain all your deposits were recorded correctly. Compare your deposit receipts with the deposit entries on your statement.
2. Be certain the correct check amounts are deducted from your bank balance. Compare each check returned in your statement envelope to the amount deducted by the bank on your statement. Anything that doesn't agree is a bank error.
3. Identify checks outstanding that have not been deducted from your account. Just check off with a red pen in your check register all checks returned with your statement. Any check register entries not marked are checks you have written that were not received by the bank by the time your statement was prepared. These outstanding checks must be deducted from the balance shown on your statement to determine the actual balance in your account at the present time.

4. Identify and deduct bank charges. Your bank will charge you for anything it can, including NSF (nonsufficient funds) checks, ATM usage, or a minimum monthly account charge. Deduct the total of these charges (once you are certain they are correct) in your check register to adjust your actual balance. By the same token, add any amounts credited to you for interest-bearing accounts and/or deposits which you have made after the statement date.

5. Contact your bank immediately if you find any errors in your account.

You should never have to call your bank to find out what your balance is. If you reconcile each statement you will know what your balance is.

Balancing Your Checking Account

Before you start, be sure you have entered all transactions **in your checkbook,** including interest earned, electronic activity, and bank charges as shown on your statement.

A. Enter Deposits **not shown on this statement** (including electronic).

Date of Deposit	Amount
_____	_____
_____	_____
_____	_____
Total A	$_____

B. Enter all checks, all withdrawals (including electronic) and any bank charges **not shown on this statement.**

Outstanding Item/Check No.   Amount

_____	_____
_____	_____
_____	_____
_____	_____
_____	_____
_____	_____

Total B	$_____
Ending balance on your statement	$_____
TOTAL A	+ $_____
	= $_____
TOTAL B	$_____
Current Balance	= $_____

(Should equal your checkbook balance)

Have a
Safe Deposit Box

Burned papers and important documents are difficult to replace. Your local bank can provide you with various sizes of deposit boxes to meet your needs. We started with the smallest box the bank had and have grown about two sizes over the years.

Many of the new homes in California come with fire-proof safety storage areas. Here is a list of important, hard-to-replace papers that may be considered for safekeeping at the bank or in your deposit area at home:

▲ Treasury bond certificates
▲ Mutual fund shares
▲ Stock or bond certificates
▲ Property deeds
▲ Automobile titles
▲ Personal property inventory list and photographs
▲ Marriage certificate
▲ Will and estate plan
▲ Birth certificates
▲ Diplomas
▲ Military discharge papers

▲ Passports
▲ Negatives of important family photographs
▲ Personal property video copy

If you use a home safe, make sure it is fire-rated and that it is securely attached to the floor for added protection. Having a safe at home is much more convenient than going back and forth to the bank.

Review Your Spending Habits

Have you found honey? Eat only what you need,
lest you have it in excess and vomit it.

—Proverbs 25:16

I've learned that if it tastes good it's probably bad for your health. Everything that's fun seems to be either fattening, immoral, or expensive! Our family tries to be cost-conscious, but no matter how hard we shop for an item, the day after we buy it, it will go on sale!

One way you can have more funds to meet your bills is by reviewing your spending habits.

▲ Stop using your credit cards except for gasoline purchases or business expenses that will be reimbursed by your employer. Leave all bank cards, charge cards, travel cards, etc. at home.

▲ Carry only enough cash for each day's needs. There's no chance of spending money if you don't have it with you. Besides, with the crime spree in our country it isn't safe to carry excess cash.

▲ Leave your checkbook at home—again, another attempt to stop your careless spending.
▲ Shop sales. Use discipline to buy only what is on sale. Store owners many times advertise a "loss leader" to get you into their store, knowing that once you are there your sales resistance will weaken and you will buy items that aren't on sale. Say NO! Don't buy nonsale items. Listed below are the months which target specific items:

When Items Go On Sale

Item:	Likely to be on sale in:
Appliances	January, July
Bedding	January, February, August
Books	January
Cars, new	August, September
Cars, used	February, November
Clothing, summer	June, July
Clothing, winter	November, December
Linens	January, May
School supplies	August, October
Televisions	May, June
Toys	January, February

▲ Don't buy state lottery tickets. The average lottery ticket buyer spends at least $250 per year for this extravagance, but never wins anything.
▲ Drop to the next lower grade in the products you use. You can maintain the same quality by purchasing generic brand products at the supermarket.
▲ Cut back on eating out. The average American spends 37 percent of his or her food budget in restaurants. The typical restaurant price is twice what it would be at home and is usually of poorer nutritional quality because it has more

fat, more sodium, more cholesterol, and more sugar. By eating at home you can better control your diet requirements.

We have found that people with poor money management have poor spending habits. Change your spending habits and you will upgrade your financial status.

PART FOUR

The Know-How for Managing Money

▲ ▲ ▲

Little Remedies for Money Headaches

Seek first His kingdom and His righteousness,
and all these things shall be added to you.
—Matthew 6:33

When you have money problems, you have to be creative in trying to get back in control. Here are several ideas that can help you think creatively.

Remedy 1: Hold a garage sale. You would be amazed at how much money you have lying around your home and garage. Lump your unneeded property together and sell it all at once. Try to coordinate a combined sale with your immediate neighbors; you'll get larger attendance and the competition will actually improve sales in most cases. Use the profits to help get financial relief; don't be tempted to purchase your neighbor's stuff!

Remedy 2: Sell any major drain on your cash flow. It might be a second home, a car, a recreational vehicle, a boat, even a main home. Whatever the drain, you might want to sell that item or items until you can solve your money problems.

Remedy 3: Check your life insurance to see if you have cash value you can borrow. Take advantage of this source if available. You may even want to review all your insurance policies and make basic adjustments if you have coverage that is unnecessary. You should also consider switching any whole life to term insurance, taking your surrender value in cash and paying off your excessive debt.

Remedy 4: Go back to the basics until you get caught up. That means carrying your lunches to work, eating at McDonald's for a dinner out, walking or riding your bicycle for neighborhood errands, and making no new purchases (that includes clothes, too). This method really hurts, but is necessary to get an immediate increase in cash.

Remedy 5: Obtain a bill-payer loan. In this method you must use great discipline. The money borrowed can't be used for anything but to pay off old bills. Many people splurge when they get this loan, but you can't. As you ease the money pain, you will be tempted to go out and use this money for frills.

Remedy 6: Put your hobby to work. Many men and women are able to put their hobbies to work. We know of people who specialize in baking bread, making gourmet desserts, carving wood ducks, sewing clothing, making alterations, detailing automobiles, doing artwork, and typing papers. Many home businesses are started out of hobbies.

Remedy7: Get an extra job. Many of our teacher friends use this skill by tutoring a few students. Accountants use their skill around tax time. If you love children you might want to babysit a few hours each day. Many parents need help before and after school hours. Working parents and single parents need housecleaning chores done so they can keep up their domestic duties. Our sister-in-law hires an elderly man to hand-water the wildflowers around her home.

Remedy 8: Use extra money to pay off debt. Tax refunds, Christmas funds, selling a car, or inheriting money from a deceased relative can be used to get you caught up. This is not as much fun as purchasing new clothes, a new car, or an expensive holiday weekend, but you must use discipline to get those bills paid.

Remedy 9: Sell any collectibles that you might have. Get an appraisal of their value and consider selling them. Many times these collectibles have become keepsakes, but when you have a debt problem, this is an area that needs consideration.

Remedy 10: Call your main creditors. Go on the offensive; don't wait for them to come to you. Creditors will appreciate you coming to them first. Many times these creditors are willing to alter their payment schedule to help you during this tight time. Most creditors don't want you to file personal bankruptcy because then they only get a fractional payment. Keeping you making payments even if it is less than they would desire is better than getting no payment at all.

> *Unless you have unlimited resources,*
> *you cannot have everything.*
> —Ron Blue

How to Get Out of Debt

Owe nothing to anyone except to love one another,
for he who loves his neighbor has fulfilled the law.

—Romans 13:8

$\mathcal{I}$t's sad to say, but approximately 80 percent of all Americans have negative net worth (which means that they owe more than they are worth). Professional marriage counselors indicate that stress over mismanagement of money is a leading cause of the disintegration of the family unit. Debt and its related problems are the banana peel that many of us slip on. Once we are down in debt, it is very hard to get out and stay out.

When you spend more money than you make, the result is debt. Unfortunately, credit cards make it possible to go into debt very easily. You may be flooded by mail indicating that you have just been approved for X amount of dollars from company Y. What an easy way to get a loan approved! When you sign up for such a good deal, you have just become a slave of that bank.

Once you have gotten into debt, how do you get out? Below are five steps to help you out of this dilemma.

1. Recognize That There Is No Easy Way Out of Debt

It's a lot easier to get in than out. Getting out takes good planning, discipline, hard work, and time. In order to get out of debt, you must also fight the added effect of interest on the loan. You not only have to pay off the debt itself, but you also have to pay off the interest on the debt.

2. Try to Increase Your Income

Extra labor doesn't always increase cash flow. In fact, it is possible to work several hours overtime and have the extra taxes cause you to receive less than if you had not worked extra at all.

By following the principles listed below you can increase your cash flow.

▲ **Avoid impulse buying.** Plan ahead for the things you need to purchase, and don't buy anything that isn't on your shopping list.

▲ **Shop comparatively.** It takes a little time to find what the best price is on an item or a service, but if you do this consistently it can really make a difference in your cash flow.

▲ **Buy at the right time.** Many prices are seasonal. Buy melons in August, not January. Buy swimming suits in August, not April.

▲ **Don't stay unemployed long.** In times of recession it pays to anticipate a job layoff before it happens and to begin job hunting before your old job expires.

▲ **Use your credit card carefully.** A credit card can be a very handy way to purchase items. However, if the account is not paid off completely each month, it can be an anesthetic used to cover the pain of debt.

▲ **Use a checking account.** If it is too difficult to discipline yourself with a credit card, destroy the card and just use a checking account. And don't write "rubber" checks!

▲ **Use banks, but don't let them use you.** Shop around for the highest rate of return on your bank accounts.

▲ **Buy quality.** Cheap goods aren't necessarily economical. In the long run, high-quality products may outlast and outperform poor-quality goods many times over.

▲ **Develop money-saving hobbies.** Many expensive services can be done by families themselves. Anything from tree trimming to plumbing can be done by handy families.

3. Begin to Pay Off Debt

By practicing cost savings techniques you should have more money to pay off your debts. Pay off the debt with the highest interest rate first, the second-highest next, and so forth.

4. Begin to Prevent Future Debt

As you pay off one debt, don't go back into debt for something else. The money you save will help you build a cushion for that rainy day. Tear up those extra credit cards that got you into trouble in the first place.

5. Dedicate Your Finances to God

Many blessings in Scripture are promised to people who dedicate their finances to God (that means assets as well as liabilities).

▲ After the slave invested the money his Lord said, "Well done, good and faithful slave; you were faithful with a few things, I will put you in charge of many things; enter into the joy of your master" (Matthew 25:21-23).

▲ Honor the Lord with your possessions, and with the first-fruits of all your increase; so shall your barns be filled with plenty, and your vats will overflow with new wine (Proverbs 3:9,10 NKJV).

▲ My God shall supply all your needs according to His riches in glory (Philippians 4:19).

▲ Instruct those who are rich in this present world not to be conceited or to fix their hope on the uncertainty of riches, but on God, who richly supplies us with all things to enjoy (1 Timothy 6:17).

Managing Your Finances in Tough Times

Where your treasure is, there will your heart be also.

—Matthew 6:21

During recessionary times, many businesses, families, and individuals struggle to keep their investments together. Though unemployment is more rampant in certain geographical regions than others, almost all Americans taste the stress of reduced income at one time or another.

Here are several ideas to be used in any economic climate, but particularly in tough times.

Idea 1: Budget Your Money

One of the hardest things to teach individuals and couples is to make a budget. They find it boring, and it gives little gratification. However, a budget is a must when we have limited income or when we lose a job.

If you don't know where your money goes every month, you probably haven't taken the time to analyze your monthly income and outgo. It is very important for you to know how much money you spend on a regular basis, and how much you owe.

For the next three months keep a diary or log of where you spend every cent (outgo) of your paycheck (income). After studying this log on a regular basis you can readily determine items that must be reduced or cut from your expenses. There are times when you must take a very sharp knife and make drastic cuts. In these situations you can't wait long; you must do it *now*. See Chapter 13 for more information on budgeting.

Idea 2: Build Up an Emergency Nest Egg

All of us must have a fund equivalent to three to six months of take-home pay to help us in case of emergencies. You might yell, "I can't do that!" I would whisper back to you, "You must if you are a manager of your money!"

If you are in a field or career that is susceptible to layoffs, seasonal ups and downs, or recessions, you should have more than six months of salary in your nest egg. You need to save at least 10 percent of your annual take-home pay for this purpose. It takes a great deal of discipline and the ability to delay gratification, but it will certainly give you a sense of well-being when an emergency hits.

Over the years we have paid ourselves first with a check to be deposited in our savings account. We also contribute regularly to our IRA plan and to a self-directed Keogh fund. Not only are these tax-deferred, but we reinvest the dividends back into additional purchases of stock. We purchase a $100 EE Treasury bond periodically at the bank and store it in our safe deposit box for safekeeping. These tools help our savings begin building for retirement.

Idea 3: Discuss Asset Management with Those You Respect

Seek out those friends whom you respect and who seem to have a handle on their finances. Question them on how they do it and what basic principles they use. Have ready your specific concerns, and write them down on paper so you will be organized when you meet with these people. This way you won't forget specific questions.

Sometimes wisdom is hard to hear, because a wise person may give you advice that is hard to take. But be receptive and not defensive when such a person gives you specifics. Be sure to write him or her a thank-you note for giving his time to you.

Idea 4: Get Rid of Your Credit Cards

If things are getting tight for you and your family, pay cash or don't buy. The last thing you need during tight times is debt, particularly credit card debt. The way business and credit is worked in America, you need at least one card in order to rent cars, verify purchases, make hotel reservations, etc., but these balances *must* be paid off at the end of each statement. If you can't do this, then don't use the card.

Watch out for credit card traps. Many banks are lowering their credit-card rates. It's about time! However, to make more money, some banks are changing the way they calculate finance charges and fees.

One trick is the so-called *two-cycle, average-daily-balance method.* Finance charges are based on outstanding balances over two monthly billing periods, which could hit those who don't pay bills in full each month. As a result, finance charges are doubled, wiping out any anticipated savings from a lower interest rate.

Another method banks use to boost cardholders' bills is

to *include new purchases* (since the end of the last billing cycle) *when calculating the balance subject to finance charge.* This penalizes those of us who pay our bill in full and on time each month.

Two other methods of calculating finance charges are based on the *adjusted balance* (the amount outstanding at the beginning of a billing period, minus payments and credits during the period) and the *previous balance* (the balance outstanding at the beginning of the billing period).

Under federal regulations, card issuers must disclose the type of method used for finance charges, but they don't have to explain how the method works. To find out, you must call the issuer and ask how the method works. You might find that you're paying much more than you think on late charges. You can get more information from these sources:

▲ **RAM Research** publishes a newsletter, *CardTrak.* Call 800-344-7714.
▲ **Bankcard Holders of America** (Herndon, VA) puts out various consumer information brochures. Call 800-732-9194 for further information.

Idea 5: Establish a Line of Credit

Not that you are going to borrow, but to have credit approved in case of an emergency. The best source of credit that is also still tax-deductible is a home equity loan. We don't recommend this as a normal way to get funds, but your home equity can be used in an emergency.

Make sure your lender gives you a line of credit with little or no up-front charges and no interest due until you decide you need the money. Start with your bank or credit union if you have been satisfied with their service.

If not, shop around; ask others who have done the same and get recommendations from them. You may check your local newspaper or the yellow pages of your phone directory to find appropriate lending institutions.

We suggest that you consider only a fixed-rate home equity loan instead of an ARM (one with adjustable rates).

Idea 6: Keep Your Investments Liquid and Safe

When times get tough, you want to keep your investments where you can get them. You usually won't be getting the highest rate of interest, but you want to be conservative and take no risks. This can be done by having your money invested in:

- ▲ Money market funds
- ▲ CD's (short-term)
- ▲ Money-market mutual funds
- ▲ Government-guaranteed securities

A few funds to help you are:

▲ **American Century Investments** (800-472-3389 or 415-965-4274). Minimum investment: $1000. It's as safe as any Treasury fund, but with an extra half-point or more in yield, plus tax advantages in many states. American Century Investments is personally my top pick for yield and safety.

▲ **Scudder Short-Term Bond Fund** (800-225-2470 or 617-439-4640). Minimum investment: $1000.

▲ **Blanchard Short-Term Global Income Fund** (800-688-7904). Minimum investment: $3000.

Idea 7: Consider Starting a New Part-Time Business

What a great time to start that dream of a business you have had for so many years! Emergencies certainly lend themselves to creativity, and now is the time to look into that possibility. We know of many couples who have started businesses in their homes during this time. Many have gone into multilevel marketing products and have done very well.

The U.S. Small Business Administration (SBA) has a number of publications designed to help new businesses. These include *Checklist for Going into Business, Developing a Strategic Business Plan, Researching Your Market,* and *Goal Setting for Small Business.* To order a free directory of publications and videotapes, call the Small Business Answer Desk at 800-827-5722 or 202-653-7561 (in Washington D.C.). In the directory you will find an order form for the booklets mentioned above, plus more.

Idea 8: Develop Your Own Strategies for Smart Money Management

▲ Pay off any personal loans you have. (Those interest charges are no longer tax-deductible.)
▲ Review your W4 form. You need not overpay your taxes to Uncle Sam.
▲ Maximize your contributions to your IRA's, Keogh's, or company pension plans.
▲ Start a nest egg fund.

Women: Shape Up Your Financial Muscles!

She goes out to inspect a field, and buys it; with her own hands she plants a vineyard.

—Proverbs 31:16 TLB

$\mathcal{I}$n our various seminars on marriage and relationships, we point out that there are emotional, physical, and psychological differences between men and women. There are also some financial differences.

▲ Women generally underrate the value of their labor.
▲ Until recently, women have had difficulty in making certain financial transactions.
▲ Approximately 50 percent of marriages end up in divorce, with women usually getting the children and the financial burden for raising the children.
▲ Most Americans living below the poverty line are women.

470

Historically women's work pay scale has been less than men's. One way to break this wage restriction is to have women take jobs which have usually been held by men, such as engineers, construction workers, attorneys, doctors, truck drivers, etc.

In order to break away from the historical limitations, there are several things you can do.

1. Improve Your Financial Position—NOW!

▲ **Increase your base salary.** You may have to ask your boss for a raise, take a second job, or develop your hobby into a paying endeavor.

▲ **Create your own line of credit.** Maintain a good credit record with your telephone company, utility company, and a gasoline credit card. Make sure you have a good reference with your bank by having both a savings and a checking account. Build a good credit history by establishing a department store charge account, adding an oil company credit card if you don't have one in your name, and applying for a small loan to be backed up by your signature or collateral. These accounts are only to help you establish credit in your name. They are not to go into debt beyond your ability to pay. Great discipline must be used in developing this strategy.

▲ **Protect your principal.** Be cautious with your money and don't speculate with your investments. At this stage you want assets, not losses.

2. Improve Your Financial Self-Worth in the Workplace

Surveys show that girls rate the importance of boys' labor higher than their own. Interestingly, boys rate girls' work equal to their own. It appears that our culture has trained women to think less of their labor. However, don't underrate yourself. Begin a fair appraisal of your worth to your company. If you feel you are carrying your part in making the company profitable, you should ask for a raise, ask for a job with more responsibility with more pay, or begin to look for a better job.

3. Take Steps to Get a Pay Increase

There are certain steps you can take to do this:

▲ **Take an inventory of your good points.** Write them down on paper. Why are you valuable to your company?
▲ **Decide how much you are worth.** Do a salary survey on your own to see how much others are making in your same job.
▲ **Ask for the raise.** If you are stalled, ask again. Here are a couple of reminders of what *not* to do:
   1. Don't threaten to quit. If you want to leave, just give your notice (make sure you have a new job first, if possible).
   2. Don't change your mind once you have given notice.
   3. Be professional and don't complain with the other employees.
   4. Don't be angry, but feel good about the decision you make.

4. Take Steps to Get a Better-Paying Job

There are certain positions within a company that more directly contribute to profitability than others. Where does your job fit into contributing to that profitability? You may want to change job classifications in order to be more important to your own company or to a new company. You might want to:

▲ **Go into sales.** Direct sales of a company's product will pay you more than being a sales clerk. Executive sales pays excellently, and it's a field where more and more women excel. As long as you can sell you will be rewarded.

▲ **Get more education if needed.** Many communities have continued education in evening classes in all areas of vocation. If you don't have a bachelor of arts degree, you might want to consider enrolling in a nearby college or university.

• **Learn a skill that pays well.** There are many such careers available in computer works, service industry, dental and medical assistance, etc.

• **Start your own business.** You can start from scratch or enter into the vast field of multilevel marketing companies. This type of business will reward you according to your production.

Single Persons Can Live Without Stress

> *Happiness comes to those who are fair to others and are always just and good.*
>
> —Psalm 106:3 TLB

*I*n America today we see an increasing number of people who would be counted as single. They fall into one of three categories:

▲ Those who have never been married
▲ Those who are divorced
▲ Those whose spouse has died.

The single person who has never been married is most often a young man or woman who is just getting started in the financial world. People are getting married later in life today; it is not uncommon to meet 35-year-olds still single by choice. This category of single usually doesn't have an income problem, but they do with outgo. If this is you, a few survival tips would be:

▲ **Establish income goals.** You have probably learned to live within your present income level. As a single you can do this with less adjustment than a married couple. Unfortunately, you may very well be adapting yourself to a low income by having inadequate savings, cutting back where you need not, and having insufficient money for vacations. Revise your income goals to be more challenging than what they presently are.

▲ **Have a disciplined budget.** Know what you need to spend, then be sure to allocate your income accordingly. (Refer back to Chapter 13.)

▲ **Don't buy too much life insurance.** For single people I recommend buying a good term insurance policy that covers burial costs and any other expenses that might be incurred following death.

▲ **Have an adequate health insurance program.** If you work for a company with a group health insurance policy, this will usually be adequate. If you are self-employed, you will need to seek out a good agent who will advise you of adequate coverage.

▲ **Save and invest.** See our chapters dealing with this topic. There are excellent no-load or low-load growth-type mutual funds which you can invest in through a monthly investment plan. Don't invest in risky investments, or respond from a telemarketing salesperson on the telephone. Only go with a sound, financial adviser who comes highly recommended by personal referrals.

▲ **Control your expenses.** Be very careful on your outgo of money. Many singles can get into a very damaging habit of living beyond their means through splurging on luxury items.

▲ **Have tax-deferred retirement savings.** Since most single unmarried people are young, they think retirement is too far ahead for them to think about: "I'll take care of that as I get older." You want to start *now*. Don't wait!

Living As a Divorced Person

This is the most difficult of the three single categories. In most cases both parties suffer financially, particularly if children are involved. As a man you will have to provide adequate alimony and/or child support. You will certainly need to budget as you have never done before. Without proper budgeting you will fall behind on your obligations and everyone will suffer.

As a woman you will struggle to be the single head of a household on an inadequate income, in most cases. You will need to build or rebuild your career goals. Here are a few things you can do to help the situation:

▲ Arrange a satisfactory alimony trust as part of the divorce settlement. Not everyone will have enough assets to fund this.

▲ You will not be able to maintain the same lifestyle as when you were married. Divorce always hurts financially. Both parties will usually have to cut back.

▲ Be faithful to your responsibilities. Irresponsibility in these areas will be the beginning of many legal and financial woes.

▲ Make sure there is adequate insurance to protect against disaster.

▲ Have a savings account to cover emergencies.

▲ Have a living trust or will made.

Those Whose Spouses Have Died

Insurance charts indicate that most women will live eight years longer than their husbands. You will need to carry on when he is gone, so don't wait until it's too late. Begin *today* to learn basic survival techniques for around the house:

▲ Where the electrical box is located.

▲ Where to turn off the gas and water.

▲ Where the list is of the repairmen.
▲ The location of savings and investments.
▲ Who handles the insurance policies.
▲ A review of monthly payments.
▲ Basic repair skills to avoid having expensive repairmen come.

There are scores of details that must be handled before the surviving spouse can carry on a normal daily routine. You might want to start a log to answer all these questions.

The largest percentage of Americans living below the poverty level are widows. Review your insurance and retirement benefits so you will have a basic understanding of your resources that will carry you through your remaining years.

Living Alone

Here are some helpful hints that will help you live alone:

▲ Learn to live economically. Protect your savings and retirement funds. If you work, continue to save if possible.
▲ Use all the resources that you are eligible for. Since you qualify, don't hesitate to use whatever benefits you have coming to you.
▲ Maintain your health insurance. As you get older, this is one of your most important coverages. Insure for the disaster.
▲ Have adequate life insurance coverage to pay for your final illness and burial expenses.
▲ If you have spare bedrooms, you might want to look around for someone to live with you. This income will help offset your expenses and will help you from becoming lonely.
▲ Continue working if you can. Even part-time work helps financially, plus it keeps you involved creatively.
▲ Have a current living trust or will made.

You Need to Be Bank Savvy

$\mathcal{C}$ onsumers need to be savvy in their use of banking services. Usually we just experience these services, but we don't take the time to sit down with an officer of the bank and ask questions which will help us to make wise financial decisions.

Consider these ideas in order to become more savvy:

1. Ask your bank for a loan on a simple-interest-payment note. This allows for monthly repayments or an installment loan figured on a simple-interest basis. You are charged interest on the balance outstanding at any point in time. On just a modest loan of a few thousand dollars you can save hundreds of dollars in the process. Some banks say they don't have this type of loan to consumers, but just for businesses. However, shop around and ask the questions anyway.

2. Stay away from credit life and disability insurance from the bank. This type of insurance is designed to pay off debt in the event that the borrower dies before the loan is paid off. You can get better terms from an independent insurance company.

3. Get to know an officer at your branch bank. It's always good to know the manager and several tellers on a first-name basis. Then if you need VIP treatment, a loan, or an out-of-town check cashed, you're more likely to get efficient assistance.

4. Rethink having a safe deposit box at your bank. Bank safe deposit boxes may not be as safe as you have been led to believe. They can be broken into, have fires, or fall to floods and other disasters. Ask if your contents are insured if such things happen. One other negative consideration is that the IRS or state government agencies can get a warrant to invade your box and confiscate its contents to pay their claims. In this case the banks must comply. One solution in which you have more control and where the long-range cost is cheaper is to buy a home safe that meets or exceeds the fire rating of your bank vault. The approximate cost of such a home vault is about $250. Look in the local yellow pages to locate your nearest safe sales store. (Your home insurance policy can cover the contents, if you properly document the contents.)

5. Automatic Teller Machines (ATM's) aren't for everyone. When this service was first introduced to the public it replaced drive-up window service and was introduced to give 24-hour service, at the same time eliminating the labor cost of this service. However, many banks now charge for this service. ATM's have become a profit center for a lot of banks. These machines have also caused an increase in crime. Most banks do not provide security guards for their customers. If you must use ATM's, exercise common sense. Make sure it's not late at night and that there is adequate lighting in the evening; have someone accompany you to the bank; make sure there is other traffic in the area.

6. Be alert to the proper use of overdraft protection. If you aren't careful this becomes just another credit card. You can get into financial trouble very quickly and end up paying excessive amounts of interest for the money advanced. This service is designed to keep you from bouncing checks (which creates fear and added embarrassment and charges). Talk to your bank official to properly understand what the service is and how much it costs.

One way to minimize this cost is to have your bank "red tag" your account and call you when you don't have enough money in your account to pay for an outstanding check. Then you can go to the bank and make a deposit to cover the amount of the check without paying any over-draft fee.

7. Shop before taking out a mortgage. Banking is very competitive, and it will pay you to shop for the best loan possible. A savings on points and interest rate will result in long-range profits for you. A 1 percent reduction on a $100,000, 30-year, 9 percent loan will save you about $25,000; a ½ percent cut will reduce your costs about half that amount. Start with your local bank, but if they won't budge, move on to another bank. You will probably find someone who can give you a big savings. It will certainly be worth your extra effort.

8. Paying off the principal on your mortgage might make sense. This is a debatable topic, since different financial planners have varying ideas on this matter. However, we are strong advocates of this idea. For almost eight years we have sent in with our monthly payment an additional sum of money (based on what we have available for this strategy). By simply increasing your monthly payment by a modest amount, and/or by making your payments early, you will be able to shorten the repayment term significantly, which will lower your total costs.

If you have a $100,000, 30-year mortgage at 9½ percent, with a monthly payment of $840.85, you will have a total repayment of $302,707.51 over the life of the loan. By adding just $50 per month to your regular payments, you will repay that 30-year loan in just 23 years and three months. The biggest factor is that you will save over $54,000.

9. Stay away from bank escrow funds for your home insurance and property taxes. Why not draw your own interest from these funds rather than having them accrue in a non-interest-bearing account? You want to be in control of this money. In some cases you will have to shop around to have this ability. Tell your bank you will not agree to an escrow account unless it pays a fair-market interest rate on your funds in that account.

These nine considerations are worth money in your pocket. Don't be timid in asking for considerations from your bank. Remember, you are the customer.

How to Be a Saver

The rich rules over the poor, and the borrower is servant to the lender.

—Proverbs 22:7 NKJV

As a young man I had a paper route, mowed lawns, washed windows, ran errands, and did all kinds of odd jobs for people. With these various incomes I was able to open a savings account at our local bank, and was also encouraged to purchase war bonds and savings stamps at my school. Those early memories made a big impact on me and certainly helped me establish my habit of saving money.

This doesn't always mean saving in a *bank;* it can also mean saving by wise shopping.

In the beginning, saving is all give and little get. Stick with it long enough, however, and your savings will help you buy a home, educate your kids, and care for yourself in your old age. Here are a few ideas on how to become a saver.

Pay in cash. This will teach you the difference between what you want and what you really need. By paying cash, you avoid finance charges. For example, by trimming your credit card balances by $500 this year, you save $93 in interest if your card issuer charges 18.6 percent.

Make bigger down payments. When financing your next major purchase—whether a new car or a new kitchen—put up as much money as you can to reduce the principal and save interest.

If you own a home, use a home-equity loan to consolidate high-rate debts. By replacing consumer debts at 18 percent with a home-equity loan at 12 percent, you will cut your interest costs by a third. In addition, the interest on a home-equity loan can be fully deducted on your income tax return. Consolidate $10,000 in car payment and credit-card advances with a home-equity loan, and, counting the tax break, a taxpayer in the 28 percent bracket will save $936.

I want to encourage you to use great discipline in using this type of loan. The equity in your home is a very valuable asset and certainly should not be abused. You *must* stick to your plan.

Eliminate one big expense a year. Skip your winter vacation, trade in your sports car for an economy car, or discontinue your health-club membership and start using the "Y."

Take that money to pay off a loan that is costing a high interest rate, or take the same money and add to a savings or mutual fund account.

Don't pay for financial services you can get for free. Using only no-fee checking accounts, mutual funds, and credit cards can save you $100 a year or more.

Save your next raise. To squeeze out money for your 401(k), earmark your next raise for it. If you earn $40,000, a 5 percent raise will give you $2000 for your account.

Take advantage of your company savings plan. If you aren't contributing to it now, you may be throwing money away. Reason: Most 401(k)s and other plans offer tax breaks; moreover, part of your contributions are often matched by your employer.

Use your flexible spending account. Don't pass up the opportunity to pay medical and dependent-care expenses with pre-tax dollars through these accounts. A family of four is almost certain to spend $1000 a year on doctors, dentists, and prescription medicines. Your savings if you pay for them from a FSA can be at least $280.

Other savings ideas can be found right in your own home:

1. Return bottles and cans for deposit. In some states, ten a week will save $25 a year.
2. Make your own household cleaners. For an all-purpose bathroom cleaner, combine two tablespoons of either vinegar or sudsy ammonia with a quart bottle of water.
3. Think cloth rather than paper. For example, use handkerchiefs instead of facial tissues and rags instead of paper towels.
4. Place aluminum foil inside lampshades to reflect more light.
5. Clean your windows each fall to reduce your heat bill by 4 percent. Dirty glass cuts off up to 40 percent of the solar energy.
6. Don't carry junk in your car trunk. Each extra pound increases the amount of gas used.
7. Join a credit union. Not-for-profit, they usually pay more interest on deposits than banks do, and charge less interest on loans and credit cards.
8. Use disposable diapers only away from home. They cost eight times more than cloth.
9. A small vegetable garden can supply enough produce to last a family a year.
10. Put heat reflectors or foil behind radiators to heat the room, not the wall.

11. Pour flat cola in the toilet bowl. Let soak for an hour to clean.
12. Slightly overpay your mortgage each month. If you have a $100,000, 30-year mortgage at 10 percent and pay an additional $23 each month, you will pay off the loan four years earlier and save $34,344 in interest.
13. Dry heavy items in the dryer first. Next, put in light-weight ones on fluff-setting. The leftover heat will dry them.
14. Grow an aloe vera plant. When someone has a minor burn, break open a leaf and squeeze the jelly-like sap onto the injury.
15. Radial tires and adequate inflation increase car stability and cut fuel consumption by 5 to 10 percent.

Save on
Banking Services

Make all you can, save all you can, give all you can.

—John Wesley

*T*hrift, like fidelity, seems a hopelessly old-fashioned word today. Yet thrift can survive in this day of the throw-away mentality. Thrift signifies a lot more than a simple desire to save for a rainy day or a vacation to Hawaii.

Thrift is a manifestation of a whole complex of still greater virtues—moderation (my favorite word), reason, self-discipline, maturity—that together make for far more than a mere bank balance. These character words make for a strong and stable life.

Thrift is most of all a sign of *personal character.* The kind of life it yields is hard enough to fashion in the best of times, but it is much harder yet to develop in times of "I-want-it-all-right-now." We live in a society in which the undisciplined endlessly pursue the unnecessary. Getting it on easy credit is not much of a challenge. Many of us go out and buy more and more and more in order to be satisfied.

We don't even have to leave our homes; we just tune into a shopping channel or browse through catalogs stuffed with the latest in high-tech gadgets.

Thrifty people save for specific goals, meaning they are less likely to buy a lot of junk in passing. They can face the tease of Madison Avenue and say, "No, thank you."

Here are some techniques dealing with banks and their services that can be helpful to your financial planning.

Banking Services

▲ If you run out of checks and stand at a merchant's cash register embarrassed, **you can write a check using your deposit slip.** Many people aren't aware of this, but your bank will accept the slip and pay. Make sure you complete it as though it were a check. Make sure you sign in the normal area of the check. In bold letters print at the bottom of the deposit slip, "*THIS IS A CHECK.*"

▲ Always make it a habit to **deposit a check immediately after receiving it.** This way you minimize your risk of losing the check. A lady once came to one of my seminars and got excited about implementing my "Total Mess to Total Rest" program. The next day, while cleaning out her desk, she found a $200 check that had been in her drawer five months! (She immediately called to let me know about her find.)

▲ Ever since I was a young boy I would **put change in a jar.** When Emilie and I were dating we would do the same after each date. At the time of our wedding we had almost $400 saved in this manner. Even today I put all my quarters in a jar. This "pot of gold" has become my "mad" money for something special for myself or a birthday gift or such. Many people faithfully deposit this money in a savings account. It's amazing how this method adds to your savings account.

▲ Since you want your money working for you, **don't keep more than is necessary in a no-interest checking account.** Even in a business checking account you can float extra cash from non-interest to interest to non-interest when it's check-writing time. A few days in the interest account will contribute extra interest over a year's time.

▲ **It usually doesn't pay to postdate a check.** If your check is charged to your account before you expect it to be, it might cause other checks that you've written to bounce. This will really cause a loss of your time to straighten it out, plus the service charges add up very fast.

▲ **Put your money in a bank where interest is compounded semiannually or quarterly rather than yearly.** Your money will work harder for you.

▲ **Only in emergencies should you withdraw funds from a savings account before the stated interest payment date.**

▲ **Have your checks printed by someone other than the bank.** Two great sources for having your checks printed at a reduced price are: **"Checks in the Mail,"** P. O. Box 7802, Irwindale, CA 91706, 800-733-4443, or **"Current, Inc."** Colorado Springs, CO 80941.

▲ **Do all you can to protect your credit rating.** This is one of your most valuable assets. If for some reason you run into difficult financial times, go to your creditors *first* and tell them what's happening. If at all possible they will try to work with you.

▲ **Try to have at least two months of income in your savings account** to help during those unannounced emergencies. Six months would be better yet.

▲ **"Pay yourself a little more first"** is a great guideline when deciding to charge or pay cash. If at all possible, pay cash and put the monthly payment into your savings account. That way you get the interest rather than paying the big bad wolf. Over a period of time this will become a normal way of thinking. You can't always do this with large items, but many items can be handled this way.

▲ **Don't pay your bills before they are due.** The extra days in an interest-bearing account will give you extra interest each month.

▲ **Banks and savings and loans are not the only institutions for handling money.** If you are eligible for membership in a credit union, you should look at this alternative. Credit unions usually pay higher interest and charge less for loans and credit cards.

▲ **Shop around for the best rates on credit cards.** This is a very competitive business, and rates do vary. If you are interested in receiving a comparison listing of over 500 banks, send $5 to **RAM**, Box 1700, Frederick, MD 21702 for *CardTrak*.

▲ **If you must have a credit card, get one that will credit your dollar purchases to airplane mileage, hotel accommodations, and even merchandise.**

▲ A great idea that pays great dividends is to **buy United States saving bonds,** either through your local bank or under a payroll savings plan where you're employed. You can build up a sizable nest egg over the years by consistently purchasing a small bond. Instead of giving another toy to an "over-toyed" grandchild, purchase a savings bond in his or her name.

▲ The key to financial success is to **spend less than is earned** and continue to do that for a lengthy period of time. Proverbs 13:11 says, "He who gathers money little by little makes it grow" (NIV).

▲ One of the basic principles of handling your money successfully is to **delay gratification.** Delayed gratification requires a long-term perspective and is the key to financial maturity. Financial maturity can be defined as "giving up today's desires for future benefits."

▲ Credit card companies estimate that **using credit cards will result in our spending 34 percent more than if we used cash.**

▲ When confronted with the opportunity to make an impulse purchase, **discipline yourself to wait at least one week before spending the money.**

▲ If you are an impulse buyer, **ask a spouse or a friend about your purchase before you give yourself the okay**

to purchase. With this accountability you will find most of your impulses going away.

▲ We have some very good friends who **freeze all of their credit cards in the freezer.** Before they can charge from them they have to wait until they thaw out. In most cases they have changed their minds while they wait.

▲ If you are really serious about curtailing credit card spending, **place your credit cards (with the exception of one for emergencies) in your safe deposit box.** By the time you go to the trouble of retrieving the cards you will know if you really need the item and will have had plenty of time to think over the purchase.

Credit Is Like Gold

▲ A good way to keep out of credit binds is to **pay off a series of payments completely before committing yourself to a new series of payments for something else.** Also, be cautious of jumping into a home equity loan. For most families their equity in their home is their retirement savings. If you deplete that fund you might seriously jeopardize some of your long-term goals.

▲ If for some reason you get a bad credit rating that has an item improperly posted to your account, **be sure to correct this error immediately.** The longer it remains on your record, the harder it is to get corrected.

▲ Are you thinking about taking out a second mortgage to finance a vacation, buy an automobile, consolidate bills, or raise money to buy stocks? Although your home could be used as security for such a loan, it's probably best to take out a personal installment loan instead. **Second mortgages should not be used for casual expenditures.**

▲ **Try not to put down less than a one-third cash payment when purchasing a car,** or to let the financing extend past 36 months. With less than one-third down, a car's depreciation is likely to reduce its market value faster than you can shrink the balance of the loan.

▲ Having trouble making monthly loan payments? Consider slicing the remaining payments in half by extending them over a longer period of time.

▲ Knowing and believing that God owns it all will provide total freedom from any type of financial bondage—the bondage of either too much or too little.

PART FIVE

When You're Ready to Make Investments

▲ ▲ ▲

How to Save Money You Didn't Know You Had

If anyone does not provide for his own, and especially for those of his household, he has denied the faith, and is worse than an unbeliever.

—1 Timothy 5:8

Do just two or three of the suggestions listed in this chapter and the money will add up fast. In many cases you may not even be aware that these possible savings are available to you.

▲ **Give up a bad habit.** Examine your lifestyle and give up a bad habit. It might be smoking, drinking, diet drinks, candies, or cookies. You'll be amazed at the savings.

▲ **Wear tights instead of pantyhose in the winter.** The tights will save you a considerable amount over the year. They are less costly and more durable. Write for a free catalog to:

L'eggs Brands, Inc.
P.O. Box 748
Rural Hill, NC 27098

▲ **Carry your own lunch.** Bring a sandwich, soft drink or juice, fruit, veggies, and a low-calorie dessert in a brown bag, and save considerably over buying lunch out. Even two or three days a week makes a big difference, and if you and your spouse both work it really makes a big savings.
▲ **Buy film and processing from a direct mail developing company.** We have used this means to purchase and process our Kodacolor film. Request information from:

Clark Color Labs
P.O. Box 96300
Washington, DC 20090

They have labs all around the country and can give you the address nearest your home.

▲ **Buy a used car rather than a new one.** The amount of savings from a one- to three-year-old used car is tremendous. You can move up to a larger, more comfortable car if you are willing to buy used rather than new. If you are concerned about getting a lemon, for a few dollars you can hire a mechanic to go over the mechanics of the car to check its condition. We are talking about thousands of dollars in savings.
▲ **Make your own coffee.** Invest in an inexpensive coffeemaker, a can of coffee, and a box of dried milk. Over a year you will save almost $200 by not buying coffee each day at the snack cart or cafeteria. Bake your own muffins instead of picking one up each morning. This will be another $150 yearly.
▲ **Save something out of each paycheck.** A savings of $50 every two weeks will give you $1300 at the end of the year.
▲ **Open up a money market account.** You want your money to be drawing interest rather than just sitting in

your checking account. Talk to "New Accounts" at the bank to see what programs are available.

▲ **Wash your silks.** Even though your silk blouses have "dry cleaning only" on the label, you should be able to wash them in cold water (except for prints, which might run).

▲ **Take winter clothes to a bulk dry cleaner.** You will be amazed at how much you can save by having your winter woolens cleaned by the pound rather than individually.

▲ **Don't spend your whole raise.** Take 75 percent of your next raise and put it into a savings or money market account. You might even want to take the raise money to pay off a loan that has a high interest rate. Discipline yourself not to raise your standard of living but to put yourself closer to financial freedom.

▲ **Make these changes in home heating:** Buy your fuel oil in the summertime, when prices are lower. Lower your thermostat one or more degrees (for each degree lowered you can save 3 percent of your fuel bill). Put an insulated blanket over your hot-water heater. Install a "day and night" thermostat which will give you more control when your furnace comes on and goes off.

▲ **Change light bulbs to fluorescents.** The fluorescents cost more initially but will last approximately 12 times longer and use about 25 percent less electricity.

▲ **Use the public library instead of buying books.** Depending upon your love of books, you can save several hundred dollars a year by getting a library card.

▲ **Rent a video rather than going to the movies.** Not only can a family save a lot of money on admission to the theater, but you can also save money on refreshments. You can also be preselective on what your family watches and not be caught by surprise because of violence or foul language. (Besides, popcorn made at home tastes better!)

▲ **Get an airline credit card.** I recommend this only for people who can properly use a credit card. If credit misuse is one of your weaknesses, don't get the card. If you sign up as a frequent flyer, you are frequently eligible for that airline's credit card. For every $1 you charge to the card (for all purchases), you earn one free mile of travel. This could save you a lot of money on that round-trip air ticket next summer.

▲ **Air conditioners don't have to refrigerate a room.** It isn't cost-effective to operate your air conditioner below 70°. If your outside temperature cools down in the evening, open a window or door to cool down the whole house. As with the furnace, you can save a lot of money on energy by installing a "day and night" thermostat. Turn the system off while you're away at work and set it to come on an hour before you arrive home so you have a cool home when you arrive. (No use cooling the house when you aren't home!)

▲ **Cook at home, don't eat out.** Our kitchens have sold out to the fast food industry. We have forgotten how to cook. Get some new recipes and take a cooking class, but stop going to hamburger havens for the next meal. Not only will this practice be cheaper, but the family will like it better and it will provide more nutritional value. Save going out for that special treat and occasion.

▲ **Use coupons at the grocery store.** Look in your magazines, newspapers, or throwaway inserts for coupons which will save you $.25 to $.50 on your next purchase. Some stores even offer "double redemption" on certain days.

Why Save?

In America we must develop the habit and good discipline of saving. Unfortunately, since World War II we have based our economy on *consumerism*—spend, spend, spend.

Here are some excellent reasons for saving.

▲ **Accumulating money so it can be put to work.** If you don't save, you will have no money for investing and lending.

▲ **Building a retirement fund.** You must have more than Social Security in your old age. It was originally intended to be only a supplement to other retirement funds.

▲ **Having money for difficult times.** You should have at least two to six months' salary set aside for emergencies.

▲ **Having money for pleasure.** All work and no play makes Johnny very boring. With good money management there must be time for fun, like a vacation, a new dress, a new suit, a second car, a boat for the lake, and to accumulate funds to invest in the stock market. You can make your own fun list!

An ideal savings goal is 10 percent of your after-tax income each year. There will be seasons in your family's life when you may not be able to meet this goal, but save *something* each month anyway.

You need to be very committed to save or you will never get started. Here are several strategies that can help you.

Savings from taxes. Many families overpay their taxes by having an inaccurate W4 form filled out with their employer. Adjust this form so you don't overpay. If you have been getting a refund each year of $800, by making a single adjustment you can have an extra $66.67 each month in take-home pay.

Sign up for your company's bond-a-month plan or stock option program. Use this $66.67 per month to invest in your company's investment programs.

Saving after paying off a loan. When you finish making that last payment on a car, a boat, or furniture, rather than going into more debt, keep sending the bank a check for the same amount, only this time, instead of a loan coupon, enclose a savings deposit slip. Since you have been getting by without this money for several months, continue doing without it, but this time save it.

Freeing up money to save. Here are three ways to reduce your expenses, which could free up hundreds of dollars per year.

1. **Check your life insurance.** Switch your whole life or straight life policy to a term policy. This is a very good idea while you are young. As you get older, term insurance rates become expensive, but by that time your money needs are less.
2. **Check your auto insurance.** Review with your agents to see where you can reduce premiums. Look at the special discount offerings: safe driver, senior citizen, multiple cars, low-mileage rates, etc. Even having your homeowner policy with the same carrier may give you reduced rates.
3. **Check your homeowner's or tenant's insurance.** Make sure your deduction is no less than $500. You really don't want to file a claim less than that. It will be a

negative on your record and cause an increase or possible cancellation on your policy.

Real savings begin when you have the right reason to save. Once you get in the habit of saving, it becomes fun. Even small amounts on a regular basis can be exciting.

▲ Save your small change in a big coin bank. When full, deposit the money in your savings account.
▲ Bank a raise or at least part of it.
▲ Bank any Christmas bonus.
▲ Bank any unexpected income, such as bonuses, tax refunds, profits, or inheritances.

Seven Ways to Get Greater Mutual Fund Returns[1]

How much better is wisdom than gold, and understanding than silver!

—Proverbs 16:16 TLB

Years ago relatively little was known about mutual funds by most people. The majority of investments were made by individuals buying individual company stock. Today's trend is that individuals are going with the professional mutual funds. Unless you have the time and resources to thoroughly research your own investment portfolio, you would be advised to invest in a reputable mutual fund.

Before you purchase any mutual fund, consider these seven areas of concern:

1. Total performance that really works for you. Don't look only at yield or capital appreciation. Factor in both figures, and then subtract the load fee, the management fee, the 12b-1 fee, and any other hidden costs of owning the fund.

2. Professional management with a proven track record. Consider the track record of the fund manager over the past three years, and the track record of the fund family. Some fund families (such as Vanguard) have a knack of doing most things very well. It's no coincidence that their funds also perform well.

3. Fund switching made easy. Markets change, and you want to be able to change funds easily and without penalty. The fund should have free or reasonable ($5) switching fees and an 800 number that isn't busy during heavy trading days. Make sure the fund has no back-end load, liquidation fee, or redemption fee.

4. Rewards that outweigh risks. Generally, mutual funds spread your risk by investing in many stocks, with professional management to check out the dangers. Not all funds promise safety, however. If you're conservative, don't buy aggressive growth funds; if you're trying to reduce taxes, steer away from funds with turnover rates above 100 percent.

5. No "dividend loads" hidden in fund. Some mutual fund families invent new ways of charging you hidden loads. One sneaky way of charging investors a sales loan is to levy a fee, up to 7.25 percent, for reinvesting dividends. If your statement says "reinvesting dividend at the offering rather than the net asset value," or "at offer," take your dividends in cash and invest them elsewhere.

6. Dividend distribution dates. Reduce your tax liability by always buying *after,* never before, dividends are distributed. Ask what dates the fund distributes its dividends. Growth funds in particular usually distribute the last month of every year. Some funds pay dividends every six months, some quarterly, some even monthly.

7. Customer service that works for you. The fund families for which I've found the best customer service are: Vanguard, Financial/Invesco, and T. Rowe Price. Polite, attentive, responsive customer service really makes a difference. Many fund families also offer a variety of service, such as free telephone switching, free dividend reinvestment plans, even IRA management.

Investing with the Long Term in Mind

Never be lazy in your work, but serve the Lord enthusiastically.

—Romans 12:11 TLB

*A*s Americans we have lost the virtue of looking at life through long-distance lenses. We want results *now*; make it fast and profitable! In the first sections of this book we have encouraged the "little-by-little" idea of accumulating your wealth.

Those who take the long view reap the rewards of significant long-term advantages.

▲ The long view tends to smooth out the short-term fluctuations and cycles of the financial markets. Long-term investors profit from long-term trends, which have always been positive for stocks, bonds, real estate, and many other investments.

▲ Continuous and periodic investing over the long term helps reduce much of the risk associated with investing. Techniques such as "dollar-cost averaging" (investing fixed dollar amounts at periodic intervals, regardless of fluctuations in price) help investors exercise the discipline required by long-term investing.

▲ For those investments that pay interest or dividends now or in the future, the positive effects of compounding escalate with time. As interest and dividends are reinvested, they generate more and more income at an ever-increasing rate.

▲ Long-term investments can help alleviate the eroding effects of inflation when the combination of capital gains and income grow at a rate that exceeds the rate of inflation.

▲ The psychological benefits of long-term investing are substantial. Investors with the long view are not panicked by short-term declines, nor are they overly zealous about sudden gains. Instead, they place these events in their proper perspective.

Principles of Long-Term Investing

*T*here are nine basic principles you need to consider when making long-term investments.[1]

Principle 1: Write Out Clear and Specific Goals

When you write down on paper what your plans are, you are more likely to put these goals into action. Ask yourself, "What am I trying to accomplish with my money?"

▲ Do I want the principal to grow over time?
▲ Do I need to reduce my tax obligations?
▲ Do I need to plan for retirement?
▲ Do I need to provide for my children's education?

The answers to such questions will help give direction to your specific investment goals.

Your second major question should be, "What is my tolerance for risk?" Are you able to live with your investment taking downturns because of market influence, variations in interest rates, changes in the economy, political changes, and changes in the tax laws?

Are you willing to assume the risks associated with an aggressive strategy that may reap significant rewards, or are you more comfortable with a conservative approach that emphasizes safety?

When you know the answer to these questions, you can begin to select the long-term investments that are most likely to meet your goals.

Principle 2: Research Your Investment Before You Invest

Long-term investing requires patience and discipline. Patience means that such investing is a long-term process. Discipline is commitment to the long-term view. The people around you will likely be short-term, thereby causing you stress because of the difference in the two ideas.

You must make investment decisions only after careful investigation, whether of stocks, bonds, insurance, or real estate. To judge value takes time. Investigate before you invest.

Principle 3: Make Sure You Understand the Difference Between Investment and Trading

Investing is when you hold an investment over a long period of time. When you buy an investment product for a short period of time and then sell it for a short-term profit or loss, you are *trading.*

Trading and investing are different things and require different strategies. Trading for short-term gains is a valid strategy for those who are willing to accept the risks and understand that it is not investing.

Principle 4: Maintain Future Orientation

The true investor is future-looking and can live with daily and seasonal swings and cycles of the financial markets. Despite short-term fluctuations, the long-term trend has always been a positive one for stocks, bonds, real estate, and other investments.

Over the last 60 years the total return of the stock market has averaged about 10 percent per year compounded annually. This compares to 3 percent inflation per year over the same period. When viewed in proper perspective, short-term fluctuations are just squiggles on a long-term line.

Principle 5: Review Your Investments Regularly

You must review your goals and investments regularly. At least once a month we analyze both of these to see if we are on target. If not, we make the necessary changes to maximize our long-term financial direction. Just because your investments are long-term doesn't mean you buy them and store them in a safe deposit box. Financial markets and world economics may fundamentally change, so you need to make changes in your portfolio when the markets change.

Principle 6: Take Advantage of Worldwide Opportunities

As a young man I was able to distinguish the various different markets in the world. There were specific boundaries where the American market started and stopped. But the global economics of the 1990s isn't that clear. What happens in Japan and Germany is often related to what's going on in America. Before you venture out into new waters, make sure you do a thorough job in researching the new market.

Principle 7. Make Sure Your Investment for the Long-Term Represents Quality

Your initial investigation must consider the organization's reputation for quality. As we know by reading many of the new business books which stress excellence, the underlying principle of business success is *quality.* Quality is not an art but a science; it doesn't just happen randomly, but must be planned for. You want companies that put high value on the future. They are willing to spend large sums of money in research and resources for the long term.

Investments with a reputation for quality will have a higher value over the long run than those that don't.

Principle 8: Use the Safety Benefits of Being a Long-Term Investor

When the total rate of return is a combination of interest or dividend yield plus capital gains, and the combination of these is greater than inflation, then we have been able to hedge against inflation—one of our long-term goals.

Principle 9: Appreciate Your Investment When Its Money Is Able to Earn Money

Many investors fail to recognize the true worth of certain investments—those in which interest and/or dividends earned are compounded over time. This is especially true if income accrues on a tax-free or tax-deferred basis.

As your principal earns interest or dividends, that new money may also earn income if you reinvest it. In effect, your income earns additional income.

As long as you continue to reinvest interest and dividends, the cycle will repeat itself throughout the life of the investment.

The Rule of 72 is a mathematical formula that dramatically illustrates the long-range time value of compounding interest and dividends. To approximate the time it will take for a given amount of money to double at a specific compound interest rate, simply divide 72 by the interest rate. For example, the long-term average compounded returned, with dividends reinvested, for common stocks was about 10 percent per year for the period between 1926 and 1987. Therefore, at a compound annual rate of 10 percent, $1000 would have grown to $2000 in about 7.2 years (72 divided by 10 equals 7.2).

Here are several long-term investments that you might want to consider for your portfolio:

Growth Investments

▲ Common stocks
▲ Direct investments in a project
▲ Partnerships in a project or group of projects

Fixed-Income Investments

▲ Long-term Treasury bonds
▲ Municipal bonds
▲ Mortgage-backed securities
▲ Corporate bonds

Growth-and-Income Investments

▲ Mutual funds
▲ Unit investment trusts
▲ Insurance and annuities
▲ Real estate

Consider a Discount Broker

*W*hen it comes time for you to expand your money management beyond your local bank and its interest-earning accounts, you will want to consider investments in stocks and bonds. When you do, you will need to consider what services you want this company to perform for you.

If you are new in this area of investments, you might want to interview various sales representatives from nationally known brokerage firms. They will use their research analysts to provide you with stock recommendations on particular companies.

This type of firm can be of great assistance, but the services will cost you more than you might be willing to pay. Also, you may not need or want all of these services. You may only need someone to help you purchase stocks and bonds for your portfolio. In that case you want to choose a qualified discount brokerage firm.

The difference in fees between these two types of firms can be significant. According to a recent survey, a full-service broker will charge an average of $218 for a particular type of transaction and a discount broker will charge an average of

$56. You might be asking, "Why the big difference?" The answer is *advice*.

Full-service brokerage houses usually provide their customers with investment reports containing buy and sell recommendations. You are paying for this service.

Discount brokers won't give you any advice on what to buy or sell. They merely execute trades at the customer's request. You can usually get printout copies of Value Line and Standard & Poor's research reports, but the discount brokers give no personalized advice.

Your decision on which type of broker to use is based on whether you need advice. You should also consider whether the full-service broker can provide some other valuable service that is worth the cost difference.

If you answer no to these two questions, you should strongly consider a discount broker, since the cost savings are considerable. The bigger the trade, the bigger the difference in price. The big discounters do not always have the lowest rates, but they do have more products to sell. In addition to stocks, they also sell bonds and mutual funds. Shopping around can be worth your effort.

You might ask, "Where do I find a discount broker?" Referrals from friends are sometimes the best. You can also check the yellow pages in your phone book or the 1992 survey published by Mercer, Inc. of New York. You can buy this discount brokerage directory for less than $40 by calling 800-582-9854. (This directory is a two-volume edition, and you need both volumes.)

Other sources to consider:

▲ **The Discount Investing Directory,** Phillips Publishing Inc., 7811 Montrose Road, Potomac, MD 20854, 800-777-5005.

▲ **Barry Murphy & Co.,** 270 Congress St., Boston, MA 02210, 800-221-2111, 617-426-1770.

▲ **Brown & Co.,** 20 Winthrop Square, Boston, MA 02110, 800-225-6707, 617-742-2600.

▲ **T.D. Waterhouse,** 9191 Towne Centre Dr., Suite 220, San Diego, CA 92122, 800-233-3411.

▲ **Marquette de Bary Co.,** 488 Madison Ave., New York, NY 10022, 800-221-3305, 212-644-5300.

▲ **Pacific Brokerage Services,** 5757 Wilshire Blvd., Suite 3, Los Angeles, CA 90036, 800-421-8395, 213-939-1100.

Your money is not at more risk with a discount broker. Your funds are just as fully protected, regulated, and insured—to at least $500,000—as with a full-price broker. Perhaps the name "discount" may be misleading. Discount brokers are not selling inferior goods for less money. They sell the same stock certificates, use the same clearinghouses, and endure the same strict SEC rules as the big boys.

Compound Interest: The Eighth Wonder of the World

He who gathers money little by little makes it grow.

—Proverbs 13:11 NIV

$\mathcal{A}$s I have shared with you in an earlier chapter, one of my friends often refers to compound interest as "the eighth wonder of the world." Two basic principles—

▲ **Earn** little by little
▲ **Save** little by little

—will help you start on the road to financial freedom.

If you can accumulate $10,000 in a savings account in the next four years and then let it grow at an 8 percent interest rate without any further additions for the next 40 years, it will be worth $217,245 (or $930,510 at a 12 percent growth rate, $3.8 million at 16 percent, and $5.3 million at 17 percent).

Look at the same situation another way. Assume that you put $2000 away into an untouchable account at the end of each year. At the end of 40 years you would have $518,113 at an 8 percent return, $1.5 million at 12 percent, $4.7 million at 16 percent, and $6.3 million at 17 percent.

Two lessons here: first, *the importance of sacrificing early in your career* to start accumulating a capital base. The time value of money is incredibly important.

Second, *the rate of return is important.* The difference of just 1 percent in the above examples (between 16 and 17 percent return) becomes substantial in the long term.

Of course, these examples assume no annual tax on earnings, so the money would have to be invested in a tax-free instrument such as an IRA, an annuity plan, or municipal bonds. You can talk to your bank or financial adviser on specific recommendations.[1]

Grow Through Reinvesting Your Dividends

Much is required from those to who much is
given, for their responsibility is greater.
—Luke 12:48 TLB

*C*an you delay your gratification? If you can patiently wait for future fulfillment you should consider reinvesting your investment dividends as a strategy to see your wealth grow. You might ask, "Why reinvest dividends?" Because the stock market has superior wealth-building power. Few other investment tools can multiply your wealth like the stock market. In the years since 1926, a single $1000 investment in money markets or bonds would have grown to between $10,000 and $20,000 (depending upon which bond you owned). But an investment in stocks, with dividends reinvested, would today be worth $535,000—over 25 times the value of buy-and-hold bonds or cash. Nearly half of these gains would have come from reinvested dividends alone.

You can enjoy this kind of gain by purchasing stocks that historically pay regular and rising dividends. By contributing a small amount of added money on a regular basis and by reinvesting the quarterly dividends into the purchase of additional stock, you can see your investment dollars grow rapidly.

By investing with companies that have a Dividend Reinvestment Plan (DRIP), you can save broker fees and commissions by going directly to the company to purchase their stock. In fact, some of the companies will even give you a 5 percent discount for reinvesting dividends or buying more shares.

If you don't presently own shares in these companies, you will need to buy one or more shares from your broker, and then you can contact the company directly. Either way, this proven method locks in superb gains from your core blue-chip stock and utilities holdings. Since dividends are usually paid quarterly, this is a great way to boost your number of shares every three months. You can also add new shares on a regular basis by investing a fixed number of dollars each month or quarter (called "dollar-cost averaging"). See the next chapter to learn about this strategy.

This plan should only be *part* of your investment strategy; it is not designed for an entire well-balanced portfolio. However, this portion of investment dollars will give you a good investment return.

Each company that offers a DRIP has a special shareholder-relations office which takes care of dividend reinvestments and new stock purchases free of commissions. Certain guidelines apply, such as minimum initial investment levels and maximum monthly or quarterly amounts.

How to Get Started

You may already own blue chip or utility stock that has a DRIP plan. If you do, you can contact the special shareholder office and request information on reinvesting. The prospectus will outline the company's requirements. Each company is different, so read the information carefully.

If you are a new investor, the best place to start is with a company that offers you *total* commission-free investing from the very first share. By simply buying one share (or more) directly from the company, you can reinvest dividends and buy as many more shares as you want *totally* free of charge. Two of my recommended stocks offer such a program:

▲ **Proctor & Gamble,** C/O P&G Shareholders Services, P.O. Box 5572, Cincinnati, OH 45201-5572, 800-742-6253 or 513-983-1100. Minimum: one share (about $85).

▲ **Texaco,** 2000 Westchester Ave., White Plains, NY 10650, 914-253-6072. Minimum: $250 to start.

With these two stocks you never need to use a broker. Buy all your P&G or Texaco shares (just $2 per fractional share for P&G) directly from the company.

DRIP Plans with 5 Percent Discounts

Some companies not only let you buy shares commission-free, but they give you a discount on your purchase!

This is one strategy that can multiply your money as rapidly as any I know of, and these high-dividend (7 to 9 percent) utilities offer better-than-money-market income, with a good chance for long-term capital gains as well. By investing in a DRIP plan with these companies, you're making money in three ways at once: high income, long-term capital gains, and zero "friction" costs from commissions.

Here are seven companies which offer discounts on shares purchased with reinvested dividends *and* which offer high dividends:

Central Maine	NUI Corp. . . . . 5% discount
Power Co. . . . . 5% discount	Public Service Co.
E'Town Corp. 5%	of Colorado. 3%
Health Care REIT Inc. . 4%	Texas Utilities Co. 5%
New Plan Realty Trust . 5%	

E'Town Corp. (OTC: EWAT; formerly Elizabethtown Water Co.) and Health Care REIT Inc. (NYSE: HCP) also let enrollees in their dividend reinvestment plans use optional cash purchases to purchase new stock at a discount to the market price (5 percent for E'Town and 4 percent for Health Care REIT).

E'Town's 5 percent discount means you could spend just $25.65 to buy a share selling on the open market for $27. Plus you save on commissions! Remember, you must buy at least 20 shares from your broker before qualifying for the E'Town plan.

Here is a condensed list of companies offering a dividend reinvestment plan.

Blue Chip Stocks

Bristol-Myers Squibb
(NYSE: BMY)
345 Park Avenue
New York, NY 10154
($10-2500/month)

Chevron
(NYSE: CHV)
575 Market Street
San Francisco, CA 94105
415-894-7700

Du Pont
(NYSE: DD)
1007 Market Street
Wilmington, DE 19898
302-774-1000
($10-1000/quarter)

Exxon
(NYSE: XON)
5959 Las Colinas Blvd.
Irving, TX 75039
972-444-1000
($10-60,000/year)

General Mills
(NYSE: GIS)
P.O. Box 1113
Minneapolis, MN 55440
763-764-3888
($10-3000/quarter)

Honeywell
(NYSE: HON)
P.O. Box 50000R
Morristown, NJ 07962
973-455-2000

IBM
(NYSE: IBM)
C/O First Chicago Trust
  Co.-NY
P.O. Box 7896
Church Street Station
New York, NY 10249
800-426-4968
($10-5000/quarter)

Lilly (Eli) & Co.
(NYSE: LLY)
Lilly Corporate Center
Indianapolis, IN 46285
800-833-8699
($25-25,000/year)

Mobil Corp.
(NYSE: MOB)
P.O. Box 8033
Boston, MA 02266-8033
800-648-9291
($10-5000/month)

Philip Morris
(NYSE: MO)
917-663-5000
($10-60,000/year)

Proctor & Gamble
(NYSE: PG)
C/O Shareholder Services
P.O. Box 5572
Cincinnati, OH 45201-
  5572
800-742-6253 or
513-983-1100

Raytheon
(NYSE: RTN)
141 Spring Street
Lexington, MA 02421
781-862-6600
($10-5000/quarter)

Utilities

Alliant Energy Corp.
(NYSE: LNT)
P.O. Box 2568
Madison, WI 53701-2568
800-356-5343
($20-3000/month)

*Central Maine Power Co.
(NYSE: CTP)
Edison Drive
Augusta, ME 04336
800-750-4000
($10-30,000/year)

DPL Inc.
(NYSE: DPL)
P.O. Box 1247
Dayton, OH 45401
($25-1000/quarter)

†E'Town Corp.
(NASDAQ: EWAT)
P.O. Box 788
600 South Avenue
Westfield, NJ 07091-0788

National Grid
(NYSE: NGG)
P.O. Box 770
Westborough, MA
  01582
508-389-2000

Northwestern Public
  Service Co.
(NYSE: NPS)
3rd Street & Dakota Ave.
  So.
Huron, SD 57350
605-352-8411, ext. 403
($10-5000/quarter)

*NUI Corp.
(NYSE: NUI)
550 Rte. 202/206, Box 760
Bedminster, NJ 07921
908-781-0500
($25-3000/quarter)

*Texas Utilities Co.
201 Bryan Tower
Dallas, TX 75201
214-812-4646
($25-3000/quarter)

Union Electric
(NYSE: UEP)
P.O. Box 149
St. Louis, MO 63166
800-552-7583
(0-$60,000/year)

*Xcel Energy
(NYSE: XEL)
P.O. Box 840
Denver, CO 80201-0840
303-623-1234
($25-100,000/year)

REITS

*Health Care REIT Inc.
(NYSE: HCP)
1 Seagate, Ste. 1500
Toledo, OH 43604
419-247-2800
($10-2500/quarter)

†New Plan Realty Trust
(NYSE: NPR)
1120 Avenue of the
   America
New York, NY 10036
212-869-3000
($100-5000/quarter)

Weingartner Realty
   Investors
(NYSE: WRI)
C/O Ameritrust Co.
P.O. Box 6477
Cleveland, OH 44101
216-737-5742
($100-15,000/
   semiannually)

Remember, every investment involves some degree of risk, so investigate any stock carefully before buying.

---

*Offers discount on reinvested dividends.

†Offers discounts on reinvested dividends and optional cash purchases.

Dollar-Cost Averaging

$\mathcal{T}$here is an old rule in buying stock which says "Buy low and sell high." That is a truism, but most of us aren't smart enough to know where the low is and where the high might be. To help you in this matter, you can smooth out market fluctuations and make more money in the long run by dollar-cost averaging your investments in stocks, whether from a regular stockbroker, a discount stockbroker, or a company offering a DRIP (Dividend Reinvestment Plan).

Set aside a certain dollar figure per month or quarter. With DRIPS, this can be as little as $10 a month or quarter. When the price of a stock or fund is down, you automatically buy more shares (or fractions of a share), and when the price is higher, your fixed contribution buys fewer shares.

For example, let's say you invest $100 per quarter in a stock. If it is selling at $10 per share today, your $100 buys 10 shares. Then let's say the market drops to $5 per share. In that case your next quarterly payment buys 20 shares. The following quarter the share price soars to $20. That means your $100 buys only five shares. Then the market returns to normal and your stock returns to $10 per share, and you buy 10 shares with your final $100 contribution.

Let's add it all up: In the course of one year you've invested $400 and bought a total of 45 shares, for an average price of $8.89 per share. Yet the average price for the year was $11.25 ($45 divided by 4). So you managed to save 21 percent per share, and you never had to outguess the market.

With most DRIP plans, you can set aside as little as $5 or $10 per month and pay no commissions.

No system is foolproof, so that you can relax and not give any thought to your investments. There is no such thing as an ideal long-term investment. Most stocks go in and out of favor with investors, and some reach their maximum efficiency as a producer of goods or services. You have to be aware of what your companies do and what their continuing potential for growth and increased earnings might be.

Market timing is crucial: The '80s were hot on computer stocks, but the '90s seem to favor biotech offerings. Every decade has one or more best type of investment.

That is why "Blue Chip" stocks are so popular; they seem to endure time and cycles of the market. Even with the "Blue Chippers," though, you have to stay awake at the wheel.

Real Estate Profits
Can Be Reduced

*E*milie and I live in California. Here real estate purchases have been a great way to increase wealth or to build a sizable nest egg for retirement. There are incredible stories of people buying homes in the '60s for $35,000, putting in normal improvements, and 25 years later selling them for over $600,000.

That's a great story if you don't have to pay the capital gains taxes! Even with the following ideas, people who live in certain desirable states will pay a large tax when they sell. However, in most of the 50 states these ideas will certainly help reduce your profit taxes.

Take a $125,000 Tax Exemption When You Sell Your Home

Special rules apply to the sale of a principal home by persons age 55 or older. If either you or your spouse were age 55 or older on the date of the sale, and 1) you owned and lived in the house for at least three of the past five years, and 2) you or your spouse have not used the exemption before, then you may elect to completely exclude up to

$125,000 of the profit from taxable income regardless of whether you buy another home. You may only use the age 55 exclusion *one time*, regardless of how much profit you realize.

If your spouse has already taken the exclusion, even if it was prior to your marriage, neither of you can claim another exclusion unless the original exclusion was revoked within three years. Within two years of selling your home, if you purchase and live in another home that costs at least as much as the adjusted sales price of the old home, your entire gain on the sale is not taxed. In that case, you should save your $125,000 exclusion and use it when you sell your second home.

But if you sell your home and purchase another home for an amount *less* than the home you sold, you might be better off taking the $125,000 exclusion now. See IRS Publication 523, "Tax Information on Selling Your Home."

Sell Your Home, Remain There, and Take a Tax Deduction Too

If you are over 55 and no longer want the problems of home ownership, you can sell your home, take the onetime tax exemption of $125,000 on the home sale, and still *stay in your house*. Here's how.

Sell your home to an investor (perhaps one of your adult children). The investor then leases the home back to you, perhaps for the remainder of your life. You'll avoid the headaches of dealing with rising property taxes, difficult upkeep, higher insurance, and major repairs. The buyer will get monthly rental income from you, plus the buyer can take advantage of tax depreciation credits and other write-offs.

Of course, you must pay a fair market rent, or else the IRS will disallow any rental deductions the buyer takes.

Make a Tax-Free Swap of Your Property

One very handy provision of the tax law allows you to use the increase in value of an old property to help you buy a new one—without paying any tax on the increase. The rule is called a "tax-free swap," and the only restriction is that both the old and the new properties must be "like kind properties"; that.is, they must be the same type of property.

Tax reducer tip: Swap your small house in an overpriced city for a bigger house in a less-expensive place. Or swap a rental property in one resort area for another rental property in a different area. Just be sure that the new properties are at least as expensive and the same kind as the old ones.

Use Your Home Equity as a Tax Shelter

Interest paid on home equity lines of credit secured by a house or vacation home is fully tax-deductible up to $100,000 annually. So one of your best bets as a tax shelter—and one of the few remaining tax shelters at all—is the home equity loan. And now a new law helps you decide what loan terms you should choose. The law will require the lender to provide:

▲ Complete information about interest rates and costs when giving you a loan application.
▲ Honest ads about home equity loans.
▲ Dependable loan terms, with no unilateral changes in due dates.

Real estate is still one of the best investments a person or couple can make. The American dream is to own a home, although each year it becomes more and more difficult for the first-time buyer to make that dream come true. None of us knows what the future of real estate will be, but with increasing population in our country, the principle of supply and demand states that desirable property will have equity-building capabilities.

Make sure that your first home fits into your ability to make the monthly payments without placing undue strain on your long-term budget. Over a long period of time, larger mortgage payments than you can reasonably make become regressive, not progressive. The extra stress will have a negative effect on your life.

House Rich, Cash Poor

Do not fear, for I am with you; do not be dismayed, for I am your God. I will strengthen you and help you; I will uphold you with my righteous right hand.
—Isaiah 41:10 NIV

As our country becomes a graying society, we will find more and more home-owners over 62 years of age who have paid off their home mortgages but now have minimal income. What do you do when you are house rich but cash poor? In August of 1989, the Federal Housing Administration entered into a pilot program with 25,000 loans available to help correct this situation.

The concept was developed to help older people from being forced to leave their homes at any future date.

This program is commonly referred to as a "reverse mortgage" and is designed to help elderly homeowners cash in on their equity. Here is how a reverse mortgage works.

▲ It is available to any homeowner who is at least 62 years of age and whose house or condo is completely paid for or is substantially debt-free.

▲ There is no minimum loan amount. The maximum loan amount is based on a percentage of your home's value and on a limit that varies from area to area.

▲ Homeowners have a choice: They can receive monthly payments, a line of credit, or a single lump sum. The older you are and the more valuable the home, the larger your monthly payments.

▲ The payments do not affect Social Security or Medicare benefits.

▲ The mortgages do not allow a lender to force you to sell or vacate your home if the money owed on the loan exceeds the value of the home. FHA insurance will cover any balance due the lender.

▲ The mortgages do not require repayment until you die, sell, or move out of your home.

If you are a senior citizen, or if you have parents who are in this situation, you can obtain additional information about this program by contacting your local HUD or FHA offices. Check the yellow pages for telephone numbers.

Should You Refinance Your Mortgage?

During the early '90s we saw interest rates plummet much lower than we ever thought possible. When interest rates go down this much, people ask, "Should I refinance my mortgage?" This chapter will help with that crucial decision.

Refinancing your mortgage is simply taking out a new mortgage on your home.

Typically, refinancing a mortgage requires the same procedures and costs associated with purchasing a new home: application fees, origination fees, and closing costs which are paid by the borrower.

In some situations, refinancing your mortgage may be a sound credit decision. Falling interest rates can be such a situation. Other factors need to be considered, however, before you trade in your old mortgage for a new one. To help you decide, consider these objectives in refinancing:

▲ **Reduce monthly mortgage payments.** By replacing your high-interest-rate mortgage with one at a lower rate, you will reduce your monthly payment.

▲ **Obtain cash by accessing the equity in your home.** For example, if you pay off a $100,000 mortgage balance and replace it with a $150,000 mortgage, you'll have $50,000 for home improvements, a college education, or a major purchase. ▲ **Take advantage of tax deductions on mortgage interest expense.** Those who own their own homes free and clear, or who have a small mortgage balance remaining, may consider refinancing to gain tax deductibility on the interest expense. According to the Revenue Act of 1987, up to $100,000 of refinanced debt, plus the amount of your existing mortgage, is eligible for tax deductibility.

When is it worthwhile to refinance your existing mortgage at a lower rate?

As a general rule, refinancing is worthwhile when your current mortgage rate is at least 2 percent higher than prevailing market interest rates. This 2 percent figure is a cost-effective margin when weighing the costs of refinancing against the savings in monthly payments.

Another consideration is how long you plan to own your home. For example, if you have a $150,000 mortgage, you would need to remain in your home for at least two years before the savings in your monthly payment recoups the cost of refinancing. The chart below can help you estimate how long it would take to realize the savings of a refinancing.

REFINANCE RECOVERY CHART

Current monthly mortgage payment $_____

Minus monthly payment at new rate   –$_____
    (See payment table below)

Monthly savings at new rate   =$_____
                     × 12

Yearly savings at new rate   =$_____
                                       (A)

Refinancing Costs† $_____
                                         (B)

Years to recover the costs of
refinancing (B divided by A)   _____

---

† Includes closing costs, application fee, origination points (approximately 2%-4% of loan amount, depending on loan size).

PAYMENT TABLE

Equal Monthly Payments to Amortize a Loan of $1000

Term Rate (%)	15 Years	25 Years	30 Years
7	8.99	7.07	6.65
7½	9.27	7.39	6.99
8	9.56	7.72	7.34
8½	9.85	8.05	7.69
9	10.14	8.39	8.05
9½	10.44	8.74	8.41
10	10.75	9.09	8.78
10½	11.05	9.44	9.15
11	11.37	9.80	9.52
11½	11.68	10.16	9.90
12	12.00	10.53	10.29

To calculate your monthly payments:

$$\frac{\text{Loan amount}}{1000} \quad X \quad \text{Payment factor from chart above}$$

For example, the monthly payment on a $100,000, 15-year mortgage at an interest rate of 10½ percent would be calculated as follows:

$$\frac{\$100,000}{1000} \quad X \quad 11.05 \;=\; \$1105 \text{ per month}$$

You may want to consult your tax adviser for advice and tax implications on this decision.

PART SIX

Good Consumer, Good Manager

▲ ▲ ▲

How to Cut Your Family's Medical Bills

If you are untrustworthy about worldly wealth,
who will trust you with the true riches of heaven?
—Luke 16:11 TLB

*I*f your health insurance rates are like our family's, they're getting bigger and bigger each year. Since we aren't covered by a group plan, we have our own private carrier, and each year the renewal premium has increased. In order to keep the premiums somewhat manageable, we have increased our deductible, knowing that our biggest concerns are coverage for major medical costs.

There are several ways to control medical expenses.[1]

Doctors

▲ Don't see a specialist if you don't have to. A general practitioner will be able to handle most problems, and his rates are usually less than those of the specialist.

▲ Don't go to the emergency room if you can go to the doctor's office instead.

▲ Consider your physician as a partner in your health care. Ask any questions you have. Don't be afraid to ask that silly question.

▲ Get advice from your doctor over the phone if you need clarification or information on such things as medications, reactions, or recurring health problems. You don't need an office visit to have something explained.

▲ Get a second opinion on anything major, such as surgery. A high percentage of second opinions don't verify the initial diagnosis.

▲ Don't overtest. Find out what alternatives you have if you refuse the test.

▲ Consider negotiating fees with your doctor. Doctors are usually willing to work out a fee and payment schedule for their services.

▲ In order to stagger the cost of health care, sequentially schedule the medical and dental checkups of the family members.

Hospitals

▲ Don't have procedures done as an inpatient that can be done as an outpatient.

▲ Ask for an itemized bill. Question what you don't understand. It helps if you can keep your own records of what you received and when.

▲ Pay your bill only after checking it over. Make sure all questions are reviewed.

▲ You can curtail hospital expenses if you try to avoid being admitted on a Friday. Friday admissions result in longer stays than admissions on another day. For the shortest stay, try to have yourself admitted on a Tuesday.

A federal law (effective December 1, 1991), called the *Patient Self-Determination Act*, requires hospitals and other health care providers to give you information (when you're admitted) about your rights to accept or refuse medical treatment, and to prepare a document that will authorize someone else to make decisions for you.

You can also get help in deciphering your hospital bills, and information on where to file complaints, by joining *People's Medical Society* (462 Walnut Street, Allentown, PA 18102, 610-770-1670, $15 a year membership fee), a consumer's advocacy organization.

Equipment

▲ Borrow medical equipment (such as canes or wheelchairs) that you may need only a short time. If you can't borrow, see if renting would be cheaper than buying. If you must buy, see whether your insurance will pay for the purchase. Check for sales. Buy only equipment with a written warranty.

Nursing Care

▲ Use home nursing care as an alternative to long-term nursing home care if possible. Staying at home is far less expensive than staying in a nursing home. Other possibilities include adult daycare and respite care, in which family members get a break by using a paid caregiver for a set time each week.

Medicine

▲ Buy generic drugs when possible. They are usually cheaper and just as effective. There are a few situations where it's important to get a brand name drug, so consult your doctor.

Generic drugs, which have the same formulation as the more expensive name brand drugs, are far less expensive, but even *their* prices vary. Large pharmacy chains and hospital outpatient pharmacies will probably be your best bargain. Shop around and buy the largest quantities advisable to get the best discount.

▲ Buy in bulk if you use regular medication. Be sure to check the shelf life of such purchases.
▲ Sometimes a mail-order service can save you money.

You can save as much as 20 percent less by ordering prescription drugs by mail. Their prices vary, so here are four companies to telephone:

▲ *Action-Mail Order*:   800-452-1976
▲ *Medi-Mail*:   800-331-1458
▲ *Family Pharmaceuticals*:   800-922-3444
▲ *Pharmail*:   800-237-8927

If you're a veteran, also check with your local Veterans Administration Office for their mail-order program. As a veteran, if you meet certain requirements, try the Department of Veterans Affairs, which operates a large mail-prescription service.

For those 55 and older, the American Association of Retired Persons, through its affiliated organization, Retired Persons Services, Inc., offers a mail-order pharmacy service for members and their families. Details: 800-456-4636, 8 A.M. to 6 P.M. weekdays, 9 A.M. to noon on Saturday. Or check your medical insurance company.

Whether you get your prescription in person or by mail, make sure you've gotten the right medication, strength, and directions. Also check the expiration date.

▲ Buy store brands when you have no strong preference. Aspirin is aspirin. It is usually made by one of the same companies in any case.

▲ If your local pharmacist isn't competitive, you might mention this to him for a possible savings.

▲ Use over-the-counter drugs whenever possible. Ask your doctor and/or pharmacist for an over-the-counter medication if it will work well. Many prescription drugs are becoming available over-the-counter; check for changes.

▲ Get longer life out of your medicines by storing them properly.

▲ Over-the-counter and prescription drugs may perform miracles when they're *needed.* If they're *not,* we're wasting money and risking the side effects. Be sure to ask your doctor for the least expensive and safest prescription. Ask for free starter samples.

▲ If you have a chronic condition for which you need medication, have it reevaluated periodically. I took drops for glaucoma for years, until refinements in the screening tests revealed that I don't have glaucoma at all! Now I have my pressure checked annually, and all is well.

▲ Don't take too many vitamins and minerals unless you need them. If you're in good health, and eat a balanced diet, save your money.

Insurance

▲ Don't overpay on your insurance. Make sure you aren't duplicating your coverages and that you aren't carrying coverage you don't need (e.g., maternity coverage when you no longer can have children).

▲ Increase your deductible to save money.

▲ If you are a nonsmoker, look for a carrier that will give you a discount.

▲ Consider an HMO or prepaid health program.

▲ If your carrier requires preapproval, make sure you get it.

▲ Pay premiums annually if you can. Be sure to pay on time.

▲ Don't abuse your company's insurance policy. The higher the company's expenses, the higher the premium costs, which affect your company's profitability.

Prevention

▲ Exercise regularly.

▲ Eat proper foods, with reduced consumption of fats, sugars, sodium, fried foods, red meats, and high-cholesterol foods. (See Emilie's book *Eating Right* published by Harvest House.)

▲ Learn stress-reduction techniques.

▲ Injury-proof your home.

▲ Wear seatbelts.

▲ Be a nonsmoker.

▲ Be a nondrinker of alcoholic beverages.

▲ Take advantage of free or inexpensive community testing health fairs.

Medical Reference Books

Be an informed consumer and have some medical background. Listed below are some excellent medical reference books:

▲ *American Medical Association Family Medical Guide* (Random House, 1987). Simple diagnostic flow charts and illustrations, with suggestions of when to use home remedies and when a doctor is needed.

▲ *American Medical Association Handbook of First Aid* (Random House, 1987). If your first aid book is as old as mine was, you'll be surprised by the changes in AMA-recommended procedures. It's important to have up-to-date information.

▲ *Take Care of Yourself,* by Donald M. Vickery and James F. Fries (Addison-Wesley, 1990). Emphasizes self-care and prevention. Not as detailed as the AMA Guide, but a good supplement.

▲ *Prescription Drug Book,* 2nd ed., by AARP Pharmacy Service (Harper Perennial, 1992). Of special interest to those of us over 50.

▲ *The Complete Drug Reference,* by U.S. Pharmacopeial Convention, Inc. (Consumer Report Books, 1991). Very detailed, includes nonprescription drugs.
▲ *The Essential Guide to Prescription Drugs,* by James W. Long (Harper Collins, 1991). Not as detailed as the above, but the price is a lot better. Good description of drug treatment for specific conditions.
▲ *The Pill Book* (Bantam Books, 1991). This book is priced low, so it's worthwhile to keep each annual edition on your shelf. Brief, clear explanations of drugs.
▲ *Getting the Most for Your Medical Dollar,* by Charles Inlander (Pantheon, 1991).
▲ *The Patient's Guide to Medical Tests,* 3rd ed., by Edward and Kathy Pinckney, M.D. (Facts on File).

Fraud Alert

Swindlers in the health-care field now cost us between $50 and $80 billion a year—affecting our taxes and insurance premiums. A few safeguards:

▲ Check all your medical bills carefully for inaccuracies.
▲ Get recommendations from your doctor for home services or equipment.
▲ Don't trust door-to-door sales or telephone pitches.
▲ Beware of offers for free checkups and batteries of tests. If in doubt, check with your doctor or hospital.
▲ Don't get involved in any shady maneuvers promising you padded insurance deals.
▲ If you suspect fraud, contact your state's attorney general's office, or your insurance company. Medicare has a toll-free hotline for fraud reports: 800-368-5779 (or write HHS/OIG, P. O. Box 17303, Baltimore, MD 21203-7303).

Ways to Stretch Your Dollars

I, wisdom, will make the hours of your day more profitable and the years of your life more fruitful.
—Proverbs 9:11 TLB

$\mathcal{I}$n today's economy we need to know as much as we can about tax laws and how to use tax deductions we have not employed in the past. This chapter will help you work within the law to stretch your dollar.

Here are a few techniques, rules, and suggestions to keep in mind.[1]

Tax-Saving Tips

▲ **Itemized deductions** can help reduce your tax bill, but watch out: You can only deduct miscellaneous deductions to the extent that they *equal or exceed 2 percent of your adjusted gross income.* You can only deduct medical expenses to the extent that they *equal or exceed 7.5 percent of your adjusted gross income* (don't forget to include transportation costs to your doctor at 9 cents per mile). But don't get too carried away with itemized deductions; you could be subject to the Alternative Minimum Tax.

▲ **Claim a deduction on Schedule C or Schedule F,** rather than on Schedule A, whenever possible. Not only will you be able to deduct 100 percent of the expense, but any deductions listed on Schedules C or F reduce your adjusted gross income, making it easier to meet the 2 percent miscellaneous and 7.5 percent medical deduction floors.

▲ **Business expense** deductions also give you a good deal of latitude. The IRS simply says they must be "ordinary and necessary." Don't overlook computer costs, supplies, subscription costs, seminar costs, etc.

▲ **Postpone income or bonus payments** until next year. Your company can still announce the amounts this year, but if payment is delayed until next year, you don't have to report it for the current year. Ask your company about exceptions.

▲ **Transfer income-producing property to low-bracket children or grandchildren.** Although children under 14 pay tax at their parents' rate above the first $1000, that $1000 can represent a fair amount of annual investment income. You could pay over $300 in taxes on it, but the youngster would pay only $75 (the standard deduction offsets any tax on the first $500; the next $500 is taxed at only 15 percent).

Ways to Minimize Taxes on Stocks and Bonds

▲ **Offset capital gains with capital losses.** Take investment losses the same year you claim gains. Such losses offset gains, and up to $3000 of ordinary income.

▲ **Give your favorite charity securities or other property that has gone up in value.** With a cash donation you merely get a deduction. But with an outright gift of an appreciated asset you deduct the full value and avoid capital gains tax.

▲ **Consider selling appreciated securities you bought on margin.** If you borrowed on margin, you are entitled to a deduction for loan interest to a $4000 limit, plus an amount equal to your net investment income. If you didn't realize enough gain to deduct all the interest paid out, consider selling some appreciated securities.

Exemptions That Can Lower Your Property Taxes

Exemptions for property tax vary from state to state, but there are several exemptions that are available in many states. Here are three that you may qualify for. (To find out more about the property tax exemptions for your state, call your local tax assessor.)

▲ Veterans often qualify for an exemption of $50 per year.
▲ A blind individual, or a surviving spouse of a blind individual, can get an exemption of up to $6000.
▲ A disabled veteran, or a surviving spouse of a disabled veteran, may be completely exempt from property taxes.

Note: For a surviving spouse to claim either of the last two exemptions, the spouse must live on the property and cannot remarry.

Maximizing Deductions to the Fullest

▲ **Pay off big loans (and the interest) with a home-equity loan.** The proceeds of up to a $100,000 loan can go for any legitimate purpose, and the loan interest is 100 percent taxfree.
▲ **Pre pay all local real estate taxes;** also, pay any estimated last-quarter income tax owed to the state or city for a deduction this year.

▲ **Turn dues into "professional expenses."** If you belong to a country club and use the club at least 50 percent of the time for business, you can deduct at least 80 percent of the expenses and 100 percent of the dues. Use the club for business lunches before New Year's Eve, or throw a "goodwill" lunch or dinner. Keep records to show that you talked business.

▲ **Increase medical deductions** so they exceed 7.5 percent of your adjusted gross income. Move up your annual physical from January to December, or pay the full amount for medical or dental procedures that start this year even if they aren't completed until next year. Stock up on your prescription drugs, medically prescribed vitamins and special diet foods (to the extent that they won't expire). Other deductions include the cost of a special mattress for arthritis or cosmetic surgery (even if not recommended by a physician); the cost of a program that prevents or alleviates a specific ailment; Medicare B premiums; room and board for an in-home nurse; the cost of orthopedic shoes; long-distance medical travel; psychotherapy; a home health spa; and computer storage of your medical history.

Three Types of Income That Require No Taxes

▲ **Gifts and inheritances** you receive are not usually taxable to you on the federal level, except for certain large amounts. (Some states have an inheritance tax.) The person making the gift/bequest has normally paid taxes, if any, on the income used to purchase the gift or to build the estate. However, income such as interest, dividends, or rents from such property is taxable.

▲ **Veterans Administration payments** and/or insurance proceeds aren't taxable.

▲ **Life insurance proceeds** paid at the death of the insured are usually tax-free, as are loans taken from a life insurance policy.

Gift-Giving As a Tax Relief Strategy

Want to make gifts that will please the recipients without giving you a nasty tax bite? Here are five ways to play angel without getting socked:

▲ **Cash gifts.** Give up to $10,000 per year per recipient in cash ($20,000 if the gift is from you and your spouse) and pay no gift tax.

▲ **U.S. savings bonds.** Consider a Series EE bond as a holiday gift. Unlike other zero coupon bonds, the tax on the annual increase in value of a Series EE is deferred until the holder cashes it in. But if the recipient of your gift is a young child, he or she may wish to report the tax annually. This could be a good idea if the amount is under $1000 and the child is in a low tax bracket; it might be better to pay a small tax each year than one big lump sum when the bond is sold.

▲ **Certificates of deposit.** Give your child or grandchild a bank CD in the child's name. Interest on a CD that matures in a year or less is taxable to the child at a lower rate when credited to the child's account.

▲ **Appreciated stock.** Give your child or grandchild stock that has gone up in value and thereby avoid capital gains tax yourself.

▲ **Charitable donations.** Donate something of value to a cherished alma mater or nonprofit organization.

Save Money on Your Travel Dollars

$\mathcal{A}$merica seems to be on the go. Everyone is planning to go someplace—now or in the future. As Emilie and I are getting older and the children are grown, we have our eyes set on New England, the South, Mexico, Canada, Hawaii, Australia, and Tahiti.

When we were younger we had the time but not the money. Now we have the money but not the time!

Last year for Christmas I gave Emilie two gift certificates to be used anytime this year: One was for a week in Hawaii and one was for a week in Mexico. So far Hawaii is scheduled but not Mexico.

When we set out to travel we want some of the best rates available. We are always looking for a deal. This chapter is specifically written to help you find that good deal. If you are a senior citizen, be sure you let agencies know this when you make travel arrangements. This age group usually has special discounts.

Travel Tours

▲ **Aerotours International**—36 E. 3rd Street, New York, NY 10003, 800-223-4555, 212-979-5000. They offer resort apartment vacations to Australia, Fiji, Indonesia, the Philippines, and Tahiti.

▲ **American Youth Hostels**—P.O. Box 37613, Washington D.C. 20013, 202-783-6161. They can accommodate access to 5300 hostels in 59 countries. Senior citizens are welcome for a minimal annual membership fee.

▲ **Grandtravel**—6900 Wisconsin Avenue, Suite 706, Chevy Chase, MD 20815, 301-986-0790, 800-247-7651.

▲ **Grand Circle Travel**—347 Congress Street, Boston, MA 02210, 617-350-7500, 800-350-7500. International travel specializing in the 50+ age bracket.

▲ **Mayflower Tours**—1225 Warren Avenue, Downers Grove, IL 60515, 708-960-3430, 800-323-7604. This tour is designed for mature travelers specializing in U.S. sites.

▲ **Outdoor Vacations for Women Over 40**—P.O. Box 200, Groton, MA 01450, 508-448-3331. Outdoor travel adventures for women of all skill levels.

▲ **Saga Holidays Ltd.**—120 Boyston Street, Boston, MA 02116, 800-343-0273; 800-248-2234. Special low-priced travels for singles, grandparents and grandchildren, and those over 60 years old.

▲ **Untours**—Hal Taussig, Idyll, Std., P. O. Box 405, Media, PA 19063, 215-565-5242. Rental apartments in Europe.

Cruises

▲ **Celebrity Cruises**—5200 Blue Lagoon Drive, Miami, FL 33126, 305-262-8322, 800-437-3111. Also discount cruises for Royal Caribbean Cruise Lines.

▲ **Premier Cruise Lines**—P.O. Box 573, Cape Canaveral, FL 32920, 407-783-5061, 800-327-7113. Cruise the Bahamas, Nassau, Disney packages.

▲ **South Florida Cruises**—3561 NW 53 Court, Ft. Lauderdale, FL 33309, 305-739-7447, 800-327-7447. They buy group allotments on most cruise lines and pass the savings to you.

Airlines

▲ **American Airlines**—800-433-7300. Call for information regarding various travel options with the best rates. They have coupon books for senior travelers (62 years old).

▲ **Continental**—800-441-1135, 800-248-8996. Request any discounts when you make reservations. Senior citizens should inquire about Freedom Passport and Freedom Trips discounts.

▲ **Delta**—800-221-1212. Request any discounts when you make reservations. For those passengers 62+, ask about the "Young at Heart" tickets.

▲ **Northwest**—800-225-2525. Request any discounts when you make reservations. For those passengers 62+, ask about the Ultra fare rates.

▲ **TWA**—800-221-2000. Request any discounts when you make reservations. For those passengers 62+, ask about the Senior Travel Pak rates.

▲ **United**—800-628-2868. Request any discounts when you make reservations. For those passengers 62+, ask about the Silver Wings Plus rates.

▲ **U.S. Air**—800-428-4322. Request any discounts when you make reservations. For those passengers 62+, ask about the Golden Opportunities coupon books.

Foreign Airlines

Contact each of these and ask for any special rates. If you are a senior citizen, be sure to ask for any programs for this age group.

▲ **Air Canada**—800-776-3000
▲ **British Airways**—800-247-9297
▲ **El Al**—800-223-6700, 212-768-9200
▲ **KLM Royal Dutch Airlines**—800-777-5553
▲ **Mexicana**—800-531-7921

▲ SAS—800-221-2350
▲ Tap Air Portugal—800-221-7370

Trains

Contact each of these and ask for any special rates. If you are a senior citizen, be sure to ask for any programs for this age group.

▲ Amtrak—800-872-7245
▲ Austrian Federal Railways—212-944-6880
▲ British Tourist Office—212-581-4700, 800-677-8585
▲ German Rail—800-308-3100
▲ Greek National Tourists Org.—212-421-5777
▲ Irish Tourist Board—800-223-6470
▲ Italian State Railways—212-397-2667
▲ Luxembourg National Tourist Office—212-370-9850
▲ Ontario, Canada, Northland—800-268-9281
▲ Portuguese National Tourist Office—212-354-4403
▲ Scandinavian National Tourist Office—212-949-2333
▲ Via Rail Canada—800-387-1144

Buses

Contact each of these and ask for any special rates. If you are a senior citizen, be sure to ask for any programs for this age group.

▲ Gray Lines—Check your local phone directory's yellow pages to assist you with the phone number in your locale.
▲ Greyhound/Trailways—Check your local phone directory's yellow pages to assist you with the phone number in your locale.

Car Rentals

Contact each of these and ask for any special rates. If you are a senior citizen, be sure to ask for any programs for this age group.

▲ Alamo—800-327-9633
▲ Avis—800-331-1212
▲ Dollar—800-800-4000
▲ Hertz—800-654-3131
▲ National—800-CAR-RENT
▲ Thrifty Rent-A-Car—800-367-2277

Hotels

Contact each of these and ask for any special rates. If you are a senior citizen, be sure to ask for any programs for this age group.

▲ Best Western—800-528-1234; Hearing-impaired: 800-528-2222.
▲ Choice Hotel International, Sleep Inn, Comfort, Quality, Clarion, Friendship Inn, EconoLodge, Rodeway Inn—800-221-2222; Hearing-impaired: 800-228-3323.
▲ Days Inn—800-247-5152; Hearing-impaired: 800-222-3297
▲ Doubletree Hotels—800-528-0444
▲ Hampton Inns—800-HAMPTON
▲ Hilton Hotels—800-492-3232
▲ Holiday Inns—800-336-6330
▲ Howard Johnson—800-634-3464
▲ Hyatt Hotels—800-233-1234
▲ La Quinta Motor Inn—800-531-5900
▲ Omni Hotels—800-THE OMNI
▲ Radisson Hotels—800-333-3333
▲ Ramada International—800-228-9898

- ▲ Red Lion Hotels—800-547-8010
- ▲ Rodeway Inns—800-424-6423
- ▲ Sheraton Hotels—800-325-3535
- ▲ Shoney's Inns—800-222-2222
- ▲ Stouffer Hotels—800-468-3571
- ▲ Travelodge—800-255-3050
- ▲ Vagabond Inns—800-522-1555
- ▲ Westin Hotels—800-228-3000

Time is money; money is time. The more you have of the one, the less you need of the other. Travel is a wonderful way to break your routine, develop a new perspective on life, gain a better sense of personal history, and strengthen your hobby if you like to play tennis, golf, paint, collect antiques, etc. It's even more fun when you can save money in the process.

Great Fund-Raising Ideas

*M*any of us are members of churches, clubs, fraternities, or sororities that are looking for ways to raise funds. About the time we realize there is a need to raise funds, we scratch our heads to think of creative ways to supplement our budget. Our minds go blank! Some of these ideas from our readers can provide real help.

Service, time, and talent auction. In this auction you don't sell material possessions but pledges for service, time, and talent. Items you might include: babysitting, a resort area condominium, homebaked cookies once a month for a year, car service to and from the airport for a future plane trip. Each donation is the generous giving of self.

Cleanup crew. A great high school or teenage project is to take the place of professional street cleaners when you need to clean the streets of the fall leaves. Charge the neighbors or business tenants a fair wage. It doesn't take many students to earn a fair amount of money for their special project.

Hill of beans. Here's a fund-raiser based on a hill of beans—kidneys, pintos, lentils, split peas, limas, and more.

Members of your club can donate these beans. Combine them into a colorful, flavorful mix, then bag them in plastic bags of two cups each and sell them for $2 each along with instructions for rinsing, soaking, and making soup. Tie a colorful ribbon at the top of your bag to provide colorful eye appeal.

Lip sync. Hold a lip-sync show. While a recording of a real singer plays, each child performs one or two songs, imitating the artists' style and mouthing the lyrics. Have rehearsals so the students can pool the songs, tapes, records, and lyrics. You can even make costumes with materials on hand and such finishing touches as feathers or jewelry. Sell tickets or take a freewill offering.

Krazy kalendar. For your special fund-raiser make up a unique calendar showing particular days of the month with specified amounts of money to put away for this fund-raising idea. In a typical week in July ask for 50 cents on Sunday "if you didn't go to church tonight," followed by "1 cent for each year of your age above 21" on Monday; "10 cents if you have a patio or deck" on Tuesday; "25 cents if you turned on the air conditioner" on Wednesday; "5 cents for each glass of water you drank" on Thursday; "1 cent for each page of a book you read" on Friday; and "10 cents if you drank lemonade" on Saturday. Deposit the money in a jar and contribute jointly for your special fund-raiser.

House numbers. Raise extra money by painting street numbers on the curbs of your neighborhood streets. Be sure to clear the idea with your local police department. Call on the neighbors to presell the orders. Depending on the economic level of your neighborhood, a fair price would be in the $3 to $5 range. Stencil black numbers in 6x10-inch white rectangles on curbs, steps, and sidewalks. You might even have local merchants donate the paint. You will find the police and fire departments delighted with the easy-to-read addresses.

Tasting bee. If you are passing up the usual barbecues, fish fries, pancake breakfasts, etc. you might want to try something different to make money—a "May Tasting Bee." At theme tables decorated with flowers, flags, and costumed dolls representing various parts of the world you can serve portions of a variety of American, European, Mexican, and Oriental foods. For a fixed price you can sample food from as many tables as you wish. The dessert table could be an extra cost if you wish. The only eating utensils needed are teaspoons and toothpicks. You could also preprint the food recipes and sell them for a nominal cost.

Twenty talents. Give your group of 20 youngsters $1 each to purchase supplies for a craft or baking project. You can also pool your money for larger projects. You can even contribute a little extra money on your own if you like. You can also use materials found around the home. In three or four weeks you can bring the crafts or baked goods to a central area in which they can be sold. You can turn the original $20 into much more by selling or auctioning off cookies, cakes, holiday decorations, aprons, stuffed toys, baby quilts, or covered photograph albums.

Seesaw marathon. Schedule a seesaw contest within your group and seesaw from a Friday afternoon until Sunday afternoon. You can presell pledges from your neighbors, friends, and family based on the number of hours the students keep going. The students can teeter-totter in three-hour shifts.

Use your own creative imagination in creating your fund-raising projects. These efforts bring out the organizational ability of the various members, and seem to bring the members closer together. Those who participate in these projects also become more familiar in the sponsoring group's purposes.

Start a Home Business

I will trust and not be afraid, for the Lord God is my strength and song, and He has become my salvation.

—Isaiah 12:2

Since 85 percent of new businesses are started by women in their homes, Emilie personally wanted to address this subject.

▲ ▲ ▲

Today's woman approaches the 1990s with much excitement. We've come a long way, women: The '80s found us making a lot of changes from home to work—stress, frustration, disorganization, and fatigue. Our priorities went out the window along with our organized homes and meals. We gave up our children to sitters and daycare and our meals to fast-food stores. Our spiritual life moved into low gear.

However, new changes are coming into focus. We are tired of the tired '80s. More women are feeling the desire to be at-home mothers and career women. We will see working women find balance between work and home and new interests in home business.

My mother became a single working parent when my father died. (I was 11 years old.) She opened a small dress shop and we lived in the back in a small three-room apartment. Home and career were mixed. Mom not only sold clothing but worked late into the night doing alterations. (Bookwork was done after-hours.) We survived because we all helped in a time of need and survival.

When our children were small I developed a small business out of our home; the extra money was for extra things. I was able to do that because I felt somewhat organized and in control of our home.

This may be the year that God will bring into *your* life the desire to be an at home woman and to develop a from-home business. Of course, to be successful it does take time, creativity, balance, and desire. Our ministry, **More Hours In My Day,** began out of our home and has stayed, there for over 11 years. Books have been written, seminars given, and mail orders sent from our door to many of yours.

Our typist, Sheri, has a typing service from her home and is enjoying better profits than ever before. A dear and longtime friend, Rose, has a small business called "Tiffany Touch," in which she goes into other people's homes in her area and does anything they need done, from organizing a drawer to hanging pictures. A mother with a new baby designed a slip over the head bib that is sold all over the country out of her home. Still another mom created designer baby bottles—she changed baby needs into cash of over 1 million dollars!

Connie Lund, out of Olympia, Washington, created a small devotional flip chart of inspiration called "Reaching Up to God." Through its sales she is sending her daughter through college. When her daughter comes home for vacations she helps collate and tie. Most at-home businesses develop family oneness, with all members working together to help with the business.

Direct sales are popular and profitable: Tupperware, Avon, Shaklee, Amway, Mary Kay, Home Interiors, "Christmas Around the World," Successful Living Books, Choice Books. From home parties to door-to-door, these are just a few examples.

One woman I read about shops for working women, buying groceries and gifts and running errands from dry cleaning to stamps at the post office. She even delivered a lunch to a school child who forgot it at home.

Another creative mom does gift wrapping for people (especially men in offices) that led to food baskets and then homemade wreaths and floral arrangements.

Another mom advertised her famous chili recipe for $1— and sold enough to buy Christmas presents for the whole family. She was very pleased and surprised. Amiee makes colorful earrings. Women saw them on her and wanted a pair for themselves. From friends to boutique shops, sales multiplied.

All kinds of arts and crafts have created many added funds to the family income.

I was visiting some friends who received an adorable loaf of bread shaped like a teddy bear. This novelty gift is now being shipped all over the state.

Nancy is a single parent who quit her computer job and started her own service in her home. She is now home with her three children and still runs a very successful business.

Nancy and Elizabeth teamed up to design and sell Christian greeting cards, business cards, and Christmas cards. They are doing very well.

Some women are working at home as an employee— sales rep, technical service rep, claim adjuster. Many others are salaried employees but spend most of their time in the field. Their employers typically don't provide an office, so their files, desk phones, etc. are in their homes. Many can do part-time employment in the same way. (You do have to ask yourself whether you have the space in your home for this type of employment.)

I have a friend who reps designer clothing out of her home four times a year. She sends out invitations with days and hours, then books appointments and helps the women coordinate their wardrobes.

As we move into the 1990s, set your desires high and chart out your goals for your future. Where would you like to be next year at this time? What will you need to accomplish to be there?

When can you start? Possibly now. 1. Your desire is to be working from home—by next year. 2. Make calls and talk with friends, family, and business associates. 3. Perhaps you need to take a class on business, sales, design, etc.

Many of you may be happy just where you are. Others may want to cut hours to be at home a little more. What do you want to accomplish in the 1990s? Start with a positive attitude, strong desire, and creativity wrapped with prayer.

My desire is to see the busy woman get back to traditional values and to use her God-given creativity wherever she may be in or out of the home.

Here are some ideas on how to begin a business at home.

Research

1. Find others who are in your same field of home business and talk with them. They can provide a wealth of information.
2. Will it benefit you to advertise in your local telephone book?
3. What kind of advertising should you use other than word of mouth?

Goals

1. Determine a time schedule to be at home with your business. Example: Within one year.
2. Sign up for a class at your local community college on simple business bookkeeping.

Finances

1. Draw up a projected budget for yourself. What will be your credits and your debits? How much money do you need to launch your business?
2. Consider the costs involved in advertising.
3. Set aside some money for start-up expenses and supplies, such as a typewriter, copy machine, furniture, and small desktop items, (stapler, scissors, etc.).
4. Start writing down hidden costs. There will always be expenses that you did not count on, so the more research you do the less likely you will have a lot of surprises.

Home Preparation

1. What area will you use and how much space do you need?
2. Can you use your existing phone system?
3. Do you need a desk, work tables, file cabinets, etc.?
4. Will any carpentry work be required?

Legalities

1. Get information on what legal matters need to be considered. Some home businesses require a business license. Check with your local county records department.
2. Obtain a resale number if needed.

3. What kind of deductions are you eligible for? Contact a CPA who is knowledgeable in the field of home business deductions.

Hours

1. Think through how many hours you can reasonably work per day, per week, per month.
2. Will you need to work around children's schedules?
3. Will you have regular business hours?
4. When will you clean your home, cook meals, etc.?
5. Don't forget *you*. Schedule time to do a few things for yourself: hair appointments, shopping, church, friends, Bible studies, etc.

As in many situations, your home business will involve a lot of trial and error. You'll learn much as you grow along, but the benefits will be great. An excellent book from one of our instructors, Donna Otto of Scottsdale, Arizona, is *The Stay-at-Home Mom* (Harvest House Publishers). It's a book that applauds the stay-at-home mom and cheers her on with practical ideas to make the journey an adventure. She has several chapters dealing with making and saving money at home. According to Donna, "Often it's the need for additional income that makes a mom take outside employment. Yet it's possible and practical to stay at home and generate income. You need conviction, discipline, and a plan."

Help!
I'm Being Audited!

Render to Caesar the things that are Caesar's,
and to God the things that are God's.

—Matthew 22:21

Over the past 15 years we have been audited three times, and I cringe each time I receive an envelope from the IRS. My heart beats faster, I get nervous, the palms of my hands get moist, and it just ruins my day. However, after going through these three audits I have gained some valuable experience that might help you get ready for this occasion.

First you need to get rid of at least four myths that the average American has.

1. The government is picking on me. Your return was selected for audit for one of two reasons: Either someone has "turned you in" or a computer has found inconsistencies in your return. It's a matter of probabilities. If your return reveals deductions that, in the opinion of the IRS, exceed an acceptable percentage in a certain category, you may be selected for an audit.

2. I must have done something wrong. Most Americans are honest when filing tax returns. IRS audits usually show no evidence that the taxpayer deliberately tried to cheat the government. Most errors are mathematical or the taxpayer can't supply proof for the deduction.

3. I'm going to be fined or receive a heavy penalty. If the IRS interprets the regulation differently from you or your tax consultant, the penalty amounts to little more than a few dollars for back taxes plus interest.

4. I'll get those guys/gals at the IRS. This is not a good attitude. Treat them as professionals who specialize in tax laws. There is no need to place the auditor on the defensive. The emotions of a pending audit take you through anger, guilt, fear, and even revenge.

While an audit is not a pleasant way to spend a morning or afternoon, you can avoid some problems if you adhere to the following eight suggestions.

1. Keep a positive attitude. As you approach your audit, eliminate all the myths you have been exposed to. Be upbeat and confident that the deductions you have taken are within the legal limits allowed by our government. The law is on your side.

2. Organize your materials. If you have followed through with many of our organizational ideas in our various books, you will have your "perfect boxes" set up which store all your records, canceled checks, invoices, and receipts to support your claim that certain expenses should be considered legitimate deductions. Many times the auditor will judge the credibility of your report's accuracy by how you keep your records and how organized you are in supporting your deductions.

3. Choose your tax preparer wisely. If you use a "short form" return you can probably get by without the help of a tax professional. However, if you choose to take advantage of legitimate deductions, hire a qualified tax expert to prepare your return.

Because of the ever-changing tax laws, you want to make sure you select someone who knows the tax laws and is also experienced as a tax preparer. (A tax preparer is skilled at preparing forms, while a tax adviser knows the tax laws and can advise you on deductions to which you are entitled.)

Seek out personal recommendations from people you respect. Word of mouth is the best way to find this person. If you don't have that type of networking you may start by looking in the yellow pages. Be sure to interview the person to make sure you feel comfortable with your respective chemistries.

4. Take your tax adviser to your audit. Even though this will cost you money, you would be ill-advised to go alone. The person who prepared your taxes is the most likely one to go with you. He or she is best trained to answer the auditor's questions. Some tax preparers recommend that you stay home while they represent you. Many times the presence of the taxpayer simply complicates matters. You must go only to give information when you are asked specifically. Don't volunteer information. Give only the facts.

5. Treat your auditor professionally. Assume that he or she is a professional and treat him with that dignity. Respect him as someone who is doing a thankless job. My experience is that he will be fair as long as you have respect for him and the system. If your return is done with fairness and truthfulness, with legitimate deductions, you will have a fairly pleasant experience. On the other hand, if you have been deceptive and inaccurate you will certainly not enjoy the experience.

6. Be confident of your position. There is no need to be intimidated by your auditor. You need not apologize for a deduction. If you are entitled to a deduction you should not hesitate to take it. The IRS not only *allows* you to take certain deductions but actually *encourages* you to do so. If you have a home business you might want to obtain "Tax Guide for Small Business" (publication #334). Call your local IRS office to obtain this publication.

7. Tell the truth. All the auditor is looking for is truthful verification of your return. He or she is trained to recognize a false receipt or a false statement. He is fairly tolerant of logical reasons for deductions, but he doesn't have much tolerance when he is lied to or deceived.

8. Be aware of appeal procedures. If you are not satisfied with the auditor's interpretation of the law, you can always appeal that decision. The auditor will be glad to familiarize you with this process

Use this process as a positive learning experience for future tax reporting. You will gain a lot of insight throughout all this. The downside is that it will cost you money—win or lose. If you win, the cost will be having your tax preparer join you in the audit and the cost of losing time off from your work. If you lose, it will also cost you the amount of tax adjustment, any interest charges, and any penalty.

Go with the proper attitude and know that the law is with you.

How to Get Property Tax Bills Reduced

One of the habits I have when we go out for dinner is to look over the bill before I pay. You would be amazed at how many errors I find on our bill. I would say that at least 50 percent of our bills have errors (which are usually over-charges).

Because of this habit, I look at all bills which come into our home. Because of the size of our real estate tax bills, I want to make sure they are right, so I spend some time making sure they are reasonable.

Your tax bill will usually state on it what the deadline for appeal is. If not, call the assessor's office to get that information.

Here are some ideas to help you review your yearly real estate tax bill:

Find out how your taxes are figured. Property tax bills are determined by multiplying part or all of your home's assessed value by a specific tax rate—for example, $5 per $100 of assessed value. Your local assessor determines that value.

If you aren't sure of the method that is used in your area, ask. A local real estate friend or the assessor's office can tell you the method used. The most common approaches include these four:

1. **The fractional method.** Your tax assessment is figured as a specific percentage of the home's full value. The assessor might figure your home's worth at $80,000, but the local tax ratio might be 50 percent. In that case the tax would be figured on $40,000. If the rate were $5 per $100 of assessed value, the bill would be $2000.
2. **The full-value method.** The tax rate is applied to 100 percent of the home's value. Usually the tax rate is lower and is proportional to the fractional method above.
3. **The construction-cost method.** Linked to how much it would cost to reconstruct that same home today.
4. **The comparable-sales method.** The assessment is based on the selling price of homes similar to yours in the same neighborhood.

Check the assessor's appraisal of your home. Legally you have the right to check records and worksheets dealing with your tax bill. When you audit these records, make sure to verify these items:

▲ Square footage
▲ Size of lot
▲ Correctly described building materials
▲ Proper school district, sanitation district, water district, etc.
▲ Check other homes in area that are similar in size to yours
▲ Number of rooms and baths
▲ Any outbuildings that no longer exist
▲ Accurate cost of improvements
▲ Right township
▲ Make sure home is properly located.

Make sure that the assessment ratio is correct. Mathematical mistakes are more likely to occur when your assessment is based on fractional versus full value rates. If your home is assessed higher than the rest of the homes in your neighborhood, you could compile your own assessment/sales ratio. Add up the recent sales prices of 12 or more homes in your tax district that are similar to yours, then look up the assessed value of those homes in the public tax records. Divide the total sales values by the total assessment to get an average assessment ratio. If this figure is substantially below the ratio used for your home, you have a good case for reevaluation of your property tax bill.

Make an informal appeal. When you can, show an obvious error. It is often possible to sit down with the assessor and get your bill reduced (and/or a refund from past overcharges) without having to go through a formal hearing before an appeal board.

Make a formal appeal. If you believe that a mistake has been made on your property taxes and the assessor does not voluntarily make the change for you, you probably have the right to make a formal protest. Check with your local office to see what procedures are necessary to file a formal appeal. When you have a set time, be sure you go to the appeal prepared. Bring:

▲ Photographs
▲ Facts you have gathered
▲ A professional appraisal of your home (this will cost you money to have done)
▲ Plans of your home
▲ Statements about property values from real estate experts

If you win, your tax bill will be reduced and you will receive a revised bill. If you lose, you may appeal to a higher court, depending upon your local laws. Yes, there is effort required, but the savings may be worth the effort.

How Much House Can You Afford?

The wise man saves for the future, but the foolish man spends whatever he gets.
> —Proverbs 21:20

The great American dream is to own your own home. Yet that dream has become more and more difficult to achieve, depending upon what region of the country you live in.

Emilie and I remember our first house hunt. Those $20,000 homes were so beautiful, with a big yard, a two-car garage, built-in appliances, three bedrooms with a living room, and a den. When the salesman told us we didn't qualify, we were heartbroken. For several weeks we didn't continue our search for the American dream. Finally we did find a home in the $13,000 range, and we were on our way.

You might be asking "How much house can I afford?" The first thing you need to know when shopping for a home is how much you can reasonably spend. For most people this converts into "How large a mortgage can I afford?"

Lenders apply underwriting guidelines to each mortgage application. One of the most common tests is the debt-to-income ratio. This ratio compares levels of income with various debt expenses. Acceptable ratios are based on what a future homeowner can spend to successfully support a mortgage and also take care of other obligations.

As a general rule of thumb, one-third of your gross income may be spent on housing expenses, one-third on taxes, and the remaining third on your living expenses (see Chapter 13 for more information regarding this).

Lenders generally like to see that your monthly housing expenses do not exceed 28 to 30 percent of your monthly gross income, referred to as a "front-end ratio." Housing expenses include principal and interest payments on your mortgage, as well as real estate taxes, insurance, and any other applicable fees, such as condominium fees.

To calculate your monthly mortgage payment, refer to the Mortgage Payment Table below. Estimates of your real estate taxes, homeowner's insurance, and miscellaneous fees can be obtained from the seller of the home or your real estate agent.

The other debt-to-income ratio considered by lenders is your "back-end ratio." Typically, your housing expenses plus other monthly payments (such as auto loans, student loans, and credit card balances) should not exceed 36 percent of your gross income.

These are general guidelines. Acceptable ratios vary by lender, mortgage type, and your unique situation.

Monthly Payment Table

Equal Monthly Payments to Amortize a Loan of $1000

Rate (%)	15 Years	25 Years	30 Years
7	8.99	7.07	6.65
7½	9.27	7.39	6.99
8	9.56	7.72	7.34

8½	9.85	8.05	7.69
9	10.14	8.39	8.05
9½	10.44	8.74	8.41
10	10.75	9.09	8.78
10½	11.05	9.44	9.15
11	11.37	9.80	9.52
11½	11.68	10.16	9.90
12	12.00	10.53	10.29

To calculate your monthly payments:

$$\frac{\text{Loan amount}}{1000} \quad X \quad \text{Payment factor from above chart}$$

For example, the monthly payment on a $100,000 15-year mortgage at an interest rate of 10½% would be calculated as follows:

$$\frac{\$100,000}{1000} \quad X \quad 11.05 = \$1105 \text{ per month}$$

Think ahead of your near-future needs and then stretch your purchase level, because you will probably be improving your financial status in the next three to five years; however, don't get to the point where all your extra funds go to a house. Then you will become a slave to the house and won't have the funds to provide extras for the home and the necessary funds for God's opportunities for your life.

We know of many families in our area who have developed great family tensions because everything goes to pay for the mortgage. When that happens, you know you have leveraged your money too much.

Plan for the future, but don't let it make you a slave.

House-Hunting Checklist

My God shall supply all your needs according to His riches in glory.

—Philippians 4:19

$\mathcal{B}$uying or renting a house, apartment, or condo can sometimes be a source of stress. By mid-summer, the anxiety of being settled before school starts can cause you to make the wrong decisions when house-hunting in a hurry.

This checklist can help you keep track of the special features of the homes you've seen. Use it to compare them and to single out that special house you want to make your home.

This organized shopping list can be kept and copies made. It will enable you to look back and compare.

If you have a Polaroid camera, take a picture of each home and attach it to the back of each checklist form.

This type of organization will certainly give you more credibility with the realtor and home-seller. They will both give you the benefit of being a wise buyer.

It's amazing how all apartments, condos, townhouses,

and homes look the same after you have spent the weekend looking at various prospects. On the back of this form keep not only a picture, but also any notes that should be jotted down.

   If time permits, drive past the schools, churches, shopping centers, malls, etc. The right neighborhood is worthy of all the information you can gather. You will probably be in this new residence for some time.

HOUSE-HUNT RECORD

Date_____

Address of home_____ Age_____

Best route to take_____

_____

Owner of Home_____ Phone #_____

Salesperson_____

House design _____

House color _____

No. of square feet_____ Size of lot_____

Asking price_____ Down payment $_____

Monthly payment $_____

Type of utilities_____ Cost per month $_____

Other costs_____

Garage? ☐ 1 Car ☐ 2 Car ☐ Larger ☐ Carport

Condition/type of roof_____

Living room: Size_____ Flooring_____

Kitchen: Size_____ Flooring_____

Dining room: Size_____ Flooring_____

Storage space: Adequate? ☐ Yes ☐ No

Bedrooms: Number_____ Sizes_____

Bathrooms: Number_____ Sizes_____ Colors_____

Fixtures and tile condition _____

Water pressure check_____

Family room: Size_____ Flooring_____

Foyer: Size_____ Closet space_____

Game room: Size_____ Flooring_____

Basement: Size_____ ☐ Finished ☐ Unfinished

Laundry room: Size_____ Flooring_____

Other _____

☐ Central Air ☐ Fireplace Location(s)_____

Overall interior condition_____

☐ Patio_____ ☐ Pool_____ ☐ Pantry_____

Distance from work: Miles_____ Time_____

Distance from shopping: Miles_____ Time_____

Neighborhood rating _____

Overall rating of home and property _____

Schools: Quality_____ Distance from home_____

Comments _____

Husband's first impression_____

Wife's first impression_____

Have the Wedding You Want While Keeping Costs Down

A man shall leave his father and his mother, and shall cleave to his wife, and they shall become one flesh.

—Genesis 2:24

When Emilie and I were married, we certainly didn't have to worry about high costs, because neither side had much money. We knew we were going to have a very modest wedding. There were no videos, limousines, carriages, garden receptions with live birds, or large entourages of attendants.

Times have changed, though, and today almost everyone wants an elaborate wedding and reception. We know of parents who have had to take out loans to pay for that wonderful occasion. According to *Brides Magazine*, the average wedding costs $16,000!

You can have a wonderful wedding and still pay only a

moderate price. Wedding bells don't have to mean wedding bills. We look at a wedding as the *event* of a lifetime, not as the *debt* of a lifetime. In order to control the cost of this most sacred occasion, you must have proper planning and a budget. Here are some ways to cut corners on spiraling costs.

Planning

▲ Establish a budget and stick to it.
▲ The longer the engagement, the more money the wedding will cost.
▲ When hiring any service, discuss in detail what is included. Don't be afraid to ask questions. Question each item and delete those items you don't want. Leave nothing to oral agreement. Be sure everything is spelled out in a contract that you read before signing. Have the vendor sign and then request a copy of the contract for your file. Make sure you read each contract so you know whether your photographer can send an assistant to take your wedding pictures, or whether flank steak can be substituted for the prime rib you ordered.
▲ The cost can be eased if you purchase smaller items gradually, such as the cake knife set, toasting glasses, ringbearer's pillow, guest book, wedding favors, etc. Purchase a little here and a little there.
▲ Decide early how the wedding reception and honeymoon are going to be paid. Historically most of the costs are borne by the bride's family, with minor costs paid for by the groom's parents. Depending on the financial situation of each, you may want to make other arrangements. Just make sure there is a clear understanding of who pays for what. If this isn't clear, there can be embarrassment and hard feelings. You don't need either on such a festive occasion.
▲ Make sure you reserve the church, pastor, reception lo-

cation, photographer, and caterers early, because wedding services are subject to the laws of supply and demand. If your wedding is planned for the last Saturday in June, demand is high. Consequently you have limited bargaining power, plus arrangements and facilities fill up early.

Wedding Consultants

▲ Many churches have wedding coordinators who can be of great assistance to you. They are familiar with the staff and facilities and have previous contacts with florists, musicians, and caterers.

▲ A friend or relative might be available to help coordinate these details for you. Make sure he or she has the proper temperament for getting things done.

▲ You may even want to hire a professional wedding consultant to help plan and coordinate this event. Consultants cost additional money, but they can usually save you more than they cost. Just make sure you have in writing what their service covers.

One-Stop Planners

▲ In many areas you can use the services of a one-stop consultant, usually associated with a chapel or garden, who will coordinate, sell bride's and bridesmaid's gowns, rent tuxedos, print announcements, and provide catering, flowers, photographs, wedding cake, music, and limousines or a horse and buggy. Look in your local phone directory for such services.

Clothing

▲ Tell salespersons your price ceiling. This is an area that can cause a lot of stress. You must be firm with yourself to stay in budget.

▲ Shop early for better selections. Negotiate prices if you've found the same dress for less elsewhere.

▲ Shop out of season. Hit clearance racks in late summer or early fall for next year's weddings.

▲ Purchase discontinued styles for reduced prices.

▲ Ask if the manufacturer will downgrade fabric; substitute polyester chanting for silk chanting or omit hand-worked beading.

▲ Get alterations quoted in writing before buying. Avoid major alterations (such as changing a neckline or waistline); these can be costly. Although most dresses need at least some minor alteration, you can limit the cost by taking careful measurements and then asking to see the manufacturer's size chart. Sizes do vary between dressmakers, and they are not likely to be the same as sizes in street clothes.

▲ Ask about the deposit. The store does need money in advance to ensure you'll really buy the dress when it comes in. But make sure you use a credit card. Why? More than one bridal shop has gone out of business, taking customers' deposits with them. If you buy with a credit card, federal consumer protection laws allow individuals to notify the card issuer and get the deposit back. If you pay by check, your chances of getting the money back are far slimmer.

▲ You might consider consignment and rental shops.

▲ Choose a fabric shoe that can be dyed after the wedding for everyday use.

▲ Some rental shops will provide the groom's tuxedo for free when you rent the ushers' tuxedos.

Time and Place

▲ Book locations in off-peak months (November through April) for possible reduced rates. Hotel deals also may be offered for weekday or weeknight weddings.

▲ You may be able to negotiate a better price if you book more than a year ahead.

▲ Check out rural sites, large garden yards, and college and boarding schools with gracious halls and libraries. Contact your state tourism board and Chamber of Commerce for addresses of mansions, country inns, or town halls. Look into parks and publicly owned buildings that may require a minimal contribution in lieu of a rental fee.

▲ Price a home wedding. You will eliminate the site fee. However, rentals of tableware and tents can be steep. You will also need to supply food and cleanup.

▲ Be careful what hour you wed. Be aware that lunch is almost always less expensive than dinner, even when the menu is the same.

Reception

▲ Limit the number of guests—that's the number one rule for savings.

▲ Plan your menu carefully. Chicken costs less than beef or veal. Broccoli costs less than asparagus.

▲ Serve food that is in season and vegetables that are grown locally.

▲ Go ethnic. Mediterranean, Mexican, German, or Chinese are often less expensive than meat and potatoes.

▲ Control your beverage offerings.

▲ The least expensive option is to have the reception between the hours of 2 P.M. and 5 P.M., when no meals are expected. An evening wedding can be followed with a "dessert reception," where guests are offered a wide array of pastries and cakes.

▲ Limit an evening reception to three or four hours to reduce beverage and labor costs. Serve hot and cold hors d'oeuvres.

▲ Consider a pre-dinner reception from noon to 4 P.M. or from 2 P.M. to 6 P.M. You might have an English high tea; hors d'oeuvres and cake; casual, open-air reception with fruits, vegetables, and cheeses; or a buffet of sliced meat, meat pies, breads, condiments, and various salads.

Guest Accommodations

▲ Negotiate a group discount if you reserve a block of rooms for out-of-town guests at a hotel. If yours is a hotel reception, check for additional discounts on room rates that the hotel may offer to your guests.

Music

▲ Consider hiring the musicians affiliated with your church or synagogue.
▲ Interview student musicians from your local college or music academy.
▲ Use a disc jockey with a good selection of records.
▲ Consider three or four musicians instead of a six-piece band.
▲ Hire a harpist, pianist, or organist for an intimate wedding.
▲ Have musicians among family or friends be part of the wedding ceremony.

Flowers

▲ Consult a florist at least three months before the wedding. In-season flowers are usually the best buy.
▲ Choose multiple blooms of inexpensive flowers, such as baby's breath and carnations worked into ferns.
▲ Use a cascade of just one type of flower and greenery. These cost less for the florist to make.
▲ Let your flowers do double duty as decorations for both the ceremony and reception.
▲ Potted plants and balloons make good attractive centerpieces.

▲ You need not decorate every row of pews or every table with flowers. Some people decorate the first few rows or every other table.

Photography

▲ Shop around, compare prices, sign a contract. Word of mouth is a good way to be satisfied.
▲ Discuss options carefully. Packages may turn out to be more expensive due to hidden costs. Negotiate prices. Arrange to take group shots before the ceremony, rather than have the photographer come to your home for family portraits, or to shoot between wedding and reception. If you want a formal portrait, ask the photographer to bring a backdrop to the reception and shoot there, saving time and money.
▲ Choose fewer prints for your album. Ask how long the photographer will keep the negatives. You may be better off to buy additional pictures in the future.
▲ Create your own albums from guests' candids.
▲ If you want a video made of your wedding, go through the same procedure as with your photographer.

Transportation

▲ Consider using sedan-sized cars of close friends and relatives for transporting your wedding party. Limousines are hired by the hour, usually with a three-to-four-hour minimum.

Honeymoon

▲ Consider a travel agency that has a wedding registry so guests can make a gift donation toward your trip. Make arrangements as soon as you set the date.

▲ Check prepackaged tours for good value, which may include air travel, hotel, food, and sightseeing.
▲ Travel off-season to get lower rates.
▲ For greater savings, book airfare, rental car, and hotel at one time. If airfares go down, be sure to have your tickets rewritten for the lesser rate.
▲ Check to see if any of your organizational memberships offer you lower rates.
▲ Use your frequent-flier miles.
▲ Let hotels know that you are on your honeymoon. Many times they have extra features with a honeymoon package.

Do It Yourself

▲ Cooperate with your friends and family to help reduce wedding costs. Get married at a friend's home, and have friends videotape the wedding. Family members can provide first or last courses to the meal. Turn your rehearsal dinner and reception into an old-fashioned potluck supper. Have a homemade cake.
▲ Fresh fruit and flowers make simple toppers. Garden flowers can be tied with ribbon and lace into bouquets. Create dried rose-petal potpourri as favors.
▲ Use artistic and musical talents of friends.
▲ Make tapes of your favorite songs as a friend stands in as D.J. Relatives can even chauffeur the wedding party.

Notes for Book II

Chapter 1: Schedule a Plan, Plan a Schedule
1. Charles J. Givens, *Financial Self-Defense* (New York: Simon and Schuster, 1990), p. 17.
2. Ibid., p. 17.

Chapter 2: Why You Do What You Do
1. Adapted from Givens, *Financial Self-Defense*, pp. 23-24.

Chapter 3: Goals: A Dream with a Deadline
1. Emilie Barnes, *Survival for Busy Women* (Eugene, OR: Harvest House Publishers, 1986), pp. 16, 43.

Chapter 4: Writing Your Financial Goals
1. Adapted from Givens, *Financial Self-Defense*, p. 28.

Chapter 9: Four Cornerstones for Money Management
1. Patrick M. Morley, *The Man in the Mirror* (Brentwood, TN: Wolgemuth & Hyatt, 1989), pp. 144-45.

Chapter 10: Four Little-Known Secrets
1. Ibid., pp. 142-43.

Chapter 12: Principles for Financial Responsibility
1. We are indebted to Charles O. White, a local Christian attorney and tax practitioner, for sharing his insight on the topics of giving, receiving, and spending. Mr. White has conducted "Personal and Family Financial Success" seminars for more than 15 years.

Chapter 15: Suggested Categories for Your System
1. From Givens, *Financial Self-Defense*, pp. 41-42.

Chapter 30: Seven Ways to Get Greater Returns
1. Summarized from Peter A. Dickinson, *Retirement Wealth-Building Guide* (Potomac, MD: Phillips Publishing, 1992), p. 17.

Chapter 32: Principles of Long-Term Investing
1. Many of the ideas in this chapter were condensed and summarized from Shearson, Lehman and Hutton's booklet "The Real Definition of Investing," #GP2043.

Chapter 34: Compound Interest: The Eighth Wonder of the World
1. These principles adapted from Merrill J. Oster, *Becoming a Man of Honor* (San Bernardino, CA: Here's Life Publishers, 1988), pp. 69-70.

Chapter 40: How to Cut Your Family's Medical Bills
1. Many of these ideas are adapted from Peter A. Dickinson, *The Retirement Letter* (Potomac, MD: Phillips Publishing, Inc., May 1992), pp. 1-4.

Chapter 41: Ways to Stretch Your Dollars
1. Many of these ideas are adapted from Dickinson, *Retirement Wealth-Building Guide*, pp. 22-24.